DATE DUE

T

DEMCO 38-297

NEW ENGLAND INSTITUTE
OF TECHNOLOGY
LEARNING RESOURCES CENTER

THE MIND OF THE NOVEL

Reflexive Fiction and the Ineffable

BRUCE F. KAWIN

PRINCETON UNIVERSITY PRESS
PRINCETON, NEW JERSEY

FOR SOPHIA MORGAN

CONTENTS

PREFACE

Sometimes a course of thought is like an evening walk. It doesn't make too much difference where we appear to be going, whether we are on a neighborhood sidewalk as the lights in the dining and living rooms start to come on, or on a path in the mountains; the important thing is the half-light, the space between the thoroughly dark and the too well known, where ideas shift costume and time frees itself from numeration. Things familiar and separate in the daylight can mingle their shadows in the evening. As we take this walk with the ghosts of the obvious, a star may come out or a night fog settle in. On a particularly fine night we might both be looking in the proper direction to see a shooting star draw its fast white line, a blessing on the flow of the intellectual fiction; traced to earth, the white path might yield only a blob of iron. But there will be other evenings, other chances, until with luck the twilight figures will reveal their paradoxical solidity, and we can agree to take our next walk on the beach, or with some other friend.

The book in your hands has taken eight years to write and is now in the odd position of presenting itself as the sequel to a work with which it was conceived in parallel, *Mindscreen* (Princeton, 1978). My first book, *Telling It Again and Again* (Cornell, 1972), related the aesthetics of repetition in literature and film to the problems of time and silence. As a study of the ways art works attempt to transcend their inherent limitations, and particularly as a way of synthesizing Gertrude Stein and Samuel Beckett, it pointed past itself toward a larger synthesis and mandated my "beginning again," as Stein would say. Indeed, one day I was teaching a class on Proust and found myself explaining his concept of the binocular temporal self and the unified timeless Self with reference to the *Republic,* arguing that Plato and Socrates were

ix

elements of a "binocular" consciousness through which a vision of the Good might be stimulated in the reader. Notions of the "second first person," the "simultaneous self," the "telescope," and the "mind of the work" all were realized in that connection, and the best way to relate them to each other and to the structures of cinematic and literary narration seemed clear at that time: to examine the phenomenology of first-person discourse and to relate that to Wittgenstein's conception of the eye as a limit of the visual field. I subsequently wrote a long book called *I/Eye* that examined self-conscious narrative structures from Melville's *Moby-Dick* to Godard's *2 or 3 Things I Know About Her* and whose organizing metaphor was refraction. It became clear that both literature and film were capable of systemic self-consciousness, that the fully realized self would be, in both modes, extrasystemic, and further, that the ultimate analogy for such a system was human consciousness. The argument hung on four basic connections: multiple points of view performed similar heroizing/obscuring functions in *Citizen Kane* and *Absalom, Absalom!;* the systemic self-consciousness in *Persona* was of the same metaphysical order as that in *The Unnamable; Shame* and *As I Lay Dying* could each, and each for the same reasons, be interpreted either as a simple fiction or as a meditation reflecting the activity of a consciousness so rigorously extrasystemic as to be called transcendental; and *2 or 3 Things* and *The Golden Notebook* showed how a self-conscious perspective could form the basis of a new approach to art as well as to politics.

Eventually the film sections of this book were rewritten and published separately as *Mindscreen,* while what was for a time called "The Ineffable in Modern Literature" and for a time "The Edge of Silence" went on to be rejected by years of publishers. Each revision has brought something new, so that by now the two books stand in their own binocular relation to the synthesis they posit, each arguing in its own way that, as Godard says, "things might come into focus through an awakening of consciousness" and that reflexivity is one way consciousness and ethics (united in Godard's term, *conscience*) are infused into an art work. This final version is twice as long as any previous one and includes, for the first time, discussions of Augustine, Dante, Castaneda, William and Henry James, Pynchon, the "higher self," the early English novel, Jabès, Wittig, Daly, Heidegger, and Derrida. What finally distinguishes this version, however, is a spiritual emphasis that is the result of living with the question of the metaphysical self for so many years, and this has led to an admittedly unconventional approach in which analysis and intuition are foregrounded by turns. In Chapter Three the encounter with the ineffable is presented in terms that may irritate the purely scholarly reader, while in Chapter Five its semiotics and phenomenology are deconstructed in terms that may appear superfluous to the mystic. I have sought to rise to the largest demands of my argument and to clarify matters in such a way as to include every serious reader. You will not need a Ph.D. to read this book, let alone one in English. This is a book that speaks from and to a sense of wholeness and love; I hope you enjoy the walk.

Some of the books dealt with here may appear to have been already talked to death—*Heart of Darkness,* for instance—and others, like *The Female Man,* may seem willfully unfamiliar. What they have in common is a peculiar inward turning of the narrative, a gaze into the cosmos that doubles back to produce an image of the gazing self. As their narrators attempt to describe the indescribable, they find language running like water through their fingers; their rhetoric accelerates like one of Einstein's trains until it nearly touches its limiting rate, which in the case of language is silence. This acceleration, this dance around the ungraspable subject, links the authors treated here in ways that point to an essentially new idea about the formal dynamics of fiction and to a very old one about the nature of the self. This is, in its own way, a book about the human condition, and its task is to suggest what we can learn about ourselves from what literature has begun to learn about itself: what it means to be

on the verge of a new sense of autobiography, of self-awareness. It is based on and attempts to demonstrate two core
assumptions: that author, text, and readers participate in the
creation of meaning and confront the limits of their levels of
awareness in response to the challenge of the ineffable, and
that opening to the ineffable is an experience not of vacuity
but of something recognized as irreducibly authentic.

This old idea, then—that the self is its own category of
absolute and that to experience it directly is to find oneself
outside any linguistic frame of reference—is very much at
odds with contemporary European thought. Jacques Lacan
and his followers have argued that the self, as an aspect of
consciousness, is a function of language, and that only as an
absence that organizes linguistic activity (itself a structure of
absences, which is where Derrida comes in) can the self be
recognized. The only self capable of discussion in such terms
is a self-image, the "imaginary." Much of my own argument depends on a related notion, but one that a Lacanian
would consider antithetical if not nonsensical: language is incapable of dealing directly with the self, but that does not
prove anything one way or the other about the absolute and
prelinguistic existence of the self. "The book is the answer
to the book," as Jabès says, and although *"once in the book"*
we are forced to work with words, we may yet be capable
of intuiting the wholeness of the book/self/universe that presents itself both as a cluster of problems and as their systemic
solution. It seems to me that the work of Lacan and Derrida—who are in any case not in agreement with each
other—can be stretched or revised to include this idea and
that it offers a valid model of the self-concept-within-lan-
guage. My proposal is simply that the reader agree for the
duration of this book to consider the possibility that the self
exists apart from any self-image, projection, or symbolic
category constructed by words and by the conscious mind.
Though there are moments when I attempt to address the
problems of why the ineffable is ineffable and of the nature
of the self that language is unable to define apart from the

projections of verbal consciousness, it should become clear that what my analysis demonstrates is the absence of the self from those texts that attempt to name it and the tendency within many of those works to project an extratextual order of presence. The self is not named in these works largely because it is extralinguistic. What is named is the problem of naming.

One connection among these books, then, is that each attempts to do the impossible; there are three further connections. First, many of them involve a hierarchy of narrators or a system of displaced viewpoints, underneath which lurks one ideal voice or stance (impossible in the novel's context). Whether extended, as by Conrad, or compressed, as by Beckett, this narrative system turns out to be analogous to the structure of the speaking/silent self. Second, the unsolvable mystery tends to be reflected in this narrative structure, so the novel often manifests a parallel to the silence it cannot name. The presentation of the structure of the mystery is sometimes the nearest approach to a solution. For that reason, these novels are almost invariably reflexive, and that reflexivity is often a function of the stimulating and doomed attempt to describe the ineffable, which is implicit in an awareness of the problem of naming. As the gaze doubles back, it reveals not only the individualistic properties of the gazer but also the fact that the gaze is itself a prime unnamable. Finally, these novels tend to be written in the first person and to manifest self-consciousness. The key to many of these works—or at least the key to the front door—is in their use of the first person. The "mind of the novel" confronts its own subjectivity with fewer resources but to much the same end as a person does: to understand its own existential base so that it can acknowledge and extend what that base makes possible. Though what "can be said" circles back to an analysis of absence and (in Derrida's terminology) *différance,* what "makes itself manifest" is a self-consuming and self-declaring intuition of presence.

Minor White once said, "No matter how slow the film,

Spirit always stands still long enough for the photographer it has chosen." My own slowness has been mitigated by the help of many friends and colleagues. Among the authors discussed here, John Ashbery, Jorge Luis Borges, Steve Katz, Joanna Russ, and Ron Sukenick have talked with me about their work. Ben Stoltzfus gave the second draft its best reading and suggested I learn something about semiotics. Judy Zatkin introduced me to brain-lateralization and systems theory. Robert Alter pointed out problems in the third draft and provided in *Partial Magic* a workable history and terminology for the self-conscious novel. Hugh Kenner and I had a week-long conversation about *The Sound and the Fury* that culminated in the present notion of "the mind of the text," and both Kenner and Sandra Gilbert read this final version for Princeton and suggested ways to improve it. Sophia Morgan led me through a world of signs, dreams, and old stories, charging me with her profound sense of visionary analysis. At a crucial point in my thinking Diane Middlebrook told me to read *Gyn/Ecology,* as David James told me to read *The Book of Questions;* Marcia Aldrich prompted me to discover the deeper levels of *Wuthering Heights* and *As I Lay Dying.* Frederick Dupee, Gladys Kadlick, Frank McConnell, Walter Slatoff, and Victor Turner taught me some of these works in school, in ways that continued to unfold. Bruce Bassoff, Martin Bickman, Melvin Buxbaum, Anna Catalana, Tam Curry, Marian Keane, Allen Mandelbaum, Ed Rivers, Regina Sackmary, Richard Schoeck, Linda Williams, and several others read late drafts of this book and made many indispensable suggestions; at one point Professor Schoeck even contributed an excellent Foreword. Carole Raphalian introduced me to Insight Training Seminars and the work of John-Roger. Francesca Erbsenhaut guided me through two Self-Realization Intensives. Sherri Hallgren suggested some of the authors and helped clarify some of the arguments and intentions of the section on feminism. Joan Gilbert worked on behalf of this book's publication for several hard years. Joanna Hitchcock and Robert Brown of

Princeton University Press have been steadfastly encouraging. The final version was proofread and the index compiled with the help of Cal Kinnear.

As a gesture of thanks for all the energy and acuity they have shared, and for the time and interest you are about to extend, the best that I can offer is this book.

Boulder, Colorado
February 1981

THE MIND OF
THE NOVEL

Love never fails. As for prophesyings, they will pass away; as for tongues, they will cease; as for knowledge, it will lose its meaning. For our knowledge is fragmentary and so is our prophesying. But when the perfect is come, then the fragmentary will come to an end.

When I was a child I talked like a child, I thought like a child, I reasoned like a child, but on becoming a man I was through with childish ways. For now we see indistinctly in a mirror, but then face to face. Now we know partly, but then we shall understand as completely as we are understood.　　—Paul, I Corinthians 13, 8–12

("Why, my God," wrote Reb Doubré, "why force us to turn to You, to pierce our walls, when You are everywhere?"

This was doubtless what Reb Tal had in mind when he noted: "Once in the book, we must use the key which words have forged for us, and which we must discover.

"Without it, we run against a locked door on each page.")　—Edmond Jabès, *The Book of Questions*

So we say, finally, we know what happens in this darkness, what happens to us while we sleep, if we allow the night, if we allow what she is in the darkness to be, this knowledge, this that we have not yet named: what we are. Oh, this knowledge of what we are is becoming clear.
　　　　—Susan Griffin, *Woman and Nature*

CHAPTER ONE

Notes on a Haunted Form

1.

> A fictional technique always relates back to the
> novelist's metaphysics. The critic's task is to de-
> fine the latter before evaluating the former.
> —Jean-Paul Sartre, *Time in Faulkner*

Some things are difficult to talk about; some are impossible.
This book deals with the attempt to talk about the ineffable
(that which, by definition, cannot be adequately verbalized)
and the related difficulties of dramatizing both metaphysical
heroism and the mysterious nature of personal identity. Although it focuses primarily on the specific approaches to
these problems adopted by Melville, Conrad, Proust, Faulkner, Beckett, Lessing, and others, this book also addresses
some of the general questions these novelists raise: what are
the limits of language? how does an artist's sense of being
embattled with these limits affect his or her[1] sense of form?
what *is* the self? Drawing on a variety of analytic methods,
I have done my best to deal with specific works in what are
their most speculative and yet their most straightforward aspects. These works seem to differ from the general run of
novels, not simply because they try to make sense out of
what makes no sense, or to take a deep breath in a vacuum,
but because to some extent each goes beyond first-person
narration into a new form that operates at the edge of silence—not out of "exhaustion," as John Barth has suggested,[2] but in search of a breakthrough. Some of them appear not just to be records of their narrators' minds but to
have "minds" of their own, as if they mirrored the structure
of the conscious self. As an artificial system, "the mind of

5

the novel" reflects and projects the artist's parallel confrontation with silence and is offered as an emblem and perhaps as a solution to or acceptance of the metaphysics of that problem. Such a structure is not conscious but gives consciousness a playground. Under the pressure of confronting the limits of their means of expression, these works appear to have become aware of their own limits as narrative structures. Although such awareness is recognized both by the author and by the reader as artificial and imitative, it remains compelling because of its systemic complementarity with the natural system of consciousness—because, in other words, it offers such a good imitation.

Reality is what exists. Our reality is a product of the interaction between what we know and what we are. Like some aspects of what we are, only some aspects of what we know can be verbalized; this dialectic of knowing and being, within which awareness functions, yields to a subordinate dialectic between analysis and intuition. To know something rationally is to be able to explain or analyze it in words; to know something intuitively is to have a sense that it is true, to see or feel the truth of it. In most cases it is easier to demonstrate than to explain what one intuits—to lead one's audience into and through a structure that mirrors the subject and precipitates the insight. This is the general pattern of metaphysical fiction. To "explain" the ineffable is to give the reader the sense that one does not respect the dimensions of the subject; even so, the fact that one is writing impels one to try to lay out the mystery in words.

A novel like Proust's *A la recherche du temps perdu (In Search of Time Lost)* demonstrates the process of seeking and discovering the self and its relation to time. In the long final chapter, however, Proust allows the narrator to explain his metaphysics. If the explanation were sufficient, the novel would be superfluous; but the demonstration and the interpretation complement each other in a way that guides the reader to intuit a synthesis—perhaps to seek in his or her own being, or in the structure of the novel, the operation of the timeless. In Beckett's *The Unnamable,* which is one long attempt to explain the situation of the narrating/narrated self, the foregone conclusion that the explanations will never be adequate to their subject becomes a demonstration in itself; the more the explanations fail, the more the reader is forced to intuit why they fail. Beckett's reader confronts a system whose limits are analogous to those of his or her own verbal consciousness. These limited systems engage each other dialectically, and any synthesis that emerges in the reader's intuitive consciousness suggests that we are more than we can name, that we have resources that transcend the verbal.

The reader of *Moby-Dick* observes Ishmael's struggle to describe what it is about the whale that makes it so urgent to define or harpoon him:

> What the White Whale was to Ahab, has been hinted; what, at times, he was to me, as yet remains unsaid.
>
> Aside from those more obvious considerations touching Moby-Dick, which could not but occasionally awaken in any man's soul some alarm, there was another thought, or rather vague nameless horror concerning him, which at times by its intensity completely overpowered all the rest; and yet so mystical and well-nigh ineffable was it, that I almost despair of putting it in a comprehensible form. It was the whiteness of the whale that above all things appalled me. But how can I hope to explain myself here; and yet, in some dim, random way, explain myself I must, else all these chapters might be naught.[3]

Ishamel does not rest at "vague nameless horror" but tries to name it. This admirable attempt leads him not exactly to a failure, nor exactly to a success, but to a "dim" middleground; and it is here that the novel finds its power. What bothers Ishmael about whiteness is "the visible absence of color . . . a dumb blankness, full of meaning." This description brings the mystery closer but does not explain it; it leads us to imagine what it is like to look at something that *feels* significant but is only a partial sign: both signifier and signified are, by turns, in some way absent. "The visible absense of color" is a null signifier; the "dumb blankness, full of meaning" points to no specific meaning and is to that extent a null signified. The attempt to describe the mystery yields to a description of how it feels to confront the mystery (an appeal to intuitive over verbal knowing), which thereby implies that language is not omnipotent, that it operates within limits. Ishmael operates between the poles of this dialectic, and the reader learns from his frustrations. But there is another mystery at work, and its power depends on its not being mentioned directly within the novel: Ishmael is himself one pole of a dialectic of masked energies. The other pole is the whale, and the synthesis is the structure of the reflexive novel, which is analogous to the structure of the self.

In *Why Are We In Vietnam?* Norman Mailer constructs a similar dynamic by splitting the narrative consciousness into two speakers who are masks of each other. One of those narrators, D.J., observes:

> The fact of the matter is that you're up tight with a mystery, me, and this mystery can't be solved because I'm the center of it.[4]

The self is the mystery at the heart of the reflexive novel. Logic teaches that no system can be entirely self-knowing; complete knowledge implies access to a view from outside the system (the seer, his seeing, and everything as it is seen). This is one sense of Wittgenstein's remark that the eye is a limit of the visual field.[5] The visual field does not include the eye; the eye can see its image in a mirror, but not itself. The eye, then, needs the mirror in order to see or deduce the nature of the complete system. This may be one reason reflexive fiction so often includes mirror imagery; it is certainly a key to the interactive awareness between such novels and their readers. It is also closely related to one of the classical proofs of the necessity of the existence of God, the systemic knower, and may serve further as an anthropomorphic projection that could help us understand God, who created a world-system (necessarily more complex and less complete than himself) so that he might facilitate and more intriguingly enjoy his own development and self-realization. If the absolute had no interest in or relation to process, we might not exist in time. Setting aside for the moment this odd conjunction of Wittgenstein, Augustine, Aquinas, Berkeley, and the Hindu philosopher Shankara, let us return to Mailer long enough to make the point: D.J., confined to his system, cannot solve its mystery—he can at best be its "D.J.," or disc jockey; this is so not just because he is inside the system, but because he *is* the system. The reader, because he or she can be outside the system of that novel, may be able to understand the mystery; the metaphysical novelist goads the reader to intuit the solution because it would devastate the novel-system to include a "comprehensive" explanation. The novel derives its power from the same means that insure its integrity: systemic limitation. These limits suggest but necessarily do not describe the means by which they may be transcended.

2.

La forma universal di questo nodo
credo ch'i' vidi, perché più di largo,
dicendo questo, mi sento ch'i' godo.
—Dante, *Paradiso* XXXIII, 91–93

Looking in my love's eyes, I know much that is not being said and cannot be analyzed. There are silences so full that they overwhelm meaning, and a silence so different from the ways the mind works that it must be described as transcendent. There is a beauty that can hurt us into joy. There is a laughter that acknowledges what "I love you" cannot say, a laughter at the wonder of the failure, at the distinctness of the systems of words and pure being.

We know that "I love you" does not express all the pain and joy of love, but we know from how we feel when we say it that these words aspire after the proper direction. When Dante tries to describe his vision of the Light of God at the end of the *Paradiso,* he says, "In its depth I saw that it contained, bound by love in one volume, that which is scattered in leaves throughout the universe, substances and accidents and their relations as it were fused together in such a way that what I tell of is a simple light. I think I saw the universal form of this complex, because in telling of it I feel my joy expand."[6] One of the biases of the book you are reading is that the ultimate vision is of a wholeness that can be called Love and that in talking about it we feel our joy expand. Analysis gives up at the instant the complex fuses into the simple. Acceptance replaces analysis as the visionary recognizes, over and beyond the fragments of language, an absolute kinship with the vision. It is not that "I love you" but that the "I am" and the "You are" fuse into the recognition that "Love is" and that a more deeply understood "I" and "You" emerge from that acceptance, with the work of the world open to do.

As if it were part of his duty as a poet, Dante offers a relatively precise image of the form of the Light: three circles that project or emblematize a concept of the Trinity and that reflexively resolve the turning threeness of the structure of the *Divine Comedy.* The best one can say about this emblem is that Dante recognizes its inadequacy to the vision and its appropriateness as a seal on the poetic system. It is a moment that can enjoy its own failure because it is underlain by a sustaining vision of completeness:

In the profound and clear ground of the lofty light appeared to me three circles of three colours and of the same extent, and the one seemed reflected by the other as rainbow by rainbow, and the third seemed fire breathed forth equally from the one and the other. O how scant is speech and how feeble to my conception! and this, to what I saw, is such that it is not enough to call it little. O Light Eternal, that alone abidest in Thyself, alone knowest Thyself, and, known to Thyself and knowing, lovest and smilest on Thyself! That circling which, thus begotten, appeared in Thee as reflected light, when my eyes dwelt on it for a time, seemed to me, within it and in its own colour, painted with our likeness, for which my sight was wholly given to it.[7]

Every detail within the *Comedy* accumulates to an analogy, an homage, to this vision; all of its complexity aspires to fuse at the end. But the poem cannot be God. The best it can do is sum itself up in an image that is a key to its own process and structure, as well as an emblem of our participation in God's self-sufficiency, and offer that whole to the reader. The poet participates in the humility of that gesture and the integrity of that structure. Because he has seen his own Light mirrored in the vision of God's, he offers a poem that mirrors its own best aspirations, looking in its own eyes and curling into the beautiful failure of language and the joy of authentic recognition.

3.

Nature is a Haunted House—but Art—a House that tries to be haunted.
                              —Emily Dickinson, *Letters*

The human being is part of nature. And it is not farfetched to describe each of us as a house haunted by an undefinable spirit. Whether we call that spirit Atman, the soul, the higher self, or even consciousness is not at this point a relevant question, although it should be noted that we can and generally do use language to express consciousness, while we generally gain access to the insights and directions of the soul or the higher self only through meditation (and what we then discover is usually neither verbal nor verbalizable).

Metaphysical criticism is a philosophic activity and is therefore liable to encroach on the territory of religion. The truths or mythologies of religion are not at issue, but its methods are. The undertaking here is to discern a means of identifying and analyzing those figures and concepts that are not included in reflexive texts but are implied by them and are necessary to any understanding of them. This is analogous to the project of recognizing spirit. It involves many of the same problems encountered in our attempts to relate the known world to the transcendent universe, and the personally experienced self to the totality of Being. It involves the problem of limits, and therefore, systems theory. To indulge in systems theory is to consider the dialectical nature of the limit of any system (an inside suggests an outside) and the ways in which systems can overlap or share a common boundary. Wittgenstein observed that the "mystical" sense arises from the feeling that the world is "a limited whole."[8] It is pointless to analyze a limited system like *The Unnamable* without attempting to indicate what it is that cannot be named; it is perverse to study Jabès' *The Book of Questions* without wondering about the answers.

A limited system cannot contain or actualize the system that encompasses it, but it can sometimes behave in a manner analogous to the behavior of the larger system; thus, language can deal with the whole of the knowable world and the range of the mind, even though language is a subsystem of the knowable world and a tool employed by the mind (although, arguably, not by the higher self). It is possible that the successful analogy depends on a structural complementarity between the contained and containing systems, as in the Zen concept of big mind ("the mind which includes everything") and little mind ("the mind which is related to something").[9]

One of the finer tools for analyzing these relationships is transcendental phenomenology. As Husserl said:

> The transcendental problem is eidetic. My psychological experiences, perceptions, imaginations and the like remain in form and content what they were, but I see them as "structures" now, for I am face to face at last with the ultimate structure of consciousness.
>
> It is obvious that, like every other intelligible problem, the transcendental problem derives the means of its solution from an existence-stratum, which it presupposes and sets beyond the reach of its enquiry. This realm is no other than the bare subjectivity of consciousness in general, while the realm of its investigation remains not less than every sphere which can be called "objective," which considered in its totality, and at its root, is the conscious life.[10]

In the course of this book, I intend to demonstrate how the means to a problem's solution may be derived from a category or level that is "beyond the reach of its enquiry." For now it is enough to observe that fiction is a system within the system of the human mind, and that the human mind either is within or often likes to see itself as being within a larger system that can be explored only transcendentally. Reflexive fiction strives to imitate the structure of the human mind and its territory—to become a limited whole. Reflexive fiction that confronts, as one of its elements or concerns, the nature of the ineffable both imitates the limited mind embattled with what transcends it and suggests the means of one solution to the problem. It is a form that tries to be haunted.

Along with "reflexivity" and the ugly, redundant "self-reflexivity," "self-consciousness" has often served as an amorphous critical term that refers to arty art without saying much about it. Used with rigor, however, it can illuminate the problem of exactly how art presents itself as haunted, so I would like to propose some terms and explore the distinctions among them.

Texts do not appear out of nowhere. An important element of reader response is to discover or decide from whom and whence the work proceeds or presents itself as proceeding. Sometimes from information provided on a book's cover, but more often from internal clues, we categorize and then respond to the work as fiction or nonfiction, as being by a certain author, and as personally or impersonally narrated. *Heart of Darkness,* for instance, can be approached on one level as an autonomous text, a system of words that significantly relate only to each other and to the story or diegetic fantasy they generate. But is more common and often more rich to anchor the activity of verbal consciousness in some construct of actual being. On this level, *Heart of Darkness* can be read as a piece of semi-autobiographical fiction written in 1898 by Joseph Conrad, and as an as-if-real account by a nameless narrator of his experience of hearing the as-if-real account of Marlow's experiences with Kurtz. Most audiences arrive at complementary postures of belief and disbelief in regard to almost any narrative system, beginning for instance by believing in Conrad and agreeing to suspend disbelief in Marlow, and perhaps going on to suspend belief in Conrad and to believe in Marlow as a condition of enjoying or becoming involved in the story.

In a self-conscious work of art, however, the task of the audience is particularly complex, for the fiction often aims to present itself as an artificial arrangement of falsehoods which are to be recognized as such, and thereby to generate the paradox that such a fiction in fact tells the truth and presents things as they are. The audience at Genet's *The Blacks,* for instance, may begin by believing in Genet and the actors while agreeing to suspend disbelief in the real (extratheatrical) existence of the characters, but it soon finds the normal option of going on to forget about Genet and the actors not available. When the characters agree that they are putting on a performance for an audience in order to distract them from the prerevolutionary social conditions outside the theatre, they speak the truth (up to a point: these remarks are exactly true of the characters but do not exhaustively describe the condition of the actors, whose relation to the world outside the theatre is more complex). Even their reading of prescribed lines reinforces rather than violates this understanding of their position, as does their admission that this performance will repeat nightly without modification.[11] Story telling has been with us for so long that the willing suspension of disbelief has become almost automatic, and a self-conscious work must induce its audience to suspend that suspension—in short, to suspend belief. One of the most exciting aspects of such work is that it may result in a confrontation with the real (like a double negative, it signifies one kind of affirmation), so that the suspension of belief results in another order of belief, that is, a direct insight into what is genuinely going on.

Deciphering a text in search of its presenter (narrator, author, culture, and so on) is a normal aspect of reader activity, but suggesting ways a text might undertake the same project raises pressing logical problems, problems that are closely related to those raised by the attempt to discover the origin and nature of consciousness itself. The problem with self-awareness is: of what is one aware? and whose awareness is it? These questions cancel each other out in the intuition that the self exists. All levels of consciousness are capable of suddenly reducing to this luminous point. Before the insight precipitates, one is in the realm of language and analysis, probing the limits of the personal system from within. And this system is formally comparable to the logically knowable world, whose limits are those of meaningful utterance. Tautology and contradiction are in this sense not "meaningful"—but self-awareness can be verbalized *only* in tautology and contradiction, from the Buddhist "Neti Neti" to the biblical "I AM THAT I AM." All this suggests that

15

self-consciousness refers in many cases to systemic self-awareness, to being aware that one is a limited system. A complex of words that has been charged by its author with an imitative awareness of the problem of naming, for instance, can be described as self-conscious.

Reflexivity and self-consciousness are not interchangeable terms. A reflexive text is set, as it were, between facing mirrors; its world doubles back on itself, often generating in the reader a paradoxical impression of limited being. Self-consciousness, a slightly higher order of apprehension, refers to the text's conceptualization of that limited being, as if on some level the text "knows" that it is a text. Between them, reflexivity suggests itself as the more general term.

Because the problem is still bound up with the audience's guided process of attributing consciousness to various levels of the text, this distinction between reflexivity and self-consciousness yields to a clearer one: that between authorial and systemic self-consciousness. Though a text cannot actually be "aware" of anything, there are of course times when an author sublimates or attributes to the text his or her awareness of what is going on. So the question for a given work is whether this awareness is presented as an aspect of the author's attitude or as an inherent property of the "autonomous" text.

In *Partial Magic,* Robert Alter argues convincingly that self-conscious fiction is as old as the novel itself and that *Don Quixote, Tom Jones, Tristram Shandy,* and *Jacques le fataliste* are central works in "the other great tradition." (In Chapter Five, I will extend this core list to include *A Tale of a Tub* and *Clarissa.*) He defines the self-conscious novel as one "that systematically flaunts its own condition of artifice and that by so doing probes into the problematic relationship between real-seeming artifice and reality. . . . From beginning to end, through the style, the handling of narrative viewpoint, the names and words imposed on the characters, the patterning of the narration, the nature of the characters and what befalls them, there is a consistent effort to

16

convey to us a sense of the fictional world as an authorial construct set up against a background of literary tradition and convention."[12] Such a novel encourages the reader to be aware of the presence of the author, of the artificiality of the novel, and of the paradoxical ways in which "the mirror held to the mirror of art held to nature"[13] functions as an intriguing analogue to nature. One such paradox has been memorably formulated by Jorge Luis Borges: "These inversions suggest that if the characters of a fictional work can be readers or spectators, we, its readers or spectators, can be fictitious."[14]

The emphasis in Alter's definition falls, I believe, on "authorial." As a construct implied by the work, the author is within the text; but as a living being, the author is inevitably extrasystemic. The author manipulates the fiction, structures its world however he pleases, because it is not, finally, the world in which he lives. We are aware, reading *Tom Jones* or *Ulysses,* of a literary craftsman who allows us to discern the game and to participate in his authorial suspension of belief, even if that suspension results in an even more intriguing and necessary trap of belief. We are allowed to remember that we are reading a novel and to integrate that distance (one aspect of the "alienation effect") into our response. The author relates to the scheme as chief game-player, usually urging the reader to share in the joke, whether he intrudes in the first person, as does Fielding, or works primarily in the third person, as does Joyce.

In some cases, the reader is aware of a particular author; in others, of a certain level of interference. The first sentence of Nabokov's *Ada,* which "quotes" the first sentence of *Anna Karenina* but reverses its meaning ("All happy families are more or less dissimilar; all unhappy ones are more or less alike"), sets up the reader for an encounter with an alternate universe—its diegetic function—but also implies Nabokov's attitude toward his own situation as a more or less Russian antinovelist. Subsequent references to "Lolita, Texas" declare that the authorial persona has some connections with

17

the author of *Lolita,* anchoring this self-consciousness in "Nabokov." If one is not so aware of the history and oeuvre of a particular author, or if the author adopts a less precise mask, one is liable to be aware simply of a joke's taking place at the authorial *level,* which is basically the case in *Ulysses* (especially in those episodes that do not include Stephen, such as "Nausicaa" and "Cyclops").

A different order of awareness and self-reference is involved in such works as *The Unnamable* and *The Book of Questions,* which more unequivocally close their systems. The various subnarrators of *Ulysses,* even when they are presented as categories of textual voice, appeal finally back to Joyce, but the labyrinth of the Unnamable's mind is congruent with that of his world, which is that of a verbal consciousness—the mind as text, the text as mind—engaged in an attempt at self-definition. Godard and Gorin's *Tout va bien* offers a cinematic example of such a structure: male and female voices declare throughout that they are engaged in making a film, discuss their options (often presenting these onscreen), and are seen finally to share their awareness of the fictiveness of the system with many of the characters, who sometimes break in with their own notions of how the film—or such a film—ought to proceed and who analyze their world as being, and being answerable to, various categories of image. All these works remind us that they are fictions; but to attribute such reminders to a character or voice or level *within* the fiction, the limits of whose awareness correspond to the limits of the knowable system, anchors the self-consciousness in that system without necessarily passing it back to the author. This is systemic self-consciousness, and it corresponds closely to human self-awareness—not because the work is autonomous, but because human consciousness is limited; the self is its own boundary, as is language. Such a work is able to imitate, and with a certain leap of the imagination, to be, a limited and self-aware signifying structure; the reader will have to suspend belief in that structure in order to consider the intentions or pleasures of the author. Beckett is almost irrelevant in *The Unnamable,* in this sense, while Nabokov is indispensable in *Ada,* for even if the Unnamable confronts many of the characters from Beckett's previous novels, he relates to them—accurately—as variants of his own situation rather than pinning the blame on their mutual and unknown author. It seems useful, then, to expand Alter's argument by introducing a distinction between authorial and systemic self-consciousness.

It is simple enough to sort out these three perspectives in the abstract, but specific examples come harder. Reflexivity and authorial self-consciousness tend to overlap, since it is often unclear how much the author wants the reader to attribute certain attitudes to "the author" rather than to "the world of the work"; and authorial and systemic self-consciousness can be difficult to distinguish for similar reasons. Nevertheless certain broad groupings are possible. Borges' "The Library of Babel," for instance, is reflexive, whereas his "Borges and I" is systemically self-conscious; the "I" of the latter is a textual Borges who attempts to sort out his relationship with the extratextual Borges, whereas the narrator of the former is presented as a person living in a library that is a universe. "The Library of Babel" can be read as science fiction, as a description of an alternate universe that is comparable to a principle of random and repetitive textuality, whereas "Borges and I" can be read as a self-regarding text whose limits are those of the immediate literary, compositional situation. "The Library of Babel" never threatens, as does "Borges and I," to make sense as nonfiction.[15]

Whereas *Ulysses* and *The Dunciad* are authorially self-conscious, continually referring back to their authors' attitudes toward literature, fallen cultures, and so forth, and ascribing their self-regarding artifices to authorial play, Márquez's *One Hundred Years of Solitude* is reflexive, for its world of mirrors/mirages is entirely self-contained. One is aware not so much of Márquez's placing this novel in relation to certain possibilities of fiction and discourse as of the characters' attempts to probe the limits of their world, whose key is Melquíades' prophetic text. The fact that Márquez's text and the world of the novel end at the same time and that the ending is synchronized with the deciphering of the final line of Melquíades' parchments suggests another reading in which *One Hundred Years of Solitude* is systemically self-conscious rather than simply reflexive. But this reading is undermined by the fact that Márquez's and Melquíades' texts are not identical; the parchments thus become only one more mirror/mirage within the world of the novel, rather than its self-describing limit. A rigorous example of systemic self-consciousness is *The Book of Questions,* in which the world and its voices are aware of creating each other and in which "to be in the Book of Questions" is to exist, as to write and to be written are variants of the same condition of being (in both a religious and a literary context). Virgil's *Aeneid,* overtly modeled on more ancient sources and complexly inter-referential, might be taken as an example of reflexivity in comparison with the authorial self-consciousness of Dante's *Divine Comedy* and the systemic self-consciousness of Beckett's trilogy; or the authorial self-consciousness of Woolf's *Orlando* might be compared with the systemic self-consciousness of Lessing's *The Golden Notebook. Don Quixote* appears authorially self-conscious in its first half, where the central problem is Cervantes' transfigurative parody of romance literature, and systemically self-conscious in its second half, which begins with the characters' confronting and refuting a false sequel (not written by Cervantes) to their earlier printed adventures. It is a question of just whose awareness of the nature of the system is foregrounded for the reader, even though the question of what exact level of self-regard is operative in a given work may finally turn on hair-splitting and conjecture. In any case, these levels tend to overlap—if not in the abstract then certainly in particular texts—and the important thing is to discover which predominates.

The novel, the self, and the knowable are all limited systems, all limited worlds; engaging one set of limits, the narrator (and author, and reader) implicitly engages the others. (The self, and perhaps the knowable, would certainly have to be regarded as "open systems," regardless of these limits, since they are capable of exchanging energy with what is outside them; if their borders were not permeable, there would be no hint of the ineffable or of other beings.) Although it is debatable whether the human self is created linguistically, it is certain that the textual self is, and it is compelling to consider the limits of self-awareness within a completely linguistic system. In this sense, Ishmael is, both as an absence and as a presence, systemically viable precisely because he does not unmask himself. If he, or his consciousness, transcends "Ishmael," it does not transcend *Moby-Dick*. The truly self-conscious novel is not only a dance around the paradoxical nature of reality; it *is* a paradoxical reality. It achieves this status precisely because the limits of its systemic awareness are analogous to those of the reader. The Unnamable can no more shake hands with the self he anticipates than Wittgenstein can or would describe what "must be passed over in silence." Confronting its limits, the self-conscious novel dramatizes the closedness of the thinking, personal system. Its tool is language. Whereas the self-conscious author, as Alter describes him, "is steadily contemplating his narrative as a fictional object among fictional objects,"[16] the narrator of a systemically self-conscious novel is obliged to consider the relation between his own limits and those of his world. He haunts the novel, perhaps unapprehended, or startling himself from behind, as the unknowable prods through the knowable, and as the mystery of identity haunts the self.

The self is not the only unnamable, but it is one of our most interesting and inescapable concerns. As I have implied above and intend to demonstrate, a substantial percentage of literature's attempts to confront or describe the ineffable—any ineffable—at some point generate (as a function of the

21

frustration of those attempts) a sense of their own limits as texts. From the perspective of the text, this is the beginning of systemic self-consciousness. This phenomenon occurs with even greater regularity when the text is narrated in the first person. This is not always a single first person either. One of the most characteristic results of the attempt to deal with what is beyond the limits of a narrative system's apprehensions or tools is the fragmentation of the narrative intelligence into parts that can examine each other (Addie and Darl in *As I Lay Dying;* Alma and Elisabeth in *Persona;* the authorial persona and his multiple surrogates in *Song of Myself*). Often the juxtaposition of these fragments projects a systemic integration, a supernarrator, a "mind of the text," a self that is the center of the mystery and whose limits are those of the work. In order to examine all this, it will be necessary to explore further the concept of limited language and the complex stance of the self-conscious narrator.

4.

Man's fate, it seems, is to inscribe the figures of
plane geometry on a spherical surface.
—Hugh Kenner, *Samuel Beckett*

Language is a system of abstract referents. As Saussure established in his *Course in General Linguistics,* the word, or linguistic sign, "unites not a thing and a name, but a concept and a sound-image"—a signified and a signifier, respectively.[17] Because a sign is a relationship between signifier and signified, it is not considered legitimate to speak of a pure signifier (that which would signify but not be part of a sign) or of a pure signified (since the signified is not "the thing itself," but a mental image evoked in the act of signification). One signifies a tree with the sign "tree" and feels, as Beckett ironically says of Watt, content. When one wishes

22

to make a more complex reference, one uses additional signs and sets up intricate relations among them—relations that function as signs on more metaphoric and structural levels of the system.

New thoughts have proved easy to express, since thought and speech proceed from the same terms—are in fact variants of the same process. New intuitions, or deeply felt experiences, are another matter, another category. The problem is, as Faulkner has Addie Bundren put it in *As I Lay Dying,*

> that words are no good; that words dont ever fit even what they are trying to say at. When he was born I knew that motherhood was invented by someone who had to have a word for it because the ones that had the children didn't care whether there was a word for it or not. I knew that fear was invented by someone that had never had the fear; pride, who never had the pride.[18]

"Motherhood" both succeeds and fails as a sign. It succeeds because a community of speakers agrees that it is the proper term for the state of being a female parent. It fails because it is only a term. Someone hearing the word may say, "yes, I know what that means"; but a person in the grip of the experience has every right to insist that the word is not adequate or even close.

To say that signs, whether singly or in system, are only terms is to imply that experience, as distinct from thought, cannot be incarnated in language. It is not to suggest that experience is unnamable. With all of its failures, the act of naming still performs its function of conceptual reference—if not of ontological correspondence.

Because of the great impact of language on consciousness and on the lived-in world, and because most writers are interested more in saying something about life than in interrelating signs within a closed system for the pure joy of it, one often finds works that are charged with frustration at

23

the limits of conceptual reference and with a drive to invent a new politics of consciousness or to go beyond naming to incarnation.

This sense of the inadequacy of language is evident both in a writer like Beckett, who is directly concerned with metaphysical problems and often sets his words in relation to silence, and in one like Agee, who in an intensely political frame of mind finds himself unable to do justice to everyday reality. In *Let Us Now Praise Famous Men* he considers offering the reader "photographs . . . fragments of cloth, bits of cotton, lumps of earth, records of speech, pieces of wood and iron, phials of odors, plates of food and of excrement. . . . A piece of the body torn out by the roots."[19] To be embattled with such failure and struggle past it is an essential aspect of the spiritual and political maturity of Doris Lessing's Martha Quest (hero of the *Children of Violence* series) and just as basic to the pessimism and self-absorption of Faulkner's Addie Bundren. It is part of the message Pynchon hears from somewhere over *Gravity's Rainbow*.

One way to see how the question of language has entered into the consideration of practically everything else is to compare *As I Lay Dying* with *The Scarlet Letter,* from which much of Faulkner's novel is clearly derived. Like Hester, Addie has a child by the local minister; like Dimmesdale, she is obsessed by the private, "secret" nature of experience. Hester's child is Pearl; Addie's is Jewel. The differences between these novels are revealed in their differing concepts of isolation: to Hawthorne, it is the "spell" of the scarlet letter, a social and theological emblem, that isolates Hester from the community; to Faulkner, it is language that isolates us all from each other. (Both agree on sin as an isolator, and both approach sin in terms of the ways it is or is not signified.) Jewel is fiery and silent; Pearl, who is fire itself, not only is loquacious but has a way of precisely articulating every major issue that confronts her. Her isolation, then, is linguistically accessible; Jewel's finds expression only in ac-

24

tion. Hester and Dimmesdale reveal their spiritual conditions in an alphabetical emblem (which in Hester's case changes its meaning when Hawthorne feels her spiritual condition has changed, so that it remains always a valid emblem); Addie speaks only from the grave, and her subject is the inadequacy of language.

The difference between these two novels is both symptomatic and prefigurative of a fall from assurance and a quest for self-consciousness. That the battlefield has become language is attributable to several things: Saussure's study of the arbitrary, unmotivated nature of the sign; a general shake-up in the model of the mind; a related shake-up in the model of the universe, beginning with Blake, Hegel, and Schopenhauer and proceeding through Nietzsche, Einstein, Heisenberg, Heidegger, and (most recently) Derrida; Wittgenstein's analysis, in the *Tractatus Logico-Philosophicus,* of the limits of language; and of course the influence of metaphysically oriented narration itself. Although he is not demonstrably an influence on the authors to be discussed in this book (Beckett claims not to have read him until late in his own career[20]), Wittgenstein offers the clearest distinction between what is and what is not namable—a distinction that corresponds to that implicit in a great deal of religious writing as well as in fiction.

In the *Tractatus,* Wittgenstein points out that "the mystical" is unutterable simply because it is inconceivable. What can be thought about can be talked about. Although illogical combinations of thought-fragments (or signs) concerning the mystical may occur in our minds, such sentences are not defensible propositions—are not, strictly speaking, thoughts. To say "God is good" is as problematic as to say "Eternity is purple," since the term "eternity" (or any term like it) is undefinable, except by tautology: "Eternity is timeless," or $x = x$. What is outside the field of logic is outside the field of language and outside the known and knowable world. Wittgenstein's advice, which is addressed to philosophers and not to poets, is simply not to make

25

metaphysical statements. A similar point was made by Chuang Tzu: "If the Way is made clear, it is not the Way."[21]

The ineffable is a metaphysical province, out of bounds. Language and thought are part of a coherent, closed system—not just a referential system, as Saussure argues, but a system that can make meaningful reference *only* to the "effable," since there is no such thing as an inconceivable concept. This does not mean that humans are incapable of feeling that there is something beyond these boundaries, but it does mean that, in language and thought, we cannot deal with that "something" directly; we can only come to terms with its beyondness. One of the most defensible and effective ways an artist can suggest that he or she wants to deal with the ineffable is to accentuate the closedness of the artistic system: to call attention to the limits of that world, and to create characters or narrators who are embattled with those limits. Hence a novel about Ahab and Ishmael, not a novel about the whiteness of the whale.

Closed-system narration has the effect of suggesting that there is something important outside the system. This poetic strategy is just as useful when tackling "thinkable" subjects. By insisting on his inability to put his feelings into adequate terms, Agee goads the reader of *Let Us Now Praise Famous Men* into attempting to imagine or generate those feelings independently, finding them in that reality in which both Agee and the reader can directly participate and from which mere books are excluded. Emily Brontë, in *Wuthering Heights,* and Faulkner, in *Absalom, Abasalom!,* use a similar tactic to make their antiheroes appear mythologically gigantic.

The system finds its calling, however, when it attempts to name not just the impressive or the intuitive but the inconceivable. As the works of Proust and Beckett demonstrate, the system itself becomes a paradox, and the namer an unnamable. The following observation from the *Tractatus* could serve as a useful gloss on the paradoxical nature of the narrator in *A la recherche du temps perdu* (though it might answer even better to the narrator of Robbe-Grillet's *Jealousy*):

> If I wrote a book called *The World as I found it,* I should have to include a report on my body, and should have to say which parts were subordinate to my will, and which were not, etc., this being a method of isolating the subject, or rather of showing that in an important sense there is no subject; for it alone could *not* be mentioned in that book.
>
> The subject does not belong to the world: rather, it is a limit of the world.[22]

The nature of the narrator in Proust's novel is of course the subject of much debate, but one of the most striking things about him is that he is not specifically anchored in time or space. There are in fact three "Marcel"s: the younger man who does the living, the older man who looks back on those experiences and tells the reader about them, and the timeless or higher self that transcends the phenomenal world. The young and old "Marcel" participate in the timeless self just as—Proust insists—the two halves of a metaphor participate in the world of essence. Each event described in the novel is looked at by the young "Marcel" as he lives it and the old "Marcel" as he puts it down clearly (reclaiming it from death, and doing what he can to communicate its "reality"). The older narrator has been sensitized to the world of ideal, or essential, reality by his visionary experience at the Guermantes' party, through which he has discovered that he participates in a timeless self. By rights, then, the timeless self ought to be narrating the novel, reclaiming "lost time" by describing the world in ideal terms. But the ideal world is ineffable, as is the timeless self. The self that sees the world *this* clearly cannot appear in the novel. Proust's solution is to present every event in double perspective—as it is seen by the young "Marcel" in his innocence and as it is reexamined and described by the old "Marcel," both in his experienced

27

worldliness and in his visionary optimism. These narrators are like the two halves of a metaphor, and the essence in which they participate is suggested by their inextricable juxtaposition. The temporally unanchored "location" of the older narrator sets the reader on a search for the impossible metanarrator, the unnamable namer, who would speak (if he could) from no discernible vantage point, and who would speak in Ideal terms about the Ideal world. There is an *I* beyond the binocular "I" of this novel: everywhere evident, nowhere included.

Hence "Call me Ishmael," not "My name is Ishmael."

5.

If it can be done why do it.
—Gertrude Stein

The namer, then, is a potential unnamable. The clearest way to explore this paradox is to analyze a series of works in terms of their narrative structures: that is, in terms of the number and nature of the narrators and of the relations that exist between them and the objects of their discourse. In parallel with this undertaking it is necessary to make some further observations about the relations between human beings and language.

I have just been watching a baby girl who is on the verge of learning to speak. At first her needs were definite and simple and crying was her way of expressing these wants. She might want Mother, food, rest, to be held, to be left alone, or a change of diaper. If she wanted food, cried, and was given the wrong kind of attention, she would cry again until she got what she wanted. A certain degree of wordless understanding between the baby and her parents was indispensable. Eventually her desires became more diversified, however: she might want one kind of food in preference to another, or might want several things at once. At this point,

28

I imagine, she discovered the need for language. She began to use the syllable "deh" in combination with various expressions, tones, and gestures; "deh" while pointing outwards often proved to mean she wanted a toy, whereas "deh" while waving up and down meant not Mother but Father.

Language comes from a desire to let others know what we want. At some point we discover that a particular sound evokes a particular response, and we learn to make that sound when we want that response. We make a sign to communicate what we mean. And although a baby is not conscious of the difference between a signified and an object of desire, it is possible that in the preconscious one internalizes the signifier/signified relationship, learning in practice not just that a given sound goes with a given thing but also— since the desire to signify is prompted by an awareness of the desire to acquire something one does not then have— that "a sound that is not the thing" goes with "a thing that is not here now." When everything desired is present— mouth, breast, and milk, for instance, all together—one has no need for reference; a baby can simply smile (which is still a sign to the mother, though it is probably not prompted by the will to communicate, at least at so young an age). The diversity of human language—or the impulse to employ it— arises out of frustration at the unspecificity of crying and gesturing; it arises from the desire to have one's needs satisfied and evolves into a practical system that, when reinforced by the evidence of communication, becomes a basic means of relating with the world. New desires lead to new signs, each of which is, as Addie Bundren says, "a shape to fill a lack." Eventually one may confront a lack for which there is no shape and find oneself face to face with the problem of the failure of even this hard-won and steadily reinforced language; and at that point (see Chapter Five, section 1) one might recognize the problem of absence that is built into all signifying systems, even that breast-filled smile. The sign is a practical relationship between "not this" and "not here," and only the impulse toward that smile—and only insofar as it is involuntary—is an experience of the unified "this" and "here." When the thing desired is not an object or action but a transcendental category for which no new term can be discovered and employed, even a highly articulate novelist may be in the position of trying to find the right nonverbal gesture to go with "deh," even if "deh" is *Heart of Darkness*.

Language is the product of desire, and it grows in response to the perception of new desires. As one matures, one's desires enlarge from wanting to have something to wanting to share something. At a certain age children begin to delight in telling stories, in sharing what they know and imagine, in making things up. Their mental worlds become more complex as language teaches them its rules and prompts them to match its range. Language is a means of satisfying frustration as well as expressing it; possibly we are linguistic simply because the world is an imperfect place and because language pulls us toward the achievement of perfection. In that sense, language expresses the condition of existing in time.

Although the frustration of not being able to express something does characterize much of the literature discussed in this book, it is also common to find reference to the complementary experience of absolute happiness and clarity; in fact these emotions often occur together, as the ineffable is experienced yet remains inexpressible. It may be that language is not equipped to deal with the fulfillment or disappearance of desire; certainly a Buddhist would say so. For many people the satisfactions of love bring this level of fulfillment, a unity of Self and Other that obliterates even that distinction and that can find expression in the language of bodies (as John Donne says in "The Extasie"), but which remains integrated and self-sufficient at the Platonic level. As a complex, temporal system, language has a tendency toward perplexity, and there are situations where this can be resolved only by the intrusion of something radically simple.

As Donne puts it:

> This Extasie doth unperplex
> (We said) and tell us what we love.

The only way to understand the silence of such lovers is to be "so refined by love" that one understands the "language" of "souls," by which point one is almost as pure and disembodied as the communion itself. Having found their communion, Donne's lovers do not speak. Only in the poem are they separable enough to be described as communicating, and even that is reduced to a mutuality of souls and an identity of intention and expression. They are joined in their eyes and hands, but even that is a sign in relation to the intercourse of their souls. The radical simplicity of ecstasy must move into other media—must be channeled into sensuality, for instance, or poetry—if there is to be communication; it must enter the less than self-sufficient world of desire and satisfaction if its absolute completeness is to be celebrated. This leaves both the poem and the lovemaking, on their own, a kind of nonsense, unless one is aware of the wholeness that prompts and infuses them. When the words are right, we feel our joy expand; when the lovemaking is right, Donne's lovers feel both the inadequacy and the appropriateness of the language of bodies. Because it represents the obliteration of the distinction between desire and satisfaction, because its communion would have to be broken down to become communication, because it echoes a prelinguistic phase of growth when all our needs were satisfied before being voiced (perhaps even before they were recognized as needs), and because its wholeness does not admit of any difference between signifier and signified, the experience of ecstasy is ineffable.

There is such a strong connection between language and the desire to communicate—especially on the infantile level, where language itself is perceived as a need—that one almost never encounters written language without positing that someone in particular is trying to express something by it.

Only when this desire to identify a speaker and a set of intentions is frustrated—for instance, when reading the output of a computer programmed to write "poetry," or a text composed on principles of random selection—does one become aware of the impulse. On a more general level than the attribution of self-consciousness to various elements of a reflexive novel, one attributes to almost any sentence some underlying or originating consciousness. It is this impulse that transforms language into narration.

Language is so uniquely a product of consciousness that it inevitably suggests to the reader that someone is using it. The reader fantasizes not simply a speaker (as in the analogy of the computer terminal) but a narrator—a deliberate employer of words, not simply a reciter. Language has the consciousness one gives it, and in the case of a narrator this may be a very particular consciousness. An entire spectrum of narration is possible here, at one end of which language "has" or reflects the consciousness of its immediate mortal speaker, and at the other end of which language "has" or appears to reflect the conscious intention to express itself or to let itself be said. When one uses one's own voice to express movements of thought and feeling, as in most nonfiction writing or in everyday speech, the mind implicit or latent in those words is one's own. When an author speaks in the voice of a persona or fictional character—as Dickens does in *David Copperfield,* for instance, or Chandler, in *The Big Sleep*—there is a play of consciousness at work. As the reader senses a manipulator behind the narrator, the words of the novel take on an added unreliability and resonance. David Copperfield is the official consciousness of his novel; his credibility as an autonomous speaker is undermined by Dickens' signature on the cover—though not by many elements of the novel itself. In a story like "Borges and I," however, the identity of the narrator is rendered paradoxical by the story's inner movement, and not even the narrator can be sure "who has written this page."[23] At that point, the only consciousness left for the reader to imagine is a mind of the text.

Moby-Dick's Ishmael functions somewhere between these narrative extremes. Ishmael does not swallow Melville as "I" does Borges, but it is difficult to consider him a neat corporeal persona like Chandler's Marlowe. Ishmael's complex disappearing acts, the depth of his insight into the thoughts of his shipmates, his knowledge of conversations he could not possibly have overheard, and his Joycean dissatisfactions with novelistic convention leave him only one reliable title. He is the consciousness of *Moby-Dick,* wearing the mask "Ishmael"—and undermining or discarding that mask whenever necessary. He is not contained entirely in the words of the novel, yet could not be apprehended or conceived apart from them. It is in this sense that he can be said not to "transcend *Moby-Dick.*" It is also in this sense that the reader's image of him includes something extratextual. If art is "a House that tries to be haunted," then *Moby-Dick* has several ghosts. Ishmael's mask is of the same pasteboard quality, and performs the same metaphysical function, as the white whale's. The logical culmination of this approach to narration (which necessarily includes Proust's "Marcel" and Faulkner's Addie) is the Unnamable, who begins by defining himself as the word "I"—or at least accepts that word until he has no need for words.

Ishmael has other unusual attributes. The very center of the novel's narrative energy, he is complexly *removed* from Ahab and the whale in a way that must be explored before the problems of self-consciousness and metanarration can be fully considered. Like Marlow in *Heart of Darkness,* Zeitblom in *Dr. Faustus,* or Sam in *Watt,* Ishmael is the paradoxical center of his novel: its consciousness, but not its hero; an eye/I whose own experience—the less intense, more verbal twin of the hero's—is his principal means of seeing, sharing, and thus comprehending the sometimes transcendent aspects of the hero's experience. Only because of this combination of shared experience and distance is he able to dramatize the other ghost that haunts the novel. (As Wittgenstein implied, Ishmael cannot describe his *own* haunting.) Although he speaks in the first person, he is actually a

33

surrogate, performing a narration that Ahab could not achieve—offering, in other words, Melville's only means of getting Ahab's insights into words. (Ahab and Pip may participate in "heaven's sense," but they are still "mad" to mortals.) To keep this aspect of the relationship between Ahab and Ishmael in focus, some term more precise than "first-person narration" seems necessary. I propose to call Ishmael a "secondary first-person narrator" and the narrative mode this gives rise to "secondary first-person narration." However useful they may prove in clarifying the Ahab/Ishmael or Kurtz/Marlow structure, these terms are not intended to apply to (and are inadequate to describe) the way in which Ishmael corresponds to the timeless self that forms a limit of the world of Proust's novel, or even the way in which he corresponds to Moby-Dick.

There is doubtless a variety of reasons so many authors decided to employ secondary first-person narration, and the influence of *Moby-Dick* (or even of More's *Utopia*) may be among them. But one of the more intriguing possibilities is that this mode suggested itself to Fitzgerald, Mann, Castaneda, and others for formal and perhaps inherent reasons, because direct recounting would inevitably have been inadequate either to suggest or to analyze the implications of their heroes' quests, whether after white whales or green dock lights, into the heart of darkness, or along the path with heart. One of the difficulties inherent in overreaching limits is that one may cease to make sense to one's fellows. This suggests the necessity of provoking understanding not through explanations but through kindred experience. Even if there were some metalanguage in which one could communicate a transcendent vision—even if one were not limited to describing experience and reactions, rather than the unknown itself—would an audience understand the words, or want to? As Plato has Socrates warn us in the *Republic:*

Now imagine what would happen if he went down again to take his former seat in the Cave. Coming suddenly out of the sunlight, his eyes would be filled with darkness. He might be required once more to deliver his opinion on those shadows, in competition with the prisoners who had never been released, while his eyesight was still dim and unsteady; and it might take some time to become used to the darkness. They would laugh at him and say that he had gone up only to come back with his sight ruined; it was worth no one's while even to attempt the ascent. If they could lay hands on the man who was trying to set them free and lead them up, they would kill him.[24]

This warning has, of course, proved notoriously apt, and in more cases than that of Socrates; there is no substitute for experience. To understand what Kurtz means when he says, "The horror!" Marlow must go through nearly the full range of Kurtz's experience himself. To recount Ahab's experience and its implications, Ishmael must lose himself in the quest for the white whale, must sense its ineffable nature for himself. But if Marlow had gone completely off the deep end with Kurtz, he would be no better than Kurtz at telling the reader what either of them saw when looking over that edge. The narrator, a kind of "secret sharer," must have slightly less heroic energy, and a more verbal bent, than the hero. To Ishmael, Moby-Dick's metaphysical and cetological nature must both become matters of obsession, yet must finally remain aspects of a physical whale. Thus the author of a secondary first-person novel is not forced to deal directly with transcendent experience but can deal with it through the mask of a compulsive narrator who has experienced as much as can be talked about, yet who urges himself, in the aim of relating the hero's experience, ever deeper into regions that can hardly be guessed at.

Metaphysical Heroism:
The Second First Person

The fountain has not played itself out, the frame
still shines, the river still flows, the spring still
bubbles forth, the light has not faded. But between *us* and It, there is a veil which is more like
fifty feet of solid concrete. . . . Already everything in our time is directed to categorizing and
segregating this reality from objective facts. This
is precisely the concrete wall. Intellectually, emotionally, interpersonally, organizationally, intuitively, theoretically, we have to blast our way
through the solid wall, even if at the risk of
chaos, madness, and death. For from *this* side of
the wall, this is the risk.

—R. D. Laing, *The Politics of Experience*

The encounter between don Juan, the man of knowledge,
and Carlos Castaneda, the graduate student taking notes on
the relations between ordinary and nonordinary reality, is
a paradigm of the relations between the metaphysical hero
and his more verbally anchored reflection, the more-than-
apprentice who attempts to tell the hero's story by describing his own encounter with the mysteries of transcendent
power. The metaphysical hero—Ahab, Kurtz, don Juan—is
a figure who has so closely touched these mysteries that he
can be said (from the perspective of the apprentice) to have
joined them, a prophet who has so unequivocally launched
himself into the silence that he cannot tell the whole of his
story but can at best encourage a kindred spirit to follow
him and thus find out the heart of that story for himself.

36

The more the apprentice reaches the master's level of understanding, the more difficult it is for him to set down what he knows; his own story becomes nearly as problematic as the master's. What stops him from becoming the same as the hero is an inherent drive to speak: Marlow's "propensity to spin yarns," Ishmael's profession as schoolmaster, Castaneda's initial desire to complete his thesis in anthropology. His learning what the master is about is a matter not so much of verbal transmission as of personal experience, so when it comes time to tell what he has discovered, he constructs for the reader a structure that is similar to that of his own quest: he focuses not on what happened to the master but on what he himself experienced, letting the reader (who is even more verbally oriented than the apprentice, in the context of this system, since the reader has no firsthand experience of the master but may have some "minimum amount of power" that would qualify him to join the quest) follow the apprentice as the apprentice has followed the master. The apprentice, having touched the mystery himself, tells his own story in the first person, yet he is not the central figure in the system: that figure is the master, whose story is exponentially related to that of the apprentice (the apprentice's experience, squared). Another way to put this might be to call the secondary first-person narrator a stepdown transformer. There is a Platonic form behind these shadows, an ideal first-person narration, and such works as *The Unnamable* have approached it. My focus in this chapter is on those works that have preferred the shadow approach, doubtless because of its great evocative power and structural neatness. Later chapters will address the problem of how the "first" person might tell his own story without the aid of his more verbal intermediary, the shadow of the figure who stands before the light.

1. MOBY-DICK

The subject recognizes the absolute substance, in which it has to annul or lose itself, as being at the same time *its* essence, *its* substance, in which, therefore, self-consciousness is inherently contained. It is this unity, reconciliation, restoration of the subject and of its self-consciousness, the positive feeling of possessing a share in, of partaking in this absolute, and making unity with it actually one's own—this abolition of the dualism, which constitutes the sphere of worship. Worship comprises this entire inward and outward action, which has this restoration to unity as its object.

—G.W.F. Hegel, *Vorlesungen über die Philosophie der Religion*

In *The Poet* Emerson proposes an ideal: "Every man should be so much an artist that he could report in conversation what had befallen him." Not all of us are so gifted, of course; the one who can put everything into words is the poet, "the Namer." A few pages later, however, Emerson acknowledges that "a beauty not explicable is dearer than a beauty which we can see to the end of." Ishmael struggles between these alternatives.

Moby-Dick begins with an attempt to confront the word "whale." At first reading, it hardly seems anything so melodramatic as an attempt at confrontation or a grope for an accurate term to contain all that Moby-Dick comes to incorporate. In fact, the chapters seem pedantic, ironic, and unnecessary. They give the reader the sense of being immersed in a catalogue, up to the ears in quotes about whales, as if Melville had decided to include, undigested, his research materials. Yet in retrospect we can recognize in these chapters, "Etymology" and "Extracts," both the introduction to Ishmael's interest in words and the beginnings of just such an effort at naming. The chapters both serve a serious intention and parody it.

"Etymology" includes three distinct arguments concerning the word "whale"—whether it entered English from the German rather than the Danish, for example—and a list of the words meaning "whale" in thirteen languages, including Hebrew and Fiji. Its material is said to have been supplied by "a Late Consumptive Usher to a Grammar School." This old man, "threadbare in coat, heart, body, and brain," would not last long on the Pequod, nor would he see beyond the word to the whaling and beyond that to the inscrutable force that may lurk behind the wall of Moby-Dick's forehead. Yet it would be pointless, if Melville wanted his reader to grasp the quest for Moby-Dick in all its suspenseful complexity, to begin his book flat out with a discussion of metaphysics. Moby-Dick must be prepared for. Furthermore, Ishmael is engaged in writing a book, and the primary repository for his insights about Moby-Dick is the word "whale." It seems proper to begin with an attempt to search that word for its magic, to seek in the study of its origins that theoretical point where the word held the virtue of the animal, and thus, perhaps, the secret of the mystery of Ahab's experience. What emerges is a list, pedantic yet portentous. The mystery is not to be found, then, in the word alone.

The next chapter, "Extracts," is supposed to have been "Supplied by a Sub-Sub-Librarian"—another caricature both of the novelist and of the researcher without insight. "Give it up, Sub-Subs!" advises Ishmael heartily; yet the chapter serves a purpose similar to that of "Etymology." It immerses the reader in "whale," and hints at a huge, even unmanageable subject. At the same time, it shows little more than that a great many people have had something to say about whales.

"Loomings," the title of the first chapter of the novel proper, is a nautical term for "objects seen through mist or darkness," or "the indistinct and exaggerated appearance of land on the horizon."[1] It too is portentous, but this time of the indistinct, the obscure, the anticipated. It announces the theme of refraction—that is, of the apparent change of size or proportion as an image passes through a medium. Moby-Dick is a mask, or wall; what he represents is refracted through the consciousness of Ahab, yet again through that of Ishmael, and finally through Ishmael's language to us. The process of indistinct exaggeration to which this chapter title alludes is basic to Melville's method of putting us in touch with Moby-Dick's energy. As should become clear later, this process both reduces that energy to a narratable level and magnifies the import of Ishmael's perceptions so that the reader is able to reconstitute the hugeness of that energy. The chapter begins:

> Call me Ishmael. Some years ago—never mind how long precisely—having little or no money in my purse, and nothing particular to interest me on shore, I thought I would sail about a little and see the watery part of the world.

"The watery part of the world," besides referring to the ocean, suggests flux and an absence of solidity. Most of the qualifiers in this second sentence are loose; Ishmael is deliberately, cavalierly imprecise about his money, his interests, his commitment to the voyage, and of course, most significantly, his location in time. On the next page, Ishmael says, "Yes, as every one knows, meditation and water are wedded for ever," giving the reader a better idea of this novel's territory. He goes on to relate the story of Narcissus, "who because he could not grasp the tormenting, mild image he saw in the fountain, plunged into it and was drowned. But that same image, we ourselves see in all rivers and oceans. It is the image of the ungraspable phantom of life; and this is the key to it all." The grasping of an image encountered on the sea is Ishmael's quest in writing this book, and he knows, even in setting out, that he must fail.

What Narcissus sees reflected, of course, is his own image. Looking over the Pequod's edge in "The Symphony," Ahab too watches "how his shadow in the water sank and sank to his gaze, the more and the more he strove to pierce the profundity." Turning to Starbuck, he sees reflected in a human eye the alternative: wife and child, land. He seizes the issue:

40

who is he? who compels him? He accepts the compulsion, the chase—and crossing the deck to look over the ship's other side, he meets in reflection the Parsee, his demonic self. Ishmael's quest is the same. In the watery world, he meets his reflections, the masks of his complex self: Ahab the metaphysician, Bulkington the man of "right reason,"[2] Queequeg, Pip and the others, and the whale. It is in search of this phantom that Ishmael goes to sea. "The key to it all" is that all of them are one self, presided over by a sense of identity, an *I* in search of itself, in search of some final, ungraspable truth of which its aspects perceive aspects.

"Call me Ishmael" could simply be a folksy way for a sailor to introduce himself; in context, however, the sentence suggests its own unreliability. "Call me" hints that "Ishmael" is a false name, chosen for its association with desert wandering (the fate of Ishmael in the Old Testament) by a country schoolmaster well versed in ancient literature. Ambiguously located in time and space, and socially liminal, Ishmael certainly deserves to be called a "wanderer" if not an "outcast." In Hebrew, "Ishmael" means "God will hear"; so the name might also suggest that the narrator desires or anticipates a perfect and metaphysically sympathetic audience. As does the narrator of *A la recherche du temps perdu,* Ishmael at times feels that his spirit "ebbs away from whence it came; becomes diffused through time and space." In pursuit of his wholeness, the incarnation of his mystery, the phantom announces himself.

Ishmael, then, is an indistinctly grasped figure from the outset. Descending into limited identity, into "Ishmael," he nevertheless proceeds immediately to suggest his kinship with the novel's other characters, notably with Ahab. Although he seems altogether more casual than Ahab, and less compulsive (he goes to sea—if we believe him—merely because he has no other pressing engagements and because he is depressed), Ishmael makes it clear that he chooses whaling because he is "tormented with an everlasting itch for things remote." He mentions "the overwhelming idea of the great whale," portraying himself as an overreacher and romantic, a man in search of the *overwhelming*. Ahab and he mirror each other. As Ahab anchors himself in humanity by his friendship with Pip, Ishmael is linked with Queequeg and delivered into life by his coffin; as Ahab is transfixed by the Parsee, Ishmael finds his darker self in Ahab. Having established that Ishmael has it in him to undertake a quest, to be enthralled by Ahab's compulsive "feud"—that he is, in Castaneda's term, an *escogido*[3]—Melville goes on, in the last sentence of "Loomings," to introduce the novel's other phantom, Moby-Dick.

Moby-Dick's major appearance takes place hundreds of pages later and ends the novel. Throughout the 131 chapters between "Loomings" and "The Chase—First Day," Ishmael prepares the reader for that colossal entrance, infusing the image of the white whale with all the suspense and meaning it can bear. This process is by turns romantic and mundane. The chapter "Cetology" sounds almost as if it were written by a Sub-Sub. Whole chapters are given to such themes as "The Right Whale's Head—Contrasted View," "The Whale as a Dish," and "Of Whales in Paint; in Teeth; in Wood; in Sheet-Iron; in Stone; in Mountains; in Stars" (a significantly expansive sequence). Ishmael is attempting to fence in Moby-Dick by relating as much as possible about whales. All these details, however exhausting, both generate a suspenseful anticipation of the whale's appearance and root Moby-Dick in the world of phenomena, thus preventing the novel from spinning off into vortices of metaphysical irony. By the time Moby-Dick appears, the reader is prepared both to be overwhelmed by him and to comprehend, as completely as possible, his physical existence. It is significant, however, that the key metaphysical chapters, "Moby-Dick" and "The Whiteness of the Whale," are centrally concerned with Ahab and Ishmael; the mysteries are simultaneous, and approach together.

Ishmael has a knack for exact description, an interest in cataloguing, and the ability to write entertainingly at great length. He has, in short, a strong verbal streak, and the urge to communicate his experience. He often experiments with narrative method and stylization—breaking into play format, for example, or transcribing the Shakespearean soliloquys of uneducated men, describing some of their remarks as "Asides," utterly failing to account for his knowledge of the innermost thoughts of these people. He refuses to be limited by the conventions of first-person narration and tells things Ishmael the sailor could not possibly know, almost suggesting that he—not Melville—can change to a ubiquitous, omniscient narrator at will. (Moby-Dick is perhaps ubiquitous.) The only alternative is to treat Ishmael's intentional stylization as retrospective myth-making—an attempt, as he sits writing all this down, to deal with his experience as if he were a novelist and to confront his nearly ineffable material on its own terms. He seems to break out of conventional narrative restrictions in order to dramatize the tendency of his subject to transcend the boundaries of ordinary discourse. He tries every prose method that will contain an aspect of his story, much in the way Joyce does in *Ulysses,* with the immense complication that Ishmael is ostensibly a first-person narrator. In fact, it is necessary for him to drop out of the tale for long periods. These disappearances make Ishmael seem paradoxically distanced—and not just by stylization—from his own experience; it appears that this distance allows him to contemplate his story. His style and his nearly phantom nature, then, become the refracting medium through which he comprehends as well as relates his material.

For the most part, the reader is limited to Ishmael's point of view. Yet of the novel's three central characters—Moby-Dick, Ahab, and Ishmael—it is Ahab who appears to be the hero. The quest is primarily his; others are infected with it by the strength of his personality. His self-destructiveness and bearing are tragic. He is central to the story—but not to the narration. Thus he and Ishmael are each central in different ways. The important point is that they are sufficiently similar people that a special relationship exists between them, allowing Ishmael to share and understand much of Ahab's experience. Their differences are equally important: because Ahab is more obsessive and Ishmael more verbal, Ishmael is chosen to return from the sunken Pequod to tell Ahab's tale.

Their kinship and difference are evident in Father Mapple's sermon (Chapter Nine), where aspects of Ahab and Ishmael add up to Jonah, and even to the preacher himself. Jonah's sin is disobedience, wickedness, defiance of God (Ahab); his origins and occupation are at first mysterious (Ishmael); when he sinks undersea, he leaves "smooth water behind" (Ahab); because he accepts his ordeal, he is delivered "from the sea and the whale" (Ishmael). Father Mapple acknowledges, by implication, the Ahab and Ishmael in himself; he is both "pilot" and "mast-head" stander. Most significant, of course, is the result of Jonah's deliverance: he becomes a preacher of God's word, a man who speaks. Ahab goes down, and Ishmael survives.

What perhaps makes this approach to narration necessary is the quality of Ahab's perception of Moby-Dick. Ahab is in touch with the "lower layer" underlying phenomena, an existential mysticism that makes him incomprehensible to most of the people around him. He regards himself as an almost transcendent figure, and Moby-Dick as a metaphysical force:

> "Vengeance on a dumb brute!" cried Starbuck, "that simply smote thee from blindest instinct! Madness! To be enraged with a dumb thing, Captain Ahab, seems blasphemous."
>
> "Hark ye yet again—the little lower layer. All visible objects, man, are but as pasteboard masks. But in each event—in the living act, the undoubted deed—there, some unknown but still reasoning thing puts forth the mouldings of its features from behind the unreasoning mask. If man will strike, strike through the mask! How

can the prisoner reach outside except by thrusting through the wall? To me, the white whale is that wall, shoved near to me. Sometimes I think there's naught beyond. But 'tis enough. He tasks me; he heaps me; I see in him outrageous strength, with an inscrutable malice sinewing it. That inscrutable thing is chiefly what I hate; and be the white whale agent, or be the white whale principal, I will wreak that hate upon him. Talk not to me of blasphemy, man; I'd strike the sun if it insulted me."[4]

The reader is never put directly in touch with whatever is behind the mask; Melville's altogether more dramatic intention is to trace "the mouldings of its features" as it expresses itself through Moby-Dick. A metaphysical hero, Ahab is trying to break out of his prison, to leave Plato's cave; even though he hints that there may be nothing behind the mask, he feels he must strike through it. "In the living act, the undoubted deed," Ahab is determined to confront that place where the ineffable most directly expresses itself. Utterly American, when he finds that place he will harpoon it.

But this paradoxical region is dark, impenetrable. Near the end of the chase, when the whale bears down on the Pequod, directly confronting Ahab and his challenge, Ahab staggers and strikes his own forehead: "I grow blind; hands! stretch out before me that I may yet grope my way. Is't night?"[5] Metaphorically, they are forehead to forehead, and Ahab is in the dark region he challenged the powers of fire to show him. "Thou canst blind, but I can then grope," he had said in defiant "worship";[6] the mystery revealed exceeds the scope of his eyes. In this moment of revelation, even Ishmael cannot see for him.

The very insight and drive that make it possible for Ahab to perceive Moby-Dick as an inscrutable force, necessarily cut him off from other men. The Parsee, who is in sympathy with Ahab's demonic nature, seems at times supernatural.[7] Starbuck, who appeals to Ahab's common humanity, thinks him mad. Pip, who has been driven mad by his own confrontations with water, death, and God, becomes his fit roommate. (Ishmael falls somewhere between Pip and Billy Budd on the scale of Inspiration, and is saved from each of their fates by his ability to articulate his visions.) Ahab does attempt to explain himself, as in the passage quoted above, but most of his deeper meditations are incoherent. Immediately after bewitching his crew with the tale of Moby-Dick and attempting to explain to Starbuck "the little lower layer," Ahab retires to his cabin and says of himself, "They think me mad—Starbuck does; but I'm demoniac, I am madness maddened! That wild madness that's only calm to comprehend itself!"[8] Understanding his own story, but raving in company, he would be a poor narrator for this novel—too ironic and fragmented. His destiny allows no leisure in which to relate his experience; he properly goes to his death, tangled in the line of the harpoon he has trust into Moby-Dick.

Ahab's meditation on his madness, delivered while he is alone in his cabin, is transcribed by Ishmael, whose last mention of himself left him on the mast-head, "with the problem of the universe revolving in me."[9] In that chapter, Ishmael used the precarious perch of the mast-head stander as a metaphor for the need to maintain one's hold on reality when indulging in metaphysical speculation. He felt it would be easy to lose his identity and sense of surroundings; such a "sunken-eyed young Platonist" might lose track of whales, and balance, and fall into the sea.

> In this enchanted mood, thy spirit ebbs away to whence it came; becomes diffused through time and space . . .
>
> There is no life in thee, now, except that rocking life imparted by a gentle rolling ship; by her, borrowed from the sea; by the sea, from the inscrutable tides of God. But while this sleep, this dream is on ye, move your foot or hand an inch; slip your hold at all; and your identity comes back in horror. Over Descartian vortices you hover. And perhaps, at mid-day, in the

fairest weather, with one half-throttled shriek you drop
through that transparent air into the summer sea, no
more to rise for ever. Heed it well, ye Pantheists![10]

Ishmael hovers around that balance point throughout the
novel. Sometimes he is a hard-working sailor, a note-taker
on the physical nature of whales. At other times his spirit,
"diffused through time and space," enters the minds of others, or adopts an anonymous, almost omniscient overview
of the Pequod's journey. This balance point is the equivalent, in Ishmael, of Ahab's "madness," and what is at stake,
what drifts, is his "identity." But whereas Ishmael is able
to recover his footing—as he does most clearly in the "Try-
Works" chapter—Ahab is not. For Ahab the physical world
is interfused with the metaphysical; so perfectly integrated
are they that he expects to wreak his hatred on the inscrutable through action.

In the "Quarter-Deck" chapter, Ishmael relates Ahab's
nailing of the gold piece to the mast, argument with Starbuck, and pledging of the crew to destroy Moby-Dick, in
the third person. In the next chapter, he transcribes Ahab's
"Sunset" meditation; in the next chapter, Starbuck's; in the
next, Stubb's. All three men are described as being alone.
The next chapter takes the form of a play and recounts the
crew's midnight conclave. These four chapters have no obvious narrator. In the next chapter, significantly entitled
"Moby-Dick," Ishmael returns. (The mysteries approach together.) He begins:

> I, Ishmael, was one of that crew; my shouts had gone
> up with the rest; my oath had been welded with theirs;
> and stronger I shouted, and more did I hammer and
> clinch my oath, because of the dread in my soul. A
> wild, mystical sympathetical feeling was in me; Ahab's
> quenchless feud seemed mine.[11]

The energy of the ineffable finds several expressions in
this novel, of varying purity and intensity. It begins as an
inscrutability behind a mask—in itself indescribable. This

energy is then imparted to Moby-Dick. In that form, Ahab has a glimpse of it. Heroically, madly, Ahab communicates not his insight but its energy to his men and drives them until they make his feud their own and are destroyed. Between Ahab and his crew on this energy scale, Ishmael alone understands the meaning of Ahab's pursuit. A man both speculative and practical, he is sucked in not simply by the prospect of heroic adventure and vengeance but by his own perception of Moby-Dick's phantom nature. The experience is one of mystical sympathy. From Ishmael, this energy is communicated to the reader—not in its complete manifestation, of course, since that would be impossible in language. This energy is communicated in much the same manner that "the inscrutable tides of God" set the sea rocking, and the motion is borrowed by the rolling ship, which then is experienced as the "rocking life" that replaces the masthead stander's identity. When in the grip of this energy, it is arguable that Ishmael has the power to enter Ahab's mind (or perhaps simply to reconstruct Ahab's thoughts), then to reenter himself.

Returned, Ishmael tells the history of Moby-Dick, simultaneously offering the hope of rational explanations for the whale's behavior, while deliberately leaving the matter a mystery. He mentions "the unearthly conceit that Moby-Dick was ubiquitous," for example, dismissing those who hold this belief as superstitious, and offering a tentative explanation of such deep sea currents as would allow sperm whales to cover improbable distances very fast; he nevertheless uses the term "mystic modes" to describe the whale's manner of exploiting those currents. In the same frame of mind, he offers a psychological explanation for Ahab's metaphysics: "Small reason was there to doubt, then, that ever since that almost fatal encounter, Ahab had cherished a wild vindictiveness against the whale, all the more fell for that in his frantic morbidness he at last came to identify with him, not only all his bodily woes, but all his intellectual and spiritual exasperations."[12] In the same paragraph he calls Ahab

48

"crazy." Then he pulls back and says, "This is much; yet Ahab's larger, darker, deeper part remains unhinted. But vain to popularize profundities, and all truth is profound." Such fencing is characteristic of Ishmael's need to have both his practical and speculative natures on call. Melville uses the limitations of his narrator's metaphysical insights to hint things that would be meaningless if said directly:

> Such a crew, so officered, seemed specially picked and packed by some infernal fatality to help him to his monomaniac revenge. How it was that they so aboundingly responded to the old man's ire—by what evil magic their souls were posssessed, that at times his hate seemed almost theirs; the White Whale as much their insufferable foe as his; how all this came to be—what the White Whale was to them, or how to their unconscious understandings, also, in some dim, unsuspected way, he might have seemed the gliding great demon of the seas of life,—all this to explain, would be to dive deeper than Ishmael can go.[13]

Ishmael then tries to explain what the whale means *to him,* and finds himself in a region of namelessness. "Aside from those more obvious considerations touching Moby-Dick, which could not but occasionally awaken in any man's soul some alarm," he says, "there was another thought, or rather vague, nameless horror concerning him, which at times by its intensity completely overpowered all the rest; and yet so mystical and well nigh ineffable was it, that I almost despair of putting it in a comprehensible form."[14] He finds that the only way he can hope to express his reaction to the whiteness of the whale is a "dim, random" one. That combination of narrative distance and temperamental sympathy which allowed him to express his insights into Ahab's mad metaphysics, and thus in a clearer way to deal with the meaning of Moby-Dick, suddenly does not apply. Attempting to explain his own feelings about the whale, he is divested of his intermediary, Ahab, and finds himself fumbling. He makes

49

a great effort, but fortunately does not abandon his knack for suggestion, as the indefiniteness of this statement shows: "there yet lurks an elusive something in the innermost idea of this hue, which strikes . . . panic to the soul." Whiteness makes bears and sharks "transcendent horrors," heightens "terror to the furthest bounds," and in a spiritual context enforces "a certain nameless terror." After revealing that he does acknowledge "demonism in the world," he arrives at his paradoxical statement of the quality of that whiteness:

> Is it that by its indefiniteness it shadows forth the heart-less voids and immensities of the universe, and thus stabs us from behind with the thought of annihilation, when beholding the white depths of the milky way? Or is it, that as in essence whiteness is not so much a color as the visible absence of color, and at the same time the concrete of all colors; is it for these reasons that there is such a dumb blankness, full of meaning, in a wide land-scape of snows—a colorless, all-color of atheism from which we shrink?[15]

He approaches it in terms of its indefiniteness first, respecting its resistance to precise formulation. When he moves on to define it as reminding him of atheism, he appears to be settling for a concrete label. What atheism may mean here, however, is the perception of a world without God, not a godless perceiver; in this sense, Ishmael's insight is reminiscent of Ahab's speculation that there may be nothing behind the pasteboard mask. But the most daring attempt Ishmael makes to explain himself is the compelling paradox of the "visible absence of color, and at the same time the concrete of all colors . . . a dumb blankness, full of meaning." (Compare Addie Bundren's "a shape to fill a lack.") This is, in fact, a perfect metaphor for the literarily almost-incar-nated unknowable: a silent blank, portentous and indefinite—and for a method of offering "all colors" by pre-senting a "visible absence." Such paradoxes, which appear not to make sense, can be comprehended only when some insight is attained of a reality that includes nonverbals and reconciles contradictions. They do not describe this reality but urge the reader on to that place in himself where he finds he understands it.

In the next chapter, "The Chart," Ishmael snares Ahab in the same imagery; the spirit that glares out of Ahab's eyes, "a ray of living light . . . without an object to color," is "a blankness in itself." From here, Ishmael retreats to his balance point. Involved with the chase even to the point of replacing the Parsee as Ahab's bowman, he nevertheless maintains critical distance from Ahab's madness. His position is best illustrated by this excerpt:

> . . . then the rushing Pequod, freighted with savages, and laden with fire, and burning a corpse, seemed the material counterpart of her monomaniac commander's soul.
>
> So seemed it to me, as I stood at her helm, and for long hours silently guided the way of this fire-ship on the sea. Wrapped, for that interval, in darkness myself, I but the better saw the redness, the madness, the ghastliness of others. The continual sight of the fiend shapes before me, capering half in smoke and half in fire, these at last begat kindred visions in my soul.[16]

The ambiguous, shrouded nature of his identity (or pose), then, is partly responsible for his ability to understand "the madness . . . of others." On the heels of this darkness, he almost loses himself in a dream, then retreats from his vision in horror to a half-optimistic realism. Thus balanced, he is able to have some firsthand comprehension of what Ahab feels, but he need not drive himself to destruction. He is able to be deeply intrigued without becoming possessed. If Starbuck, rather than Ishmael, had survived to tell this tale, the reader would have little idea what all the fuss was about, and the narration would not be involved in its own battle with limits.

This refractive method of narration serves both to intensify and to moderate transcendental statements. The most direct statement about the ineffable must necessarily evade its subject matter if it is not simply to be tautological, paradoxical, silly, or meaningless. To be dealt with in language, and particularly in literature, such resistant material must be filtered, or masked, and approached in part. In *Moby-Dick,* the whale himself is such a filter; as it is experienced by Ahab, the energy is filtered further, to the point where it can be comprehended and expressed by Ishmael, who is the mask through whom the energy reaches us. By now the energy is so multiply filtered that we can look at it, as if these three characters were the successive layerings of optical filters through which we can gaze at the sun without being blinded. In that sense the energy is diminished.

On the other hand, this material, however moderated from its unnarratable original, makes feverish reading. Our comprehension of Ishmael's insights, which themselves beat at the boundaries of expressibility, allows us to guess at the intensity, and comprehend the meaning, of Ahab. The manifest presence of the filters allows us to imagine the brightness of the image we would see if we removed them—a brightness that must be even greater than what we have encountered so far. Removing the Ahab filter, we can almost conceive the energy of the whale, and beyond him, whatever lurks in his whiteness, whatever "puts forth the mouldings of its features from behind the unreasoning mask."

2.   *HEART OF DARKNESS*

> The road suddenly became a mirror gallery. You no longer saw landscape, but faces. I watched mine advancing.
> —Edmond Jabès, *The Book of Questions*

Five men sit in a boat on the Thames. All are old friends, with seagoing experience. One of them is Marlow, the long-winded storyteller of *Lord Jim;* another is the anonymous narrator of *Heart of Darkness.* Marlow tells these men the story of his journey into the Congo and his encounter with Mr. Kurtz, an agent in charge of a trading post, who had changed inexplicably from an idealistic capitalist to a sort of demigod dictator over the natives who brought him ivory. Marlow had attempted to bring Kurtz out of the Congo, but Kurtz had died on the way; and his last words had been, "The horror! The horror!" Marlow suggests that what Kurtz discovered in the Congo, and in himself, was a "heart of darkness." By the end of the tale, told in the dark, the narrator has been brought to feel that the Thames itself "seemed to lead into the heart of an immense darkness."

Heart of Darkness corresponds to *Moby-Dick* in several ways. Ishmael felt himself chosen by fate to join the crew of the Pequod, suggested that some "infernal fatality" charmed the crew into adopting Ahab's obsession, and observed finally that he was ordained by "the Fates" to replace the Parsee as Ahab's bowman and thus to survive the wreck. Similarly, Charlie Marlow, on the way to the job interview with the Company, which will send him to Africa, passes something like the Fates in an outer office. In both novels these appeals to classical mythology prepare the reader for supernatural dealings; in both cases fate corresponds to the "power" that recognizes the *escogido's* latent talents and difference and that "selects" him.

More stikingly, there is the hierarchy of transcendent experience: the heart of darkness, Kurtz, Marlow, narrator, reader; cosmic inscrutability, Moby-Dick, Ahab, Ishmael, reader. Conrad's tale dispenses with the Moby-Dick stage and adds a secondary narrator.

Marlow is self-conscious about his task as a narrator. He is aware of the difficulty of communicating experience, whether nonverbal or simply personal. He despairs of being able to show his audience the man behind the work "Kurtz," for example, or the exact reality his words are trying to express. As he puts it, the only thing that makes his attempt easier is the fact that he is talking to friends who know him and may be able, through that knowledge, to divine the meaning of his experience:

> "This simply because I had a notion it somehow would be of help to that Kurtz whom at the time I did not see—you understand. He was just a word for me. I did not see the man in the name any more than you do. Do you see him? Do you see the story? Do you see anything? It seems to me I am trying to tell you a dream—making a vain attempt, because no relation of a dream can convey the dream-sensation. . . . No, it is impossible; it is impossible to convey the life-sensation of any given epoch of one's existence—that which makes its truth, its meaning—its subtle and penetrating essence. It is impossible. We live, as we dream, alone. . . ."
>
> He paused again as if reflecting, then added—
>
> "Of course in this you fellows see more than I could then. You see me, whom you know. . . ."
>
> It had become so pitch dark that we listeners could hardly see one another. For a long time already he, sitting apart, had been no more to us than a voice. There was not a word from anybody. The others might have been asleep, but I was awake. I listened, I listened on the watch for the sentence, for the word, that would give me the clue to the faint uneasiness inspired by this narrative that seemed to shape itself without human lips in the heavy night-air of the river.[17]

It is as difficult to see the man in the name as to feel another's dream-sensation. Even so, the "faint uneasiness" that the narrator feels is a sign that Marlow has managed to communicate some of the feeling of his experience. For Marlow, as for the narrator, Kurtz and the tale begin as words whose signifieds are to be discovered. (The quests are parallel and include that of the reader, now self-consciously "seeing" only words.) The "subtle and penetrating essence" that Marlow despairs of putting into his words has somehow been partially conveyed—whether through Marlow's tone of voice, through the narrator's will (a deliberate act of imaginative empathy), or through more verbal devices is not said. As in *Moby-Dick,* it is presumed easier to comprehend the unknown through the medium of a personal acquaintance who has more deeply explored that territory ("You see me, whom you know"). The narrator invests his own retelling of Marlow's tale with two particularly unsettling details at this point. Because he cannot see Marlow, but can only hear his voice, he gives us the sense that he is in the presence of a narrator completely possessed by his story, that Marlow is in fact only a voice. (The parallels with Faulkner's *Absalom, Absalom!* are striking here; this is very much the way Quentin and Shreve are possessed by the story of Sutpen.) He tops that by suggesting that the story "seemed to shape itself without human lips"; in that sense, the narrator directly confronts the mystery simply by listening to the autonomous tale.

Conrad skillfully prepares the reader for a story so intimately connected with the unknown and the nonverbal that its very telling seems to involve extraverbal agencies. Kurtz, Marlow, and (from the reader's perspective) the narrator are all, primarily, voices. This is a story that could marshal the elements to get itself told, and that finally evokes on the Thames something like the darkness of which it speaks. The ineffable surrounds the words. In the following passage the narrator makes it clear that the meaning of Marlow's tale is not contained in its signs:

> The yarns of seamen have a direct simplicity, the whole meaning of which lies within the shell of a cracked nut. But Marlow was not typical (if his propensity to spin yarns be excepted) and to him the meaning of an episode was not inside like a kernel but outside, enveloping the tale which brought it out only as a glow brings out a haze, in the likeness of one of these misty halos that sometimes are made visible by the spectral illumination of moonshine.[18]

The haze can be many things: the deeper meaning of an event, the "subtle and penetrating essence" of a personal experience, or an unknowable. In this case the heart of darkness is all three. The structure of the telling, however—not just the tale—is the glow that brings out the haze: the system between the episode and its meaning. There is no other way to illuminate this halo.

The narrator's primary functions here are to retell Marlow's story and to be its perfect audience. Like the narrator/transcriber of *The Turn of the Screw,* this narrator feels special sympathy with the teller and his tale; this is how he is "selected" as an *escogido* of the next level. Through his reaction to the tale, and as a matter of his own personal experience, the listener/narrator demonstrates the story's evocative nature and describes the bringing out of the haze—thus allowing Conrad's short novel to develop more of the latent material in Marlow's story and to approach more closely a demonstration of the workings of those forces that it could not hope to contain entirely. This telling of the telling of the tale, this setting of one narrative system within another that reveals its nature and power, is the indicator and basis of *Heart of Darkness*'s reflexivity.

As the central symbol of a complex work, the heart of darkness has many aspects. First, it is the potential for uncivilized behavior. "Civilized" behavior in this novel is rarely admirable, however: sometimes brutally imperialistic and sometimes merely stupid, ignorant both of the value of human life and labor and of the "dark" side of reality. While Kurtz consciously explores the darkness in himself, his countrymen do evil without confronting its root in their own nature. So the heart of darkness is also the destructively selfish aspect of human character, freed from sublimation in the Congo just as the Freudian *Id* is freed to express itself most clearly in dreams. (One reason Marlow presents his experience as being dreamlike is that the Congo has quite literally become an imperialist nightmare.) Above all else, this heart of darkness is obscure, difficult to formulate, not so much a particular threat as a category of experience.

Kurtz feels no urge to tell anyone much about this monstrous negativity. His basic reaction is to feel horror but not to change his ways. Finding the report he had written on the "Suppression of Savage Customs," he scrawls across it, "Exterminate all the brutes!" This note does little to communicate to any potential reader the relations among "savagery," "civilization," and Kurtz; it is a warning from hell, but against what? When Marlow arrives to take Kurtz back to Europe, he describes him as a man whose "intelligence was perfectly clear" but whose "soul was mad." Chasing him into the jungle, Marlow finds Kurtz in an almost transcendent state: "He had kicked himself free of the earth. Confound the man! he had kicked the very earth to pieces. He was alone, and I before him did not know whether I stood on the ground or floated in the air." Kurtz's state of being, then, is contagious; yet he is alone. His soul is "an inconceivable mystery . . . struggling blindly with itself."[19] In all these respects Kurtz resembles Ahab.

Just before he dies on Marlow's boat, Kurtz has a vision, a "supreme moment of complete knowledge. He cried in a whisper at some image, at some vision—."[20] This cry appears to Marlow to be both a summation and a judgment of what Kurtz sees. But the words, "The horror! The horror!", do not describe that vision; they can communicate only to someone who knows their context intimately. And it is Marlow's role to comprehend them as it was Ishmael's.

Conrad is at pains to suggest that Marlow's journey into the Congo is analogous to Kurtz's on virtually every level and also that Kurtz goes irrevocably deeper into each stage of that journey. Whereas Kurtz dies, Marlow nearly dies; even Marlow's way of relating that fact suggests that his collapse is related to Kurtz's: "the next day the pilgrims buried something in a muddy hole. And then they very nearly buried me. However, as you see, I did not go to join Kurtz

57

there and then. I did not. I remained to dream the nightmare out to the end."[21] Their journeys in are parallel, then, but only Marlow journeys back.

Before Kurtz's death Marlow had observed: "His was an impenetrable darkness. I looked at him as you peer down at a man who is lying at the bottom of a precipice where the sun never shines."[22] Marlow's own collapse allows him to penetrate some aspect of this darkness. Stepping over the edge of life, Kurtz had his revelation. When Marlow nearly dies, he not only appreciates Kurtz's vantage point and feels the weight of his pronouncement but, in fact, undergoes Kurtz's experience—almost as if he had been allowed to *become* Kurtz:

> "Since I had peeped over the edge myself, I understand better the meaning of his stare, that could not see the flame of the candle, but was wide enough to embrace the whole universe, piercing enough to penetrate all the hearts that beat in the darkness. He had summed up— he had judged. 'The horror!' He was a remarkable man.
> . . . And it is not my own extremity that I seem to have lived through. True, he had made that last stride, he had stepped over the edge, while I had been permitted to draw back my hesitating foot."[23]

If, as Marlow says, "we live, as we dream, alone," then the only way another's private experience can be comprehended is for one almost to become the other. If one is ever to share the experience with a wider audience, words or something like them must be used. Yet Kurtz's insight cannot be deeply comprehended by someone who simply listens to his words; one needs a figure through whom to dramatize and experience the comprehension. So Marlow necessarily undergoes a less intense crisis than Kurtz: he draws back his foot from the edge. If he had gone over, he would have become as dense a source as Kurtz—not because he would be dead, but because his insights would more effectively resist verbalization. On his return to England, Marlow is, of course, hardly in a communicative mood.[24] Conrad apparently found it necessary to force him to betray his insights (by having Marlow lie to Kurtz's fiancée[25]) in order to reverse his course.

As Marlow finishes the tale, he is described as "indistinct and silent, in the pose of a meditating Buddha."[26] This tells much about how he has chosen to deal with his knowledge. He has to some extent withdrawn, in the manner of sages and monks who wish to keep in touch with the ineffable and avoid distraction; he is "apart" even from his audience. His indistinctness almost suggests that he is on the boundaries of physical existence, a creature of the haze like his vision. It is clear that he has given the story time to settle before attempting to relate it, at what loss of its integrity one can only speculate. All this is set up in the narrator's first description of Marlow: "He had sunken cheeks, a yellow complexion, a straight back, an ascetic aspect, and, with his arms dropped, the palms of hands outward, resembled an idol."[27] He is like a medium, if not a spirit, and the context is Eastern. Because his audience is in a meditative mood, and because Marlow insists that they listen past his words, the stage is set for metaverbal communication. The heart of darkness not only impresses the narrator but appears to surround the boat.[28]

Marlow is still not detached enough from his insight to be able to write it down, even if he does put most of it into words. So the narrator—a less intense version of Marlow, as Marlow is of Kurtz[29]—is necessary if the story is to reach paper. Another way to say this is that Marlow is here as deeply in touch with his experience as the narrator is with his own but that because the narrator's is one step further removed from Kurtz's than is Marlow's, it is sufficiently filtered to admit of literary expression.

The narrator's experience of the heart of darkness is rooted in words, even if those words appear to speak themselves, but it also has nonverbal aspects. He is made ill at ease by the story (or its "haze") and feels the presence of "an immense darkness" at the end of the Thames and in the weather, even as Marlow had felt it in the wind when he visited Kurtz's fiancée. From this equivalent, however less intense, of Marlow's breakdown—which in itself was a less intense analogue to Kurtz's—the narrator is able to grasp the "subtle and penetrating essence" of Marlow's experience. Because he has personally felt all this, he is able to provide his own resonant reduction of the story rather than simply to transcribe the monologue. Since the darkness he imagines to be at the furthest reach of the "tranquil waterway" is also at the hidden center of the tale, the Thames becomes the narrator's metaphor for the revealing indirection of his own narrative structure.

The narrator's closeness to Marlow is made clear in several ways, some of which also emphasize Marlow's closeness to Kurtz. The clearest of these is Marlow's appearing to the narrator as only a voice. Several times Marlow, too, refers to Kurtz's voice, once even saying, "I made the strange discovery that I had never imagined him as doing, you know, but as discoursing. . . . The man presented himself as a voice."[30] At the beginning of the story, the narrator mentioned that he, like Marlow, had been a seaman; Marlow, of course, had also shared professions with Kurtz, going off in the employ of the Company. One of the subtlest connections is so offhand that it may be a mistake on Conrad's part: Marlow seems able to read the narrator's thoughts, or somehow to be in touch with the latter's narration. At the beginning, the five sit silent, meditating. The narrator thinks, but does not speak, of the "great knights-errant of the sea," who had colonized the Thames. Two pages later, Marlow says, "I was thinking of very old times, when the Romans first came here, nineteen hundred years ago—the other day . . . Light came out of this river since—you say Knights?"[31] The narrator has said nothing, and nothing in Marlow's speech suggests that he has been interrupted at this point by the narrator with his bright comment about Sir Francis Drake. Together with the meditative mood and the Buddhist pose, this odd remark suggests how much further this tale-telling may be from spoken language.

60

From Kurtz, to Marlow, to the narrator, then—though all three attain similar ethical insights and all three have severely unsettling confrontations with darkness—there is an increase in verbalization and a decrease in transcendental intensity. In one sense, this is the same filtering process used in *Moby-Dick:* the narrator is relating Marlow's experience, Marlow is relating Kurtz's. Kurtz is unable to say coherently what he knows, because he is too close to it; Marlow can find words to talk about Kurtz and himself, although he is unable to describe their vision except in metaphor; the narrator can write about Marlow's experience, and within that, Kurtz's, because they are contained within the story of his own experience of uneasy listening.

Each character tells, however partially, his own story. *Heart of Darkness* itself is the story of one man's listening to another named Marlow; it is the record of the narrator's experience. He insulates the manifestation of the ineffable with "seemed to" and "appeared to," yet one feels he has been as deeply touched by the atmosphere of a story as one can be. In telling his own story, he must try to communicate that sense of uneasiness aroused in him by both the verbal and nonverbal aspects of Marlow's narration. He is not simply a transcriber of Marlow's words, but must manage to evoke the quality of his own nonverbal experience as well. (The question of transcription will be more fully addressed in Chapter Four.)

Marlow's task is essentially the same: he must tell what he discovered and felt during that period of his life which included a confrontation with the heart of darkness. Because he is closer than the narrator to the edge of verbalizable experience, his response to that confrontation is initiated not by his tongue but by his whole system: he nearly dies, then becomes antisocial, and finally withdraws into himself.

Kurtz feels even less of an urge to communicate than Marlow did in the London streets. His remarks are not descriptions but exclamations. Kurtz has no filter through which to confront that horror which he sees underlying all life. Although he is capable of great eloquence when writing im-

61

peralist pamphlets and is well versed in several arts, language—and the urge to speak—fail him here. Put in a context that readers can understand, his exclamations are all the more chilling for that "failure."

It is, as Marlow first observed, impossible to "convey the dream-sensation" by relating the dream. Inevitably, any verbal formulation of experience must remain a verbal formulation and will lose some of the quality of its model. In spite of what it may gain in poetry, it is not a primary experience of the sort it describes; rather, it is a primary *poetic* experience. If this were not so, and if it were possible to communicate the heart of darkness itself, directly, in words, then both Marlow and the narrator would be as shaken as Kurtz. Instead, each successive relation dilutes the primary experience. In this way, the unrelatable material is reduced to relatable terms—specifically, the emotions felt by a friend in his nonverbal moment, as comprehended through kindred experience. Through this and other means, the narrator is able to grasp the meaning that envelops Marlow's tale and in his turn to show us how to find the meaning that envelops his own.

3. WATT, DOCTOR FAUSTUS, AND PALE FIRE

Spirit is not something having a single existence, but is spirit only in being objective to itself, and in beholding itself in the "Other," as itself. The highest characteristic of spirit is self-consciousness, which includes this objectivity in itself. God, as Idea, is subjective for what is objective and objective for what is subjective. When the moment of subjectivity defines itself further, so that the distinction is made between God as object and the knowing spirit, the subjective side defines itself in this distinction as that which belongs to the side of finiteness, and the two stand

at first so contrasted, that the separation constitutes the antithesis of finiteness and infiniteness.
This infinitude, however, being still encumbered
with this opposition, is not the true infinitude; to
the subjective side, which exists for itself, the absolute object remains still an Other, and the relation in which it stands to it is not self-consciousness.

> —G.W.F. Hegel, *Vorlesungen über die
> Philosophie der Religion*

In his study of *Moby-Dick, Heart of Darkness,* and *Absalom,
Absalom!,* James Guetti argues that Ishmael and Ahab represent two different modes of cognition, two sets of existential
expectation:

> For Ishmael the imagination begins and ends with lan-
> guage, and he is aware of the existence of something
> beyond his ordering imagination only in the sense that
> he fails to express it unequivocally. But what is ineffable
> for Ishmael is not so for Ahab; for him the world be-
> yond the artifices of the visible—the supposed reality—
> is not unknowable but only unknown; it is potentially
> perceivable and, indeed, assailable through agents like
> the white whale—agents which, therefore, are them-
> selves revelations.[32]

Ishmael and Ahab, then, have different expectations of
Moby-Dick. Ahab, although willing to chance the discovery
that "there's naught beyond," is in search of some transfiguring principle or order; Ishmael, the man of words, holds
on to the possibility of ordering his narration by deliberately
accepting his inability to understand all that "the whiteness
of the whale" connotes. Because Ishmael himself displays
some of the aspects of this "whiteness," as narrator,[33] Melville is able to make manifest his novel's central and paradoxical perceptions without having to explain them. The

whale may not be a definitive revelation, but Ishmael is, and he succeeds in projecting his own "whiteness" precisely by *not* discussing or calling attention to it.

Guetti argues that Ahab's expectations are dismissed, if not parodied, by his death and that Ishmael's position is vindicated. I would like to suggest, however, that Melville is actually dramatizing two ways of getting at the ineffable (one of which allows for perspective and survival) and that Ahab, in his sudden "blindness," is learning not that there is no transfiguring order, but that such an order may be unknowable. Ishmael's position is vindicated, but not at the expense of Ahab's essential insights: that there *are* masks, and that something may be behind them. It is probably impossible for Ishmael to realize the way in which he himself participates in this mystery, and it is dramatically effective for Melville to displace onto Ahab the quest for absolute metaphysical knowledge. Ishmael confronts the whale-mystery through Ahab; the reader confronts the language-mystery through Ishmael.

It cannot, of course, be determined whether any language-mystery can ever clarify the mysteries of the universe, but it can be observed that *Moby-Dick* maintains its hold on clarity by displacing—and, in some cases, refusing to discuss—the process of revelation. What I should like to demonstrate here is the evocative utility of secondary first-person narration as a technique of displacement, a method of indirection that has helped a surprisingly large number of authors to goad their readers "to find directions out." The novel is the province of the narrator; the narrator is a hero of language, and must deal with and within its limits.

Like *Madame Bovary,* Samuel Beckett's *Watt* is a first-person novel whose narrator has a tendency to disappear from the reader's consideration, yet whose painstaking attempts at objectivity only make more clear the narrator's emotional commitment to the characters and their problems.[34] The narrator of Beckett's novel is named Sam, but any other points of contact between narrator and author seem obscure. Sam is presented as a devoted, if occasionally inaccurate, transcriber of the long monologue of his friend, Watt. He makes little attempt to interpret the meaning of Watt's experience or to describe his own reactions to the tale. But the deliberateness of his transcription of the maddeningly permutative monologues shows that he has been hooked. Like Watt, he must mention everything.

During the time of their acquaintance, Watt and Sam live in corridored "mansions" and meet in a garden fenced off by barbed wire; at one point, Watt is "transferred to another pavilion" and has to crawl through this fence to tell Sam the rest of his story. Finally, exhausted by the many years of relating his life story, Watt returns to his pavilion forever. Sam attempts to write down what he had heard, until he is overcome by "fatigue and disgust." Watt uses several unique narrative methods, such as speaking in apparent gibberish while walking oddly, but Sam proves able to decipher each language and to continue to get it all down in his "little notebook."

What Watt has gone through is a long, eerie confrontation with the mysteries of the universe as they express themselves in the household of Mr. Knott, where for most of his story Watt is employed as a servant. Watt is a peculiar man, who thinks he knows how to smile because he has seen it done so often, yet who imitates one so badly that he affronts or confuses people. His "way of advancing due east . . . was to turn his bust as far as possible towards the north and at the same time to fling out his right leg as far as possible towards the south, and then to turn his bust as far as possible towards the south and at the same time to fling out his left leg as far as possible towards the north,"[35] without bending his knees. He is also very bad at making generalizations and at putting his intuitions into words.

The novel opens with Watt's journey to Mr. Knott's house, where he is greeted by the servant whom his coming displaces. This man attempts to give Watt some idea of what he is getting into, as a previous servant had done for him

65

when he had arrived. The servants, he says, become aware that they are involved in unknowable matters while working for Mr. Knott—that employer, house, and rituals are part of a mystery. This mystery is of the sort considered by Wittgenstein (and before him by Augustine, the mystery religions, and so on): its resistances to comprehension and to language are related. As the outgoing servant puts it, "what we know partakes in no small measure of the nature of what has so happily been called the unutterable or ineffable, so that any attempt to utter or eff it is doomed to fail, doomed, doomed to fail."[36] Even though he is himself "imbued" with his "dearly won" insights from head to foot, he finds himself unable to explain them. But he does not stand in any hierarchical relation to Watt, as Kurtz does to Marlow; he and Watt are educated in much the same way by their direct personal experience of the household. The hierarchical relationship exists between Watt and Sam.

The second part of the novel describes Watt's life as downstairs servant. The third part, which also includes a flash forward to his friendship with Sam, describes his service upstairs. In the fourth and final part, Watt leaves Mr. Knott's employ when a new servant appears. Neither this new servant nor Watt has any idea how either got into the house. Watt knew he himself came in the back door, but not how it happened to be open; nor had he seen the previous servant leave. The new man knows only that one moment he was out, and the next he was in. This suggests that one enters Mr. Knott's territory by means of a sort of quantum leap, as if the precipitous succession of servants were intended as a symbolic parody of transcendence.

One day during Watt's employ Mr. Gall and his son arrive to tune the piano. Their visit upsets and confuses Watt. As Sam puts it: "What distressed Watt in this incident of the Galls father and son, and in subsequent similar incidents, was not so much that he did not know what had happened, for he did not care what had happened, as that nothing had happened, that a thing that was nothing had happened, with

66

the utmost formal distinctness. . . ."[37] In this incident, then, Watt confronts the manifestation of something parodistically ineffable: "a thing that was nothing"—comparable, perhaps, to the "dumb blankness, full of meaning" that upsets Ishmael. But it is characteristic of Watt that he is unable to rest with a paradox or to accept (as it is said the previous servants had been unable to accept) the unknowable as a fact of life. He must try to explain it in nonparadoxical terms. For Watt, as Sam says, an explanation is an exorcism. He is not troubled by whatever can be explained; the logically unformulatable upsets him, however. To speak of a nothing stymies him: "For the only way one can speak of nothing is to speak of it as though it were something, just as the only way one can speak of God is to speak of him as though he were a man."[38] (This "man," or "full grown . . . foetal soul,"[39] may even be—or resemble—Mr. Knott.)

The following excerpt sets forth Watt's problem most clearly:

Not that Watt desired information, for he did not. But he desired words to be applied to his situation, to Mr Knott, to the house, to the grounds, to his duties, to the stairs, to his bedroom, to the kitchen, and in a general way to the conditions of being in which he found himself. For Watt now found himself in the midst of things which, if they consented to be named, did so as it were with reluctance. And the state in which Watt found himself resisted formulation in a way no state had ever done, in which Watt had ever found himself. . . . Looking at a pot, for example, or thinking of a pot, at one of Mr Knott's pots, of one of Mr Knott's pots, it was in vain that Watt said, Pot, pot. Well, perhaps not quite in vain, but very nearly. For it was not a pot, the more he looked, the more he reflected, the more he felt sure of that, that it was not a pot at all. It resembled a pot, it was almost a pot, but it was not a pot of which one could say, Pot, pot, and be comforted. It was in vain that it answered, with unexceptionable adequacy, all the purposes, and performed all the offices, of a pot, it was not a pot. And it was just this hairbreadth departure from the nature of a true pot that so excruciated Watt.[40]

Sam goes on to explain that if the "departure from the nature of a true pot" had been greater, then Watt would have been able to say that he simply did now know the name of this utensil. The problem with this "pot" is that there is no possible name for it. Accurate terms cannot be applied to it. Because many things in Mr. Knott's household have this unsettling quality, as if something unknowable were manifesting "the mouldings of its features from behind the unreasoning mask," Watt finds that his entire situation resists verbalization. Furthermore, he finds himself alone in this particular aspect of his unease: "For the pot remained a pot, Watt felt sure of that, for everyone but Watt,"[41] just as for Starbuck Moby-Dick remained a whale.

Watt's strategy for explaining, and thus exorcising, his situation is to describe it in many conflicting ways, trusting that one of them must be right. He rounds up all the variables that might apply to the situation in question and then combines them in almost every possible arrangement, often regardless of sense. Even if one of these combinations should happen to correspond to the truth, Watt would have no way of recognizing it; his only satisfaction is that somewhere in his thinking he may have hit on that permutation which correctly expresses the situation.[42] The problem, and the cause of Watt's despair, is that *no* words in whatever sequence can apply to those manifestations that really trouble him. He persists in an attempt doomed by definition, and he suffers.

Years later he tries to communicate his insights to Sam. His method of explanation is still permutational. He describes the routines of the household by mentioning every relevant detail in every combination, so as to overlook nothing. The beginning of one of these two-page descriptions reads:

As for his feet, sometimes he wore on each a sock, or on the one a sock and on the other a stocking, or a boot, or a shoe, or a slipper, or a sock and boot, or a sock and shoe, or a sock and slipper, or a stocking and boot, or a stocking and shoe, or a stocking and slipper, or nothing at all. And sometimes he wore on each a stocking, or on the one a stocking and on the other a boot, or a shoe, or a slipper. . . .[43]

Watt is not able to generalize, or to say, "Mr. Knott wore socks and stockings, boots, shoes, and slippers, or nothing at all, at various times and in various combinations." He is safe only if he describes each combination. This limitation is part of the reason he is so upset by occurrences that demand intuitive comprehension. (It is not that Watt is not intuitive, but that he is upset so long as those intuitions cannot be precisely verbalized.)

When these catalogs fail to capture the essence of his experience, Watt begins to perform permutations on the English language, inverting with mathematical precision first the order of the words in the sentence, then that of the letters in the word, and so on. Because he is still dealing with the language, however, he fails here too. He stops only because of exhaustion.

But Sam has been touched. The reader must infer that Sam has a permutative streak in him, too, because Watt's catalogings are usually reproduced whole. Although he does seem more articulate, Sam cannot put unutterables into language any better than Watt can. His transcription of a monologue such as the following, uttered by the servant who leaves at Watt's arrival, suggests his own unwillingness to condense and generalize: "Mary . . . remained there quietly eating onions and peppermints turn and turn about, I mean first an onion, then a peppermint, then another onion, then another peppermint, then another onion, then another peppermint,"[44] and so on for half a page. Sam describes himself as an incompetent narrator, unreceptive to Watt's communications as well as untalented at conveying them to anyone else.[45] He attempts to overcome his limitations by taking notes, and he does, in fact, prove better able than Watt to knock his revelations into shape. In this sense he is like the narrator of *Heart of Darkness,* who is able through his emotional and intellectual sympathy with Marlow—as well as his distance from Kurtz—to transform the monologue from the groping utterance of a withdrawn man into a printed narrative. Sam's similarity to Watt is made most clear in those moments when he speaks in his own voice and is seen to belabor every element of his own statements. He muses once, "To think, when one is no longer young, when one is not yet old, that one is no longer young, that one is not yet old, that is perhaps something."[46]

We can extend the parallel with *Heart of Darkness.* Mr. Knott, or the ineffable that manifests itself in his household, is comparable to the heart of darkness, while Watt is, however comically and inadvertently, a metaphysical hero—an adventurer with elements of both Marlow and Kurtz, who is upset by his intuitions but unable to find a format for their expression. Sam is the narrator, with elements both of Marlow and of Conrad's anonymous transcriber, whose confrontation with the mystery has not been firsthand, yet who is sufficiently like the primary adventurer to be able to share his experience and sufficiently word-oriented to be able to record it. (We shall see later how Beckett returns to this structure in *Molloy* on the way to a more direct confrontation in *The Unnamable.*)

This narrative pattern can be identified in numerous other novels. It suffers interesting variations in such works as *Wuthering Heights, Absalom, Absalom!, The Great Gatsby, A la recherche du temps perdu, Frankenstein, The Turn of the Screw,* and *The Republic.* It occurs quite straightforwardly in Thomas Mann's *Doctor Faustus,* where the story of Adrian Leverkühn, a composer who may have made a pact with the devil and whose music seemed the product of superhuman insight, is related by his bookish friend, Serenus Zeitblom. Leverkühn expresses his experience in his music; what he must have gone through personally can only be guessed at by Zeitblom. But Zeitblom is in his own way living through the equivalent of that bout with the devil in the narrative present, for he begins writing in 1943, in Nazi Germany. Although he begins the novel by protesting that he intends to remain in the background, and although in a significant concluding note Mann identifies Leverkühn as the tragic hero of his novel, Zeitblom's experience continually claims the reader's attention. In the Epilogue he describes himself as "an old man, bent, well-nigh broken by the horrors of the times in which he wrote and those which were the burden of his writing."[47] The two plot lines relate to each other just as do the two main characters. Zeitblom goes on to explain how he turned out to be the man to write this account, and in so doing he clarifies the workings of secondary first-person narrative: "A task has been mastered, for which by nature I was not the man, to which I was not born, but rather called by love and loyalty—and by my status as eyewitness."[48] A man of words, only peripherally involved in Leverkühn's tragedy, Zeitblom is hardly a man possessed by the supernatural. In order to intuit the essence of the story, he must live through a modified version of its central aspect. This the war forces him to do, and Mann is careful to point out to the reader the moral kinship between Leverkühn's and Nazi Germany's dark energies. Zeitblom is surrounded by demoniacal behavior, as Leverkühn was; his present experience coordinates with and illuminates his retracing of the past. At one point he says, "My tale is hastening to its end—like all else today."[49]

Zeitblom's modesty, paradoxically, is not self-effacing; this is typical of many secondary first-person narrators. As a means of directing the reader to the grandness of the central character's deeds or insights, the narrator often downplays the importance of his own experience (for a parodistic converse of this, consider the indirection of Stein's *Autobiography of Alice B. Toklas*); most readers, however, are alerted by such downplaying and make a point of paying special

71

attention to the narrator's experience, which often turns out to be the main avenue of exploration and explanation available to them. In rare instances, such as Boris Pasternak's great autobiography, *Safe Conduct* (which is notably concerned with the life and thought of Mayakovsky),[50] the narrator is sincere in this gesture. More often, however, the narrator is simply hiding behind the cliché dichotomy between "literature" and "life": Ishmaels write books, Ahabs defy the gods.

It is characteristic that a secondary first-person narrator be a man of words and blame his "inability" to deal with or adequately convey the hero's experience on his own moody bookishness; it is also characteristic that this specific limitation is his chief asset. Ishmael presents himself this way in "Loomings"; Marlow implies much the same thing in the ironic yet accurate reference to "my hesitating foot"; Zeitblom practically apologizes for opening his mouth. Perhaps the definitive example of this deceptive self-effacement is to be found in the opening of Conrad's *Under Western Eyes,* a novel likely to have influenced both Mann and Nabokov:

> To begin with I wish to disclaim the possession of those high gifts of imagination and expression which would have enabled my pen to create for the reader the personality of the man who called himself, after the Russian custom, Cyril son of Isidor—Kirylo Sidorovitch—Razumov.
>
> If I have ever had these gifts in any sort of living form they have been smothered out of existence a long time ago under a wilderness of words. Words, as is well known, are the great foes of reality. I have been for many years a teacher of languages. . . . To a teacher of languages there comes a time when the world is but a place of many words.[51]

I mention Nabokov here because *Pale Fire* seems, in its own reversed way, to be a limiting case of secondary first-person narration. Its "hero," the more or less visionary poet

John Shade, is presented to the reader both directly, in his poem "Pale Fire," and indirectly, through the parodistically academic notes on that poem written by his "dear friend" Charles Kinbote. The problem is that Kinbote is crazy. Although he adopts the guise of an Ishmael and offers all the "correct" disclaimers, it is evident that Kinbote fancies himself a pseudomythical king and that Shade is the bemused academic.[52] Instead of opening up a concealed heroic adventure, the secondary first-person structure of *Pale Fire* operates in a precisely negative fashion, reflecting if anything a second, impossible Kinbote: Charles II, "last king of Zembla." When Kinbote calls attention to himself, it is with a perverse sense of power:

> Let me state that without my notes Shade's text simply has no human reality at all since the human reality of such a poem as his (being too skittish and reticent for an autobiographical work), with the omission of many pithy lines carelessly rejected by him, has to depend entirely on the reality of its author and his surroundings, attachments and so forth, a reality that only my notes can provide. To this statement my dear poet would probably not have subscribed, but for better or worse, it is the commentator who has the last word.[53]

Whereas the reader of *Doctor Faustus* relies on Zeitblom to open up the mystery of Leverkühn, to expand upon the little that is known, the reader of *Pale Fire* relies on Shade's poem and other concrete evidences of what "really" happened in order to unscramble the mystery Kinbote *creates*. The secondary first-person narrator is usually more sane than the hero and offers the reader his own experience for illustrative purposes; Kinbote adheres precisely to the pattern, but calls attention to his own position both to enlarge on his *own* madness and to obscure whatever Shade might have been getting at. (His first serious mention of himself, for example, is: "There is a very loud amusement park right in front of my present lodgings."[54] The context is a description of

73

Shade's manner of composition.) It seems inappropriate for Kinbote to become, as he does, the central character of *Pale Fire,* until one considers the appropriateness of Ishmael's and Marlow's becoming the paradoxical centers of their own narrations. Kinbote is simply being true to the demands of the form.

4. THE TEACHINGS OF CARLOS CASTANEDA

Have you ever seen a saint wearing a watch?
—Pablo Picasso

Carlos Castaneda is the central figure in his multivolume investigation of the world of the Yaqui Indian sorcerer. In the first volume, *The Teachings of Don Juan,* the emphasis is on don Juan, the sorcerer, and on the attempts of Castaneda, a graduate student in anthropology, to learn from him the uses of hallucinogenic plants. This volume, which may actually have begun as an academic project and which was published as straight anthropology by the University of California Press, includes such parodistic paraphernalia as a structuralist appendix and closes with the suggestion that Castaneda, having reached a certain plateau in his apprenticeship, is afraid to continue further.

Behind all this scientific and empirical reportage on the uses of peyote, the rituals associated with gathering roots and mushrooms, and so on, something else is clearly developing—the theme of Castaneda's apprenticeship. Don Juan has recognized through an omen from Mescalito that Castaneda (even though not an Indian) is to be one of his apprentices. At this point, the wily reader will recognize two literary paradigms of long standing: the careful disguise of scholarship (which goes back at least to Swift's *A Tale of a Tub* and whose major contemporary practitioner is Borges), and the displacement device of secondary first-person narration. There is, of course, the possibility that everything Castaneda says happened to him did in fact happen just as he says it did, which would then suggest that these literary devices surprisingly correspond with the ways mysteries are revealed and heroism conducted in the real world. In any case, it is the apprenticeship and not the sorcerer that emerges as Castaneda's focal subject.

In the second volume, *A Separate Reality,* Castaneda drops the academic devices and concentrates on what it means to "*see*"—to be aware that there are two levels of reality, one of which is not accessible to ordinary perception. In the introduction to this volume, he insists that he is reporting things he did not understand at the time he first encountered them, and which to a great extent he still does not understand—from which we learn that these volumes are supposedly being written from the developing perspective of an author who is still an apprentice rather than with the dramatic irony (and good memory for innocent perception) of a master. He also insists that his work is free of literary devices.

In the third volume, *Journey to Ixtlan,* Castaneda suddenly changes the subject and announces a reinterpretation of the material contained in the first two books. The important point now is that there are two realities; power plants (natural drugs), which helped open and reeducate Castaneda's perception, are now thrown into the background so that the crucial aspect of don Juan's teachings—the metaphysical perspective—can occupy the foreground. By the end of this volume, Castaneda expects that someday he will become a sorcerer. (We shall leave the next volumes for another chapter, but it might prove helpful for the reader to consult, at this point, the chapter entitled "The Strategy of a Sorcerer," in *Tales of Power,* for another perspective on the early stages of the apprenticeship [no citation from Castaneda's works is permitted].) In this analysis, I shall be working on the assumption that these are Borgesian—or at least Conradian—disclaimers and that Castaneda has been a master, if not all along, then at least since the time he began to write the second volume. To clarify some of the ironies involved, I will use "Castaneda" to refer to the author of these books and "Carlos" to refer to the persona/protagonist, who is to some extent a fiction.

Whether or not he began as an overweight and overlimited student of anthropology in 1960, and whether or not he underwent an apprenticeship to the Yaqui sorcerer whom he acknowledges he is only calling don Juan, it seems likely that by the early 1970s Castaneda was behaving like a hunter and like a warrior. Stealthy, secretive, self-contained, he has been hooking his audience by its own preconceptions, suppressing his personal history, avoiding routine, and keeping in touch with his power. He has presented himself as a fool on a quest, almost like Parsifal (within his narrative), and as a solitary bird (in the epigraph to *Tales of Power*). The secondary first-person format has suited him perfectly, allowing him to split his knowledge into a teaching figure and a learning figure, an explainer and an asker, a master and an apprentice who is more than an apprentice. The first requirement of this narrative structure is that the Marlow figure go down much the same path as the Kurtz figure so that he can present the metaphysical hero's experience in terms of his own more verbally anchored experience; that is precisely how Carlos began, and it is the key to the structure of indirection so impeccably maintained in the first four books. He has not, however, maintained the secondary first-person device in the two most recent volumes, *The Second Ring of Power* and *The Eagle's Gift*, and it is arguable that the more Carlos is presented as a sorcerer in his own right, the less effective Castaneda's works have become.

One of Castaneda's most effective means of keeping his true actions and sources in doubt is to assert that his apprenticeship was factual, with only a few names and places changed. In this respect, his writing kin are not A. L. Kroeber and Ruth Benedict, but Nabokov, Borges, and especially Plato (whose Socrates is a pseudohistorical figure incarnating Platonism). Unlike the lady in *Hamlet*, however, Castaneda does not protest enough. He would not have his readers take all this as fantasy, yet he keeps using the techniques of ironic fiction. When he begins *The Second Ring of Power,* for instance, by saying that he returned to Mexico because he had trouble believing that he had done what he said he did in *Tales of Power* and then launches into a matter-of-fact rendition of things even more incredible, that opening is not so much an appeal to conventional perspective or scientific context as it is, like the opening to a *Frankenstein* sequel, an explaining away of the apparent finality of the previous conclusion. Castaneda is a trained anthropologist, but he says he always wanted to be an artist.[55]

All this has manifest stylistic advantages. When Castaneda says "I actually saw" a separate reality, the "actually" so stands out from his usual flat presentation that it is convincing without hyperbole. In the first two volumes, he has no serious problem with credibility because he is dealing mostly with drug-induced experience, and under a drug one can see or feel sure that one has seen many things; here the flat style is an advantage. But when in the later volumes he presents himself as leaping off cliffs, "talking" with coyotes, *seeing* the lines of the world, and so on, all without drugs—in other words, when he no longer needs the drug subject matter to win an audience and can get to his point about the actual existence of nonordinary reality and in the process present himself as a potential sorcerer—then the flat style implies that Castaneda has long since abandoned the reference points of scientific anthropology. He simply *behaves* like a researcher.

In fact, what Castaneda does is to put the reader in the same position with reference to Carlos that Carlos occupies with reference to don Juan. We begin by requiring explanations, structural analyses, assurances that Carlos really saw or did what he says he saw or did—and then, after awhile, we go along for the ride, shift our perspective, seek in ourselves the power he describes, and perhaps even find it. (A large percentage of Castaneda's audience has doubtless attempted to duplicate Carlos' experiences—to cross the eyes in a certain manner, to take peyote under carefully described circumstances, and so on.) All that is necessary now is to deduce that Castaneda has constructed the figure of don Juan and the caricature of Carlos on these same principles: that he has made both out of himself, and that he is exploiting secondary first-person narration because of its usual advantages. Rather than write a single book about sorcery and from the perspective of the sorcerer—a book that would either not find a publisher or win him a berth in the nuthouse—Castaneda writes a series of books from the prespective of a literal-minded outsider who is taking notes on a sorcerer's practices. He leads the reader as don Juan leads him, until at last he can assert that the heart of darkness is, so to speak, just down the Thames.

This is the reflexive aspect of Castaneda's work, the cunning at its base: its urging the reader to take it literally and as a work of fiction, at the same time and in the same terms. (His books become their own "doubles," and the reader is left to guess which interpretation or structure is *"dreaming"* the other.) This is one of his means of demonstrating directly that our sense of the world depends on our habitual way of explaining phenomena to ourselves—our acceptance of a certain "description" of things—and that those habits can be abandoned. Just as we have to exert equal effort—depart to the same degree from *what is*—to make ourselves happy as to make ourselves sad (one of don Juan's more widely embraced maxims), we have to exert equal effort to interpret Castaneda's matter-of-fact text as literally true as to interpret it as a carefully researched metaphor. The best way to proceed, then, is not to interpret it at all, if we can be comfortable in that position. In any case, we know that Castaneda, the impeccable warrior in the world of words, is not going to explain the game or relax his stance. To confront a paradox in its own terms, to accept it and go on from there, is, of course, what his books are all about and

78

the first task they set the reader: to confront not the paradoxes they refer to, but the paradoxes they are. We find that in Castaneda, as in Melville and Nabokov, secondary first-person narration and reflexivity tend naturally to reinforce each other.

It is possible, of course, that Castaneda's cunning came on him by degrees, that his artistic confidence grew with his audience. It is certainly possible that he served an apprenticeship to a Yaqui sorcerer, that he learned how to *"see,"* and that he is accurately reporting his experiences of *"stopping the world."* My point is the same whether these things are true or not. Secondary first-person narration is viable because it allows the ineffable to be framed and, within that frame, examined; this is the case whether or not the ineffable's manifestation is a fiction.[56] It makes no difference whether Castaneda recorded teachings he could not understand[57] or cast himself in the role of someone who did not understand what he transcribed. Nevertheless there are many hints that Castaneda has been behaving with the reader as don Juan behaved with Carlos, and an essential element of that behavior is that it is strategic.[58]

The founding principle of that strategy is the same as that of the apprenticeship structure and thus of the secondary first-person narrative structure that keeps don Juan at one pole and the reader at the other: one must have power in order to learn about or to manipulate or even to get power.[59] Carlos is not a mere apprentice but an *escogido*[60]—one who has been selected as a fit apprentice because he already possesses some of that power he wants to learn about, one who is already different from other men. (This would be a *Catch-22* situation except for the fact that the issue of being different is a red herring—everyone has some degree of power,[61] so the real issue turns out to be that an *escogido* is *selected* by power because of the power he already possesses.) Ishmael is already a kind of Ahab and a kind of masked energy like the whale; Marlow is telling a man like himself about a man whose characteristics, in however reduced manifestations, they clearly share; Marlow and Ishmael are selected by Fate the way Carlos is selected by power.

Power exists by itself as a pure force. Don Juan is able to manipulate it expertly. Carlos finds that power and its uses in himself as he strips away his verbal defenses and his stubborn, sometimes childish or frightened need for explanations. The reader brings to the text his or her own sense of personal power, though the approach is at first entirely verbal (the act of reading).

Castaneda's strategy is to outline this hierarchy of power: from power as it manifests itself in the wind at twilight, for instance, or in allies; to the sorcerer's ring of power as it is manifested in don Juan's or don Genaro's acts of *"will"*; to power as it is discovered in Carlos the *escogido*; to power as the reader seeks it in himself. Castaneda allows the reader to adopt the position of apprentice and knows this strategy will succeed because everyone has some degree of power and because to commit oneself to reading all these volumes is virtually an act of allowing oneself to be selected—to open oneself to the possibility of "an appointment with knowledge," to become a minor *escogido,* to agree to experiment with abandoning traditional explanations of the nature of reality.

The reader is capable of understanding don Juan at first through the intermediary of Carlos ("through a glass, darkly") and then face to face—but the face by then (perhaps in the as-yet-unwritten final volume, perhaps in some category of the reader's imagination) is that of Castaneda, the achieved sorcerer. Or the face is that of the reader—who may, like Carlos, have encountered as part of this initiation into "sorcery" the totality of the self, an encounter that is a necessary aspect of the discovery of the nature of the universe.

CHAPTER THREE

The Simultaneous Self

We cannot look around our own corner.
—Friedrich Nietzsche

Reflexivity is a transcendental problem. To become aware
of the self is to become aware of its limits, and to engage
those limits is to question the validity of language and of
belief—the validity of intrasystemic modes of understanding, which may be inapplicable to whatever goes on outside
the system and may not even be capable of analyzing their
own functions within the system.

The human being is an open system in that it can interact
and exchange energy with the environment. A text is a
closed system; it cannot grow, and more to the point, it cannot know. In the category of self-consciousness, the best a
text can manage is an imitation: a limited structure reflecting
and perhaps even discussing its limitedness. But people are
always pleased by analogies to their own situations, and so
the reflexive text is awarded its own paradoxical response:
suspension of belief. We suspend disbelief to the extent that
we agree to forget that the text is a closed system incapable
of self-consciousness. We suspend belief to the extent that
we agree to listen to the text not as an alternate reality, but
as a text; rather than look through it we look at it. When
the text says "I see I am a text," we are then in a position to
say that it is accurate and that in spite of the fact that a text
cannot see or know anything *we* can see or know a great
deal, including the fact that we too are limited systems. We
try to understand ourselves and the universe, and we play
with a full deck—but what we play with is only a deck.

The problem of the ineffable and the problem of the self

81

are closely related in a number of ways. A text's awareness of systemic limitation can engage the reader's sympathetic identification and stimulate an investigation into how his or her own system understands what is within and without itself. A text's attempt to go beyond its limits—to discuss the ineffable, for instance, or to engage its author or reader in spontaneous conversation—has the effect of foregrounding those limits, and that foregrounding often has the further effect of focusing the reader's attention on the nature of the narrator. Under the pressure of a comparable authorial attention the narrator is liable to undergo a split into several elements.

Sometimes these narrating elements will be able to pay attention to each other, will discuss or interact with or contradict each other (as in Stein's *Identity A Poem*). Sometimes the narrator will discuss his own subselves (Proust). Sometimes a character will be split into person and ghost (Quentin in *Absalom, Absalom!*) and have a dialogue with himself about what it is he cannot understand, or what he cannot understand he is. Sometimes a hidden element will surface and establish domination over all the others (Atman, for example) and then prove itself to be undiscussable. The point is that one way to describe the self is as a colony of subselves, all of which exist at once and some of which use language. Another way to describe the self is as a functioning relationship between two categories of being—the knowable and the unknowable—organized by and around two categories or means of understanding—analysis (language and the logically systematic) and intuition (which ranges from the absolute understanding based on direct or shared experience to the "sense" that something is true, and which can embrace the chaotic or affirm the "impossible").

This chapter is concerned with the structure of that colony of subselves and some of the ways those categories of understanding relate to each other, both in fiction and in the emerging discipline of transpersonal psychology,[1] a disci-

pline that has made it both easier and somewhat more legitimate to discuss metaphysics, the self, and literature in similar terms and contexts. This will necessarily involve an
attempt to investigate the actual nature of the self, of the
universe, of the limits of language. Some readers may find
this presumptuous and self-defeating, but I hope it will
prove exciting.

It is tempting to describe the universe—especially as it exists in relation to human perception—as a coin with two
sides: the knowable and the unknowable, the analyzable and
the intuitable, the phenomenal and the noumenal, matter
and spirit, language and silence, the conscious and the unconscious, the imaginary and the symbolic, the tonal and the
nagual, physics and metaphysics, Brahman and Atman, the
left hemisphere and the right hemisphere, the secular and the
sacred, sequence and timelessness, heads and tails. Logicians
and metaphysicians tend to agree that from the left side of
that dichotomy (language, and so on) it is possible to know
everything about the left side except its absolute ontology,
and virtually nothing about the other side: hence the word
"ineffable." Some of these people go so far as to say that
because they cannot know anything about the right side,
they are unable to participate in it; others argue that there is
a different kind of knowing (intuition or direct experience)
that can render the other side accessible but still leave it undiscussable.

Another aspect of this argument is that from the right
side, the left side is knowable—to become oriented within
the unknowable is to become capable of living in and "understanding" the totality of the universe. Mystics like Shankara then go two steps further and argue first that it is important to remember that the two-sided system is in fact one
coin, and second that those two sides are actually identical
(Atman is Brahman). In such a context the proper image is
not a coin, then, but a Möbius strip or Klein bottle. On the
way into the heart of this problem, I would like to take up

83

one of the more remarkable split structures the system appears to present: the tonal and the nagual, which are central to what Castaneda calls the sorcerer's explanation.

1. CASTANEDA: THE SORCERER'S EXPLANATION

You cannot rule men nor serve heaven unless you
  have laid up a store;
This "laying up a store" means quickly absorb-
  ing,
And "quickly absorbing" means doubling one's
  garnered "power."
Double your garnered power and it acquires a
  strength that nothing can overcome.
If there is nothing it cannot overcome, it knows
  no bounds,
And only what knows no bounds
Is huge enough to keep a whole kingdom in its
  grasp.
But only he who having the kingdom goes to the
  Mother [Tao]
Can keep it long.
This is called the art of making the roots strike
  deep by fencing the trunk, of making life long
  by fixed staring.

—Lao Tzu, *Tao Tê Ching*

Tales of Power begins by foregrounding the figure of don Genaro, who is Carlos' benefactor as don Juan is Carlos' teacher.[2] The teacher's function is to talk with the apprentice, to work on his reason, to convince him both that there is an absolute distinction between two categories of existence called tonal and nagual—and that the apprentice knows nothing whatsoever about the nagual. The effect of this is to clear away all preconceptions or novitiate arrogance concerning the realm of the unknown, to create a conceptual

84

and experiential vacuum that is labeled nagual. The benefactor's function is to give this protégé irrefutable and direct demonstrations of the existence and uses of the nagual, to fill the vacuum without explaining it. (Don Juan and don Genaro would here agree with Wittgenstein in the *Tractatus:* "What can be shown, cannot be said."[3]) The organizing center of the tonal is the *reason,* whereas the organizing center of the nagual is the *will*; each of these is a ring of power, whose function is to effect a description of the world.

Tonal is the organized, analyzable world; it is a reflection of an order that exists in the universe, not a sheer controlling misrepresentation or willful projection of the logical mind onto the alogical cosmos. The tonal is the latter in one way, however: it does like to believe that it accounts for everything, that all phenomena are knowable in the way that it knows. In this respect, the reason is controlling and defensive, and to this extent, it is in error. Reason accounts well for whatever is on the "island of the tonal," everything that can be named or discussed. But the nagual cannot be discussed. The nagual is a reflection of a paradoxical and all-including category that also exists in the universe. The only way to deal with the nagual is to tap or enter or synchronize with it, in some cases by tapping or entering or synchronizing with the nagual that appears to be inside oneself—the *will* or arational center. There are two categories of perception associated with these two categories of being or universal structure: seeing and *seeing,* dreaming and *dreaming,* sequentiality and timelessness, physicality and luminosity, and so on.[4] Both are rings of power.

The world is a description. Ordinarily one succumbs to the tyranny of reason and accepts the way it organizes phenomena as being the way phenomena are actually organized—saying, for instance, that the laws of cause and effect apply universally. The tonal supports its description of the world by continually explaining and restating things to itself by means of what is called the internal dialogue. (The tonal always proves itself right, admitting into evidence only tonal units.) There are two major ways of short-circuiting the reason and stopping the internal dialogue. First, one can overload the perceptual centers, introduce so much data—by unfocusing the eyes in such a manner that the entire visual field is available for processing, by taking certain drugs that expand the perceptual spectrum, and so forth—that the internal dialogue cannot keep up with it and becomes stymied. Second, one can present the reason with something paradoxical and incontestable, something it simply cannot explain but also will not allow itself to deny. Don Juan accomplishes the former by giving Carlos drugs and setting him certain perceptual tasks. Don Genaro accomplishes the latter by confronting him with the problem of the double, which involves being in two places at once. When the internal dialogue ceases, when the tonal's world description is short-circuited, then the experience of *"stopping the world"* (that is, stopping its description) occurs, and another description or world is able to foreground itself. The nagual becomes observable.

The terms of this other description are not linguistic, so the mind's condition at this point is comparable to that of emptiness or silence; the whole range of alogical phenomena suddenly forces itself on the attention and compels acceptance rather than analysis. It becomes clear, for instance, that although the tonal prefers to believe that don Genaro is a physical body occurring in linear time and therefore capable of being in only one place at a time, the nagual shows that don Genaro is an organization of awareness and luminosity held together by the life force and capable of organizing itself wherever and whenever it chooses, that the notion of sequential time is inapplicable in this category (nagual has its own time), and that don Genaro is therefore entirely capable of being in two places at once. Carlos at first tries to explain the double to himself by wondering whether one don Genaro is physical and the other an illusion. But he discovers later that both manifestations are categories of *dreaming* whose simultaneity is a nagual characteristic that will not submit to such tonal terminology as "physical body" or even "illusion."

The only way to integrate tonal and nagual in tonal terms is to say that the universe includes all things, some of which occur in systems—which is to say that order is a self-perpetuating partial system. In *The Second Ring of Power,* one of the capsule definitions of tonal and nagual says that the nagual supports and surrounds the organized tonal.[5] To be a sorcerer is to know how to enter the nagual. The sorcerer's apparently impossible feats remain inexplicable but nevertheless occur; they are acts of *will,* which means that they are neither caused by nor routed through nor understandable by the rational center. Since the body, for instance, is simply an organization of layers of luminosity (or a cluster of awarenesses or feelings),[6] it is a simple matter for the sorcerer to arrange himself into the appearance of a crow or into the appearance of a Yaqui Indian or into his own double. Whereas the tonal arranges data, the nagual can actually create "something" out of "nothing"; and whereas the sorcerer can accomplish all these things, he is still fundamentally a witness to the nagual and does not understand how any of this works.[7]

When Castaneda leaps into the nagual and back again at the end of *Tales of Power,* he acknowledges that the unspeakable is truly unspeakable.[8] The two most important aspects of this last stage of his initiation are: first, that he experienced the premises of the sorcerer's explanation in his own person rather than simply hearing about them (a corollary of the assumption that the sorcerer's explanation makes sense only when one is ready to understand it, that is, when one has stored enough personal power; and an effect of the double-leveled initiation process, where the reason is convinced that it can't explain everything and the *will* is then directly involved in impossible events); and second, that at a crucial moment something inside him, some aspect of his perception (which was being trained all along), suddenly realized his own nature, experienced directly that he was pure awareness.[9] If that awareness is analyzable, it is possible to analyze it only into a cluster of awarenesses that are temporarily committed to associating with each other. That coming together is the way elements within the nagual organize themselves into beings; beings get distracted by the area of organized being (the tonal) and allow themselves to forget their true nature, allow the tonal's description of the world to dominate their assumptions. (This is similar to Marvell's joke that the spirit is "blinded with an eye."[10]) This leads to two basic metaphysical conclusions: no one can be talked into a perception of the ineffable, and a direct experience of the true or transcendental self is an irrefutable transcendental event.

It may be simple to contact the self, but it is certainly not easy. It is as simple as it is direct, but it is as difficult as it is difficult to put away one's customary means of interpreting—that is, being in—the world. The long-term goal of Castaneda's first four volumes is to prepare the reader to distrust the absolute and final authority of the tonal and to confront the fact that the nagual is a mystery. In this respect, he is still the reader's don Juan, his teacher. He cannot be the reader's benefactor, for he cannot present the reader with irrefutable evidence of the nagual. No author can. These volumes are just tales of power. The secondary first-person structure can lead a reader only so far. Castaneda helps the reader rearrange the elements of the tonal (everything known or discussable), then asserts—which is not the same as showing—that Carlos leapt into the nagual and there discovered the totality of his being. The option that opens for the reader is to discover the totality of his or her own being, which may have the side-effect of showing the reader how to leap into the nagual. Leaping into the nagual, however, is in this context a relatively trivial matter—a side trip. It seems unlikely that someone who has gone into the center of the self and discovered the life force that organizes the universe would at that point be overwhelmingly interested in performing magic or turning into a crow. When one can pull oneself out of a hat, who needs a rabbit?

The totality of one's being is a relationship between the organized self (tonal) and the indescribable colony of awarenesses (nagual). It is not that the nagual is more true than the tonal. The tonal, however, must recognize that *it* is not the whole story, as the nagual has realized that the tonal is a beautiful and efficient way to function. Sequence, logic, mind, body, time, language, and so on are all aspects of the tonal; they are organizers that reflect their having been organized. They reflect an organization that exists in the universe, but they are powerless to explain that organization. The final aspect of the sorcerer's explanation is that the world of reason is as unknowable as is the chock-full void of the nagual. Thinking does not understand itself; logic has never yet explained what makes logic logical. As we shall see in a moment, much in modern philosophy supports these observations; the *Tractatus,* for instance, admits that it amounts to a tautology.[11]

When don Juan insists that there is no real Carlos, he means that the physical body is a temporary organization of forces rather than a fundamental object. The self is not real the way a brick is real—but neither is a brick. This is almost like crossing over from Newtonian to Einsteinian physics, or like discovering that matter is an organization of incredibly small units of energy whirling around each other in a near-void. Carlos could be told this over and over, and even learn to live with it; but once he has personally experienced it, he will never be able to accept the tonal as the entire universe. One can be convinced of something through rational argument; but the process Carlos goes through is one that *compels* conviction, which is another matter entirely—comparable to the spiritual experience of conversion. What he has learned can be translated into a set of observations and assumptions (definitions of the tonal, "definitions" of the nagual, and so forth). But the reverse is not true; the analy-

89

ses and axioms cannot precipitate the direct experience, which is a matter of insight rather than one of deduction. The universe and Carlos are real in the same way. There is no benefactor in these volumes to show the reader irrefutable evidence of the nagual—and there is considerable doubt whether the story told here is true in any respect, let alone the magical[12]—but there is the reader's self, and that is capable of being opened to perception.

Castaneda serves as the teacher, then, and the reader serves as his or her own benefactor. But one is not able to *read* oneself into a state of transcendental apprehension. One can approach the tonal from the nagual, but not the other way around; what Castaneda calls the "bubble of perception" has to be opened from the nagual side, once all the knowables have been gathered on the side of the tonal.[13] (This may be similar to the Unnamable's "door that opens on my story.") The reader's self will have to step forward of its own accord, once the mind and its roles have stepped out of the way.

That stepping forward poses many logical and metaphysical problems. There is no way to know that what has stepped forward is the transcendental self, an expression of divinity, a key to the cosmos, or anything more identifiable than a change of blood flow within the brain (a quantifiable phenomenon associated with certain states of meditation[14]). If this is a revelation, it does not constitute proof; it is an experience of *having* to be convinced. There remains a difference between logical proof (knowing) and direct comprehension *(knowing),* between what can be demonstrated with words and what can only demonstrate itself. I shall now attempt to clarify the structure of that distinction and its bearing on Carlos' initiation.

Castaneda implicitly raises the question of the relation of the sorcerer's explanation to contemporary research into the structure of the brain.[15] Don Juan dismisses the fruits of that research as simple indications that something is going on, rather than explanations of what is going on; he says something similar about logic and language, maintaining that we think and talk without knowing how or why, that we have no idea where thoughts come from, and so on. Without refuting those statements, I would like to point out to what extent the split between tonal and nagual corresponds to that currently posited between the left and right hemispheres of the brain, and how some of the processes and problems Castaneda describes imply that brain lateralization theory might prove relevant.

No one is sure whether hemispheric specialization is reflected in behavior, or even in thought patterns; every single brain cell has something like one million connections with other brain cells.[16] But in the normal right-handed subject, the left hemisphere of the brain is dominant for speech and related sequential/analytical processes, while the right hemisphere is dominant for spatial perception and related processes—holistic apprehension, gymnastics, and so forth. (For purposes of discussion, it is common to assume a right-handed population, noting that these hemispheric functions are often reversed in left-handed subjects.) Dreaming seems to be closely associated with an area in the right hemisphere that corresponds to the left hemisphere's language areas. Some evidence suggests that dreaming is a nonsequential activity, a spatial arrangement of timeless "events" that the dreamer organizes into a sequential "story" upon awakening simply because the left hemisphere is unable to conceptualize this sort of simultaneity. Nonsequential time is outside the left hemisphere's realm of comprehension, impossible to express in sequential terms. So although the human brain may be able to deal with two sorts of time, the language center cannot, and when the dreamer wakes up and rationality reasserts its dominance, it becomes necessary to organize the events of the dream-world into the terms of the waking world.

This interpretation is comparable to what Castaneda describes as the basic activity of the tonal, fitting all phenomena into its own terms for order (its description of the world) and ignoring or falsifying whatever does not fit. One of the last elements in don Juan's explanation to Carlos of what he has undergone consists of forcing Carlos to see that two particular sets of events happened simultaneously. In one set Carlos leapt back and forth from cliff to gorge, and in another set don Genaro and Carlos went through some horseplay over Carlos' hat; both sets were continuous, and the leaping set involved the further problem of Carlos' being at the top of the cliff and the bottom of the gorge at the same time. [17] The point is that Carlos later finds himself remembering each set as continuous and so cannot manage to work all the events into a coherent sequence (hat tricks while on the top of the cliff, between leaps). In other words, he is forced to acknowledge the simultaneity in spite of the fact that it makes no sense. His impulse is to impose a sequence on the spatial, as if his left hemisphere were asserting its interpretation of the dream-world; don Juan makes him see that this impulse is both normal and fruitless. The implication is that "nagual's time" is similar to the spatialization of "events" characteristic of the dreaming right hemisphere, or to the holistic nature of waking right-hemisphere interpretations of the world. The double will never make sense to the left hemisphere, but the right hemisphere might be able to grasp it, as long as it is not pressed to put its visualization into sequential or linguistic terms. (It is basic to linguistic process to break the world into fragments and then put one fragment after another; this is the essence of the connection between language and time.) The two common modes of knowing—analysis and intuition—may thus be closely related to left- and right-hemisphere activity, respectively. This is, of course, not a new idea, and it is one that is easily overstated and overemphasized (Western culture is left-hemisphere dominant, Eastern culture is right-hemisphere dominant, and so forth), but it may offer a useful way of looking at the limits of language and the ways in which humans can transcend those limits.

The other aspect of Carlos' initiation that may relate to

brain lateralization is quite farfetched. Research has determined that the right ear sends information to the left hemisphere, and the left ear to the right hemisphere. When don Juan and don Genaro "split" Carlos so that he can discover the nagual, don Genaro whispers into his left ear (addressing the right hemisphere; they call it the "whispering of the nagual") and don Juan whispers something different into his right ear.[18] Carlos has the sensation that his left ear is open to a larger field, a spatialized auditory sharpness. What I am wildly suggesting here is that the sorcerers functionally disengage Carlos' corpus callosum—the bundle of nerves that interconnects the two hemispheres—reducing him to the level of a split-brain subject and freeing his right hemisphere to range independently of his tonal processes. (A split-brain subject can hold a pencil in the left hand and know what it is but not be able to come up with the word "pencil," because the left hand's information is being sent only to the right hemisphere; holding the pencil in the right hand, the patient has no trouble naming the object.) This phase of Carlos' initiation does not cause him simply to pay attention to the nagual rather than to the tonal; it somehow allows him to pay attention to both at once. When asked two questions simultaneously, he comes up with an answer that uses terms from both questions, but which is basically a piece of self-contradictory nonsense.[19] After that he gives up trying to organize the input and feels the split take place. I am not suggesting that Carlos' reactions be analyzed in any laboratory context; in the first place, it is unlikely that the reported reactions occurred. What is significant here is the metaphor of split attention (one of whose way stations is paradoxical or nonsensical language) and the immediate effect of that split: an ability to operate on both levels of awareness, to process both ordinary and nonordinary reality at once, and to experience in that condition the totality of the self.

It does not undermine the validity of Castaneda's report that this is a metaphor—in fact, that is one of its advantages.

Since the ineffable cannot be discussed in rigorous philosophical (let alone anthropological) language, but can at best be talked around, one may as well discuss its manifestations metaphorically and via literature. One of the things Castaneda most pointedly reveals is the categorical overlap between philosophy and literature: they depend on many of the same structures, and they often provide the same kinds of evidence. One can discuss *Moby-Dick* and the structure of a simple sentence with the same rigor and to the same ends; one can discuss Castaneda's books as attempts to report on ineffable experiences, as fantasies about ineffable experiences, as philosophy or anthropology or fiction—and still be doing the same level of analysis. Once one accepts the notion that the world is a description, it makes little difference to which set of rules that description answers (fiction or reportage, and so on). As Ron Sukenick has observed:

> The world of the sorcerer is a stage and in Castaneda's books don Juan is the skillful stage manager. What he is trying to teach Castaneda is not the primacy of one description over another, but the possibility of different descriptions. He is teaching Castaneda the art of description. And in so doing he breaks down, for the alert reader, that false separation of art from life, of imagination from reality that in our culture tends to vitiate both. This lost connection, which is the essence of primitive cultures, is maintained in our empiricist civilization only in the arts, where it is allowed to survive as in a zoo. . . .
>
> Once philosophy was stories, religion was stories, wisdom books were stories, but now that fiction is held to be a form of lying, even by literary sophisticates, we are without persuasive wisdom, religion, or philosophy. Don Juan shows us that we live in fictions, and that we live best when we know how to master the art.[20]

The question is: what is one left with when one sees that the universe is a description—what is one left with, that is, in addition to some wonderful description? One is left, first of all, with an attitude: to live in the moment, accepting the island of the tonal as a convenient organization rather than as fundamental reality. Second, one is left open to the nagual—to the disorganized and all-inclusive nonsystem that exists before and under all description. This opens one to the insight that the self is both tonal and nagual.

There is more to Carlos' leap, then (at the end of *Tales of Power*[21]), than an unusual level of communication between his left and right hemispheres. The analogy of the brain is useful only up to a point: Carlos does learn how to go back and forth between two categories of perception, one of which is, like the left hemisphere, linguistic and sequential—the tonal (the nagual, however, has implications far beyond those of right-hemisphere processing, and to do justice to Castaneda's system, it might be more proper to relate the tonal to the "description" provided by the normal and integrated behavior of both hemispheres). The vital detail is that he discovers that he is a cluster of awarenesses joined together by the life force and that under that structure is something that corresponds to pure awareness. The experience is one of discovering totality. It can be experienced but not explained, because it involves contacting absolute unity, and language depends on differentiation. It is to feel empty and filled at once, everything and nothing, here and nowhere. It is to feel complete, to feel happy, to feel permanent and instantaneous, to transcend all categories, and to remain clear. With the skill and understanding of a master, it is at this point in his narrative that Castaneda introduces the issue and the grounding fact of love.[22]

It makes no difference whether there is a tonal and a nagual, any more than it matters whether Castaneda is a novelist. What compels attention is the skill and apparent authority with which the conclusion of *Tales of Power* describes

Carlos' experience of discovering his true self. The humility and acceptance that inform this passage—what might be called the precision of its exuberance—are found throughout the literature of the ineffable. Like many other writers, Castaneda here accepts that words fail and finds the best words he can to describe how it felt to Carlos, and might feel to others, when the whole self opens: when the distinction between matter and spirit makes no sense and when the impossibility of explaining that sensation or insight is the quintessence of triviality.

Carlos' discovery of self is comparable in every important aspect to what William James called the phenomenon of instantaneous conversion.[23] The feelings that accompany such conversion are regularly described as those of assurance, peace, completeness, love, newness, surrender. The assumption that conversion represents a sudden experience of the Deity remains an assumption. It is somewhat less of an assumption that the convert is suddenly opened to contact with a subliminal or preconscious mental field, an area of the self that is not usually accessible (not to say repressed). This "uprush" of "energies originating in the subliminal parts of the mind," which upsets "the equilibrium of the primary consciousness," is sometimes associated with visions but always involves "a sense of astonished happiness, and of being wrought on by a higher control."[24] James's term for the whole category of sudden subliminal intrusions is "automatism." His comment on the metaphysics of this experience is impeccable:

But if you, being orthodox Christians, ask me as a psychologist whether the reference of a phenomenon to the subliminal self does not exclude the notion of the direct presence of the Deity altogether, I have to say frankly that as a psychologist I do not see why it necessarily should. The lower manifestations of the Subliminal, indeed, fall within the resources of the personal subject: his ordinary sense-material, inattentively taken in and subconsciously remembered and combined, will account for all his usual automatisms. But just as our primary wide-awake consciousness throws open our senses to the touch of things material, so it is logically conceivable that *if there be* higher spiritual agencies that can directly touch us, the psychological condition of their doing so *might be* our possession of a subconscious region which alone should yield access to them. The hubbub of the waking life might close a door which in the dreamy Subliminal might remain ajar or open.[25]

This excellent and useful perspective may serve as a guide to Carlos' peak experience at the end of *Tales of Power* , when the "hubbub" of the tonal is silenced long enough for the self to experience its totality. We shall see later how closely such a description might apply to Proust.

First, however, it will be necessary to arrive at a firmer sense of what such terms as "the totality of the self" and "the ineffable" are attempting to indicate. From here on, I shall be using the term "higher self" to refer to that subliminal or "subconscious" region whose function may be to communicate with spiritual agencies, and which may be a spiritual agency itself. By comparing Castaneda's perspective with those of Wittgenstein and the ancient Hindus, and by tying that in with our observations on narrative structure, we may arrive at a tentative structural synthesis between the literature of the ineffable and the philosophical and spiritual structures that literature addresses. The point, for now, is not so much that the higher self might be nagual as that both the universe and the self can be referred to as absolute wholes—and that from the perspective of the referential system they may be, for just that reason, absolute holes.

2. Another Look at the Ineffable

The first service man can render is to give thought to the Being of beings. . . . The word ["being"] says: presence of what is present.
—Heidegger, *What is Called Thinking?*

97

That would be a blessed place to be, where
you are.   —Beckett, *The Unnamable*

As Alan Watts points out in *The Book,* one characteristic
of a metaphysical question is that it "cannot quite be formulated."[26] A question that can be formulated is one that
obeys the rules, or conforms to the structure, of logic; any
such question can have a logical answer. A metaphysical
question cannot be formulated because it would have to be
answered in alogical terms—which, Wittgenstein points out
in the *Tractatus,* do not exist: "It is as impossible to represent in language anything that 'contradicts logic' as it is in
geometry to represent by its co-ordinates a figure that contradicts the laws of space, or to give the co-ordinates of a
point that does not exist."[27] It is possible to speak nonsense,
but it is not possible to mean anything by it; it is possible to
stimulate the hearer's imagination with metaphor and paradox (the sound of one hand clapping, for instance), as long
as one realizes that one is not really saying anything, that
some term in the statement is inadequately defined or mis-
used (clapping requires two hands). It is impossible to think
illogically. It is impossible to make a meaningful statement
about the ineffable.

Such an argument does not imply that there is no such
thing as the ineffable; it simply "defines" that area by exclusion. The ineffable is not in the world, not knowable, not a
matter of "facts in logical space."[28] The world so defined,
and language, share the same limits—in fact, they determine
each other's limits.[29] What Wittgenstein does in the *Tractatus*
is to "signify what cannot be said, by presenting clearly
what can be said."[30]

The structure of the *Tractatus* is a great poetic achievement, and the work has a good deal more humor and simplicity than it is usually credited with. One way to describe
what Wittgenstein does is to say that he creates the world in
six major propositions and then declares the sabbath in his
seventh proposition and closing sentence: "What we cannot
speak about we must pass over in silence." Another way to

describe it is to say that he organizes the formal logic of everything that can be known (as if on one side of the bubble of perception), making it clear that all of that is the tonal, so that the nagual becomes an absolutely empty category that can be understood only from outside the tonal. (In Beckett's rather than Castaneda's terms, one could say that Wittgenstein leaves "in the silence" that which cannot be thought about, that which is outside the limited whole of the world, that is, outside of the text.) The similarities between Wittgenstein and don Juan are uncanny, particularly in the matter of strategy.[31] Their basic point of agreement is that thinking is limited to the tonal and that thinking works (logic proceeds logically) because "propositions *show* the logical form of reality. They display it."[32]

Logic is a limited system. What the correspondence between language and the world indicates is simply that they share a structure. The totality of facts in logical space, like the language that can discuss it, is a set of terms that reflect termness and describe the terminological. The logical form of a proposition is, from this perspective, a manifestation of something inaccessible to logic:

Everything that can be thought at all can be thought clearly. Everything that can be put into words can be put clearly.

Propositions can represent the whole of reality, but they cannot represent what they must have in common with reality in order to be able to represent it—logical form.

In order to be able to represent logical form, we should have to be able to station ourselves with propositions somewhere outside logic, that is to say outside the world.

Propositions cannot represent logical form: it is mirrored in them.

What finds its reflection in language, language cannot represent.

What expresses *itself* in language, *we* cannot express
by means of language. . . .
What *can* be shown, *cannot* be said.[33]

Language and logic amount to a point of view. A point of
view cannot observe itself. That is one reason why absolute
self-knowledge cannot be discussed—it involves a point of
view outside the knowing self, which is a contradiction in
terms. The self *shows* what it has in common with the whole
of reality.

The concept of "self" is crucial to this discussion, because
from *The Cloud of Unknowing* to *The Unnamable* the experience of self-realization has been affirmed to be ineffable. The
self is a limited whole, and to "know" this fully is to transcend the phenomenal world, to become the "knower" on
another level. Some describe self-realization as an experience
of discovering that one is divine, or of becoming one with
the higher self (even these discriminations reflect a "fall" into
the search for terms). The self so contacted cannot be described as an element of personality, because its essential feature is an overarching wholeness. The Hindus argued that
Atman (the higher self, or that to which the higher self can
open) and Brahman (the self of the universe) are identical;
Shankara went on to define Atman as Brahman-within-the-
creature. The self *shows* and cannot *say* what it has in common with the nature of Being. This philosophical paradox is
relevant to the structure of self-conscious texts, many of
which are given the task of attempting to describe their own
(of course, imitative) awareness of their being limited systems. Not surprisingly, many such texts are organized
around the attempts of a first-person narrator to define his
own processes and end, as *The Unnamable* does (or peak, as
does *As I Lay Dying*), in a silence that cannot be analyzed.
The self is the most present manifestation of the ineffable
with which any human can deal.

Everything within the logic/language system—the totality

of facts in logical space, which is the world—can be expressed. To see the system whole, one would have to be outside the system. That is a functional description of transcendence. Reflexivity climaxes in the experience of absolute self-knowledge, the system's observing itself. What it observes, it cannot say. Beckett's *The Unnamable shows* that it is a text; what it *says* is that it is having trouble naming itself and has to wait for some kind of "door" to open from the other side of what it cannot identify as textuality, or even as the limits of logical space. The special brilliance of that novel lies in Beckett's having kept rigidly coterminous the limits of textuality and the limits of the verbal consciousness of the narrator (a discipline that makes it possible, as we shall find later, to speak of a "mind of the novel").

The conversion experience involves sudden access to the whole self and therefore suggests to the convert such terms as "higher control," because the experience can "make sense" only in terms of a system higher than the personal system. The experience might well be one of systemic self-knowledge, but that does not make *sense*; it is easier to conceptualize this wholeness as proceeding from the "Other" of God and then to ascribe to God that radiant completeness. Some critics impoverish *The Unnamable* by identifying the "Other" as Beckett rather than as the narrator's projection of his own intuited wholeness and thus tend to miss the positive implications of Beckett's having presented a limited whole that is embattled with the failure of language. It should be clear that Beckett is presenting the human condition at the edge of silence, that his "failures" are comical, necessary, and charged with the energy of what cannot be said. His despair is adequate to his vision. Unlike the majority of writers who have dealt with these problems, he simply does not cheat; the silence remains extratextual.

One meaning of silence is: a category outside language, not simply an intermission within language. Silence can indicate that language has been stymied and can thus point

past itself to another aspect of experience.[34] It can also, stymied, mark a uniquely intriguing and valuable barrier. The
genius of Wittgenstein, in this respect, is threefold: he realizes that it is a misuse of the mind to ask metaphysical questions, to attempt to define the undefinable; he uses the mind
to clarify logic's limits from within, by showing what language can do; and he shows in this manner exactly what the
mind cannot do. To put this more colloquially, Wittgenstein
defines an area by not entering it, shows the hole in the
doughnut by frying the batter; when all this is clear, he eats
the doughnut, leaving two kinds of hole: the hole of the
nagual, which used to be the one surrounded by doughnut,
and the hole of the tonal, which used to be the doughnut.
By linking Wittgenstein with Castaneda and Beckett, I am
attempting to demonstrate that the ineffable is a category of
extrasystemic awareness and that the limits of the personal
and textual systems are analogous. The ineffable is the All,
both of holistic intuition and of the universe—an All that is
regularly identified as God but that can as easily be considered an irreducible Oneness. When God defined himself to
Moses (Exodus 3:14), he said, "I AM THAT I AM," and in
that tautology mirrored the self-evident and nonsensical
quality of metaphysical statement just as he identified the
gist of the conversion experience. Offering the same words
that a comparably enlightened human might use, God implicitly linked his own self-knowledge with that of man—
who is, one might argue, made in God's image as reflexive
texts are made in man's, all of us sharing the same quality of
systemic completeness that is the absolute and prime characteristic of the *universe*. But to speak of an undifferentiable
wholeness composed of wholes is to misuse the mind.

All the propositions of logic "say nothing."[35] The entire
Tractatus turns out to be "nonsensical" (much as the tonal
turns out to be unknowable), but only once it has "been
understood"; its propositions have to be transcended if the
world is to be seen correctly.[36] One might say that the *Trac-*

tatus self-destructs. Wittgenstein climbs the ladder so it can be thrown away; he articulates the boundary of silence, leaving the silence its integrity and the mind its job.

To climb the ladder, in this sense, means to gain access to a view somewhere outside the world. Wittgenstein's propositions do not appear "nonsensical" to the logical mind engaged in reading his book; rather, they show how things are. Their limitation is that they too belong to the logical world and therefore cannot say anything about the system that contains them. The *Tractatus* is an internal view of the interior. In other words, because these propositions are propositions, they can make only logical statements; one must see the system they describe from the outside of that system—make an imaginative leap. To consider what it means to say "the whole of logical space" or "the totality of propositions" is to begin to feel "the world as a limited whole," which Wittgenstein identifies as the mystical perspective.[37]

From that perspective, Wittgenstein's propositions simply manifest their limits; they are not so much nonsensical as they are tautological, asserting that $x = x$. They show that they say nothing, like all tautologies. One has the illusion that $x = 2$ really *says* something, represents an advance in scientific knowledge or whatever, only as long as one forgets to notice that it is the form of the statement—that it is an equation—that determines the statement; $x = 2$ is instantly reducible to $x = x$, which is self-evident. (This shows exactly how mathematics is a language.) Tautologies are not pictures of reality, Wittgenstein asserts, because they "admit all possible situations"; they do "not stand in any representational relation to reality"; they are "unconditionally true." They are not nonsensical, he argues, but they are "part of the symbolism," like the 0 in math.[38] (In this sense, the *term* "silence" is part of the symbolism of language.)

The problem here is that a tautology is an excellent description of reality, whether or not Wittgenstein chooses to call it a "picture of reality." Reality is what exists, and we have no way of knowing whether reality admits "all possible situations." The mystical insight consists primarily in seeing that although logical statements operate logically on the logical world there may be more going on. There are wonderful equations written on the blackboard, but the blackboard vanishes—or better, the equal signs reveal the equality of signs. This is comparable to the Hindu insight that the universe is equal to itself, a statement that says "nothing" as it opens the possibility of everything. One way to get to this insight is to answer "all possible scientific questions" or to describe the inevitable form of all meaningful statements (the project of the *Tractatus*, whose coincidental parody is *Watt):*

> Scepticism is *not* irrefutable, but obviously nonsensical, when it tries to raise doubts where no questions can be asked.
>
> For doubt can exist only where a question exists, a question only where an answer exists, and an answer only where something *can be said.*
>
> We feel that even when *all possible* scientific questions have been answered, the problems of life remain completely untouched. Of course there are then no questions left, and this itself is the answer.
>
> The solution of the problem of life is seen in the vanishing of the problem.
>
> (Is this not the reason why those who have found after a long period of doubt that the sense of life became clear to them have been unable to say what constituted that sense?)
>
> There are, indeed, things that cannot be put into words. They *make themselves manifest.* They are what is mystical.[39]

Eliot expressed a related insight in the *Four Quartets:* it is "Only by the form, the pattern," he said, that words can "reach / The stillness."[40] Meaning is made manifest in form, the way something looks from the outside and the way it feels itself from the inside; in terms of the *Tractatus*, the form of the whole shows the reader that it is limited but makes no mystical or exterior-viewpoint statements. The same is true of each of its propositions, whose "nonsense" or tautology factor is manifest, but which make sense when one enters them (that is, reads them with the intention of understanding, thinks with them, shares their limits). These propositions manifest logical form but cannot describe or discuss it; logical form is self-evident in them, and therefore, ineffable. Here we arrive at the crux of the problem: the ineffable is self-evident.

As Eliot says, words "reach into the silence" only "after speech." Words move "only in time." But they have an atemporal dimension as well, one in which they are not moving and cannot die. The quality of that nonmovement, Eliot insists, is not "fixity,"[41] but rather a gathering together of all time into an eternity that is necessarily present, a stillness around which movement and time are organized and from which they proceed. This "still point" makes itself manifest in dance, for instance, which cannot represent that point but could not exist without it. Its verbal counterpart is silence, the timeless gathering together of the inexpressibly unified universe, the water of which we notice the wave forms, the space that contains no paradoxes because there are no limited terms to be tricked into apparent self-contradiction. In terms of normal logic and the normal world, a paradox appears contradictory (for example, to say that one feels here and nowhere), but in an alogical context, as when one is in the grip of a conversion experience, this paradox may be self-evidently accurate. A paradox has one kind of meaning in the logical world, which might be called the world of time (to borrow Eliot's metaphor), and another kind—based not on what it says but on what it is—in the world of the still point. In the logical world, a paradox is a tension between what is said and what is trying to be said; the former is usually a contradiction, the latter a transcendental insight or category-smasher.

Words reach into the silence only after being spoken—to use "after" not in the sense of temporal sequence but rather in the sense of overtone, vibration, additional function. Their sound may still be going on, but their form addresses the silence, manifests the still point, on another level than that of logical meaning. Wittgenstein explains that process as one of formal complementarity: propositions share logical form with reality and make it manifest. One might say that they vibrate at the same frequency, as if there were a tuning-fork relationship between propositions and reality.

There are many ways to deal with the ineffable, but two suggest themselves at this moment. One way is simply to *be*. In that condition, there is no need for language, and in fact, no language. Everything exists; nothing requires expression. The problem, as Wittgenstein says, has vanished. This may amount to beatitude. The other way is to enter time, which is to enter the fragmentary (one moment at a time, rather than all time at once) and to accept its conditions, one of which is partial expression and another of which may be the illusion of separate personal identity, death, and so forth. Fragmentary expression involves dividing the universe up into separate terms and then putting them one after the other, like frames in a movie projector, in order to form in the mind of the listener a single, more unified image or concept; the listener performs this integration by understanding the ways the words go together and what they mean as a unit, that is, what they point toward. In the world of time, then, the way to deal with the ineffable is to *speak*. Often one proceeds by using language against itself, making it aware of its boundaries, spinning paradoxes and metaphors and myths, setting images before or between mirrors, trying to get the words to see past themselves or the listener to join their battle on that level until he or she can jump levels, climb Wittgenstein's ladder, and see the world correctly.

The way Eliot puts this, one enters time in order to conquer time. That insight is similar to Shankara's view of the universe: as a game whose object is to understand that it is a game and that everything is actually One—that differentiation is an illusion.[42] God creates or enters time in order to discover himself behind all the masks and so to return to atemporal oneness. Language behaves the same way, has a complementary structure—except that it cannot achieve insights or return to its original nature. (One might say that language needs man in order to discover itself and that reflexive fiction provides one of the better playgrounds.) We may use language, then, as a mirror for ourselves and our roles in the game, and see it in relation to the ineffable and to silence; we may watch it enter the category of expression and manifest the category of logical form while it points past itself to the undifferentiated, the whole, the silence.

The ineffable is so only from the point of view of language and the logical mind. That which is ineffable, however indescribable, is also inherently self-evident: it makes itself manifest; it is a property of the system. A conversion experience involves discovering the obvious. It transcends not terms but termness; it is universal but incommunicable. This accounts for the gulf between the convert and the skeptic. The skeptic can always say, "If it is so obvious and present and simple, why can't you tell me what it is?" and the convert can always say, "You have to discover it for yourself, but it would help if you adopted a perspective above this level"—to which the skeptic can, of course, reply, "That makes no sense." (These terms need not be taken in any religious context; the convert is one who has had a conversion experience.) It is easy to get lost in terms and to feel that they account for everything, but with a shift in perspective it is simple to see that terms are one system and that they are barred from representing the aterminological; the next step is simply to experience the silence, the self-evident, whatever you want to call it.

To step outside the whole of logical space may not be as impossible as it sounds, if it is at least partly a matter of shifting perspective to observe that which a logical perspective has obscured. Two exercises in shifting Wittgenstein's own perspective may be useful here:

Propositions show what they say; tautologies and contradictions show that they say nothing.

A tautology has no truth-conditions, since it is unconditionally true; and a contradiction is true on no condition.

Tautologies and contradictions lack sense.

(Like a point from which two arrows go out in opposite directions to one another.)

(For example, I know nothing about the weather when I know that it is either raining or not raining.)[43]

The first shift is from the world of poetry. In his poem "A Boy," John Ashbery presents the state of contradiction as a poetic object, one that corresponds to the main character's state of mind:

It had been raining but
It had not been raining.[44]

The fact that much of this poem does not make sense is to its advantage. The lines tell us "nothing about the weather," but they manifest a state of contradiction that is both self-evident and their point.

The second shift is from the world of science. "A point from which two arrows go out in opposite directions to one another" does not necessarily lack sense. It lacks sense if the space on which the point and arrows are drawn or conceived is flat. If space is curved, however, the arrows could eventually go out to one another. The term "opposite" makes sense only in a universe where space is defined as flat; it also depends on such subconcepts as the axis and the "straight line." In this sense, the argument of the *Tractatus* is overlimited, and this is perhaps the reason Wittgenstein went on to write his *Philosophical Investigations*: "the limits of language" needed to be rephrased as "the limits of a language."

Wittgenstein argues in the *Investigations* that it is proper to speak not so much of language as of a particular "language game." A language game has particular rules. Using the example above, we could say that one language game includes the condition of curved space, while another does not, and that "opposite" will mean or behave differently in each game. Many philosophers embraced the *Investigations* as a refutation of the *Tractatus*, taking their cue from Wittgenstein himself. It seems to me, however, that the issue of the ineffable was not at all dismissed by Wittgenstein's change in perspective. What he did was to complicate the presentation of what goes on within logical space, introducing a relativist perspective in which language games have meaning in relation to one another.

There may well be more than one kind of meaning and more than one way of achieving meaning. Each particular language game will limit its world. Each game plays by various internally consistent rules, and these rule-systems validate each other within the totality of games. There may even be a game that does not proceed logically (abstract film, for instance, a right-brain structure that remains open to semiotic analysis). An alogical game would not have meaning in the sense that the *Tractatus* defines meaning; it would have meaning in the terms in which *it* defines, manifests, or rejects the possibility of meaning; I cannot describe such meaning here because I am using a logical language game. What the *Investigations* implies (Wittgenstein does not really discuss this problem) is that "the ineffable" might be a relative term—that from the perspective of language game five the statements that are possible in language game seven might not make sense. This may, in fact, be an accurate description of the universe. It is also possible that the conversion experience represents a shift in language games, like that from flat to curved space.

I am suggesting here that the language games outlined in the *Investigations*, and the many others that follow from those, operate within logical and public space because they are languages, have rules, make particular statements. They may appear illogical to one another. But there is still no language that is silent, that *has* to be silent—no language that can dispense with fragmentation and sequence or allow a point of view to observe itself. The ineffable remains outside *all* language games, unless a single syllable like *Om* is defined as a complete language; for that to be valid, *Om* would have to be the sound that is the universe and not just a reference to it. The rules of that game would include that the Hindu perspective was correct. There would be no way of making any other statement (there would be no otherness) and certainly no way of writing fiction (there would be no fictions and no way of making discriminations or recombinations). A necessary property of this language would be that signifier and signified are identical. The literature of the ineffable, in contrast to the language game of *Om,* accepts the conditions of time and fragmentation, turning the necessary failure of its means of expression into a way of goading and guiding the audience to an intuition of that whose not being included or explicable is one aspect of its perfection.

One way to summarize all this and consolidate its relevance to the problem of the self is to refer briefly to Henri Bergson. In his *Introduction to Metaphysics,* Bergson endorses the distinction between

> two profoundly different ways of knowing a thing. The first implies that we move round the object; the second, that we enter into it. The first depends on the point of view at which we are placed and on the symbols by which we express ourselves. The second neither depends on a point of view nor relies on any symbol. The first kind of knowledge may be said to stop at the *relative;* the second, in those cases where it is possible, to attain the *absolute.*[45]

The first mode is analytical, the second intuitive. Metaphysics is the science of direct and perhaps absolute knowledge, "the science which claims to dispense with symbols."[46]

Symbols are incapable of dealing with the infinite; in the following passage he both clarifies the reasoning behind that statement and expands on the difference between analysis and intuition:

> When you raise your arm, you accomplish a movement of which you have, from within, a simple perception; but for me, watching it from the outside, your arm passes through one point, then through another, and between these two there will be still other points; so that, if I began to count, the operation would go on forever. Viewed from the inside, then, an absolute is a simple thing; but looked at from the outside, that is to say, relatively to other things, it becomes, in relation to these signs which express it, the gold coin for which we never seem able to finish giving small change. Now, that which lends itself at the same time both to an indivisible apprehension and to an inexhaustible enumeration is, by the very definition of the word, an infinite.
>
> It follows from this that an absolute could only be given in an *intuition*, whilst everything else falls within the province of *analysis*. By intuition is meant the kind of *intellectual sympathy* by which one places oneself within an object in order to coincide with what is unique in it and consequently inexpressible. Analysis, on the contrary, is the operation which reduces the object to elements already known, that is, to elements common both to it and other objects. To analyze, therefore, is to express a thing as a function of something other than itself.[47]

Bergson goes on to give an example of one "reality . . . which we all seize from within, by intuition": the personal self. Intuition is a matter of direct knowledge, of insight. (Love is, in this context, the paradigm of intuition; for "an object" in Bergson's second paragraph, substitute "the beloved," keeping in mind that the beloved need not be a person.) Bergson argues that science best proceeds by building on new information that might be acquired through intuition and that the metaphysical experience is complete in that it does not in itself require any subsequent analysis; he points out that "from intuition one can pass to analysis, but not from analysis to intuition."[48] The great advantage of intuition is that it is able to keep pace with the changing reality it enters into (time, for example, or the "duration" of the self in time). The task of metaphysics is "the constant expansion of our mind, the ever-renewed effort to transcend our actual ideas and perhaps also our elementary logic."[49] Metaphysical intuition is the preferred method for understanding a changing subject and for performing "*qualitative* differentiations and integrations."[50] One can know what it is to be a self in time, and perhaps even be unable to put that knowledge into scientific terms, yet remain free from the charge of relativism: "What is relative is the symbolic knowledge by pre-existing concepts, which proceeds from the fixed to the moving, and not the intuitive knowledge which installs itself in that which is moving and adopts the very life of things. This intuition attains the absolute."[51]

In effect, Bergson asserts a dualism in knowledge that corresponds to Wittgenstein's and also to that of many religious thinkers and contemporary psychologists. Analytical approaches yield analytical results, which are capable of being expressed logically and scientifically, and which are therefore capable of being shared with an audience that listens to words. Intuitive or direct knowledge may prove impossible to render in terms; it may be self-evident in a way that can only be directly experienced, with the result that such knowledge is not verbally communicable. This is, of course, where transpersonal psychology finds its characteristic approach, which if it may be generalized at all is to lead the client through a process that might precipitate an insight or an "unfoldment in being."[52] It is also where metaphysical fiction and poetry enter the field, as guides for the reader through an imaginative structure, a sense of whose wholeness (projected via its reflexivity) might stimulate an intuition. And it is clearly the basic issue in Romantic poetry, particularly in the work of Blake, Wordsworth, and Coleridge.

Although the words in a metaphysical fiction are first understood primarily by the left hemisphere of the brain, the image the reader forms on the basis of those words probably involves more right-hemisphere work (events in space, and so on), with the result that a fiction is able to address more than the propositional or analytical aspects of the reader's mind and perhaps of the subject matter. Even within the verbal level, the meter of a poem is likely to be processed by the right brain,[53] and it is arguable whether certain of the leaps involved in understanding metaphors and paradoxes can be handled by the left brain at all. It may be possible for the right brain to leap to a perception of what "makes itself manifest" in a given form and is not set forth in terms. The basic distinction here is between the left brain, which is analytical and verbal, and the right brain, which is spatial and holistic; whether or not this implies that the right brain is also the site of intuition, and whether or not any of these distinctions prove literally physiological, the "left and right hemispheres" are useful as metaphors for these aspects of human consciousness. It is possible, in any case, that language is primarily a left-hemisphere function and that certain uses of language may transcend or bypass the range of the language center without becoming lost to intuition. It is also possible that the ineffable is accessible only to that subliminal faculty William James discussed, which may be a spiritual doorway rather than an element of the "personality."

However it happens, there is a remarkable concensus about how the experience of absolute intuition feels, and one could cite Zen and Sufi masters, Gnostic scrolls, Metaphysical and Romantic English poets, and even California psychologists to this effect, were there not already a well-established understanding that "the 'unitive' experience of the mystic . . . is found in almost all cultures at all times. This experience is the transformed sense of self."[54] The basic

113

differences between the seers and the scientists who have attempted to write about this phenomenon seem ultimately rhetorical. Most of them agree—whether or not they consider it valid or valuable—that the mind must step out of the way or be stymied if the higher self is to step forward (or the blood flow to change). The "transformational psychology" of Dr. Brugh Joy, for instance, represents an attempt to make the realization of spiritual wholeness a valid therapeutic goal, a way of allowing the patient to receive and channel positive, healing energies. Joy's rhetoric itself ranges from the clinical to the vague: "your Beingness is you on *all* levels of reality."[55] When Shankara, at the other professional extreme, wrote to much the same effect about the experience of personal completeness and the related sense of the wholeness of the universe, he argued that beyond the illusions of Maya (a self-sustaining relationship between ignorance and "world-appearance") was Brahman, the "one Reality which appears to our ignorance as a manifold universe of names and forms and changes"; he maintained that Brahman was also "the innermost self, the ceaseless joy within us . . . absolute existence, knowledge and bliss."[56] The personal self is subject to Maya just as Brahman is; "the ego-sense . . . creates the impression that 'I am the actor, I am he who experiences,'"[57] but the true self is Atman (that is, Brahman-within-the-creature) and the roles as well as the ego-sense itself are illusory. Atman and Brahman are the same, and seeing through or beyond Maya (the illusion of multiplicity and fragmentation) puts one in touch suddenly with both, which reveal their identity.

Grafting onto all this the more rigorous rhetoric of Wittgenstein, one might describe the experience this way: logical space *and everything else* suddenly becomes tautological. Tautology, which "opens the whole of logical space" and *"shows"* that it "says nothing," also allows for the possibility of ubiquity and universal oneness. Tautology can be taken as the basis of personal identity (I am I) and the formal meaning of all equations (x = x). Repetition, as a literary device or as a mantra, is one celebration of this unity.[58] Silence may, on the intuitive or private level, be its manifestation. Neutrality may be its tone, and love, its process.

The experience of needing to be silent can arise in many ways. One might be filled with absolute bliss and thus be totally beyond the reach of language. One might feel frustrated and stymied, feeling the transcendental to be just out of reach—not yet experienced and yet still beyond expression. And so on. The first description applies most often to the intuitive seer; the second, to the analytical mind in search of (or suddenly and perhaps involuntarily involved with) a breakthrough or solution. One cannot move from analysis to intuitive understanding any more than words can achieve silence, and it is possible for someone focused on the verbal or analytical level to feel frustrated—like Beckett's Watt in some ways, and Faulkner in many.[59] Problems and solutions are parts of the same system, and "the solution of the problem of life is seen in the vanishing of the problem"—an option that must seem absurd (or in any case, out of reach) to the analytical mind.

When Gertrude Stein was dying, she kept asking herself and her companion Alice B. Toklas, "Alice, Alice, what is the answer?" Finally she laughed and died, saying, "In that case, what is the question?"

3. The Higher Self in Stein, Whitman, and Proust

The word "self" seems to put people off.
—Abraham Maslow,
Toward a Psychology of Being

What is really important for philosophy is to know exactly what unity, what multiplicity, and what reality superior both to abstract unity and multiplicity the multiple unity of the self actually

is. Now philosophy will know this only when it
recovers possession of the simple intuition of the
self by the self.
—Henri Bergson, *An Introduction to Metaphysics*

I have called this chapter "The Simultaneous Self" in order
to call attention to a paradox: the self is often perceived or
conceptualized as an aggregate of personal systems, or subselves (the body/mind/spirit is a familiar triad). And many
literary texts depend on the audience's realizing that certain
characters are each other's doubles, secret sharers, alternate
selves, complements, and so on. This sometimes has the implication that these component selves must integrate with
each other if the work is to achieve dramatic resolution,
though it is more common to encounter a work like *The
Brothers Karamazov* in which the possibility of the characters'
adding up to an integrated self (basically a Gestalt therapy
approach to literature) is latent in the novel's structure as
psychodrama but is not part of the diegesis. For the self,
then, as for certain literary structures, there is the option of
transcending subcategories and discovering the wholeness of
the system. In some cases, this involves the simultaneous
perception of the real existence of all the subselves, immediately succeeded by a sense of absolute integration. In the
instant between these perceptions, one is both an irreducible
unity and a complex of personal systems; the experienced
inconceivability of that state of awareness may be one reason
it often leads so directly to a transcendental intuition.

The first step toward this paradoxical state is to manipulate the partial selves into simultaneity—which Proust accomplishes through the practice of involuntary memory, although there are other ways. The next step is for that
simultaneity to act on itself, as in the analogy of a critical
mass. On one side of the flash (when matter reveals itself as
energy) there are simultaneous selves; on the other, the immersion in pure and undifferentiated being. As a nonsensical
term, the "simultaneous self" attempts to open for the

reader one aspect of the chain reaction and to introduce a discussion of several approaches to the nature of the multiple self, beginning with Gertrude Stein's marionette play, *Identity A Poem*.

The primary discipline to which Gertrude Stein subjected her awareness when she wrote portraits was to focus on the object of her attention so completely that she would lose all consciousness of self. Free of egotism, free of remembering, and to a great extent free of what she called "human nature," she could *see*—not the accidental, nor even the visual aspects of the portrait-subject, but the being-in-itself that made the subject what it was. Her exact intelligence paid attention to the *entity*, the nameless center, and disregarded the *identity*, the birth certificate. In *Identity A Poem*, she turned this almost Buddhistically neutral yet rigorously and detachedly scientific gaze on herself. In the course of writing that play and *The Geographical History of America* (an extended meditation on "The Relation of Human Nature to the Human Mind," which includes a longer version of *Identity*), Stein discovered that the writing of masterpieces—works that in themselves are timeless and free of identity—demanded that the author herself become pure entity. She had to forget who she was and abandon being-in-relation; she had to free herself from causality, necessity, politics, time, memory, her name, everything associated with human nature. In so doing, she would rest in the human mind, the entity that "gazes at pure existing," as Thornton Wilder put it.[60]

Applying the discipline of the portraits to the project of self-analysis, Stein achieved not autobiography but philosophy (a distinction that then, of course, vanished). At the center of this self-portrait lies something anonymous and wise, the entity that is independent of her name—"an existence suspended in time" but with no sense of time:[61] "The human mind can write what it is because what it is is all that it is and as it is all that it is all it can do is to write."[62]

"The human mind" here refers not to consciousness but

to pure consciousness; it is the part of the self that is totally independent of relation. It is what you are when you forget what you are.[63] It is a constant. When it writes, it addresses itself, and in its own terms, paying no attention to audience (that is, relation).[64] It does things (writes, plays, notices) for the sake of doing them. Human nature, on the other hand, is the self-in-relation; it is the self that desires, that starts wars, that eats, that is noticed by others, that has a sense of time and so can remember itself and so cannot write masterpieces. In other words, "identity" is used here not in the sense of $x = x$, but in the sense of $x = 2$; "entity" is closer to $x = x$. The mind frees itself from identity, the name of its body or the relational aspects of its own activities, just as Beckett's Unnamable frees itself from Molloy and Malone and Mahood, in order to find the door that opens on itself: the clear, anonymous, universal *I*. From this base, the entity of the human mind "plays because it plays"; awake, in the present, without remembering, without ties to the birth certificate of human nature, it can produce works that are at their own centers timeless, anonymous, unhurried, true— that are, as Stein defined them, masterpieces.

Identity A Poem[65] leads the reader through a process of discovery. It begins with the problematic statement, "I am I because my little dog knows me." This is a statement of identity. It is all very well to be recognized by one's pet, or by any exterior agency, but what is being recognized is the self-in-relation and not the inside mind. Only the mind can be alone, can forget its identity and exist in autonomy; neither human nature nor any dog can be alone in this way. Human nature cannot write masterpieces (which proceed from "knowing that there is no identity and producing while identity is not," as Stein puts it in the essay, "What are Masterpieces?"—acknowledging that this kind of "knowing" is "extremely difficult"[66]), although masterpieces can tell stories about human nature. Human nature can desire but not play. The human mind gets excited where human nature gets nervous.

118

Stein implies that there are two categories of art, each distinguished by its originating consciousness. A work by the human mind can be about human nature, or it can show "the essence of what happened" or "the excitingness of pure being";[67] the distinguishing factor is not what it treats, but that it is by the human mind. At this point in the argument, Stein sets herself the task of demonstrating the difference between "a play with human nature and not anything of the human mind" and "a play with just the human mind."[68] She tries and, characteristically, starts over.

This series of inner plays leads Stein to the perception that "dogs and human nature have no identity" to the extent that they can sometimes become totally immersed in what they are doing ("Not any dog can say not ever when he is at play").[69] She also observes that "Nobody knows what the human mind is when they are drunk." Although a dog can behave as an entity under certain circumstances, it cannot go through the process of knowing that it is doing so. The place where human nature and the human mind mingle is in the first realization that the self is internally validated: that I am I regardless of what my little dog knows. This realization initiates a dialectic (acted out on the page) between identity and entity: the search for and retreat from pure being.

In the world of the mind, any number can be a "one"; it need not "remember" that it is the second in a series that accumulates to "two." By the same logic, the self can forget its identity and become an "I," and then lose even "I" in the act of clear seeing (this is what happens when an entity writes). It can behave "as one is one,"[70] that is, with the same groundedness in pure being as that manifested in the equation $1 = 1$. In the play of identity, any scene can be scene 1; in the continuous present, each moment is now, is the first. It is in this spirit that the scenes in *Identity A Poem* cavort with their numbers until they achieve "Scene 1" and finalize their analysis.

In Act 1, Scene 3[71] Stein repeats her opening line, beginning again. "I am I because my little dog knows me," she

119

says, is the way she "had played that play," but it is not a good identity base, not connected with the place where "one is one," not carried out with the conceptual rigor of "one is one" analysis. She goes on to pick up an argument from *The Geographical History:* "we in America are not displaced by a dog," because we come from a wide, flat land, an open scheme where the mind can range freely; a dog's recognition of us is not as strong or clear as our mind's self-knowledge. We cannot be kicked out of our own mental province. The dog, now seen choking over a ball, is not very bright anyway—and where would we be if we needed our dog to recognize us and he did not? ("I would not be I. Oh no oh no.")

Stein goes into the mind, then, where the play can play. At this point, she introduces two voices, "Chorus" and "Tears." It hurts (brings tears) to let go of memory, of dogs, of companionship, of human nature, and it is difficult to argue with or lead along a clever audience (chorus) or the recalcitrant side of one's nature (chorus). Nevertheless she proceeds. (This conflict and its resolution were announced in the first lines of the piece: "I am I because my little dog knows me. The figure wanders on alone.") There are two ways of knowing: to know that something or someone is related to something else (this involves remembering, keeping "left and right" distinct); and to know something as an independent entity (like the mind itself). This takes us back to Bergson. But what does it mean to be in the human mind when the awareness of being in that state can so easily constitute thinking-in-relation?

Chorus   There is no left or right without remembering.
    And remembering.
    They say there is no left and right without remembering.
Chorus   But there is no remembering the human mind.
Tears   There is no chorus in the human mind.[72]

The epistemological problem is so complex that only the chorus, and not the mind, can comment on it. The mind functions without remembering, without comparing; that is the secret of its success in the continuous present and in the realm of entity. The chorus points out that the mind itself cannot be remembered, or analyzed in terms of something else, any more than it can analyze itself in terms of something else. The chorus can say this because it is *not* in or of the mind; it is at this point a voice of 'nature and identity. For the chorus, the mind is an object of speculation, something exterior to simple human nature.

A tearful voice responds that this paradox is not insoluble from the perspective of the mind, because "There is no chorus in the human mind," because the faculty that wants and needs to conceptualize in terms of resemblance and memory is not part of the system of the human mind in the first place. The mind functions easily in this area of primary being and timelessness and can simply accept and work within it without having to classify it. Entity, as Stein dramatizes it, is absolutely centered and self-sufficient. What is unique about her formulation is that entity is not silent; its perfection can express itself in the play of words; its insights are so clear and so unmediated that they can find a language suited to that clarity. Frustrations at the phenomenology of the ineffable are not part of the entity's burden. This does not necessarily mean that as pure entity Stein could express the ineffable—though her project of remaining in contact with an interior essence and being able to notice and articulate the essence of what is present does touch many of the same problems and stands as a tribute to her optimism and to her vision of an essentialist language (the human mind's). Her point is a related one: that the human mind cannot conceptualize the structure and limits of its isolation because it would have to think like the chorus in order to notice the problem.

The chorus, however, turns out not to *be* human nature but only to share some of its perspectives. In the longer version of this play in *The Geographical History,* Stein shows that any identity has the problem of wondering what it really is; this is logical, for the characteristic of entity is that it is what it is, pure and simple, and so does not (at this point in her demonstration) have to worry about self-knowing. Here is part of the long version:

> Dogs and birds and a chorus and a flat land.
> How do you like what you are. The bird knows, the dogs know and the chorus well the chorus yes the chorus if the chorus which is the chorus.
> The flat land is not the chorus.
> Human nature is not the chorus.
> The human mind is not the chorus.
> Perspiration is not the chorus.
> Tears are not the chorus.
> Food is not the chorus.
> Money is not the chorus.
> What is the chorus.
> Chorus.   What is the chorus.
> Anyway there is the question of identity.
> And that has also to do with the dog.
> Is the dog the chorus.
> Chorus.   No the dog is not the chorus.[73]

The chorus' asking "What is the chorus" *is* or *shows* "the question of identity." The revelatory humor of this kind of game-playing justifies Stein's method: the question of identity is better shown than directly explained, for just the reasons Wittgenstein and don Juan have advanced. Stein is leading herself and the reader through a revelatory process.

Having brought the reader to this point, then, Stein is free to complicate the argument drastically. It is not legitimate to assert that the human mind has no problem understanding its own nature simply because it is entity. On her way to the "Scene 1" that will demonstrate the problem, she consolidates what she has discovered so far. The chorus has said earlier that her little dog's knowing her "does not prove anything about you it only proves something about the dog." Now she says that "a little dog knowing me does not really make me be I no not really because after all being I I am I has really nothing to do with the little dog knowing me, he is my audience, but an audience never does prove to you that you are you."[74] Here "being I" means being in the "I am I" or entity state.

The problem is, "When I am I am I I." Here is the scene:

SCENE I

I am I yes sir I am I.
I am I yes madame am I I.
When I am I am I I.
And my little dog is not the same thing as I am I.
Chorus   Oh is it.
With tears in my eyes oh is it.
And there we have the whole thing
Am I I.
And if I am I because my little dog knows me am I I.
Yes sir am I I.
The dog answers without asking because the dog is the answer to anything that is that dog.
But not I.
Without tears but not I.[75]

When Stein is entity and has no awareness of self, then, she cannot *know* that she is herself; to say "I am I" would break the state, shift attention.

Stein only appears to be stopping at the Montaignesque question, "Am I I," however. It is not that she doubts her being, but that she understands she cannot settle the question of her being's existence; no referential system can come to her aid. (This applies to the entity state; she has to ask the same question for different reasons in the state of relation.) It would be comparable to asking a logical proposition to describe logical form (what it must have in common with reality in order to represent it). The proposition simply has or shows logical form. Similarly, the human mind manifests entity. In that state, finally, it accepts itself and its inability

123

to achieve self-description without surrendering the ability to play and "without tears." There is no point in crying over her aloneness, her absence of relation; the final step in her demonstration, the one that allows her to proceed to a little dance around the notion of ending the piece "after giving," is her abandoning that sadness. Her kinship with the dog is that she too is the answer to herself. Though Stein would not have used the terms, this amounts to an acceptance of the ineffable in the context of a secular experience of the higher self (as well as a means of showing how people can validate each other through an understanding of each other's systemic integrity); its crux is the impossibility of describing entity. Hence she offers not an explanation, but a dramatization of the problem, an essentialist play rather than a lecture.

As Stein explains this in "What Are Masterpieces?"—part of whose point is that in order to create a masterpiece one must be free of conceptions of time and identity—"At any moment when you are you you are you without the memory of yourself because if you remember yourself while you are you you are not for purposes of creating you."[76] There is an analogy here with Heisenberg's Principle of Indeterminacy: one can *be* something or define it, but not both at once. As Stein observed in "Henry James":

> I am I not any longer when I see.
> This sentence is at the bottom of all creative activity.
> It is just the exact opposite of I am I because my little dog knows me.[77]

Deep into being, she can see and can create, but she has no awareness of self. This being-not-in-relation does not provide a rationale for writing incomprehensibly, as some of Stein's critics have charged; it is a phenomenological isolation within which she has the duty to be absolutely precise and clear, as she always insisted she was. What she asks is that the reader be simple and share her play, particularly her sense of time.

It was necessary for Stein not to pay attention to the audience while she was writing, but it is clear nevertheless that she wanted her work to be read and understood:

> If you do not remember while you are writing, it may seem confused to others but actually it is clear and eventually that clarity will be clear, that is what a masterpiece is, but if you remember while you are writing it will seem clear all the time to any one but the clarity will go out of it that is what a masterpiece is not.[78]

The clarity of a masterpiece and the clarity of entity are of the same order. As pure entity, Stein's relation to time and identity is on an "as if" basis:

> . . . to go on being not as if there were no time and identity but as if there were and at the same time existing without time and identity is so simple that it is difficult to have many that are that.[79]

Her paradox is, as usual, exact; for its precedent, one has to look back almost to *The Cloud of Unknowing*. To be in this state of clarity is the essence of simplicity—complication cannot enter it except as an object for the higher attention to play with (for instance, while writing a novel that includes characters and a developing story line). But it is difficult to find this simplicity, let alone the courage to function in a state that the Lacanian "identity" would consider self-absence; so there are few writers of masterpieces.

Returning to Shankara for a moment, we can notice the metaphysical significance of the "as if" relation. The ultimate interior self, the pure consciousness that witnesses everything the person does, knows that the phenomenal universe is a game, an integrated series of illusions perpetuated by ignorance and laziness. We need to learn to see through the illusions of time and matter, to see that each person is a portion of the energy of God. We exist in eternity even as we are embodied in time, and we need to learn how to open to that whole spectrum and focus it in acts of creation and in an attendant heightened awareness of pure being. Shankara felt that the universe had disguised itself as phenomena in order to have the pleasure of discovering its true nature, even if that required many incarnations or steps. To clarify his argument, we might use the analogy of energy's manifesting itself as matter, but it would be more precise to say that energy, matter, thought, and so forth, are all kinds of vibration and the universe is a wave pattern. This concept has been argued well, with reference to contemporary physics, by the late Itzhak Bentov in his entertaining and ingenious book, *Stalking the Wild Pendulum*. One of his notions is that "a continuous spectrum of realities arises due to the ability of matter to contain consciousness" and that these relative realities constitute a hierarchy that culminates in a state of being that is "the absolute."[80] Shankara's perspective on this hierarchy is reductive but perfectly consistent with Bentov's conclusions. And though Stein would probably disagree with both of their cosmological answers, it is clear that she is committed to similar questions.

Shankara claims that the game exists but is not real in the ultimate way Brahman is real, although both have existed at least as long as the world. The game exists as a set of appearances; it vanishes when one has a direct experience of the irreducible and universal One. The game is not "real" in Shankara's strict sense of the term because nothing that could cease to exist can be real; the only reality is therefore the One. This renders logical and livable the notion that the world of time and change is "illusory," a notion that can easily alienate people who have a deep experience of living in the world. What Shankara means, in other words, is that the world is an illusion in that it changes. God is not subject to change and thus is not an illusion in that Being is a constant (energy is conserved), though it is arguable that God's self-knowledge is capable of some undiscussable quality of process. To be illusory means to change, and to change means to exist in time. To be illusory, then, means to exist in time. Absolute Being must be extratemporal. Obviously, our world is temporal, although the infinitesimal instant may somehow be congruent with eternity. We cannot say (in terms; that is, with inherently temporal fragments; that is, from a mortal perspective) just how the unillusory eternal is with us, unchanging, "while" we are in time—but it is entirely possible that that is the case. All Shankara wants to do is to turn our attention from what changes to what might underlie and sustain what changes, and that does not entirely invalidate mortal experience; it simply offers a shift in context.

How is the "enlightened" person to continue in the world after seeing it as a set of appearances (or a "description")? Clearly, one must approach phenomena both on their own terms and on an "as if" basis. One need not confuse a brick wall with ultimate reality in order to avoid walking into the wall. In other circles, this is called "being in the world but not of it," or being "harmless."[81] One lives with the knowledge that one is part of the universal Self and is considerate of others who may not share that perspective, helping them to realize their potential and living in the reality of unconditional love. This is a world-view basic to many religions, but it is also a workable analogy to the human mind's attitude toward the events in the novel it may be writing: it treats them as if they were as real as itself, while realizing that they are not.

Whether or not Gertrude Stein was a closet mystic—and she would have insisted that her orientation was strictly scientific—the point remains that her observations on the human mind are comparable to those of many students of transcendental consciousness. The central or centrist mystical assertion, for our purposes, is that some element of the self exists as pure entity in a timeless condition and is so completely realized that it has neither the need nor the capacity to conceptualize that condition. It simply manifests its condition; it functions and it is. It might be described as pure consciousness, or as what you are when you forget who you are. In this discussion, I am calling it the higher self.[82]

127

The higher self is complete. It is not fixed or rigid but is self-sufficient, inexhaustible, and in a state of becoming though not of imperfection. It can step forward when the mind steps out of the way. It can be evoked by words but not contained in them—that is, it can choose to step forward, and sometimes this will feel like an act of grace. It guides the conscious and physical aspects of the self without appearing to intervene overtly; some mystics[83] say that it is the part of us that knows what our karmic path is and what we have to do to fulfill it.

When the higher self does step forward, that can produce a rise in energy—as if one were a spark that had been fanned into flaming, or as if the whole self were an energy field whose center had begun to pulse and glow or warm up, or as if one were simultaneously clear and dizzy. This energy can wash through the body and fill it with vibration; directed through the hands, it can heal. It is like the air in a balloon. It is a center of impersonal and unconditional love. Sometimes its vibrations feel audible, or as if they ought to be audible; sometimes they feel like a light.

The odd thing is that although the mind can attempt these descriptions, it realizes them as nonsensical; and although it has nothing to do with the higher self's stepping forward, the mind can continue to function on its own level while the higher self is manifest (the key to Dante's joyful failure). The point is that the higher self and the mind operate on different levels and that the higher self is not a verbal or conceptual experience.

The higher self is neither the body nor the mind but loves them both and patiently lifts them to its unconditional, timeless (that is, absolutely present), and perfect state. On the other side of the barrier of words and time and preconceptions, it waits to be discovered—but without the impatience implied by "waiting" because (like Godot rather than the tramps, if you will) it has no sense of time. It can also be described as waiting on the other side of the "bubble of perception." It cannot be named, but will answer. It acts for the highest good, to which it is attuned as if to a kindred frequency. It can also attune to the higher self in others and share its love. It exists in a condition of wholeness, love, and creative power. To discover it is to undergo a transformation of consciousness, in fact, a transformation past consciousness into a more assured sense of being: to discover that one is the focusing point of a flow.

Becoming aware of the higher self is not, however, the same as discovering the One. The higher self is one of our elements; in some circles it is considered not the soul, but an intermediary or gateway. It often happens that one will make contact with the higher self and not find it necessary to remain silent, whereas absolute immersion in the One renders all terminology useless. It is possible to speak *from* the higher self, to say what it might want to say if it could speak. (This is the "as if" approach in reverse—to speak of the truth as if it were possible to speak of it, rather than to speak of human nature, events, and so on, as if they were fundamental realities.) Hence Yeats can present a "Dialogue of Self and Soul," which climaxes with the stepping forward of the heart energy of the higher self as resentment and remorse are cast out, in an acceptance of incarnation that allows his heart to fill with a perception of universal blessedness.[84]

The higher self embraces life and moves the whole self toward fulfillment, accepting time and phenomena as vehicles for action and thus for self-improvement and attunement. When it steps forward in *A la recherche du temps perdu,* the narrator is flooded with a joy that he interprets as timelessness. Whitman manages to sustain, for virtually the whole length of the first and best edition of "Song of Myself," the simultaneous presence of his conscious and higher selves, often speaking from the higher self on an unstated "as if" basis. The "Me myself" that Whitman speaks of stands "Apart from the pulling and hauling . . . compassionating, idle, unitary . . . both in and out of the game."[85] Accepting this watchful, waiting consciousness (called the "witness" by some mystics), he finds that the self-evident is unnamable:

A child said, What is the grass? fetching it to me with
  full hands;
How could I answer the child?....I do not know what
  it is any more than he.[86]

Whitman's best guesses as to the nature of the grass include the notions that it is the "flag" of his own disposition, "the handkerchief of the Lord," and "a uniform hieroglyphic" or one-sign language whose signified is universal equality. He finds that he and all others are "immortal and fathomless," whether or not others realize it; and to help others realize it, he offers "hints," words that "itch at your ears till you understand them.[87] He is deathless, not contained between his hat and his boots, loving, accepting, complete, all-embracing, *and* articulate (because he is saying what the higher self might say if it could). He acknowledges that he is up against a mystery, but he embraces it and is clear about it; it is as evident as a handful of grass and just as undefinable.

Whitman's simultaneity here is of two kinds. The first is the simultaneous presence of his higher and conscious selves (which must have been necessary to the composition of the poem). The second is a phase in the development of the poem's persona, "Walt Whitman." He begins as a first-person single subject who intends to celebrate himself and to take on ("assume") a universe of characteristics as a way of demonstrating the unity of the self and the diversity of its manifestaions; he announces at the very outset that he and the reader are complementary in nature. (This is obviously a good deal more than an expression of the ideals of democracy.) He then goes through a phase of cataloging everything that he is: he is a poet, he is a fireman, he is a man, he is a woman, and so on. He is all these things, and yet he is the "unitary" self; with regard to the other lives, he is "both in and out of the game," just as he is Walt Whitman but not contained between his hat and his boots. As he inventories these aspects of his self, these simultaneous alternates, he both embraces them and is freed of them. Each role, each mask, each identity rises in him, truly represents him in that moment, and then is released back into the heart of life. At a crucial point, he confronts "touch" and realizes that he is one among many universes;[88] he realizes that he and the cosmos survive together and achieve balance by sending out energy—that he gives as much as he receives, and in the same coin. He thus becomes not a fireman, but a primal energy. He becomes the pure voice of the poem, the reader's companion; then he gets up and leaves. On the way out, he accepts death and reincarnation and gives the definition of the "Me myself"—the higher self, the soul, Atman, or even the mind of the text—there is no way to tell—his last and appropriately most inarticulate shot:

> There is that in me....I do not know what it is....but I know it is in me.
> [. . .] I do not know it....it is without name....it is a word unsaid,
> It is not in any dictionary or utterance or symbol.
> [. . .] Do you see O my brothers and sisters?
> It is not chaos or death....it is form and union and plan....it is eternal life....it is happiness.[89]

At this point he "dies" and becomes ubiquitous; he becomes the meaning of his poem. (We can take this as another instance of the recurring connection between discovery of the unnamable self and systemic reflexivity in literature.) He has struck through the mask, to quote Ahab, but from the other side.

Proust's narrator in *A la recherche du temps perdu* discovers that perceptual repetition (involuntary memory) short-circuits the phenomenal world and allows the timeless self to step forward. As we shall see, the crucial element is that at least two selves (the narrator now and the narrator then) become simultaneous, in an instant that is immediately transfigured out of time. The tonal, if you will, is silenced long enough for the self to experience its totality; the narrator is transfused with happiness and simply *finds* that he is free of death and that anxiety and loss can be the portion only of those parts of him that exist in time. This is an experience of the higher self, and its demonstration begins with an appeal to fluidity in time and reflexivity in the text.

Proust's nameless "I" is first encountered in a pseudotimeless state, describing a semiconscious condition. At only two points in this seven-volume novel is the narrator given a name (Marcel). So much art and attention is devoted to his not having a name through these thousands of pages, however, that the two "Marcel"s might well be considered oversights. It seems arguable that Proust intended to create a persona unique in the history of literature: an "I" that would dominate the text as anonymously and fundamentally as the reader's sense of identity (in Stein's term, "entity"; in Whitman's, "Me myself") dominates his or her own being. Returning to Wittgenstein's distinction between what makes itself manifest and what can be said, we can observe that the pronoun "I" *shows* self-conscious identity, whereas the words "self-conscious identity" *say* it. Proust's narrator is, through the complexity of his presentation as both witness and witnessed, the first literary consciousness as unknown and total as that of a human being; in this sense, Proust's immediate heirs are Stein and Beckett.

The novel's first sentence, "Longtemps, je me suis couché de bonne heure," has two possible translations: "For a long time I have gone to bed early" and "For a long time I went to bed early." This widely noticed ambiguity (which could have been avoided, for instance, by Proust's having used the imperfect tense) is significant, because it makes it difficult for the reader to decide whether the narrator is describing a state of affairs that no longer exists or one that persists. In other words, the narrator declines to locate himself in time.

The narrator goes on to describe the ambiguity and freedom of consciousness he experiences on either edge of sleep:

Sometimes, when I had put out my candle, my eyes would close so quickly that I had not even time to say "I'm going to sleep." And half an hour later the thought that it was time to go to sleep would awaken me; I would try to put away the book which, I imagined, was still in my hands, and to blow out the light; I had been thinking all the time, while I was asleep, of what I had just been reading, but my thoughts had run into a channel of their own, until I myself seemed actually to have become the subject of my book. . .

He hints here that *A la recherche* might have a reflexive structure: that this book is being narrated by its subject—not just in the standard first-person-narrative sense but in the sense that the narrator's "I" is that not of a person but of a completely text-bound and text-created entity. Alternately, he hints that *A la recherche* incarnates the autobiographical fantasy of a semiconscious being. He even manages to suggest that this act of effortless and free-floating narration is noticed from within the book, so that the scene of waking up that follows the hint can be taken as an event within the dream (and this makes sense, since the dream—that is, the text— does not cease). The self has become the subject of the book; the subject of the book is presented as a self that is half-aware that it may be, or be in, a text.

A la recherche begins, then, on the verge of systemic self-consciousness and continues throughout its length to manifest (through its sequence of associations as much as anything else) a flow of being. There is, of course, the possibility that this hint is only a teaser and that the whole novel is a long *saying* rather than *showing* of the process of becoming freed from the destructive action of time—but frankly, I hardly think so.

. . . but my thoughts had run into a channel of their own, until I myself seemed to have become the subject

133

of my book: a church, a quartet, the rivalry between François I and Charles V. . . .

One implication here is that *A la recherche* can be full of events and characters and still be, underneath and alongside all that, nothing but one consciousness—a consciousness that from the perspective of those characters and events would be considered extrasystemic. The narrator, even in his moments of self-awareness, would be like "Alice" in the looking-glass dream that is being dreamed by Alice—a dream that can include speculation about who might be dreaming it (the Red King, according to Tweedledum) without breaking open the structure.[90]

The only thing that would break open the structure would be for the dreamer to wake up, that is, for the bubble of perception to be opened from the outside. The outside, in the case of a novel, is extratextual. In the case of the conscious self, the outside signifies the unnamable self. The verbal self cannot wake itself up (end the dream from within) any more than analysis can lead to an intuitive breakthrough. The intuition happens on its own; the higher self chooses, autonomously, to step forward. The mind's only option is to step out of the way, to create a vacuum for the higher self to fill. Until that happens, "waking up" is only another event within the dream.

One way to create that vacuum is to go silent; another is, according to Proust, to experience involuntary memory (a process of sudden and total reexperience, to be discussed below). In this case, the higher self is like Shankara's God dreaming the game of the universe, manipulating its terms until his true and timeless being has an unmasked experience of itself. It might also be argued that the author is like God and that the higher self, like the phenomenal world and the events of the novel, is a mask in search of the face that gazes from behind.

. . . the rivalry between François I and Charles V. This impression would persist for some moments after I was

134

awake; it did not disturb my mind, but it lay like scales upon my eyes and prevented them from registering the fact that the candle was no longer burning. Then it would begin to seem unintelligible, as the thoughts of a former existence must be to a reincarnate spirit; the subject of my book would separate itself from me, leaving me free to choose whether I would form part of it or no; and at the same time my sight would return and I would be astonished to find myself in a state of darkness, pleasant and restful enough for the eyes, and even more, perhaps, for my mind, to which it appeared incomprehensible, without a cause, a matter dark indeed.[91]

In the concluding phrase of this first paragraph of the novel, the narrator introduces the issue of the "incomprehensible," and to some extent, also resolves it. The dark world appears "without a cause," yet the reader has just been told that the free-floating consciousness deliberately chose this incarnation rather than the one it had been dreaming previously. (Shankara would observe that the deluded ego-sense chooses to be deluded.) The solution to the darkness is the realization that the spirit has chosen to be there in the dark, that it is the cause of its own condition. Its goal now is to free itself from darkness, time, and death, through a direct experience of its own timeless nature. Its problem appears incomprehensible until, as Wittgenstein says, "The solution of the problem of life is seen in the vanishing of the problem," which is precisely the experience of Proust's narrator at the party that closes the novel.

On the verge of sleep, as in his dreams, the narrator is nearly free in time and space. He can return effortlessly to an earlier stage of his life, or imagine that the bedroom is in any city. In the moment of waking up, he has to decide, or remember, to have a certain name and address: to "put together by degrees the component parts of my ego."[92] Man creates his own limits, then, partly out of the demands of habit and partly because of his failure to analyze and appreciate these moments of freedom (hence the analytical project of *A la recherche,* an analysis that begins—following Bergson—with intuition). The narrator's identity, anonymous and transcendent, inhabits him as his body does the dark bedroom. Beckett's Unnamable occupies its timeless, spaceless place in much the same way—just as each self-conscious "I" inhabits its particular novel.

The main tension in *A la recherche* is between time lost and time refound. "Time found" is simply the process of living, but time found after it has been lost is the key to a transcendent existence. For six and a half volumes the narrator goes on to describe (or dream) the cycles of idealization and disillusionment that have been his life. An extraordinary richness of perception is counterpointed by a deadening need for habit. As a child he is bookish and dependent. He dreams of visiting the places and meeting the people he hears or reads about; he becomes infatuated with a girl his own age, and with an older woman whose family dominates polite society. Above all, he wants to become a writer. Years later, when he has seen the disappointing places, been accepted by society, and survived an obsessive, deceptive love affair, he sees himself as a failure.

He has lived through the gap between signifieds and signifiers, "places" and "names." He appears to have gotten everything he had wanted, but in fact he has only their shells. Some are not as beautiful as he expected, some are drained by habituation, some have grotesquely aged. He finds language as ineffectual as life; both disappoint the expectations they create. What has stopped him from becoming a writer is not just the failure of will of which he is so aware, but this sense that language is a failed system. (His left brain does not know what the right is doing, so to speak.) What he wants is a way of directly evoking a place that incarnates the essence implied by its name; the language he wants is magical, transcendental, totally effective. He wants to be analytical and holistic at once, but feels cut off from both. What he has missed in life is the *essence* of people and events that his youthful imagination (goaded, among other things, by his reading *and* by the images in stained-glass windows and magic lantern slides) had led him to desire. This essence must necessarily be free from the destructive action of time; it is virtually a Platonic "form." At the end of the novel, the narrator has a right-brain, holistic vision of this essence, discovers a method for keeping in touch with it, overthrows the domination of habit (in terms to be examined more fully in the next chapter, the action of the "basic self"), and declares himself ready to become a writer. The vision is of time refound, and one of the most important and little-noticed aspects of that experience is that the "place" is *not* brought forward by the "name." Language is not capable of containing the timeless essence; the ineffable remains ineffable. But language can create the conditions for the timeless to manifest itself, and this Proust explains as the structure and task of metaphor.

Metaphor, "by comparing a quality common to two sensations, succeeds in extracting their common essence and reuniting them to each other, liberated from the contingencies of time."[93] Although Proust might have meant to imply that the essence is actually contained in the metaphor, his larger argument necessarily implies that the metaphor presents the two common elements in such a way that the essence will manifest itself dialectically in the mind of the reader—hence the recurring device of synesthesia in this work, for instance, and of metaphors that juxtapose different frames of reference. Certain works of art, he argues, put the reader directly in touch with the "Realms of Truth" by presenting his or her "spirit" with "immaterial" elements that transcend the "senses" ("things, that is, which the spirit can assimilate to itself").[94] The elements of the metaphors that fill this book, like its events and characters, are apprehensible by the senses no matter how Symbolist they become; one must therefore conclude either that Proust failed to understand the implications of his own argument or that he intended the reader to see past what the novel said to what it showed and to apply the imagination toward an intuitive understanding of what is so extensively analyzed. Proust did, after all, read Bergson, and the climax of his novel is a transcendental intuition.

Time and language are renewed together by the narrator's direct intuition of the timeless essence that transcends them both. Until he has this intuition and successfully analyzes it (precisely the sequence Bergson recommended), he is out of touch with his past. His memory of it is artificial, deadened: a wax museum of facts. Because he can call any of these moments to mind at will, he calls this his "voluntary memory." In the last volume, he discovers that another kind of memory has been prodding at him: an instantaneous recall of pure sensation. These instants fill him with joy and peace and banish the fear of death. He discovers that this is not a deliberate memory process but perceptual reexperience triggered by an outside stimulus, a magical and nonverbal invocation. Because he cannot control it, he calls it "involuntary memory." The happiness it brings is categorical freedom, and the problem of will vanishes as he is infused with purpose, just as the problem of habit vanishes in the face of radical authenticity. This freedom is an aspect of William James's conversion experience. Involuntary memory itself is an experience of repetition, with the complication that the original and repeated percepts all happen at once; it is an instance of what is implied by the statement that repetition is a timeless state.[95] It is also a right-brain event—although that term does not exhaust its description—and a transcendental as well as practical unraveling of the problems of will and habit.

An unsuspected stimulus, common to two points in time and not noticed by the will (deliberate attention), has the power to bring the earlier moment to life. For example, the adult narrator dips his madeleine in tea and feels inexplicably happy; after a while, he recognizes the taste as one he enjoyed in childhood. At first, he identifies his joy as that of rediscovering a happy moment, but eventually he realizes its deeper cause. (The madeleine episode occurs early in the first volume, the full realization late in the seventh.) In such an instant, he is not simply reliving the past but experiencing the moment's essence. He is not simply flashed back, but flashed *out* of time. Freed from chronology, he is not weighted down by death; freed from the banality of his former perceptions, he is in touch with the essence of being. In short, he discovers his capacity for transcendence:

> I experienced them at the present moment and at the same time in the context of a different moment, so that the past was made to encroach upon the present and I was made to doubt whether I was in the one or the other. The truth surely was that the being within me which had enjoyed these impressions had enjoyed them because they had in them something that was common to a day long past and to now, because in some way they were extra-temporal, and this being made its appearance only when, through one of those identifications of the present with the past, it was likely to find itself in the one and only medium in which it could exist and enjoy the essence of things, that is to say: outside time.[96]

Because the narrator is not remembering but reliving a moment from his past, he feels he has literally moved out of the present. Because he is experiencing the common stimulus *in* the present, however, he remains paradoxically in and out of both moments with his whole being. His younger and older selves are both present; both of their moments are linked. The selves are resolved in a transcendent self, a "giant plunged into the years."[97] The moments are linked by their mutual essence.

The timeless self, who perceives these essences, is alive in both the older and younger selves, but it can be brought to full consciousness only when the other two are joined by a common experience. It is a drastic violation of normal chronology to experience one's older and younger selves at the same instant; it short-circuits the course of the temporal self

139

entirely, and that creates the conditions for the higher self—complete, joyful, eternal—to step forward. This allows the narrator to experience what he calls "a fragment of time in the pure state," which involves both using and transcending his senses.[98] The timeless self notices these things continually, but is autonomous and inaccessible to the sensual, timebound aspects of the self. Yet it infuses the personal system. It is the mystic being that looms (in Melville's sense of the term) beyond the sense of identity and boundlessly reveals itself in that paradoxical instant when the other elements of the self become, for whatever reason, simultaneous.

This timeless self is, quite appropriately, not contained within Proust's novel but is only described in terms that Wittgenstein, for instance, would call nonsensical (if it has any "direct" presence, it is as the system's dreamer). What infuses the novel, however, is the sense that both Proust and his narrator have had the experience of which they speak. This leads to a final remark on the condition of being verbally stymied, of feeling that one cannot talk about something and must either let the ineffable manifest itself or fixate on the failure of language.

This condition can be painful and frustrating or blissful and exuberant. It appears that the frustrated author or persona is one who has not yet had the unitive metaphysical experience and feels separated from truth by a wall of words (Ahab trying to break through the mask, Addie trying to make direct contact with her students by whipping them, Vladimir and Estragon waiting for Godot) and that the joyful persona or author is one who, like Proust or Whitman, has found this joy while having the metaphysical experience. It depends on which side of the bubble of perception one feels based.

CHAPTER FOUR

Frames under Pressure

FARMER: The village lives in fear. Ruepp says
he's seen a Giant. The time of the Giants is
coming back.

SECOND FARMER: The Giant breaks the trees and
beats our cattle. He's tearing out our bowels
whenever he sees us.

YOUNG FARMER: He is licking our brains out.

HIAS: Tell Ruepp that there is no Giant. Next
time he has to pay attention to the angle of the
sun. The sun had gone down. The Giant was
just the shadow of a dwarf.

—Werner Herzog, *Heart of Glass*

In this chapter, we shall pay attention to the angle of the
sun: a few narrative structures that help to give the impression that we are making contact with giants. Literature, like
any sign system, finds its characteristic energy in the tension
between the poles of signifier and signified. It has one foot
planted squarely in the limits of language and the other in
the complete range of experience. It inevitably returns to
words, even if its author has had an intuition that transcends
the verbal system. It rewards those who see only as far as
words and logic will let them see, and those who return to
the cave to share with their companions their insights about
figures that are not shadows.

Although there is a long history of the visionary experience in literature—much of it depending on tautology and
nonsense for "direct" expression and on tropes, traps, and
systematic exclusion for indirect expression—there is a par-

allel and complementary body of work that deals in many of the same ways with the experience of *almost* having a vision, or retreating from one, or obsessively failing to communicate one. The latter system is entirely appropriate—rather than deliberately negativist or self-defeating—since it acknowledges literature's basis in the effable, in language. It is this attention to the nature of its medium that makes the frustrated or overreaching structure so prone to a reflexive approach, and that therefore leads eventually to systemic self-consciousness, which is one of the most elegant and successful means of actually resolving the problem, manifesting an identity it cannot in any case explain.

Even the metaphysically comfortable author will often generate a "frustrated" narrative structure in order to hook the reader with shadows and lead him out of the cave; something of this approach is basic to novels as diverse as *A la recherche du temps perdu, One Hundred Years of Solitude,* and *Moby-Dick* and to such films as Bergman's *Shame,* Duras' *India Song,* and Malick's *Days of Heaven.* But it is more common to find the author in much the same position as his text—that is, as his basic tool—working without much metaphysical irony in an area that is for him too "a matter dark indeed." The apotheosis of these two approaches' occurring at once is probably Werner Herzog, who shortly after finishing *Heart of Glass* woke from a dream and tried to shoot a film in the dark.[1] What shows up more often is a dialectical presentation of the simultaneous views from each side of the barrier of silence: *As I Lay Dying,* for instance, with its maddened Darl and its silent/speaking Addie; or *Wuthering Heights,* with its civilized and uncivilized pairs of children regarding each other through a "window." There are times, however, when the barrier cannot balance the work or the ironies of its metaphysical perspective. When this happens in *Absalom, Absalom!,* the novel is nearly exploded by the energy of its rhetoric. When it happens in *Gravity's Rainbow,* the light burns out in the projector (for the novel, for the characters, and perhaps for the author, who are all presented as "preterite" and whose stories are apocalyptically unresolved[2]) and the book just stops.

The attempt to talk about the ineffable puts the work under pressure, whether or not the author approaches the task in a state of hopeless frustration. Works that attempt to deal with the mythic and the supernatural regularly encounter many of the same pressures and hit on similar solutions. The shared problem is not just to describe what cannot occur in the logical world but also to generate a sense of mystery and scale, not just to fail to capture but also to create or outline the elusive figure.

The effect of this pressure is often to call attention to the narrative structure or frame of the work. This is true in the frustrated work of Faulkner and Beckett, in the playful work of Carroll and Borges, in the elegant meditations of Henry James, or in the "mad" digressions of Swift. One of the only outlets for this pressure, short of sheer rhetorical excess, is a reflexive awareness—the text's discovery that it is a text. This approaches from the other side of the mirror, if you will, the pattern observed in the previous chapter, where the self begins with a reflexive perspective and goes on from there to discover that it is confronting an ineffable.

Sometimes this pressure is manifested as a sense of distance, separation, framing—as if something were keeping the observer in a different place or on a different level from that of the figure or problem observed. This distance has the double effect of including and excluding the figure or problem, of setting it at a remove that goads the reader's imagination into placing it even further away and thereby, paradoxically, closer. I will be using the term "telescope" to make this complex double action more clear, but first it will be necessary to expand on the relations between the angle of the sun and the impression of gigantism (and please keep in mind that whether or not he is a dwarf, Herzog's shadow figure certainly *behaves* like a giant), between intermediary narration and the generation of myth. Here myth is a function of distance, and form, of balanced stress.

143

1. I/EYE: SOCRATES, *GATSBY,* AND OTHERS

> Hail to the only, the universal Truth. We try to
> reach it by innumerable roads whose indirection
> we are. Truth is in the movement toward it. It is
> also in the coming of a counter-truth wrapped in
> mystery.
>
> —Edmond Jabès, *The Book of Questions*

First-person narration offers a character the opportunity to
speak of his own experience, but it does not necessarily
make it possible for him to do so. Because it presents the
experience and viewpoint of a single character, first-person
narration puts the reader in a rich position: of deciding
whether the narrator is telling all he knows or being mis-
leading (and there are cases, like Machado's great *Dom Casmurro,* where there is no correct answer to that one), and
going on from there either to accept the story as presented
or to deduce, from what the narrator says, what is "really
going on." The "real" story may reveal that more is going
on than the narrator understands, or perhaps that more is
going on than the narrator wants the reader to realize (the
general term for all this is "dramatic irony"). An example of
the deliberately deceptive narrator is the killer who pretends
to be trying to solve the mystery in Agatha Christie's *The
Murder of Roger Ackroyd;* an example of the narrator who
does not quite understand his own story is the good friend
and loving husband in Ford Madox Ford's *The Good Soldier.*
But to the extent that the reader trusts the narrator, he or
she assumes that intimate experience is being portrayed sincerely (if not necessarily "accurately," allowing for the dis-
tortions created by point of view).

This sense of being in close touch with a person who is
trying to tell us about himself is most often lost in third-
person writing, except in quoted monologues or other sorts
of first-person inserts. In this regard, Dickens' *Bleak House*
is an utterly successful and appropriate balancing act, alter-

nating third-person "omniscient" passages written in the present tense with the first-person past tense sections of "Esther's Narrative." Esther describes her experience after it has happened, employing a naive, self-effacing, and loving perspective; the other narrator, by using the present tense, appears independent of the constraints of time—he can go to events as they are happening—and vents an anger that would be inappropriate in Esther. What makes this particularly interesting is that the third-person narrator's "time" is the time of narration and that his sarcastic perspective is not at all objective, so that on the whole *Bleak House* presents two varieties of self-aware discourse, each of which is personal and incomplete while each makes claim to scrupulous accuracy. In addition to filling out the details of Esther's story, then, the "omniscient" passages participate in a critique of the possibility of omniscience and objectivity—and all this contributes to Dickens' critique of the so-called objectivity of the legal system.

When a character cannot put his experience into words, even to himself, no third-person narrator is likely to do a better job. (If words fail, it hardly matters whose they are, but it is more believable to read "I cannot say what I felt in that moment" than to encounter a third-person narrator who cannot say what the character felt, although the point-of-view approach—"he did not know what he felt," and so on—can be quite evocative.) This issue arises when the narrator is trusted and stymied. Its dynamics and logic, which this elementary discussion is attempting to illuminate, explain why so much of the literature of the ineffable is written in the first person. In addition to the fact that limited perspective is a determining factor in the very existence of the sense of the "mystical" (in Wittgenstein's sense of the word), and the effectiveness of making an appeal (under the pressure of talking about these matters) to the reader's own sense of impotence, first-person narration has the manifest advantage of being able to shift from the analytical to the intuitive at will.

When the narrator is stymied both analytically and intuitively, some literary device is needed that can shift the terms of the discussion from unknowns to knowns, at least long enough for a meaningful dramatic context to be established ("Maya" implies that the world is a "meaningful dramatic context"). In secondary first-person narration, that device is the filter of another "I." The logic of this bears repeating at this point: the more one is in touch with nonverbal experience (unless one is in the privileged position of being a medium for the higher self), the less able one will be to find words for it. But if one waits to describe the experience, it often loses its clarity and one's description runs the risk of great inaccuracy. One needs to have the immediacy of experience and yet be somehow removed from it. A second "I"—someone who is able to live through a less intense version of the event and who can speak of his own muted experience—can provide the necessary distance. By relating his own story, he provides the something through which the nothing can be discussed. Here the ineffable is being dealt with in a less direct manifestation; it is being framed and filtered at once. The second character, however, confronting the heart of darkness that envelops a monologue, or demonism in Nazi politics rather than in an actual deal with the devil, can speak of his own experience in such a way that it illuminates by implication what the central character has undergone. The story of his initiation provides a dramatic context through which the reader can comprehend or imagine the richer but less precisely described vision of the hero. Conversely, the presence of the hero makes it unnecessary to limit the range of the tale to a conventionally apprehensible level.

Behind most secondary first-person novels, then, is a first-person novel that could not have been written effectively, if at all, in that mode: *Heart of Darkness* narrated by Kurtz, *Moby-Dick* by Ahab, the autobiography of Adrian Leverkühn. These overreaching figures cannot tell their stories, not because they are inarticulate, but because (as it is said of

Watt) words do not apply to their situations. There are other secondary first-person novels—*The Great Gatsby*, for instance—where the story that the hero might tell about himself would simply be boring, because he would not have the distance from himself to appreciate what might be interesting about him.

So there are two sides to this problem, both of which result from the centered isolation of the overreacher, so centered that he cannot place himself in relation to society or see himself from the outside. When Ahab speaks of himself in his cabin, he is "madness maddened" yet says he can contemplate himself and his madness with "calm."[3] When Sutpen explains his "design" near the end of *Absalom, Absalom!*, he is matter-of-fact.[4] On the one hand, we have the prospect of the raving metaphysical hero whose insights would have to be toned down by the narrator, and on the other, the silent, private type—Gatsby or Sutpen or Heathcliff—whose perspective would have to be brought forward and embellished by the narrator. Either way, the outside view is necessary. The narrator is some kind of eyewitness to the hero's story, either through suffering alongside him or through hearing it from him under special circumstances. He is also an I-witness in that he undergoes a version of the crucial experience in his own person (or is stirred to comparable insights). Thus he is both an observer and an experiential center, an eye and an I.

It is possible to stretch a metaphor here and call this the literary equivalent of binocular vision: two slightly different views of the same object (Ahab's and Ishmael's views of the whale, for example) are compared by the brain (the reader), which deduces what the spatial (actual) relationships among the elements of the object must be and produces for itself the illusion of a three-dimensional image. One eye cannot see a three-dimensional image, but the brain can compare two points of view and arrive at a whole. Literature cannot contain the ineffable, but two complementary points of view can suggest to the imagination how to generate the condition or object that might underlie or manifest itself in this complex of impressions. With input from two I's, the reader may find it easier to intuit what neither one can completely say.

If we examine the workings of this structure in *The Great Gatsby* and Plato's *Republic,* we should be able to understand more clearly the double action of toning down and transfiguring up the experience or perspective of the metaphysical hero, the process that I have suggested is often active in the generation of myth and that is one effective formal response to the pressure to do the impossible. This will provide a useful perspective on intermediary narration as a whole, which we shall go on to examine in *Wuthering Heights, Absalom, Absalom!, The Turn of the Screw,* and related works. There are times, after all, when this mass of tactical doublings, substitutions, and filters is the only effective means of treating the condition of being in which we find ourselves, when it feels more appropriate to confront Faulkner's view of history rather than Shankara's and the fragmented Quentin rather than the simultaneous Whitman. At this point in the argument we shall reenter that dark tunnel, for the sake of the light at its end.

Filtering a hero's experience through that of a concerned observer makes the obscure aspects of that experience more accessible. These obscure elements may appear transcendent, superhuman, uncivilized, demonic, and so on—or they may simply need bringing out. The story of Fitzgerald's Gatsby, like that of Conrad's Lord Jim, only gradually reveals its dramatic interest; the reader's impression of each of these apparently failed idealists has to be guided by an intermediary who has a personal, intuitive impression of the hero's greatness. (Conversely, Conrad's Nostromo does not need this kind of bringing out—he is heroic and flawed in more obvious ways—so *Nostromo* is written in the third person.) Most of the people who have direct contact with Gatsby, who attend his extravagant parties or speculate on his underworld connections, consider him interesting but hardly "great," and a reader of some third-person history of Gatsby might be expected to share that perspective or go on to judge him pathetic. What distinguishes Gatsby is perceived only by his short-term neighbor, Nick, and what Nick shows us is not Gatsby but his seeing Gatsby.

Nick describes himself as "a normal person" whose open-mindedness has encouraged people to confide in him so that he is "privy to the secret griefs of wild, unknown men."[5] Nick admires Gatsby for his "heightened sensitivity to the promises of life . . . an extraordinary gift for hope, a romantic readiness such as I have never found in any other person and which it is not likely I shall ever find again."[6] Gatsby's romantic idealism classes him with those other over-reaching heroes whose awareness and energy isolate them from the comprehension of their fellows—Ahab and Kurtz, Heathcliff and Sutpen—and Nick's susceptibility to Gatsby, which reveals their basic similarity in character, is very much like Marlow's to Kurtz.[7] A further link between Gatsby and the other four heroes is his obsessiveness—what Sutpen would call his "design." Like Heathcliff, Gatsby falls in love while poor, then makes his fortune and moves into a big house, hoping to seduce his lover away from her husband. Like Sutpen, he makes that fortune in antisocial ways and directs his extravagance toward the vindication of his youthful impulses. Like Kurtz, he has (socially innocent) idealistic plans for himself, at least at first, and like Ahab, he commits himself to "the following of a grail."[8]

When he makes his fortune, Gatsby creates himself in the image of what he has wanted to be—a "Platonic conception of himself" that has taken shape in "a universe of ineffable gaudiness."[9] He attaches this self-concept to another of his creations, the image of an ideal Daisy, his former girlfriend. Speaking of the short affair Gatsby finally manages to have with her, Nick observes: "There must have been moments even that afternoon when Daisy tumbled short of his dreams—not through her own fault, but because of the colossal vitality of his illusion. It had gone beyond her, beyond

149

everything."[10] The fact that Nick is Daisy's second cousin and recognizes her for a selfish coward (not that he is hostile to her) and Gatsby's taste as "vulgar and meretricious"[11] makes it even more clear that what he values in Gatsby is the quality and not the object of his grail-following, a perception that elevates the whole story into the category of metaphysical heroism, the attempt to live in two realms at once.

In an Arthurian context, Gatsby might easily be recognized as a hero who would not need an intermediary presenter; he is a violent innocent like Parsifal and an honorable adulterer like Tristan or Lancelot. For Gatsby, Daisy is the goal of a chivalric quest so fervent as to constitute a personal religion. But cut off as he is from a heroine or a religious emblem that his Waste Land culture might consider worth the struggle, and compromised by his own good nature and the misinterpretations of others, he is easy to dismiss as an unscrupulous fool. Even his self-image seems limited to that of a nice person with big ideas and a great capacity for love. But Nick sees something more in him: the illusion that has gone "beyond everything," the implicit Platonism of his self-concept, and so on. He even describes Gatsby as a literal "son of God," in a tone that is only partly ironical.[12] And although Nick is enough like Gatsby to recognize (or project, in the Gestalt sense of the word) these elements of his personality, it is still important to remember that Nick is a more *normal* person and this novel is his own more accessible story—something Fitzgerald emphasizes, for instance, by having Nick think about his own birthday during one of Gatsby's climactic scenes, although it is equally to the point that until he mentions it, Nick has forgotten that it is his birthday because he has been so caught up in Gatsby. One of the more interesting paradoxes about secondary first-person narration, then, is that it allows the discussion of the hero as a being-in-relation (Gatsby through Nick, which is also Gatsby-*and*-Nick, a variant of the simultaneous self) while stimulating the reader to conceptualize the hero as entity, Gatsby as what Gatsby means on a higher level.

At the end of the novel, Nick imagines what Gatsby must have felt when he first saw, from the lawn of his new mansion, the green light at the end of Daisy's dock; he compares this to the first settlers' view of the unspoiled New York landscape, when man was "face to face for the last time in history with something commensurate to his capacity for wonder."[13] It takes a man like Nick to see this in his hero and transfigure him: to bathe Gatsby in that green light it took Gatsby to appreciate.

Just as Nick creates Gatsby in the image of Gatsby's idealism, Plato creates Socrates. It often happens that a hero is made over by his disciple in the light of the hero's own insight, and sometimes this gives him a special resonance. A familiar example is the Jesus of the Gospel of John, who is transfigured and transfused by Light and the Logos. Or one might call Boswell's Johnson a literary invention who incarnates Samuel Johnson's talents.

In the area of fiction rather than biography, it sometimes happens that a hole in the story becomes the resonating center of the narrator's inventions, leaving the reader to decide what the hero is really like and what he may really have done; sometimes the narrator will cover this hole not with information, but with an appeal to myth (to say, for instance, this is how it might have happened or been explained in "the time of the Giants"). Such asserting/concealing is evident in the hints about Heathcliff's origins. One of the reasons Leverkühn's encounter with the devil is only suggested (so that the reader never knows whether it actually occurred) is to leave open the possibility that Zeitblom is falling back on myth to articulate the denser aspects of his impressions of his friend. The relativity of this transfiguring process is clear in *Absalom, Absalom!*—as in its film complement, *Citizen Kane*—where Sutpen is made over by several obsessed observers.[14] As portrayed by Miss Rosa, Sutpen incarnates

151

the demonic power she saw in him; for Mr. Compson, he is not simply compared to but turned into the tragic king of whom he reminded Compson, and so on.

The *Republic* provides another clear example of this transfiguring process. It recounts a conversation in which several people, including Socrates, attempt to define Justice. They never do entirely define it, but they do describe the workings of a just society. This strategy of examining Justice in terms of its secondary attributes—or reflections—is only partially satisfying, but to good effect, because the reader is goaded by dissatisfaction to continue seeking Justice in ways that analysis cannot. The reader's intuitions, which are teased by what is *said* in the dialogue, are attuned by what the dialogue *shows,* for Justice is manifested in the structure of that dialogue as well as in the figure of Socrates.

Justice is an Idea or Form, which in Plato's metaphysics can be only imperfectly analyzed. One cannot directly discuss it; one can discuss only its shadow on the cave wall. If one has attained to a high philosophic consciousness, one has the option to tell a story about it (the myth of Er in the final book, for instance—and, of course, the *Republic* itself); but there is no point in blinding one's companions, and probably no way to do so short of leading them directly (and gradually) out of the cave. Rather than describe Justice, then, Plato creates a character who incarnates Justice. Socrates is transfigured by his perception of the Ideas or Forms. Throughout the *Republic,* Socrates does not simply discuss the just society (a manifestation of Justice rather than the Form itself); he also behaves justly: attempts to help others to a perception of the Good, answers hostile questions good-naturedly, and conducts a dialogue. (There are many points, of course, where Plato presents Socrates less idealistically and where dialogue proceeds in a manner more crafty than "just.")

Logos, the rational or creative principle in the universe, is a possible root of the Greek word for dialogue. Dialogue is the vehicle by which speech and reason participate in their higher manifestation, Reason.[15] Speech is guided by Socrates into dialogue, out of which ideas emerge, and these ideas incarnate or manifest Ideas. In the just society, similarly, dialectics helps to lead the students to a direct perception of the Good—or more properly, leads them to the point where they are ready to intuit the Good with "the eye of the Soul."[16] The Logos makes itself manifest in the dialectic of the logos (dialogue), leading the participants (from whom the reader is at only a slight remove) through analysis to intuition by example.

When Socrates does offer a definition of Justice, it is as a proper ordering of elements—a definition that reduces itself quickly to: "the power which produces states or individuals" that behave justly or are properly arranged.[17] He is still falling back on tautology and indirection, giving an extensive description of the image in the mirror as a way of defining X as the object that casts that reflection. Justice turns out, in any case, not to be the ultimate object of the quest; there is a supreme Form that manifests itself in the Idea of Justice as well as throughout the universe, and that Form is the Good. Socrates' companions ask him for a definition of the Good, even on the level at which he had defined Justice, but Socrates says he simply cannot give one.[18] His companions must settle for another series of analogies and reflections, but the hint has been planted that "an inquiry such as ours"[19] cannot touch the subject. Dialogue is appropriate to a certain stage of enlightenment. The ultimate goal, however, is to educate the immortal soul.

Without ever calling attention to its own behavior as a just structure (behaving and organized in accordance with a higher principle of proper order), the *Republic* manifests what it does not quite discuss (like a proposition that displays but cannot analyze logical form), leaving itself open as an object for intuition. This is the reflexive aspect of the text.

The same principles are evident in the characterization of Socrates, and this is the mythic aspect of the text—the hero made over in the image of his own insight, presented in terms of the extraordinary areas to which he has access. These areas may be outside normal experience, outside civilization, before recorded time, outside recordable time, underneath conventions or definitions, and so on.

Socrates is the intermediary between the world of essential Form and Plato, and Plato is the intermediary between Socrates and the reader. In addition, they share an interest and aptitude for dialogue and philosophy. These are the secondary first-person aspects of the text. Socrates' vision of the Good demands to be treated the same way as Gatsby's of the green light and Kurtz's of the heart of darkness. The intermediary structure both filters and reflects or manifests the essence it cannot discuss; it becomes, whether as a text or as a structure implicit in the text, a valid object of the reader's primary attention.

2. *WUTHERING HEIGHTS* AND *ABSALOM, ABSALOM!*

> Are you trying
> to "describe" me, boy?
> —Ed Dorn, *Gunslinger*

Intermediary narration has two predictable effects: it alerts the reader to the subjective aspects of the rendition, and it boxes in the subject matter. As it is passed from hand to hand, the story becomes more manageable, its basic elements more distinct at the same time as they are more in the distance. (Something similar happens in the darkroom: successive generations of prints increase in contrast.) This process can be useful in effecting a temporary reconciliation between myth and the novel, making it possible to couch the heroic intensity or primal experience of an extraordinary figure in the civilized pages of books.

Form is the result of an interaction between what in many esoteric schools is called first and second force—"initiative" and "resistance," respectively. "Form" is the third force, and "result" is the fourth:

> These four forces may be more easily understood through the use of an example: the making of an iron kettle. In the tangible world, the initiating force is the molten iron.
>
> To clarify what resistance is, we shall compare it to the mold which is used to make the kettle. The molten iron is poured into the mold. The mold is passive resistance. It passively resists the free flow of the molten iron.
>
> We see that the kettle represents the force of form. The kettle itself exists because of the interaction between the molten iron and the mold.
>
> The result of the iron kettle is its uses. The kettle could not be used unless there had occurred the interaction of the first three forces.[20]

This is, among its many applications, a useful way of describing how novels achieve form. Even on an internal level, their interest often depends on the ways they resonate between the poles of anarchy and control. They often give the simultaneous impression of spontaneous life (characters that are not robots, events that seem to develop) and willed structure. The form of a sentence—this one, for example—arises from the interaction between what its author wants to say and what the words, the circumstances of writing, the implicit demands of the audience, and a number of other instances of second force will allow him to say.

The greater the first force is, the greater the second force must be if the form is to come into being. The attempt to discuss the ineffable or even the activities of heroes puts extreme pressure on the expressive situation and requires a strong containing structure—one buttressed by successive levels of narration, for instance, or stylized by intensely poetic language (as in an epic poem with a heroic or mythical subject). One cannot pour thirty pounds of molten iron into

155

a half-inch thick sand mold and expect to form a kettle. The resistance characteristic of second force must frustrate the initiating force to some degree, and this battle is evident in the third force of form: one can deduce molten iron and mold from the kettle. The difference between a field of alfafa and a big jar of sprouts is the quality and degree of resistance (earth vs. air) that the initiating seed has encountered.

Novels like *Absalom, Absalom!* and *Wuthering Heights* are clear examples of how an intense first force demands a strong second force. This dialectic is manifest, for instance, in Faulkner's characteristic oxymorons, his description of Rosa's "static rage,"[21] or the long passages of italics, and in Brontë's involuted wrapping and unwrapping of the story of Heathcliff and Catherine.

Novels are not just about people in society, but they do often treat the conflicts that arise between the individual and the larger culture (*Crime and Punishment, War and Peace, Middlemarch,* and *Madame Bovary* are obvious examples, but even the "total subjectivity"[22] of Robbe-Grillet's *Jealousy* adopts as its vehicle the theme of adultery among members of the upper class and as one of its targets the nature of colonialism). And their form is often the result not only of the interaction between language/medium/genre and expressive intention but also of that between the first and second forces of the individual and society. To this extent, every novel, whether or not it is concerned with social issues, tends to socialize what it discusses.

This may involve stating an issue in such a way that it will be comprehensible to a member of the author's society. Or it may involve stating an issue, period. Ineffable subjects must be modified or framed if they are even to be conceptualized by the intellect rather than "passed over in silence." They must be "made" (or treated as if they were in some way) logical, or rendered approachable through such devices as metaphor. Most events and characters in novels have already been civilized in this fundamental sense. Transcendent material may or may not demand to be interpreted in a fictional social context—that is a question of literary convention. But it must be modified or channeled in such a way that it can be referred to in the first place and received by an audience. Anything written about logically, then, has been made comprehensible: civilized into words. In fact, this is true whether or not the writing is logical in Wittgenstein's tight sense of the word, as even the most Surrealist poem demonstrates (since it is a poem and makes its own kind of sense to an audience).

Emily Brontë's half-Romantic, half-Victorian *Wuthering Heights* offers a striking example of the process of socialization on several levels. It manages to remain a well-formed novel while telling a primal story about emotional and natural chaos. It also describes and dramatizes the exorcism of this chaos, both in the story of the shift from Wuthering Heights-ness to Thrushcross Grange-ness and in its use of intermediary narration. In all these respects, it manifests both socialization and sublimation, the latter term referring both to the mechanics of repression and alternative expression and to the generation of the sublime. We shall see later how much the same is true of *Absalom, Absalom!;* this dialectic of socialization, active in both novels, further justifies their being described as mythic—but in Lévi-Strauss's sense, as a key to the scheme of oppositions and contradictions that structure each one's society.

The Romantic aspects of *Wuthering Heights* include Heathcliff's unknown, perhaps demonic origin; the excesses of Catherine and Heathcliff's passion; the role of raw natural elements in the characterization of Wuthering Heights itself; and the pure sense of energy that pervades the novel's central scenes. It is Victorian not simply by virtue of its date of composition (c. 1847) but because of the spirit in which it controls its Romantic material. Many Victorian novels give one the sense that uncivilized forces are ready to break through whatever social structures are containing them. Steven Marcus' studies of Dickens and of Victorian pornography are convincing on this matter,[23] but even in the work of

Thackeray, Eliot, Carroll, Browning, Arnold, Carlyle, and Hopkins (who were all able to make stress work in their favor), anarchy, lust, crime, madness, materialism, and other elements of perverse destructiveness are a constant undercurrent. The structure of *Wuthering Heights* amounts, at least in part, to an exorcism of such uncivilized energy.

This exorcism is accomplished in two ways: by the complexities of narrative framing, and by the history of the second generation of characters. Both involve the transmission of energy from an original source to a more passive agent, a process in which some of that energy is lost (eventually to free-float in the imagination of the reader and across the moors; energy is, after all, conserved) and what remains is more containable. The differences between Nelly Dean and Lockwood are comparable to those between Catherine Earnshaw and Cathy Linton. There might even be a case that Nelly and Lockwood are, like the Catherines, two stages of one role. The simultaneity of Cathy's birth and her mother's death, and the similarity of their names, make it possible to see the one character as a less energetic continuation of the other, as if this were a demonstration of reincarnation and karma, or perhaps an exothermic reaction.[24]

Wuthering Heights is conceived in twos: two Catherines, two generations, two narrators, the "two children figure" discussed by Dorothy Van Ghent,[25] Wuthering Heights and Thrushcross Grange, *in* and *out*. In some cases, these are polarities; in others, simply pairs. But most can be related to the novel's organizing principle: a hierarchy of energy. At its height is the pure and uncontainable energy in which Heathcliff and Catherine's love participates; at its base is Lockwood, the citified narrator. The uncivilized energies cluster about Wuthering Heights, nature *(out)*, the supernatural *(out)*, and Heathcliff; civilization is represented by Thrushcross Grange, storytelling, and the indoors. The major plot line begins with Heathcliff and Catherine at Wuthering Heights, and ends with Hareton and Cathy at Thrushcross Grange. But there is a double movement here, too, for the novel also ends with a mention of Heathcliff and Catherine's ghosts walking the moor *(out)*. By that mention, the novel maintains its Romantic/Victorian duality while achieving its predominantly indoor conclusion—an achievement that is also manifested in the fact that the novel has managed to get written and its story to be effectively communicated to Lockwood.

The first generation of couples, including as it does the elder Lintons, has no monopoly on *out* energy. The generational contrast operates primarily in terms of four couples: Catherine/Heathcliff and Catherine/Edgar in the first generation; Cathy/Linton and Cathy/Hareton in the second. Catherine/Edgar and Cathy/Linton are for differing reasons unsuitable couples; they are perversely transitional in the move from the Heights to the Grange. Catherine is not suited to life at the Grange: she is too fiercely emotional, too deeply identified with Heathcliff. She cannot transfer her energy from Heathcliff to Edgar without being torn apart, without dying into a different life (since these men are actually the two sides of her own nature, which is why and how they incorporate the poles of her sexual taste); she cannot make the shift in one lifetime and still be herself. It would be like asking Victor Frankenstein to choose between Elizabeth and the Monster. Thus a second Catherine (more muted, and thus more integrated) is needed. Conversely, Cathy is not suited to life at the Heights, nor to loving Heathcliff, and she is even less likely to succeed at loving Heathcliff's terrified, selfish son, Linton. Yet Catherine is drawn to the Grange as Cathy is drawn out of it, in the novel's intriguing balance.

These two women complexly occupy the half-defined ground between the energies of Heathcliff and Hareton. The shift from Catherine to Cathy is thus the hinge-point of the story, where the midpoints of the hierarchy and of the novel's development are reached simultaneously. Heathcliff personifies those extremes of violence and will, tenderness and longing, hatred and need, that resist or subordinate all societal bounds and are utterly indifferent to morals (not to say ethics). Hareton is honorable and strong, and has it in him to become a good husband and gentleman farmer. Cathy and Hareton are dynamic and loving, an admirable couple who have suffered much and fought hard; they are not likely to roam the moors after death, or to appear to introverted gentlemen in violent nightmares. (Another way of saying this is that they are not the kind of image that might correspond to the projections of Lockwood's darker self, whereas Catherine and Heathcliff certainly do.) It is not simply that Catherine and Heathcliff's energy has been reduced to a level where it could function happily at the Grange (although that is partly what has happened), for Cathy and Hareton are not Lintons. Cathy and Hareton, in command of their energy, can be expected to bring life at the Grange up to their level. Rather than a projection of the darker side of the self, Cathy and Hareton are an ideal of healthy integration. *Wuthering Heights* is a parable of the *vitalization* of social institutions as well as an exorcism of uncivilized impulse. This double movement is also at work in Brontë's infusion of filtered mythic energy into the acculturated institution of the novel.

Because it acts as a medium between these two opposing ways of life, allowing both their integrity, this novel is comprehended by its own central symbol: a window. It is through windows that the *in* and the *out* have knowledge of each other, and it is in windows that their images are contained. Catherine and Heathcliff see Edgar and Isabella through a window, as an old man at the novel's end sees Catherine and Heathcliff's ghosts "out of his chamber window." There are numerous other examples, familiar to any reader of the novel, and there is no point in belaboring what Dorothy Van Ghent has made so clear in her excellent discussion. The point here is simply that the novel's strict "framing" has allowed it to become a window on both these energies.

The reader enters this violent, at times unearthly story

160

through the mind of Lockwood, the introverted city dweller whose very name suggests repression. His lack of insight into his new surroundings is comical. To the end of the novel, this self-styled misanthrope—a voyeur too timid to return the glance of a girl at the seashore—considers himself a capital match for Cathy. His desire for solitude is quickly exposed as egotism, his professed love of rusticity is undercut by his reaction to Joseph's housekeeping, and his air of civility is revealed by his dream that first night to be simply the mask of a man who does not know himself. In that dream, the ghost of Catherine appears at his window, begging to be let *in;* and to be rid of the child, he rakes her wrist over the jagged glass of the window he has broken.[26]

Lockwood needs to let the Catherine in himself come to the surface, but his initial response is one of anger and fear. (To reverse this: Catherine appeals to Lockwood rather than any other character because his unconscious readiness to develop—no matter how out of touch with that beginning maturation he may be—and his place in the narrative-energy hierarchy make him her proper vehicle for gaining entry into the more contained, natural, effable, social world of the living—in other words, for getting her story told as well as for ending her metaphysical isolation. The subject of the novel selects its proper medium, in all senses of that word.) Lockwood is irritated into breaking the dream-window and encountering the unknown, even if his conscious motive is to get rid of the unknown; what he finds, first of all, is his capacity for cruelty and violence, and his susceptibility to fear. His vital energies are out of balance; he is out of touch with his primitive emotions. He is not an integrated outdoorsman like Edgar. In short, if he were a little smarter, he would be Emily Brontë's ideal audience: one who needs to see both *in* and *out* clearly and to come to some personal integration. The fact that he is less intelligent and less perceptive than that ideal audience makes him instead Brontë's ideal narrator, for dramatic irony—the framing of what is not said—is the heart of this novel's effectiveness.

161

For such a man, and the conventions he represents, to come in touch with the meaning of Catherine and Heathcliff's experience, some drastic obliquity is required. So little able is he to comprehend Heathcliff directly that Lockwood at first mistakes him for a kindred spirit—not at all proud, a reserved and private man, who would love and hate in secret—but eventually Lockwood recognizes that he is only projecting. In his need to be told everything, and in his passive stance, he is more akin to the seated, word-oriented novel reader than to Heathcliff. He is, in fact, a surrogate reader, intermediary between Nelly and the Victorian audience as Nelly is between him and the central characters. It seems inevitable that Lockwood fail to understand much of what he transcribes. He may understand the words, but he does not have the openness or insight to achieve an emotional comprehension—let alone a reliving—of the primary experience.

The device of transcription is perfect in this context, because it allows Lockwood to repeat words he could never speak for himself. That is, in fact, the most common reason for its use: to get onto paper a story that its teller either could not or would not write. In other words, transcription helps overcome traditional limits of discourse as they apply both to what one might feel would be appropriate or possible to write down and to what a text might be expected to contain or address. *Frankenstein* and *Heart of Darkness* show this process clearly: neither Frankenstein nor Marlow would write his story down, and this way neither is forced to put himself in a writing—or a censoring—frame of mind. In addition, the reader is allowed to imagine the teller's being almost past or beyond conventional storytelling, offering instead a testimony that is somehow "beyond the pale." The final advantage is that the words on the page take on the quality of being framed, of being one level removed from their original nature and therefore less in contact with the indescribable or extraordinary event—a Platonic distance that, as we shall see, works entirely for their credibility and stimulates the audience to work past them.

Without thinking about transcription and framing in these terms, it is difficult to see why Nelly Dean needs Lockwood, though it is perfectly obvious why Lockwood needs her. The action mandates some kind of secondary narrator who has access to the principal scenes, since the primary characters could not or would not verbalize their experience and since an omniscient narrator could not provide the necessary balance of involvement, identification, and detachment. None of the most dynamic scenes could have taken place in Lockwood's prescence—Heathcliff would murder him first—nor could Lockwood be expected to interpret what he sees with even Nelly's insight. Without Nelly, Lockwood would never discover the story.

Since Nelly answers all these requirements so well, the question arises: why was Nelly not chosen as the novel's sole narrator? It would, after all, be credible that she should write down what she has seen, perhaps for the benefit of Cathy and Hareton. There seem to be three answers: Lockwood's repressed figure clarifies much of Brontë's symbolic and cultural message while making it easier for the reader to relate to the situation (as discussed above); the power of first force here demands a more dense and involuted second force; and the multiplicity of this narrative structure contributes greatly to the intensification of the *out* material as well as to the stability of the *in*.

Nelly Dean is not a secondary first person, but a bystander—at times, in fact, she is more meddler than onlooker. She is involved in the story but not possessed by it. She, like Lockwood, communicates more than she understands; because of her conveniently excellent memory, the reader hears the actual words of the primary characters and is able to see past her moralizing reactions and achieve a deeper interpretation of what she has witnessed. The paradox of this transcriptive method is that (whether the recording medium is Lockwood's notebook or Nelly's memory) the reader is both spatially and temporally removed from events that are being dramatized directly in his or her imagination, as if these events were going on at that moment. To be reminded of this distance is powerfully disorienting.

The most blatant example of such disorientation can be found in the opening to Chapter 16. Engrossed in the scenes leading up to Catherine's death, the reader is suddenly jerked away to the narrative present: "About twelve o'clock that night, was born the Catherine you saw at Wuthering Heights."[27] This deliberate invocation of Lockwood (the "you") could hardly be surpassed as a mood breaker, but we are led even farther away from the past by Nelly's personal philosophizing and her attempt to engage Lockwood in a thin discussion of the afterlife. The effect of this irritating digression, which reminds us of the narrative situation and the drastic differences in insight and energy that exist between the original protagonists and these talky outsiders, is to relax whatever tension might have been built up in the reader. The timing is crucial: Cathy's birth is the novel's axial event and most powerful shift. Brontë gives us a break, to set us up for more; she also stimulates our reflexive awareness by yanking us out of one fantasy-level into another.[28] By such methods, the narrative structure allows for the generation in the reader of an unusual emotional intensity without the danger of overload; this is in many ways the novel's major achievement and distinguishing characteristic.

Because as readers we are always liable to be made aware of the narrators, our experience of the central events becomes involved with our consciousness of the frame. The events are contained by Nelly's sense of them as her rendition is contained by Lockwood's writing (I use "contained" in the double sense of presenting and limiting or restraining). These frames restrict the range of the immediate narration. Nelly is in no position to put Heathcliff's emotion into words, although she can repeat his dialogue; his dialogue will not, however, explain him very deeply. Heathcliff is too close to his own experience, and too close-mouthed. He and Catherine are the overreachers whose experience requires a more verbal outsider if it is to be set down. (Their dialogue is intelligible, but so reduced and fundamental that it has—read on its own—nothing like the power of the emotional energy behind it until it is contextualized and framed.) Nelly and Lockwood have the verbal bent and the distance; they are different from Ishmael and Marlow, however, in that they lack the imagination to enter the central characters' experience or genuinely to share it. The result is that they are a different kind of intermediary than the secondary first-person narrator, and have the primary function not of mirroring but of interpreting the heroic action—sometimes even to the point of outright error.

Told so little (and distrusting some of that), the reader has more to imagine. Because our tensions are built up and relaxed so skillfully, we are able to approach the heroes' level of experience with our intuitive and critical faculties intact and our tolerance or capacity for intensity increased. Because of all it does not say, *Wuthering Heights* suggests the hugeness of its territory without exploding its own civilized structure.

One way to realize the effectiveness of these evocative manipulations is to compare this novel with the unfortunate movies adapted from it, all of which omit the second generation, and some of which contain no vestige of the Nelly/Lockwood narrative device. Without these two passing-down devices, there is *less* intensity. There is a love story, but hardly one capable of threatening the culture or possessing the audience the way the novel does. This has nothing to do with the fact that these are films; it has to do with the narrative structures of these particular films.[29] The issue of Catherine and Heathcliff's physical relationship, for example, when presented directly appears to be a question of morals or sentiment, but when filtered and framed, it addresses the transcendental implications of amorality and the limits of the personal system. In these movies, the emphasis is on sexuality, "romance," frustration, excitement, and patriarchal convention; one might say that the story has been *over*civilized. In the novel, one has the sense that sexual intercourse could not begin to deal with Catherine and Heathcliff's need for each other; they *are* one another. Their love incarnates, as Van Ghent puts it, an "anonymous natural energy" and its mythology. In short, these films present sentimental melodramatic versions of what Nelly might think was going on or was at stake, without identifying these as Nelly-ish views or foregrounding the Nelly-figure in such a way as to alert the audience to the ironic limitations of this perspective.

Nelly and Lockwood operate on a different level of expression than do Catherine and Heathcliff because of the difference in their levels of experience. This eventually becomes the same issue as that of their position within the narrative spectrum; the issue is still the hierarchy of energy. The advantage of Nelly and Lockwood's position is that it allows them to obscure, reduce, and clarify (through contextualization) the actions and statements of the primary characters.

Catherine and Heathcliff do speak about themselves and their position, but what for them are obvious and simple reports on their condition are to the logician nonsensical and to the reader unclear without contextual distance. Heathcliff says, "I cannot live without my life," with the same intense, clear sense of what he means that Catherine has when she says, "Nelly, I *am* Heathcliff." These ultimate statements manifest the limits of the romantic love system, where the beloveds are one self. It is important to note that those limits involve a paradox, and that the lovers' statements might easily be compared to the attempts at reflexive awareness of a simultaneous self. It is precise to call *Wuthering Heights* a metaphysical romance.

Nelly and Lockwood use qualifiers and speak at length because they are more or less normal people, which is, of course, why they occupy their particular position in the narrative spectrum (at one end of which is the reader, and at the other, the "anonymous natural energy"). The bringing-out and filling-in that Nelly and Lockwood provide is of two kinds: they offer the background detail that lets Catherine and Heathcliff's words and behavior make sense to the reader, and they set the story at an experiential distance that goads the reader to open the matter beyond what is being said. The reason for the latter tactic is, of course, that this allows the novel to transcend its own limits as a conventional narration, almost to violate the limits of verbal transmission. It succeeds here because it never transgresses the limits of language; here, much more than in *Heart of Darkness,* the sense of the story envelops the tale, precisely like an aura. One does not think in terms of the limits of language here because no character focuses on the difficulty of expressing the metaphysical. The usual limits-of-language situation involves a speaker, like Beckett's Unnamable or Watt, who knows almost what he means and realizes he is failing to say it. In *Wuthering Heights,* the narrators are so dense and miss the point so often, that what they say is exactly and uncomplicatedly what they mean; they are not even trying to say what cannot be said. This leaves the reader imagining what they ought to have been trying to say, and that is the key to this novel's success. It operates as a goad, working its way past every barrier into the center of the reader's imagination.

If Nelly were more imaginative, saw the story whole and tried to put its mythic dimensions into words, the novel would simply turn Gothic. She would try to make Lockwood grasp the essence of the relationship, probably through hyperbole. (She might, in other words, behave like Faulkner's Miss Rosa.) The audience would have no work to do and would not bring its own experience (from which the fantasy has ultimately to be generated) to bear; if anything, we would tend to tone her down. Instead, her method of diluting, oversimplifying, and missing the point allows the audience to achieve the necessary reconstruction, while her literalness insures that the basic facts will be available in recounted dialogue and action.

To summarize: from the primary experience—as it might eventually be reconstructed by the reader—to Nelly, to Lockwood, there is a decrease of energy and a progressive obscuring of the story. The obscuring is accounted for by the cultural preconceptions of the transmitter. In addition, there is a layering on of narrative tenses, of framing scenes, of narrations within narrations (like Isabella's letter), of pastness, and of involuted presentational sequence; all of these function as filters and containers, binding and reducing the energy of the story. The density of these filters indicates to the reader how little of the original we see directly (and what *is* presented directly is hardly bland or ineffectual writing), and therefore how much reconstructing we have to do.[30] The filters are a measure of the reader's distance.

This structure might be described as muting or intensifying, depending on how one approaches it. What the reader encounters is less intense than the hypothetical primary material. On the other hand, the metaphor of passing down and the ironic keys to reconstruction make it clear that this story is far more intense than what appears within the frame, allowing the adumbration of an image of extraordinary power. As a double process, this might be compared to the action of a refracting telescope, which magnifies or reduces according to which end is looked through. The extraordinary subject is reduced to narratable bounds by the same process that provokes the reader to intuit the nature of the original. It is in this sense that *Wuthering Heights* is both an exorcism and an invocation of primitive energy, and by this means that the novel is able to act as a window between civilization and chaos.

When Proust was accused of examining life with a microscope, he replied that he examined it with a telescope. His critics meant that he paid too scrupulous attention to minor details; his retort implied that the things he was looking at were huge and remote. What intermediary narration does is provide a way of looking at giants, placing a tiny image in the eyepiece and informing the mind that the signified that goes with this signifier is immense.

Faulkner's *Absalom, Absalom!* demonstrates how the complexities of intermediary narration not only generate heroes and make it possible to observe giants but also can stimulate self-consciousness in the work of art. This novel also makes good use of the simultaneous self, turning most of the characters into aspects of one self-addressing and self-telling system. Its indebtedness to *Wuthering Heights* is obvious, not just in the similarities between Heathcliff and Sutpen or in the uses of involuted reminiscence, but in the sense that the achieved form of the novel reflects each author's most heightened sense of contemporary civilization. In Faulkner, that form is more tight and straining, more obviously obsessed and compulsive than in Brontë, because the later culture is more overtly on the verge of self-destruction. Although it is more complex than in *Wuthering Heights,* the second force in *Absalom* appears only barely able to contain the first force of Sutpen's and Quentin's respective obsessions. Whether in Rosa's italicized and metrical raving or in Mr. Compson's dipsomaniacal, classical nostalgia, the third force in this novel seems always on the verge of explosion or implosion, a tenuous balance between the centrifugal and the centripetal. Its frenzied complexity both indicates the intensity of the first force and contains or reduces it. The intermediary narrators amplify and explain Sutpen as Quentin's various selves and surrogates attempt to deal with his own mirrored self-destructive obsessiveness; as in *Wuthering Heights,* these explanations and filterings function as a telescope. The difference is that Faulkner's storytellers are sometimes presented as guessing or inventing, and the reader's task becomes not one of looking through the narrators to the intact evidence, but one of attempting to resolve a relativist image whose central figure and whose medium of transmission have somehow created each other. The reader is forced to look at the telling as the story, and the novel reinforces this by turning reflexive.

One important difference between *Wuthering Heights* and *Absalom, Absalom!* is in the ways the narrators relate to each story. Nelly and Lockwood, who often miss the points they indirectly reveal, are able to tell the story calmly and to draw away from it when it becomes too tense. Rosa Coldfield, Mr. Compson, and Quentin, however, have each let the story grow inside them—whether for a few months or for generations makes little difference, since what matters is how fundamentally they are hooked—and have charted it through their own deepest emotional tangles, from which it emerges elegiac, romantic, or hysterical. Even Shreve, the reader-surrogate, becomes a temporarily obsessed cocreator (but like the reader, he can withdraw at the end if he chooses). If these narrators "miss points," it is not from lack of trying or lack of insight.

Faulkner's narrators are often more verbal forces than speaking characters, and in this novel some of them are overwhelmed by their awareness of the inadequacy of language to create order (whereas in *As I Lay Dying* the focus is on language's inability to signify, or to establish deep interpersonal communication); their anxiety is reflected throughout the text. Communication is no problem here— in fact, the narrators come virtually to share their visions and to participate in a self-narrating system—but order is at best a charged dynamic and at worst a crashing façade. The dominant rhetorical device is the oxymoron, which asserts a state of viable contradiction, a dialectic of what Faulkner would call "unresolution," and the structure of the novel as a whole is both unresolved and complete, apparently scattered and formidably well-arranged.

The nearest that *Absalom* comes to a resolution is its ending on a note of sustained ambivalence[31] and its generating what might amount to an ultimate yet composite image of Sutpen (in other words, a coherent dialectic). Looking past each partial image—the best that each narrator can achieve—

the reader has the opportunity to synthesize the object of the narrators' evocative quest. By the time the simplest and most convincing image of Sutpen appears (the hillbilly innocent who reveals himself to Quentin's grandfather), it is capable of being expanded like the simple self-image of Gatsby or Heathcliff, but it bears the additional function of anchoring the whole complex of contradictory images it neither echoes nor dispels. Sutpen is the elephant who appears to the proverbial blind investigators as taillike, footlike, trunklike, and so forth, depending on what part each has grabbed hold of; and like that elephant, his self-image is simple rather than dialectical (compare Bergson's discussion of the simple/infinite arm movement). The "blind" reader can make sense of this complex of impressions only by integrating all the views, including Sutpen's, and what emerges is not a metaphysical spirit, but a childish giant. *Absalom* is a mythological, not a transcendental text. The basic difference between *Absalom* and *Wuthering Heights* is not in *Absalom*'s more complex use of the telescopic frame, nor in its attempt to sustain and conceptualize the distance between the giant and the reader, but in its more troubled concept of the medium. As in *Wuthering Heights,* the novel is a window, a frame for an image—but the image here is contradictory, and chaos is on either side. The ordinary distinction between *out* and *in* fails to hold, and the frame is under considerably greater pressure. That frame consists of both the novel and the narrators, and in a larger sense, of Faulkner's view of the culture. *Absalom* is, quite simply, a modernist *Wuthering Heights.* And as a culture goes through major changes, confronting the collapse of one order and the possibility that no better order might arise to replace it, its assured concept of language is subject to, and reveals, the same stresses. For many modernists, dialectics was a viable response to cultural fragmentation; this is as evident in the major works of Pound, Joyce, Eliot, and of course, Eisenstein as it is in Faulkner. The difference is that Faulkner's dialectics did not regularly lead to a new sense of cultural viability but often dramatized the logic of what he enjoyed calling "doom." Whereas *Ulysses,* the *Cantos,* and the wildly enthusiastic *October* have a good working relationship with the fallen world, *Absalom* is a more desperate masterpiece.

In the periods of essence and origin to which mythologies often aspire, when gods were gods and heroes were heroes and time did not accumulate into history, a Sutpen could simply go about his business. If it happened that his "design" brought about his ruin, he might achieve tragic awareness and elevation. If not, he could happily build up his house and consolidate his rule. Sutpen is based on this sort of hero—Agamemnon and David, in particular, but also Shakespeare,[32] one of Faulkner's favorites. In the world of history and class and money, however, such a hero has to surrender his innocence but may not get much in return. And further down into history, when heroism itself is a kind of fantasy or dim memory of the culture, it may be nearly impossible for a single mortal to do more than grab on to the tail of the elephant, characterize the whole being as rope, and start to climb. The number and obscurity of the filters (masks and interpretations and recourses to tone) between the giant and the various levels of audience is, as in all such telescopes, the fundamental indicator of distance—cultural, temporal, epistemological, and phenomenological.

Anyone who tries to talk about Sutpen confronts this distance, which expresses itself characteristically in long, fast, driven outpourings of charged language. The speakers are, except for Shreve, psychologically rigid: tense, fixated, resistant to change. This tension is the primary locus of second force in the novel. The pushing stream of Rosa's words, for instance, is an index of the forces condensing them, as if they were water from a hose, shooting farther with greater, more stinging pressure from an increasingly contracted nozzle;[33] but it might also be thought of as the sand mold that has to be thick if it is to stand up to a great deal of molten iron. Mr. Compson's personal failures, which partly determine his view of Sutpen, are diverted into a rhetoric that, if less compulsive than Rosa's, is still informed throughout by prolixity and a sense of failure. Both Rosa and Mr. Compson have long stopped doing anything that might be called personal growth or creative living, and Quentin—as established in *The Sound and the Fury*—is on the verge of killing himself so that time and change will not lead him to outgrow his obsession with Caddy's betrayal of his concept of honor. The issue, however, is not the neuroses of the storytellers, but the inevitability of Sutpen's provoking this driven response from anyone who tries to interpret his experience.

It might appear at first that Sutpen's absence is what most provokes this response in the narrators. A recurring pattern in *The Sound and the Fury, As I Lay Dying,* and *Absalom, Absalom!* makes this a likely guess. All three novels employ a complex of narrators, each of whom is centrally concerned with a powerful figure who is physically or temporally absent: the Compson brothers are obsessed with Caddy, the Bundrens with Addie, and the inner narrators of *Absalom* with Sutpen. Each novel raises the question of order by setting at odds the forces of chaos and rigidity, and each looks back to a time that was relatively more integrated.

It turns out, however, that even Quentin's grandfather, who is healthy and who has Sutpen directly in front of him in both time and space, is stymied into rhetoric in *his* attempt to deal with Sutpen's actions, so absence cannot be the determining factor (unless one speaks of a Derridean absence, as we will in the next chapter). Discussing his design with Compson (Quentin's grandfather), Sutpen speaks clearly and deliberately: "You see, I had a design in mind. Whether it was a good or a bad design is beside the point; the question is, Where did I make a mistake in it, what did I do or misdo in it, whom or what injure by it to the extent which this would indicate. I had a design. To accomplish it I should require money, a house, a plantation, slaves, a family—incidentally, of course, a wife."[34] And even without the distancing factors of time and hearsay and death and cultural shifts, let alone mental illness, Compson throws Sutpen's words back at him in a frenzy:

"Conscience? Conscience? Good God, man, what else did you expect? Didn't the very affinity and instinct for misfortune of a man who had spent that much time in a monastery even, let alone one who had lived that many years as you lived them, tell you better than that? didn't the dread and fear of females which you must have drawn in with the primary mammalian milk teach you better? What kind of abysmal and purblind innocence could that have been which someone told you to call virginity? what conscience to trade with which would have warranted you in the belief that you could have bought immunity from her for no other coin but justice?"[35]

Suddenly adjectives come in pairs, figures of speech intrude, clauses are stacked—and for no discernible reason. (Compson could simply have spat tobacco and shaken his head.) The reader can only infer that Compson, shocked, is trying to deal with Sutpen's innocence through language. It is not legitimate to attribute this rhetoric only to Quentin (who is telling this part of the story), as if he were recasting the original dialogue in the light of his current state of mind, because *Sutpen's* words are clean and simple.

The nature of the distance between Sutpen and the people who interpret his experience, then, is not primarily temporal or cultural so much as it is *linguistic*. The issue—and the nature of the telescope in this novel—is the disparity that the narrators perceive or demonstrate between language and being, between attempting to speak and achieving an absolute or even adequate expression of the case. What makes Sutpen heroic is his attitude toward action. He can confront—or incarnate—his own experience and its assumptions directly; mere mortals find themselves thrashing about for the right words. Sutpen confronts many of the same problems he poses: the social system, for example, is an incomprehensible order that destroys him along with his efforts at controlling or reinventing or imitating it. But he attempts to master that order, and the universals it reflects, through action and not through language. Sutpen's attitude toward language is the same as his attitude toward action: he simply does it. In a modernist context, that makes him both a fool and a hero, an admirable and dangerous giant; it also makes him the true kin of Addie and Caddy.

Language is not, however, doomed to an absolute stymie point by the attempt to deal with Sutpen. It discovers a most interesting way out of the cramp: it vanishes into silence *and* achieves clear communication by precipitating a simultaneous self into reflexive awareness. The narrators are the elements of that self and the vehicles for the text's near self-transcendence.

In the following passage, Rosa's rigidity and drive appear to force language past itself into a direct and silent presentation of the signified:

> and opposite Quentin, Miss Coldfield in the eternal black which she had worn for forty-three years now, whether for sister, father, or nothusband none knew, sitting so bolt upright in the straight hard chair that was so tall for her that her legs hung straight and rigid as if she had iron shinbones and ankles, clear of the floor with that air of impotent and static rage like children's feet, and talking in that grim haggard amazed voice until at last listening would renege and hearing-sense self-confound and the long-dead object of her impotent yet indomitable frustration would appear, as though by outraged recapitulation evoked, quiet inattentive and harmless, out of the biding and dreamy and victorious dust.[36]

The signified is evoked through outraged repetition, which causes Quentin's linguistic attention to back off and turn in

175

on itself. What is achieved is a short-circuit, and the vision rushes in to occupy the vacuum created by the disappearance of language.

In order to describe what Quentin sees in this vision, Faulkner has recourse to the oxymoron. He compresses opposites into simultaneity, a use of dialectical montage that can sometimes evoke in the reader's mind a synthesis for which there is no term. (Eisenstein said that dialectical montage in film was useful in generating a synthesis that would be "graphically undepictable."[37]) Faulkner describes a "quiet thunderclap," "attitudes wild and reposed," an earth that is at once "tranquil and astonished," and so on, and casts Sutpen virtually in the role of a patriarchal God.[38]

When Quentin shifts into the next level of apprehension, he becomes two selves who try to explain Sutpen to each other and do so in something that is not exactly language:

> creating the Sutpen's Hundred, the *Be Sutpen's Hundred* like the oldtime *Be Light.* Then hearing would reconcile and he would seem to listen to two separate Quentins now—the Quentin Compson preparing for Harvard in the South, the deep South dead since 1865 and peopled with garrulous outraged baffled ghosts, listening, having to listen, to one of the ghosts which had refused to lie still even longer than most had, telling him about old ghost-times; and the Quentin Compson who was still too young to deserve yet to be a ghost, but nevertheless having to be one for all that, since he was born and bred in the deep South the same as she was—the two separate Quentins now talking to one another in the long silence of notpeople, in notlanguage, like this: *It seems that this demon—his name was Sutpen— (Colonel Sutpen)—Colonel Sutpen.*[39]

It is not even correct to say that Quentin becomes two selves here, because he is at least three; the third one listens to the other two. Eventually, Quentin and Shreve take up these two voices, with Quentin taking the role of ghost most of the time, so that the energy of the storytelling is dialectical from first page to last, and the synthesis—a linguistically undepictable perfect narration—is projected outside the system of the novel, existing either in the reader's integrative consciousness or in the transcendental periphery of the linguistic world. The metaphysical element in *Absalom, Absalom!* is not Sutpen, but the narration, a "limited whole" whose inner rule is dialectics and whose synthesis transcends its limits. On the way to this projection of limited wholeness, the narration has its elements address each other and reveal themselves to the reader as united by the task of defining or linguistically responding to Sutpen; as the sign that the system is on some extratextual level integrated, it offers in the title of the novel that tragic self-awareness that eludes Sutpen and all of the narrators.

Quentin's first grasping of Rosa's image of Sutpen, which amounts to a possession, happens without or in spite of hearing. His later outpouring to Shreve continues (like Marlow's) in a "flat, curiously dead voice,"[40] as if Quentin were a medium, or in any case, the vehicle for the story rather than its originator. Quentin and Shreve move together in one thought—a thought that is the pure narrative energy of a story that compels itself to be told:

> They stared—glared—at one another. It was Shreve speaking, though . . . it might have been either of them and was in a sense both: both thinking as one, the voice which happened to be speaking the thought only the thinking become audible, vocal; the two of them creating between them, out of the rag-tag and bob-ends of old tales and talking, people who perhaps had never existed at all. . . .[41]

Elsewhere, Faulkner calls the things that Shreve makes up "probably true." The point is not that Shreve is a good guesser, but that he has been caught up in a narrative drive that is as infallible as any storytelling can be: a pure inspirational source, the mind of the story. He is a medium for

177

an autobiography, the story that tells itself. Faulkner presents himself as not knowing any more than Shreve does; he will commit himself only to a "probably." Most of the narrators' conjectures are accepted as true and end up in the novel's Chronology and Genealogy. The implication of all this is that the story exists somewhere and is managing to get itself told. It listens to its subvoices as Quentin listens to the two Quentins. It functions as a simultaneous self (much like *As I Lay Dying*) and offers for its own consideration and in the service of the growth of its self-consciousness a series of partial views of its own system. When the subselves have completed their presentations, the novel ends.

The level that is aware of all these narrators as a simultaneous self is integrated and silent, and therefore outside the novel. As we shall see in *As I Lay Dying*, Faulkner's titles are crucial signs of what his novels mean—often of their central and impossible or absent subject (sanctuary in *Sanctuary*, for instance)—and expressions of an extratextual periphery. What this integrated self says is "Absalom, Absalom!"—something that is never *said* in the novel, but that is manifested or *shown* throughout. This is a subtle but definite instance of systemic self-consciousness in a tragic context, and it will be shown in the next chapter to be an example of "the mind of the text"; for now, it should be sufficient to explicate Sutpen's tragedy, which is the "pasteboard mask" from behind which the textual self "puts forth the mouldings of its features."

Sutpen begins as a West Virginia hillbilly. In the early 1820s, his family leaves the mountains and takes up work on a plantation. Like the biblical David, Sutpen is an innocent, without any concept of property or social hierarchy. When he is sent around to the back door of the big house, his sense of self-worth is violently insulted and he runs off to a cave (again like David) to think. He concludes that if he is ever going to be able to live with himself he will have to become like the man who owns the plantation. This "design" begins as a demonstration of his own human worth and dignity, but through the rigidity of its conception, it evolves into a force that depends for its success on the denigration of others. Sutpen's crucial error is to turn others away from the door of his own big house. This rigidity destroys him, his mansion, and his children; it also dominates the principal narrators. And it accounts for the initial success of his design.

The hint for *Absalom*'s basic trope—that of interpreting the Civil War in terms of the Trojan War—probably came from O'Neill's *Mourning Becomes Electra,* which predates the novel by five years. Sutpen resembles Agamemnon in several ways, most notably in his decision to sacrifice his children to the success of his patriarchal design. Agamemnon's sacrifice of Iphigenia for the sake of his military effort, of course, brought about the fall of his house as well as his own death. O'Neill's Agamemnon, Ezra Mannon, shares with his prototype and with Sutpen the desire to return from war to a stable household and finds like them that the household has become, largely as a result of his own compulsive empire-building, the most fatal battlefield. The conspicuous difference between Mannon and Sutpen is that Mannon is willing to change and is capable of acknowledging his errors.

II Samuel records that David's son Absalom had a sister, Tamar, and a half-brother, Amnon. After Amnon seduced and abandoned Tamar, Absalom killed him and went into exile. David's cry on hearing of Absalom's death in a later revolt is, of course, the source of Faulkner's ironic title. If Sutpen had been able to put his children's interests before his own—or even his own best interests before the demands of his compulsive design—neither Henry nor Bon would have been forced to play their roles at the gates of Sutpen's Hundred. Instead the unsounded cry, "Would I had died for thee, O Absalom, my son, my son!" rages beneath each sentence of Faulkner's novel. It makes itself manifest.

Most tragic heroes bring about their own destruction through the operation of the same character traits that have made them great. It is an essential element of tragedy that the hero realize how he has destroyed himself. Oedipus makes plain this recognition when he blinds himself not with the nearest stick, but with his mother's brooches—and in the choice of blinding as his action—as Lear does with his use of touchingly simple (not "kingly") language when he is reunited with Cordelia. In this sense, both *Wuthering Heights* and *Absalom, Absalom!* are failed tragedies. Heathcliff and Catherine never attain this kind of self-knowledge; their problems must be resolved by another generation, almost karmically. Sutpen doggedly fails to find the "mistake" in his design. The difference between the two failures is that the narrating force of *Absalom* achieves the recognition of Sutpen's tragic flaw. The title is not simply an author's overview of the situation, but the mind of the novel's crying out, as Sutpen never does, its ironic recognition of the right to charity and acceptance of the innocent at the door, and the self-destructiveness of compulsive rigid drivenness; it alludes to the former by its choice of the term "Absalom," and to the latter by its tone. Although Sutpen fails, the novel itself approaches tragic awareness.

3. FROM *Frankenstein* TO *Gravity's Rainbow:* A CLUTCH OF HORRORS

When you try to sew Orpheus back together what you get is Frankenstein.
—Ron Sukenick, *98.6*

Horror is a major category within myth and within the literature of the ineffable. It tends to deal less with the inconceivable than with the extraordinary, the supernatural, the primordial, the unspeakable—in other words, with the more threatening aspects of the metaphysical as they intrude on the everyday. Because the supernatural or monstrous comes in most cases from outside the known system (even if its source is the unexplored regions of the psyche, as in the story of Jekyll and Hyde), it flourishes under many of the narrative devices that deal with the ineffable—those that at once say and do not say, or that frame in order to invoke and exorcise in the same presentation. The literature of horror includes many examples of complex framing structures and of reflexivity. As often occurs in metaphysical writing, the attempt to describe or discuss the limit-smashing experience puts the language and structure, or framing systems, under pressure. In the literature of horror, this pressure manifests itself with surprising regularity as the need to *fence in* the horror object—not in a literal cage but in a narrative frame, a story within a story—and what often goes on to happen from there is that the frame itself becomes a horror object.

In many ghost stories, for instance, the horror experience regularly referred to is not that of seeing a ghost, but that of hearing a ghost story. In Poe's "The Man of the Crowd," the narrator compares his insoluble mystery (not the piece he is writing, but its subject) to a complexly closed text:

> It was well said of a certain German book that *"er lässt sich nicht lesen,"* it does not permit itself to be read. There are some secrets which do not permit themselves to be told. Men die nightly in their beds, wringing the hands of ghostly confessors, and looking them piteously in the eyes; die with despair of heart and convulsion of throat, on account of the hideousness of mysteries which will not SUFFER THEMSELVES to be revealed.[42]

This may begin as a joke at the expense of an unnamed German stylist, but it changes immediately into an appeal to the reader's sense of the self-consciously forbidden text, the book that would be dangerous or horrible to read. It also yokes the threat to silence, saying that certain mysteries are unutterable, that they *choose* to be so, and that when they do present themselves it is in silence—making silence a category

181

of frightful communication. Before examining some of the more conspicuously reflexive instances of the textual horror object, like *The King in Yellow*, let us take up the subtler problem of the dreadful journal, charged with the aura of what it records.

The central question about Henry James's *The Turn of the Screw* is whether the governess is mad—in other words, whether the ghosts have any existence outside her own mind. According to Wayne Booth (whose reductive reading has been superseded by Shoshana Felman's, among others), this question was not central to James—who apparently intended to present the governess as reliable—but is nevertheless an important and regular aspect of the book's impact on its audience.[43] The late Frederick W. Dupee argued convincingly that *The Turn of the Screw* deals in "possibilities rather than facts" and is a tale "of total irony" that is "concerned with the difficulty of *making sense*, of piercing the moral and metaphysical mysteries."[44] Those critics who have tried to read this short novel as an investigation of sexual pathology have, in their over-literalness, missed an obvious and important point: this is a ghost story, and part of the essence of confronting the supernatural is to be unsure of just what is going on, since the intrusion violates one's normal interpretive and experiential categories. That which transcends ordinary reality is dramatically most effective when it is left, on some final level, out of bounds. It was within genre expectations for James to have partially undermined the governess' reliability; it was a daring extension of that decision to decline to give the governess a name and to make her an interface between the haunting ghosts and possessed children. What haunts *the story* is her own potential unreliability, and it is this which gives the final turn to the screw, making the text an unsettling object for the reader to confront, an unknowable in its own right. What makes it so compelling is that the elements of the story that are not clarified are those that could not *be* clarified, given the subject matter and the observer, and that the governess is so honestly attempting to describe and understand her experience. The reader who adopts a superior or Freudian attitude toward the governess, taking all this as a matter of repression and dramatic irony, is simply defending himself against a mystery. The point is not to explain away the mystery but to share the governess' uncertainty as well as her clarity.

The Turn of the Screw shares with *Heart of Darkness* the device of the long-delayed telling and an emphasis on some special sympathy between the teller and the final, anonymous transcriber/narrator. (Since both works were written at the same time, these correspondences suggest not influence but something more interesting: that James and Conrad each recognized the inherent appropriateness of this narrative structure to the problem at hand.) The central story—the governess' memoir—is written down at an unspecified time and entrusted much later to Douglas. Like Marlow, Douglas waits a long time before sharing the story, and when he does, he singles out one of his friends as best qualified to understand its essence. That friend—the first-person narrator of *The Turn of the Screw* as Marlow's best listener is the first-person narrator of *Heart of Darkness*—is so taken by the story that he transcribes the governess' memoir word for word—again, some considerable time after he has heard it read by Douglas. He then waits an unspecified time before writing *The Turn of the Screw*. The effect is to isolate, frame, and fence in the "dreadful" story, to distance it from the reader both in time and in levels of narration.

Just as in *Wuthering Heights* and *Absalom, Absalom!*, the object (event, protagonist, telling) distanced in this manner tends to become mytholgical and implicitly unapprehensible. This happens, in other words, both to the governess' tale and to her telling of it, since both are set at a great distance by the same telescopic framing devices. The first implication is that the encounters between the governess and the ghosts, and the consequent death of Miles, are so unsettling as to require viewing from a distance; the second is that the memoir itself may be a horror object (which would be the case if

183

it showed but did not say something horrible of which the governess were not aware: that *she* was the nameless and destructive force) meriting the same sort of enclosure and distance. The story is further charged by Douglas' saying that it had made an indelible impression on his heart, that he had no need to put that into words.[45]

Within the governess' narration, the process of framing continues. Her first sight of Quint shocks her with "the sense that my imagination had, in a flash, turned real."[46] This may be a hint that she is imagining the ghost, or it may be a natural reaction to seeing something unusual that partly resembles her romantic fantasy of encountering a stranger— but it is also a division between conceptual levels, one of which concerns the familiar and one of which will employ distancing as a means of dealing with the extremely unfamiliar. If anything, such distancing increases the immediacy of the perception (the double action of the telescope): "I saw with a stranger sharpness. The gold was still in the sky, the clearness in the air, and the man who looked at me over the battlements was as definite as a picture in a frame."[47] My emphasis falls on that "frame" and on a twist in the next paragraph: "So I saw him as I see the letters I form on this page."[48] What she means is that she saw him distinctly, but what James might have meant is that horror and text are inseparable and perhaps the means of each others' creation. This may, in other words, be a conspicuously reflexive observation. A further implication is that here in the inner sanctum, here in the fenced-in memoir, the ghost is as directly confronted as is the text itself: hence the best reason for the need to distance that text from the reader with so many frames.

The governess is a metaphysical hero and knows it. At the edge of ordinary reality, she suspects, of course, that words fail her: "I scarce know how to put my story into words that shall be a credible picture of my state of mind; but I was in these days literally able to find a joy in the extraordinary flight of heroism the occasion demanded of me."[49]

She also puts her finger on another basic characteristic of the metaphysical hero: "It was in short a magnificent chance. This chance presented itself to me in an image richly material. I was a screen—I was to stand before them. The more I saw, the less they would."[50] She is describing herself not as a *shield* between the children and the ghosts, but as a screen, a filter. Because she is closer to the horror, she sees it more clearly than do others—and because she stands between the horror and other mortals, they see the little they do see of it *through her,* just as Marlow gets his first sense of the heart of darkness through the medium of Kurtz. The governess masks and transmits at once; her memoir screens us from the enormity of what she sees, and simultaneously projects that horror onto the screen she becomes, so that the horror appears at times to be part of her very being. As the frame and medium for this ghostly possession, she appears from the reader's perspective to be its partial site and possible point of origin (as in the analogy of an image "in" a mirror).

It is interesting that the governess finds both her highest exultations and her greatest fears equally impossible to verbalize; the issue is not the positive or negative quality of the experience but the degree of its extremity. Two of these negative moments deserve mention in closing. At one point, she and Quint face each other silently and without moving:

> The moment was so prolonged that it would have taken but little more to make me doubt if even I were in life. I can't express what followed it save by saying that the silence itself—which was indeed in a manner an attestation of my strength—became the element into which I saw the figure disappear.[51]

Again, what the governess may simply be saying is that she was strong enough to make the ghost vanish, that he disappeared into the silence she had been powerful enough to maintain—but what James may be implying is farther-reaching. If Quint is a horror at the level of the text, his disappearance into the silence is a brilliant gesture. Any text is surrounded by silence, but texts that deal with the supernatural or the ineffable are particularly charged by that silence, which is the goad to their effort and the measure of their failure. It is just as well that the governess finds in the silence an indication of her personal strength rather than the manifestation of an occultist medium that threatens every frame she is managing to maintain; for the reflexively oriented reader, this is one of the story's most complexly unsettling moments.

The governess' confrontation with the worst horror comes, of course, at the end: "I seemed to float not into clearness, but into a darker obscure, and within a minute there had come to me out of my very pity the appalling alarm of his being perhaps innocent. It was for the instant confounding and bottomless, for if he *were* innocent, what then on earth was *I?*"[52] The two destructive powers—the ghosts on one hand, and she on the other—are confronted in much the same terms; they are also mutually exclusive. Her crucial words are "confounding and bottomless," and they indicate that the possibility of her being destructive is at least as great a horror and threat as any ghost. Such a line of thought would, bottomless, have to be followed forever —would be, in its own dreadful way, another window on the infinite.

James shares with Poe and H. P. Lovecraft the distinction of having written the finest of American supernatural fiction, and it is interesting to note that both later authors share with and perhaps learned from Poe (in spite of James's avowed hostility to Poe's work) two important devices. First, Poe often makes his narrator an acquaintance of the doomed metaphysical hero, and second, art or an art object is often the key to or site of the supernatural event. These two devices yield a third: a reflexive *and* diegetic use of the fenced-in, horrifying text. On a small scale, Poe's "The Oval Portrait" is a clear example of the latter devices: the narrator, intrigued by a woman's portrait, discovers a description of its creation and lets that (transcribed) narration present the climax; a fenced-in text describes an art object whose creation destroyed its subject, the painter's wife. (Godard uses this story reflexively in his film *Vivre sa vie,* retelling it just before he stages a scene in which the heroine, played by his own wife, is killed—through the agency, of course, of the script Godard has written.) On the largest scale Poe ever attempted, the *Narrative of A. Gordon Pym* can be seen to operate in much the same manner, although the burden of the structure here lies more in what the narration refuses to say rather than in what it, in spite of all framing, finally presents.

Pym's record of his voyage to the Antarctic (made after the voyage and left incomplete at his death) closes with the vision of a huge white figure. In his "Introductory Note," Pym says that he let Mr. Poe write the first few chapters as if they were fiction but composed the rest himself. A third author is presented as having written the appendix; he amuses himself by pointing out some aspects of Pym's story that Poe (who, this author says, did not believe the latter parts of the story in any case) has failed to understand, most of which suggest the possible identity of the white giant, the significance of its whiteness, and the secret meanings of the shapes of the canyons Pym explored (they form words). There are, then, two fenced-in texts: Pym's gradually less credible memoir (similar to the governess' both in its being bracketed and in its subtly increasing appearance of unreliability), and the signifying rock formations.

Lovecraft and Borges are equally indebted to Poe's wonderful conclusion. Breaking off as it does at the moment of maximum tension, Pym's memoir allows the horror to present itself in silence—not only its own, but also the text's. Any explanation of the horror (the nature of the Antarctic and its ghostly inhabitants) comes from the author of the appendix, the distanced scholar—but even he confines himself to lining up the next level of evidence and does not actually draw conclusions. The Borgesian twist—the suggestion that Poe missed the point—calls attention to this

187

bracketing of the memoir and thus compounds the mystery, forcing the reader to check out the memoir more carefully (especially in relation to the appendix) while undermining the reliability of that memoir (since Poe is announced as one of its authors) and, of course, making a doubly reflexive joke. The first level of reflexivity calls attention to the paradoxical status of the text and makes the reader examine his own attitude toward that text; the second is precipitated by the reader's recognition that Poe is, of course, the true author of all three segments and could hardly have missed the point.

One of the things Lovecraft took from Poe in general and *Pym* in particular was the device of the secret text. Although Lovecraft is sometimes unfortunately literal in his presentation of the bestial, describing what simply should not be described and waxing geometrical when he ought to remain allusive, he is often good at suggesting the feel of an encounter with the unknown. He is not consistent in his restraint, however, nor in his ability to use reflexivity; thus "The Unnamable,"[53] which with a little care might have been effective, is one of his silliest stories, despite its promising notion of having Lovecraft take a positivist thinker to the site that had inspired one of his derided, published fictions. On the other hand, his short novel *At the Mountains of Madness* (which is typical in that it is compelling only until the monsters are revealed) makes an interesting, reflexive use of the secret text.

Throughout Lovecraft's work, someone is always discovering "the dreaded *Necronomicon* of the mad Arab Abdul Alhazred."[54] The *Necronomicon,* of which there is only one surviving copy, is the key to the Cthulhu mythos and to other monstrous aspects of prehistory; none of its readers is left unchanged by it. Its power resides first in the horrors it treats and second in its own isolation, as a forbidden text, from the everyday world. It is itself a fenced-in horror object, an interface between the visible and the hidden (as Borges' Encyclopedia of Tlön is an interface, and an evoker of what it describes, although Borges' tone is more playful[55]); it is appropriate that Lovecraft rarely if ever quotes from it, at least in English. *At the Mountains of Madness* performs an elegant twist on the implicit reflexivity of the textual horror object by suggesting that Poe's *Narrative of A. Gordon Pym* is another such text, that it is a key to actual horrors presented, as Poe said, *"under the guise of fiction."*[56]

Lovecraft's narrator leads an expedition into *Pym*'s Antarctic regions and discovers not just similar monsters (and more) but also similar clues—in particular, the exclamation *"Tekeli-li!,"* which was identified in *Pym*'s appendix as having something to do with the whiteness of the mythological horrors. This leads him and his only surviving companion to speculate about "unsuspected and forbidden sources to which Poe may have had access when writing his *Arthur Gordon Pym* a century ago."[57] Since Lovecraft's and Poe's works are both approached by the reader as fictions, these speculations create in the reader's mind the possibility that they are equally *not* fictions but instead forbidden texts, keys like the *Necronomicon* to unknown regions. So in this case, the reflexivity is used to undermine the reader's suspension of belief—to increase the impact of the horror story by implying that it is only pretending to be a story. Lovecraft turns the canon of horror literature into something more closely resembling the canonized books of the Bible: a series of pseudohistorical glimpses into the ways the supernatural impinges on ordinary reality, to be consulted for their "accuracy" as much as for their beauty. It is one thing to set a fiction like the *Necronomicon* at the heart of one's fiction, and quite another to set there the actual and accepted works of Poe.

The linking figure between Poe and Lovecraft, a minor American novelist named Robert W. Chambers, hit on a variation of these devices that is, as a reflexive structure, even more satisfying. *The King in Yellow* is a collection of stories, three of which leave their respective narrators dead, mad, or possessed as the result of their exposure to a book called *The King in Yellow*. This inner text is not a book of stories, but a yellow-bound verse drama, acknowledged by those unlucky enough to have read it as a "beautiful, stupendous creation, terrible in its simplicity, irresistible in its truth"; its words contain "the essence of purest poison"; it is banned, yet spreads "like an infectious disease."[58] As a language game, then, this inner text is defined by its effectiveness—by its effecting what it signifies—and by its irresistibility. (Appropriately, it has at its heart a semiotic killer, the Yellow Sign.) One of its readers, who fancies himself—or perhaps is—the heir to the earthly domain of the King in Yellow, tells how "those poisoned words had dropped slowly into my heart, as death-sweat drops upon a bed-sheet and is absorbed."[59] Even those who try not to open the book are doomed to read it through. It describes, in an allusive Gothic rhetoric imitated by Lovecraft, the awful land of Carcosa, the King and his Pallid Mask, and that deadly emblem known as the Yellow Sign.

The first story, "The Yellow Sign," is presented as "an unsigned letter sent to the author"—unsigned, as it turns out, because its author (Scott) had died in mid-sentence. In that letter, Scott tells how he and his model, Tessie, discovered in the street outside Scott's New York studio a grublike church watchman; this watchman had appeared to Tessie in a dream, driving a hearse with a glass-windowed coffin in which she had seen Scott. Scott soon had a dream in which he was in that coffin (compare J. S. Le Fanu's *In a Glass Darkly* and Carl Dreyer's *Vampyr*) and saw Tessie watching him. From his position in the street, near the church whose organist played "like a fiend in human shape," the watchman called three times to Scott, "Have you found the Yellow Sign?" Tessie soon presented Scott with a love token, a brooch she had found shortly before her nightmares began. Then she read *The King in Yellow,* and against his better judgment (shades of Adam), so did Scott; they realized then that the golden character on the brooch was the Yellow

Sign. The watchman burst in on them and seized the brooch. Tessie died of fright, and Scott "killed" the watchman—who turns out to have been dead and decomposing for months. Scott died soon after; his last act was to write this "confession." At one point, he says the reason he had been afraid to read *The King in Yellow* was that he had heard of "the awful tragedy of young Castaigne, whom I knew."[60]

The tale of Castaigne is told in the first person in the next story, "The Repairer of Reputations." This story is set in a futuristic (1920) America, where suicide chambers dot the streets of New York and where the repulsive Mr. Wilde manipulates hundreds of disgraced clients in his project of establishing the legitimate King in Yellow in dominion over the earth; his power emblem and sometime death warrant is the Yellow Sign. His own secret text, "The Imperial Dynasty of America," identifies Castaigne as a potential legitimate successor. Mr. Wilde is torn to pieces by his cat, and Castaigne (after an unsuccessful attempt to destroy his own cousin) writes this story and dies in a madhouse.

The final relevant story, "In the Court of the Dragon," is set in Paris. It is the first-person account of a man who, after reading *The King in Yellow,* goes to a church to calm his nerves. He finds himself terrified of the organist and leaves the church, but the organist pursues him to his apartments and closes in on him. At that moment, the narrator finds himself again in the church. He understands that the pursuit was not a simple daydream and that his escape was not final; he has recognized the organist and implies that that figure is the King in Yellow. Then the church vanishes, the man sees the towers of Carcosa, and he sinks into flames as the King whispers to his soul the words of his damnation.[61]

The three stories relate to each other in an intricate manner. The story of Castaigne establishes that the world described in the inner *King in Yellow* is not (from the characters' point of view) fictitious, that it is some kind of alternate universe. It also explains the function of the Yellow Sign, whose signified is the power and immanence of the King in

Yellow. Scott is a friend of Castaigne; although he begins by being afraid that reading the yellow book had driven Castaigne mad, he finds when he receives the Yellow Sign that the King's world does exist. Scott mentions that the organist at the nearby church plays in a fiendish manner. The narrator of the final story finds either this or a similar organist in Paris and is destroyed by him; this is rather like Ishmael's suspicion that the whale is ubiquitous. All three stories reinforce each others' discoveries, and each of those discoveries is precipitated by a reading of *The King in Yellow*, a book whose greatest power inheres in its simple language.

The terror here is that the ineffable *can* be described, and that such description cannot, once confronted, be forgotton or escaped; behind the clear verse of the occasionally cited play lurks the greater danger of the Yellow Sign, a character not in any human language but *absolutely effective*. It is the Ur-sign at the heart of the forbidden text, and the implicitly reflexive title of Chambers' book of stories necessarily generates in the reader the sense that he or she is confronting a reduced but complementary danger in reading this *King in Yellow*. It is as if Chambers' book were a higher circle in hell, or as if *it* played secondary first person to the overreaching verse drama. The book of stories refracts the drama, is the lesser image through which the original can be considered. Chambers' book uses English to frame the language game whose effectiveness is typified by the Yellow Sign, and whose Rosetta Stone is the verse play, *The King in Yellow*.

Aside from the fact that each of them is written in the first person, the conspicuous linking feature among the *Narrative of A. Gordon Pym, The King in Yellow, The Turn of the Screw,* and *At the Mountains of Madness* (to set them in their order of composition) is that of the textual horror object. In *Pym* and *The Turn of the Screw* the central narration is more paradoxical or problematic than specifically horrific, but that paradox, that unreliability, is still the key to the nature of the horror. In *The King in Yellow* and *At the Mountains of Madness,* as well as in *The Turn of the Screw,* books not only identify the horror figures but come reflexively to incarnate them, obsessing the reader if not actually proving destructive. Among these four, the book that comes closest to systemic self-consciousness is *Pym,* yet each of them to some degree presents itself not simply as a description of horrors but also as a horror object with a fenced-in text at its center.

The converse of this pattern is more familiar: a cluster of relatively innocent texts with an often silent horror at their center; this is the case in Bram Stoker's *Dracula,* for instance, and also in Richardson's *Clarissa* (whose horror is the illegitimate use of patriarchal power against its heroine) and Faulkner's *As I Lay Dying.* One of the most unsettling aspects of *Dracula* is the fact that one never hears from Dracula but only hears about him; he keeps no journal, writes no letters, makes no recordings, while his victims and investigators are desperately setting down the little they know. The reader often feels an urgency about, for instance, Jonathan Harker's journal—if only the other characters could read it!—that indicates how successfully this novel is constructed around the problem of partial evidence, limited point of view, metaphysical and experiential perspective. If the texts are assembled and the experiences collated, one will be able to say that Dracula is a vampire. One will have, then, a larger view of the situation. One will *not,* however, have an inside or direct understanding of the supernatural; one will have neither Dracula's perspective (he presents himself either in silence or in an aristocratically menacing allusiveness) nor a metaphysically satisfying explanation of the phenomenon from the "other side" (a term for the spirit world that Pynchon uses effectively in *Gravity's Rainbow,* making the barrier between life and death also a barrier between categories of apprehension). Clarissa's rape and Dracula's nature are horrors that will not "suffer themselves to be revealed" but can only be guessed at through their effects. We shall see that *As I Lay Dying* requires a more complex analysis, but for the moment

193

we may note that the dying Addie is silent and is the main object of the other characters' attention, and that her silence and the fact of her dying are more compelling than the sick-joke aspects of her decomposition (which simply attract comment rather than obsessive attempts at understanding).

To clarify the role of secondary first-person narration and the question of the fragmented self in horror fiction, it is helpful to consider Mary Shelley's *Frankenstein*. The narrator, Robert Walton, is presented in the most explicit terms as an inspired overreacher who shares Frankenstein's "madness" and who regards him as a potential friend and brother.[62] It is also clear that Walton is not as compulsive a hero as his passenger and is finally willing to pilot his ship back out of the polar region rather than push on to glory or destruction. (Frankenstein's advice on that matter—despite his earlier warnings to Walton not to venture too far into his respective field, lest he destroy himself and his loved ones as Frankenstein had—is *not* to turn back.[63]) Walton's relation to Frankenstein, then, is precisely that of the secondary first-person narrator: a slightly less over-the-edge version of the hero, chosen to transcribe the hero's story. The fact that Frankenstein, like Marlow (but unlike Ahab or Leverkühn), is able to relate but not write down his own tale illuminates how similar *Frankenstein* is to *Heart of Darkness,* both in narrative structure and in choice of horror. Just as Marlow's listener records the tale of a civilized man's search for the split-off, uncivilized aspects of his own nature, Walton transcribes the story of Frankenstein's relationship with the "monstrous"—not so much terrible as rejected—aspects of his own nature. And just as all three major characters in *Heart of Darkness*—the listener, Marlow, and Kurtz—are comparable and related, there is a clearly intended complementarity among Walton, Frankenstein, and the Monster. One could add up Frankenstein and the Monster and have something resembling an integrated person: a figure who would in fact resemble Walton, who is an overreacher with both scientific and poetic interests (whereas the Monster is

194

devoted to language and Frankenstein is indifferent to it[64]). What this synthesis would add to the figure of Walton is the element of tragic experience. We may also note that Frankenstein tells his story only for the benefit of his secret sharer (suppressing the scientific details, to insure that his experiment not be repeated) and does so in an isolated narrative situation, the polar ice-cap, where he expects to die and from which he can hardly expect his audience will return.

Framing in time and in narrative level operates here, too, keeping the Monster's story within his creator's story and both of them within Walton's. The Monster's story is the horror "text," but for a surprising and twofold reason. From Frankenstein's perspective, the Monster is certainly the horror, and to confront him directly and at length is the event he would be most prone to insulate within narrative levels; he does the same thing with the letter that describes William's death, reciting the text rather than simply telling Walton about the murder. For the attentive reader, however, the Monster is not the fearsome creature Frankenstein considers him, but a once-beautiful mind in a gross body, and the horror is in how the Monster has been treated, both by his creator and by other men. So it is still the burden of the Monster's tale that is the central horror, and it is still appropriate that this revelation be fenced in, but there is considerable irony here on Shelley's part.

The horror, then, is not the Monster but the terrible story of how his *tabula rasa,* his innocent mind, is schooled in rejection and hatred by nearly all humans, the failure of whose compassion is the atrocity. *Frankenstein* is not about the dangers of creation as much as it is about the responsibilities of the creator. The Monster is Frankenstein's split-off self, the poetic and linguistic side with which, as a compulsive scientist, he is out of touch, and the unhappy childhood that he did not experience. The Monster's behavior is a dramatization of how one side of Frankenstein's nature turns destructive when it is not sufficiently loved; the Monster is,

195

quite clearly, Frankenstein's inner child—not his son, but his own child nature. (From the outset, Frankenstein's plan is to create a being like himself.)

Frankenstein cannot declare himself simply a conscious, fine person and reject his emotional self without ceasing to be whole; the emotions will respond to this rejection and have their revenge. It is no wonder that Frankenstein never consummates his marriage to Elizabeth, that she is simply a beautiful and loving "sister" whom he admires and needs but never gets around to actively wanting—the Monster always comes first. And because the Monster is not accepted and understood, he destroys the conscious self's rather flat and lovely plans for an untroubled life organized around a love that is not sufficiently confronted to turn passionate; only hatred and rejection are passionately confronted here. So the quest of Frankenstein's life is, or ought to be, to "re-own the projection" (in Gestalt terms), to take the Monster back into himself. That is a wholeness, however, that he cannot bring himself to accomplish because of the extent of his fear, and eventually his hatred, of that lonely, poetic, unbeautiful child. He imagines that his task, then, is to destroy the Monster with whom he is inseparably linked. The Monster, who understands all this much better than Frankenstein does, allows his creator to determine the nature of the game: if they cannot be loving beings together, either as creator and creation or as husbands with wives, then they will simply have to die together.

The ultimate act of compassionate love in this novel is the Monster's suicide. It is not an act of remorse for causing the death of Frankenstein, but an acknowledgment of their mutual dependence. The Monster even agrees with Frankenstein on the importance of the experiment's not being repeated and addresses Walton directly, making it even more clear how similar he is to his creator.[65] Appropriately, even though this apparent climax of the story is allowed to happen in the narrative present, with Walton's transcription's being interrupted by the events, the love climax—like the other major events in the lives of the Monster and his creator—does not happen in Walton's presence but is, with the Monster in the final sentence, "lost in darkness and distance."[66]

It is of considerable relevance that the Monster's politics and strategy are very like Sutpen's, despite the fact that Sutpen is less compassionate or aware. The Monster weeps over the fate of what he calls the "original inhabitants" of the American hemisphere (innocents like Sutpen and himself, vilified and relegated to the subhuman by the forces of official culture) and forms a design of finding acceptance in the terms offered by the oppressor. If he cannot have "high and unsullied descent united with riches,"[67] he can still fixate on finding his creator (to establish his descent) and securing a wife.

Sutpen, the Monster, and even Gatsby share the psychology of what is sometimes called the "basic self"; and this is to say more than that they are childish, emotional, or fixated. The term "basic self" means more than, for instance, "child" does in transactional psychology (*Games People Play*, etc.), and more than "child" does as a stage of physical growth, but it is closely related to both. It signifies the consciousness of the physical being, the emotional self full of physical desires. The basic self is a body-consciousness that is dominant in children, and its primary task is (according to some mystics) to anchor the self on the planet, to see that the body is kept alive and satisfied.

The basic self is part of an interesting system, most recently set forth by John-Roger,[68] that conceptualizes the self on three primary levels. Since we have devoted so much attention to the notion of the higher self, and since this study is concerned with the limitations and aspirations of consciousness to make sense of what is beyond its scope, it is appropriate to present the core of the system, a metaphysical psychology of considerable usefulness:

> *Higher Self:* the link to the Soul, and the inner witness to experience, in touch with the karmic path and charged with guiding the self toward fulfilling and re-

197

leasing that karma; perhaps independent of cause-and-effect thinking and of linear time; a psychic connector, transpersonal.

Conscious Self: the linguistic, abstracting, and often holistic mind, which develops to the point of autonomy and sometimes to the point of control, late in childhood.

Basic Self: the emotional, physical, and often spontaneously creative aspects of the self; dominant in children; the site of habit-formation; and the usual medium through which the higher self finds expression (since the mind rarely pays attention to the higher self and is too well-equipped to deal with effables to work in terms of unconditional, loving unity).

To a great extent, what is going on in *Frankenstein, Absalom, Absalom!, The Great Gatsby,* and *Wuthering Heights,* not to mention *Citizen Kane,* is that the destructive or heroic figure, who is perceived as uncivilized and in search of loving acceptance, is dominated by his basic self and is perceived as a mystery by the more verbal elements (conscious self, narrators) that surround and would like to suppress or sublimate him. One way to consider the literature we have examined so far, and a fairly rewarding one, is in terms of the conscious self's attempts to deal linguistically and in a civilizing manner with the higher self (which it finds it must approach intuitively or else stand aside for) in the literature of the ineffable, and with the basic self (which it often conceptualizes as anarchic, lower class, dark, illegitimate, menstrual, bestial, or *Id*) in the literature of the childish overreacher, which includes horror, much of myth, and much of what is still appropriately termed metaphysical heroism. If the higher self does sometimes find expression through the basic self, it follows that an overreacher like Ahab—a fixated and compulsive child if ever there was one—may well be in touch with the ineffable, even if his quest does boil down to a temper tantrum. The same logic can be applied to Slothrop's erections and Parsifal's foolishness. This leaves Socrates in a different category of metaphysical heroism in that he operates through the conscious self until he finds or reveals that even he is wordless—though his basic self is notably active in the *Symposium*. Proust's narrator in *A la recherche du temps perdu* is embattled with the problems of will and habit (negative aspects of the conflicted basic self) until the higher self, working through and past his physical senses, frees his creativity and creates his freedom, allowing all aspects of the self to function positively and to enrich each other.

Frankenstein is a parable of the conscious self's absolute need for the basic self and of the tragedy that attends an irresponsible rejection of the innocent, creative, poetic, angry, emotional, sexual, hungry, and vulnerable being inside even the most disciplined person. Shelley's underlying vision here is of a drive toward personal wholeness, of the integration of creativity and compassion, industry and spirit. We shall see later how, in *The Female Man,* Joanna Russ uses Gestalt psychology quite self-consciously as a means of indicating the political and personal meanings of wholeness; but for the moment, we are concerned not with a feminist utopia, but with a tragedy of the patriarchal and industrial age. Before examining Thomas Pynchon's nightmare view of the full range of what it means to be cut off from wholeness while the destructive aspects of the basic self scream toward us with their burdens of warheads and murdered lovers, let us take one more glance at horror in general.

Horror literature, to be of enduring interest, must be both terrifying and transcendental. The merely violent or disgusting does not qualify. Horror opens a window on the mythic, on the dark, on the basic self, on the mysterious, on transformation, on death, on undeath. A rigidly limited sense of the conscious self presents the mind as being cut off from that which is beyond conception and from that which is emotionally extreme, both of which may have ties to the metaphysical and both of which function in the greatest of

199

horror literature, from *The Turn of the Screw* to Hedayat's *The Blind Owl*. But both the higher and basic selves must be integrated with the conscious self—not incorporated into it but embraced alongside it within one larger, holistic system—no matter how indecipherable or dangerous their territories might appear. That larger system is the realized, unified, harmonious, effective self. In a Jungian context, horror allows the reader to confront certain archetypes in the service of a larger integration; in Gestalt terms, the task is to recognize the archetype, and so on, as a projection, a split-off aspect of the whole self, and to re-own it. It often happens that a narration constructed according to the principles of the simultaneous self—where the unifying character energy is scattered among several versions of the same self, as in *A la recherche du temps perdu,* where the scattering occurs in time, or *Absalom, Absalom!,* where it is the function of a Fall, or the *Republic,* where it is a convenience for the self-expression of the Logos (and all three of these complex fragmentations are aspects of the Fall into language)—will re-own its projections, unify its multiplicity, by coming to systemic self-consciousness. It will declare that it is, as a system, a whole self, the unity of its parts, and (on an "as if" basis, since it is still a text) a self-aware, self-directing, self-perfecting "consciousness."

Many texts function on the edge of this integration; *Frankenstein* is a notable example. One of the greatest and perhaps most optimistic horror stories of our time, *Gravity's Rainbow,* takes place on the border that separates time, diversity, and cause and effect from eternity, unity, and synchrony; it maintains an energetic suspension of interlocking elements, which are a Gestalt of the narrating persona as well as the simultaneous self of the mind of the text. The term "suspension" is appropriate here because it is important that all of Pynchon's plot elements not lock into an overdetermined system (because that would then make the novel part of the "They-system," an agency of the Plot, a controlled and controlling delusion) yet not deteriorate into utter randomness (a perhaps blissful "scattering" like that of Slothrop's personality, but one that would let no novel have form). At the end of *Gravity's Rainbow,* with the future both of the characters and of the audience left open, the suspension at once declares itself and comes to a halt, refusing to let the story find conventional resolution while neatly interrelating the many symbolic threads in an image that is both authorially and systemically self-conscious. It seems entirely appropriate to think of this in terms of horror fiction, since the Rocket (whether as missile, spacecraft, or Passover Angel) is an archetype of transcendence and terror, a grail-image that can be used "to kill people" or "to transcend."[69]

The arc of the Rocket's flight path is a symbol with that same kind of doubleness: first, it represents both the sign of God's covenant with the chosen people and the sign of "the fire next time"; second, it defines a border between "this side" and "the other side," between the mortal and the spiritual. And more than a border, it becomes an agency of paradox, which in the Herero view is "the law of experience" and one aspect of a cosmology in which "opposites can be reconciled and men can be individual selves and yet parts of a larger self, members of a human and a cosmic community."[70] This is not to forget that we could easily blow ourselves to radioactive bits and that the theatre on whose screen (the mindscreen of the "narrator"[71]) the novel is being "shown" is managed by a man Pynchon compares to Nixon. The Rocket, in both its positive and negative aspects, resembles Frankenstein's Monster, and the quest for the "A 00000" is a quest for wholeness. It is also a quest for the Zero, which can be the level of the "deeper and true self," a "pure . . . informationless state" associated with "great serenity,"[72] or the Pavlovian's point of extinction, or even the modern politician's site of extinction—ground zero. It might be the silence that attends the ineffable or the perverse silence of universal death. In its dialectical presentation of the Plot and the Counterforce, *Gravity's Rainbow* becomes one of the counterculture's weapons against the

201

neat, compulsive murderers, liberating its readers into a vision of the free self in process. There is no space here for a complete analysis of this novel, but a few general observations on its uses of the reflexive and the ineffable are in order.[73]

Gravity's Rainbow presents two extreme categories of preconscious experience: the world of spirits, and the world of emotional anarchy. The former manifests itself in séances, the Herero vision, the Kirghiz Light, the epigraph from Von Braun, and so on; the latter accounts for the oral, anal, and sexual perversions rampant in the lives of the major characters and is evident in the destructiveness of warfare. The high point of the spiritualist subplot is the séance with Rathenau,[74] whose views on time and synthesis help to clarify other discussions of what it means to move "beyond the zero—and into the other realm"[75] and to be free of "the idea of the opposite";[76] The high point of what might be called the basic-self subplot (in this case an emotional overreaching in the service of transcendence) is Blicero's enshrouding his lover Gottfried in Imipolex G, the first erectile plastic, and launching him in the abortive Rocket.[77] Both of these extremes defy the consciousness and paralyze its expression into a vision of lostness that is a kind of hope, a firing squad whose guns *might* shoot paper flowers. They mandate an emphasis on paradox, on punning, on flight from the overdetermined systems that paranoids see too well; they mandate what the psychic Prentice calls "creative paranoia,"[78] the "visionary slapstick" of the Counterforce, the vaudevillian reflexivity of this novel's humor; they are at the edge of a vision of unity, resolution, synthesis, synchrony—but they are not there yet. They are trapped in a dream just before the bomb either falls or does not, just before salvation either happens or does not.

As the reader pushes through this long novel, expecting a resolution—expecting, for instance, Tchitcherine and Enzian to have a showdown rather than simply to pass each other on a road—he is like a prison guard at an electrocution, his hand on the power switch. But the novel short-circuits, refuses to climax in anything but its levels of reflexivity and symbolic interconnection (Slothrop scatters, the Rocket miscarries, the bulb burns out). At that point, the reader suddenly discovers that it was *he* who was sitting in the electric chair. The short circuit—which has not been achieved in the modern political world since the reader is still being conditioned, is still living under the arc of the Rocket, is still waiting for the novel to find conventional resolution so he can have his Behaviorist reward for skittering through Pynchon's labyrinth, is still cutting time into instants and frames with calculus and movies and partial attention and plotted trajectories—that short circuit is the one thing that has saved him from oblivion, from the plan. The problem in reflexive fiction is to make the "short" function as a valid circuit.

The world of *Gravity's Rainbow* is split in a great many ways (like the good and evil Rocket and the "Primal Twins" Enzian and Blicero[79]), the most political of which is the split between the fascistic, destructive, Behavioristically conditioning forces of the Plot (who enjoy Beethoven) and the erratic, mystical, creative Counterforce (who enjoy Rossini). To allow the novel to find a "chase scene, chase scene, wow yeah Douglas Fairbanks"[80] resolution, to indulge those aspects of the audience that enjoy "Kute Korrespondences"[81] (even if they hope "to zero in on the tremendous and secret Function whose name, like the permuted names of God, cannot be spoken" by means of that string of noticed correspondences and interconnections) would be to come out on the side of control, which is death in this context. To undermine a controlling fantasy system is a creative political act. To do so not by destroying the novel but by turning its processes back on themselves, so that the novel rises in awareness as it turns reflexive, is a fundamentally ethical gesture, because it attempts to heighten the self-awareness of the audience.

Pynchon announces at the beginning of the novel's final hundred pages that he is, as the organizer of the novel's system, embattled with cause and effect, even though the novel may be answerable to other means of organization. "You will want cause and effect," he says to the reader. "All right."[82] Then he rattles off some previously unmentioned events that tie parts of the plot together. But the tone of that "All right" has done in the reader's suspension of disbelief; whether or not we choose to accept these details as "what really happened," we cannot avoid the feeling that they have been made up to satisfy reader demand and not simply supplied because the reader needs everything spelled out. This, of course, implicates the entire diegesis as an authorial construct rather than a reported event and makes the reader self-conscious along with the author.

Later, Pynchon suggests that the story is out of his control—not like a normal story, which might be presented as having really happened, with the narrator merely the recorder and not the controller (part of what the reader pretends to believe when suspending disbelief), but like a self-conscious system that obeys its own laws. The reader is left facing a relationship in process between the author and the fiction, with each element having some degree of self-determination; to an extent, the author here is watching the novel unfold, is a witness to it, quite as much as the reader is. And this is no more a pose on Pynchon's part than respect for the Muses (who would sing *through* the poet) was a mere literary device in the ancient world.

He offers first an old story about systems theory, about the way parts can accumulate into something more than the sum of those parts. He describes the assembly of the "A 00001" (the second in its series) as "a Diaspora running backwards, seeds of exile flying inward in a modest preview of gravitational collapse," then tells the "story about the kid who hates kreplach." The meat, the frying onions, all the parts are lovely and fun, but the minute the kid recognizes the system into which they accumulate, he rejects it. The novel is coming together, too:

> "Now, I'm going to roll the dough out, see? into a nice flat sheet, now I'm cutting it up into squares—" "This is *terrif,* Mom!" "Now I spoon some of the hamburger into this little square, and now I fold it over into a tri—" "GAAHHHH!" screams the kid, in absolute terror— "*kreplach!*"

> As some secrets were given to the Gypsies to preserve against centrifugal History, and some to the Kabbalists, the Templars, the Rosicrucians, so have this Secret of the Fearful Assembly, and others, found their ways inside the weatherless spaces of this or that Ethnic Joke. There is also the story about Tyrone Slothrop, who was sent into the Zone to be present at his own assembly— perhaps, heavily paranoid voices have whispered, *his time's assembly*—and there ought to be a punch line to it, but there isn't. The plan went wrong. He is being broken down instead, and scattered. His cards have been laid down, Celtic style, in the order suggested by Mr. A. E. Waite, laid out and read, but they are the cards of a tanker and feeb: they point only to a long and scuffling future, to mediocrity (not only in his life but also, heh, heh, in his chroniclers too, yes yes nothing like getting the 3 of Pentacles upside down covering the significator on the second try to send you to the tube to watch a seventh rerun of the Takeshi and Ichizo Show, light a cigarette and try to forget the whole thing)—to no clear happiness or redeeming cataclysm.[83]

I have no idea whether Pynchon actually laid out the Tarot to find out how the novel should end or what the destinies of his characters would be, or whether this is a device attributed to the narrating persona, but it seems to make little difference either way. There is a clear sense that the story has its own destiny, its own metaphysical logic. The novel will not have a punch line. The Counterforce will not band together, smash the bad guys, do something creative with the "A 00000" or "A 00001," declare a sexual and political paradise. Enzian and Tchitcherine will not recognize each other on the road; Enzian and Blicero will not battle to the death; the Rocket, launched in the final pages, will not fall in Prentice's dream of the opening pages and will not fall on the theatre of the very last page; the Zero, in other words, will not be manifested within the novel. Any expression, any novel, will always be "delta-t" away from the Zero, as a word is delta-t away from what it signifies[84] and as any instant is delta-t away from eternity and silence; those are the conditions of being in the world, of being in time, of being in language. The actual Tarot cards, which suggest that Slothrop will not succeed in his quest, also indicate "mediocrity . . . in his chroniclers," sending the narrator to watch the Japanese equivalent of—who knows—Ozzie and Harriet, as the novel scatters under his hands. But the story of Slothrop, who was sent into the Zone to be present at his own assembly and that of his time—systems in search of their own coherence—is not so much a failure as it is, like the inner meaning of the kreplach joke and of this phase of the novel, a "secret." There will be "no clear happiness" (perhaps the victory of the Counterforce) and no "redeeming cataclysm" (the fall of the Rocket, an apocalyptic beginning to a new age, a metaphysical shake-up): but that is exactly Pynchon's real success. What there is instead is a coming to consciousness.

As the bulb burns out on the final page, what keeps going is "a film we have not learned to see." It happens at "the last delta-t," on the infinitesimal edge of unity, eternity, white light, the Zero, silence; it makes one aware of the absolute present, which is the closest thing to timelessness a mortal can experience and which involves an immediate attention to what is. What is, at this point, is a stopping novel, and the pure white light, just now burning out, yields to a blankness of screen and page:

The rhythmic clapping resonates inside these walls, which are hard and glossy as coal: Come-*on! Start*-the-*show! Come-on! Start*-the-*show!* The screen is a dim page spread before us, white and silent. The film has broken, or a projector bulb has burned out. It was difficult even for us, old fans who've always been at the movies (haven't we?) to tell which before the darkness swept in. The last image was too immediate for any eye to register. It may have been a human figure, dreaming of an early evening in each great capital luminous enough to tell him he will never die, coming outside to wish on the first star. But it was *not a star,* it was falling, a bright angel of death. And in the darkening and awful expanse of screen something has kept on, a film we have not learned to see . . . it is now a closeup of the face, a face we all know—

And it is just here, just at this dark and silent frame, that the pointed tip of the Rocket, falling nearly a mile per second, absolutely and forever without sound, reaches its last unmeasurable gap above the roof of this old theatre, the last delta-t.[85]

This concept of the delta-t is introduced along with a cluster of major symbols about six hundred pages earlier, in the context of an argument between Leni and Franz Pokler. When the two of them see Fritz Lang's film, *Die Frau im Mond* (in which, Pynchon notes, "the countdown as we know it" is first used), Leni sees "a dream of flight" and Franz comments on the special effects. Leni's insight is that "Real flight and dreams of flight go together. Both are part of the same movement. Not A before B, but all together. . . ." She calls her husband "the cause-and-effect man" and sounds as if she shared some of Rathenau's perspective on synchrony and synthesis, spirit time, the larger sense of flow. Her way of describing life in the moment is:

Δt approaching zero, eternally approaching, the slices of time growing thinner and thinner, a succession of rooms each with walls more silver, transparent, as the pure light of the zero comes nearer. . . .

But he shook his head. "Not the same, Leni. The important thing is taking a function to its limit. Δt is just a convenience, so that it can happen."[86]

In his attempt to rule out the paradoxical constructs that delta-t suggests, Franz is in Pavlov's camp, attempting to prove that everything can be reduced to cause and effect; if he knew about them, he would be disturbed by such paradoxical or ultraparadoxical phenomena as Slothrop's erections. He also falls asleep in movies, whose illusion of motion depends on the chopping up of flow into fragments (a calculus of movement with disturbing application to the process of analysing "the trajectories of cannonballs through the air,"[87] one of the basic connections between the imagery of movies and of the Rocket in this novel), a habit that irritates Leni into one of her best arguments: "How did he connect together the fragments he saw while his eyes were open?" Integrating the fragments (frames into a fantasy of movement) is a holistic mental act, not so much the reflex action of "persistence of vision" but a preconscious activity called the "phi phenomenon" (something of which Pynchon may not have been aware, but which was analyzed by Hugo Münsterberg, one of Gertrude Stein's teachers and a colleague of William James[88]), a decision to make sense out of the stills by interpreting them as aspects of a single motion. The right brain, at least, aspires to a sense of wholeness. Franz makes sense through analysis, and so is cut off from Leni's perspective: " 'Not produce,' she tried, 'not cause. It all goes along together. Parallel, not series. Metaphor. Signs and symptoms. Mapping on to different coordinate systems, I don't know . . .' She didn't know, all she was trying to do was reach."[89]

All one *can* do in this territory is reach. "Symptoms" are the root of the science of semiotics. "Metaphor" is a raid on integration. "Mapping on to different coordinate systems" is the basic method of this novel; it is a way of presenting many interpretations of experience and variations or polar systems of character encyclopedically, accounting for everything while maintaining the "secret" in suspension and the Primal Twins in their dialectic—keeping the "0" and the "1," the ineffable and the effable, inseparable and opposed because only together can they function as a signifying system, the basic binary language not just of computers but also of anything in the universe—electrical, subatomic, biological, pendular—that has a pulse.

The countdown of the Rocket, for instance, can be mapped onto the coordinate systems of the Kabbalist Tree of Life and of cause and effect. As one of the characters explains:

> "Now the Sephiroth fall into a pattern, which is called the Tree of Life. It is also the body of God. Drawn among the ten spheres are 22 paths. Each path corresponds to a letter of the Hebrew alphabet, and also to one of the cards called 'Major Arcana' in the Tarot. So although the Rocket countdown appears to be serial, it actually conceals the Tree of Life, which must be apprehended all at once, together, in parallel."[90]

Seriality, placing one thing after another, is the syntagmatic aspect of language and a basic tool in the left brain's analytical processes: this cause now has that effect later, one is before two, and so on. But there may be more going on in the universe than linear time, as there is more than logic can make sense of. Making sense in language involves plotting a word by means of both the syntagmatic and paradigmatic axes (the one-after-the-other, and the wholeness from which aspects of thought and experience are derived), which are comparable to the x and the y axes that together account for the graphable point. The ungraphable, the ineffable, is not axial, not in time; it is not syntagmatic, and it transcends the notion of paradigm just as Socrates' Idea of the Good was beyond even the other Forms. *Gravity's Rainbow* does not occur at the "pure light of the zero," nor at ground zero; it does not attempt to "represent by its coordinates," as Wittgenstein said, "a figure that contradicts the laws of space."[91] It shows one ascent that is "betrayed to Gravity"[92] or mortal failure, and it generates some enthusiasm both for transcendence and for natural freedom, but it does not suggest which of these perspectives will prevail. It maps the possibilities, in parallel and in series.

On first page and last, the novel presents its story and the world as "all theatre" and through dreams; everything it presents might be considered a hyperextended dream, a reflexive instant sliced into the delta-t of events, Maya. Should the Rocket fall, time would stop; it would be transcendence or detonation; the novel is a dream that happens before, or a fiction suspended between dreams.

The "last image" on the movie screen is of a familiar face in its dream of eternity, seeing "the point of light" in the "true moment of shadow." The Lone Ranger is not going to show up, but neither is the Rocket going to impact. Pynchon leaves the reader with the option of joining in a hymn whose imagery is hopeful in a Puritan/Herero/Tarot paradoxically integrated sort of way, but which is also presented within an image of media control of the audience, "Follow the bouncing ball."[93] Zero and One are no longer flickering one after another in the binary language of the movie shutter; the imagery of the fiction has stopped. But the Plot vs. Counterforce dialectic is continued up to the last instant, as is that of the Zero of the white page and the One of the narrator's voice. The reader can quit yelling *"Start*-the-*show!"* and investigate what it might mean to be free of the bouncing ball.

CHAPTER FIVE

The Mind of the Text

I am the silence that is incomprehensible . . .
I am the utterance of my name.
— *Thunder, Perfect Mind*
The Gnostic Gospels

When the "show" stops, the audience notices the theatre.

Because it is possible to argue that *stopping the world* allows a direct perception of the nagual to supplant the world-description of the tonal, or that to recognize oneness with the universe is to escape the tyranny of the world-description of Maya, it makes sense to suggest that a fiction that suspends belief in its own system of illusions creates a void that can be occupied by another category of perception. The complaint that there is nothing really going on in self-conscious fiction ("Come-*on! Start*-the-*show!*") is a function of metaphysical and political conditioning as much as it is the reflection of a natural desire to be entertained. Most good stories take us both out of and into ourselves, and re-flexive fiction does much the same thing by taking us into and out of itself.

Offering a volume of blank pages would be like selling seats in an empty theatre. Even in the most self-conscious fiction, however, the show never completely stops; although its focus is (to borrow Eliot's metaphor) "the still point of the turning world,"[1] it is nevertheless a dance. No silence discusses the ineffable. Silence is, in any case, a conceptual or metaconceptual category rather than a sensory event; deprived of outside stimulation, the ear will hear its own blood flow. Even John Cage's famous four minutes and thirty-odd seconds of programmed silence (a period in which a piano is not played) is an exercise in noticing the "musical" quality of those unprogrammed sounds that come to occupy the concert hall and an occasion to redefine what is meant by "music." Books with blank pages are sold, but mostly to be used as journals: they have an unstructuredness that often prompts self-examination. More to the point here are the lacunae in *Tristram Shandy* and the resonant blank page that is the "Sappho" entry in Monique Wittig and Sande Zeig's *Lesbian Peoples: Material for a Dictionary.*

The literature of the ineffable is always a literature, and this book has been attempting to deal not so much with the unnamable itself as with what happens within texts that try to name it. (For years people have been asking me whether this book would be blank!) Another reason it is appropriate that these texts not be silent is that to recognize Maya is not to abolish it but to learn how to live with it; it is to be in the world but not of it, to adopt a certain attitude toward illusion. The point of Ron Sukenick's *The Death of the Novel and Other Stories,* for instance, is not that the artist has nothing to say except that he is writing but that reality and imagination are mutually enriching and mutually sustaining categories; in some of his stories, art and life are symbiotic, while in some, they create each other. In the Kabbalist terms borrowed by Edmond Jabès, the "black fire" of the Torah is written on the "white fire" of the silent parchment; the unsaid allows and underlies the saying. Both the still point and the white fire can be taken as metaphors for the "underlying ground of Being" (to borrow from Heidegger), and the texts to be discussed in this chapter are those that attempt to allow the silences at their centers to come to the reader's intuitive attention.

So far this book has concentrated on two narrative patterns that arise in response to the difficulty of discussing the silence: secondary first-person narration and the literature of the simultaneous self. The first has the advantage of displacement, allowing the author to present a framed dramatization of the experience of vision—an advantage shared by the "telescopic" and "fencing-in" strategies of the literatures of myth, horror, and failure. The second brings the inquiry closer to home, casting the metaphysical hero and the observing verbal consciousness as aspects of the same being. Each of these devices makes it possible to write around the experience of wordlessness, filtering the insights and describing their effects. The question now is what happens when the filters are set aside and the telescope is collapsed, when the distinctions among the levels of the self are recognized only in the instant of their vanishing, when the self overtly attempts to confront its entire being—an attempt that, for a narrator within a fiction, necessarily includes an acknowledgment of textuality. This inquiry will involve a look at the beginnings of stream of consciousness narration in the eighteenth-century novel; a demonstration of the almost inevitable reflexivity of fictions that imitate the processes of consciousness; and a suggestion that in the radical fictions and semiotics of contemporary feminism, in which the pretextual self is both a quest object and a prodding "absence" that motivates a reexamination of all structures, the political as well as the psychological and philosophical implications of self-conscious narration are clarified.

1. LOGOS, DIFFERENCE, AND THE "SECRET" OF THE INEFFABLE

We say amisse,
This or that is:
Thy word is all, if we could spell.
—George Herbert, "The Flower"

The "film we have not learned to see" is always with us. It is often said that "the breath is the life," and this is meant in a double sense: the act of breathing, and the presence of spirit. All living things "breathe"; whether or not they me-

213

tabolize oxygen, as open systems they participate in a chemistry of exchange with their environments. Attention to the act of breathing can be useful (in yoga, for instance) as a means of focusing on the absolute present and eventually of recognizing the God-presence inspired/breathed into man. A series of breaths can in no way explain Being but may help lead the breather to a clarifying experience. The systemically self-conscious speech act may, in a similar manner, open on a manifestation—or a sense of the presence—of its own underlying ground of Being, the white fire. Even if the circumference of this unexpressed presence appears to be nowhere, its center—as St. Bonaventure observed of the conception of God in the universe—will be everywhere.[2] Although this is not commonly recognized as an aspect of the experience of reading self-conscious fiction, a comparable holistic vision has been central to nearly every major religion for thousands of years; and it is legitimate, I think, to apply some of the religious terms and insights to what I am suggesting is a comparable system—as they have recently begun to be applied within psychology and physics. From Sufism to Zen, from Jesus ("The kingdom of Heaven is within") to the Upanishads, it is taught that the route to vision is inward and that one of its aspects is a direct experience of an inner, ego-free awareness, a transpersonal completeness and neutral inner mastery that vanish into a sudden perception of absolute unity: the self as universe, the universe as self.

This is more than a roundabout justification for investigating the metaphysics of first-person reflexive fiction, but it will serve. Textuality is the functional equivalent of mortal perspective; the limits of its language are the limits of its world. The limits of human perspective are those of experience, and not all experience can be set out in terms. The *Tractatus* falls within the category of what Stanley Fish calls "self-consuming artifacts" in that it leads the reader past what it can say, obliterating its absolute authority as it proceeds.[3] Mortal consciousness may also be a self-consuming artifact. The signifying system of a text may—and in the novels I have chosen for discussion, regularly does—attempt to project an understanding of the being the text manifests, which is most easily localized in its narrating persona. Although it can stop the inquiry at the point of finding a name (David Copperfield, for instance), or go further into a locus of ambiguity ("Call me Ishmael"), many texts take the risk of proceeding even further, at the risk of annihilation or nonsense, in search of the irreducible selfness that makes speech possible, in search of the spirit that breathes. As a text confronts the limits of its system, certain insights become possible and the sense and strategy of the whole may be transmuted. This "literature of consciousness" points not to the apparent dead end of having nothing but talking to talk about, and not to terminal narcissism, but to the foundations of a humble and brilliant self-awareness, to a literature of enlightenment. This does not mean the enlightenment associated with any particular religion so much as it suggests the groundwork of a new sense of textuality—but it may well contribute to the authentic self-knowledge of the reader.

Self-consciousness offers a link between Leni's "different coordinate systems," between sequence and synchrony, between textuality and silence. A more familiar link is the term "Logos," which attempts to point to a link between Being★ and Saying. Before tracing the growth of the literature of consciousness from Samuel Richardson to Edmond Jabès, and its implications for the literature of radical feminism, let us take a brief look at some aspects of the thought of Hegel, Heidegger, and Derrida.

In her Introduction to Heidegger's *Identity and Difference,* Joan Stambaugh points out that "we cannot leave metaphys-

---

★Throughout this chapter, Being is capitalized to refer to "the underlying ground of Being" or a comparable absolute; in lower case, it signifies individuated consciousness.

ics by a series of reasoned conclusions. We must simply leap out of it."[4] Metaphysics, which incorporates ontology and theology into a potentially unified discourse,[5] constantly threatens to obliterate Heidegger's hard-won distinctions—and the more Heidegger attempts to reject metaphysics, the more he founds an even more essential metaphysics, based both on an insistence on a difference—or holding back, "perdurance"—that allows things to happen (comparable to Pynchon's "delta-t") and on the fundamentality of Being in general.[6] Although he rigorously avoids "mysticism" as well as any "vicious subjectivizing of the totality of entities,"[7] Heidegger continually addresses the same questions that the mystics do and comes close to arguing analogies to their insights—that fundamental Being is actualized in time, for instance.[8] Whereas many Western philosophers find they cannot reason themselves *into* a metaphysical position, and that language is necessarily addressed to the facts of logic, Heidegger declares that Western languages are basically metaphysical, an insight to which he may well have been led by his scrutiny of the terms "Being" and "Being-there," through all their tangled mirrorings:

> That difficulty lies in language. Our Western languages are languages of metaphysical thinking, each in its own way. It must remain an open question whether the nature of Western languages is in itself marked with the exclusive brand of metaphysics, and thus marked permanently by onto-theo-logic, or whether these languages offer other possibilities of utterance—and that means at the same time of a telling silence. The difficulty to which thoughtful utterance is subject has appeared often enough in the course of this seminar. The little word "is," which speaks everywhere in our language, and tells of Being even where It does not appear expressly, contains the whole destiny of Being.[9]

One reason Heidegger finds it difficult to make a nonmetaphysical statement about Being is that he admits into his vocabulary the term "Logos," which is not only the root of "logic" but also an appeal to "what is meant."[10] What is meant cannot always be adequately formulated, and this leaves Heidegger in the position of attempting to refute Hegel's *Phenomenology of the Spirit,* for instance, in a language that does not have Wittgenstein's built-in safeguards against "nonsense."[11] This make his work especially fascinating, almost heroic in the manner of Beckett, where insight and a sense of rules seem to clash beneath the sentence. The difference between acknowledging the existence of God and demonstrating the "precomprehended question of Being" may simply be one of perspective. When (in *The Question of Being*) Heidegger finds that man, as "Being-there," is the "zone" where the question of Being—necessarily answered in advance if the question is to be asked—is asked, and finds the answer given not only in advance but "nonverbally, nonnominally, and without agency," he insists that this is (to quote Gayatri Spivak) "not mysticism. It is the baffling result of an examination of the obvious, the lifting of the most natural forgetfulness."[12]

Although Heidegger would resist the notion, it is possible to relate such ubiquitous forgetfulness to the action of Maya (or its Kabbalist complement, Malkhuth, or Sufism's Mukti) or to follow both Wittgenstein and Buddha in considering these limits of apprehension to be functions of operating within a system. To stop forgetting may be to transcend or bypass the system and to find that at least one basic religious assertion is obvious: that absolute Being is precomprehended and manifests itself in the process and continum of space, time, matter, and energy. We shall return to this question of the simplicity and obviousness of the conversion experience in connection with Derrida's notion of the sign as the site of a difference, or the trace of an absence, that opens the possibility of thought.

Before continuing with Heidegger, however, it is important to give some idea of the philosophy with which he was embattled and to suggest, through a quick look at Hegel and

Lacan, just how embattled the concept of the self is in Western philosophy. After all, it is a simple matter to find in spiritual writings any number of endorsements of the existence of the absolute self; the twofold challenge is, on the one hand, to do direct "research" on one's own inner being, and on the other, to integrate poetic and spiritual assertions with the more scientific investigations of philosophy and psychology as well as with the revelatory tropes of literature.

Hegel's primary orientation was Romantic, and from Goethe to Schiller, his favorite poets were concerned with the integration of the rational and the sensuous as well as with the metaphysical spectrum of the self. In the twentieth century, Hegel's writings on logic and on the dialectical aspects of history have been far more respected than has the spiritual conviction that was the foundation and end-point of those writings. It is with the more or less discredited aspects of Hegel's philosophy that I find myself in agreement.

Hegel considered the dialectic of history to be a process in which the *Geist* (absolute Spirit) strove for self-consciousness. As long as time and history continue, Spirit expresses itself as the spirit of a particular epoch (the *Zeitgeist* or time spirit). The "thesis" of the French monarchy, for instance, gives rise to the "antithesis" of the French Revolution, and the conflict between thesis and antithesis results in a "synthesis"—in this oversimplified example, that of Napoleon—which becomes in its turn a new thesis. The dialectic continues until a final synthesis is reached, and that synthesis is the absolute self-awareness of Spirit. It is at that nearly inconceivable point that history would end. Although this view of history was inspired by Hegel's Christianity, it has great similarity to Shankara's notion that the goal of the universal game is for the "many" to realize that they are masked cells of the "All"—in other words, for Spirit to come to absolute awareness of its nature. (It is not enough for the universe to be One; it wants to *know* that it is One.) Hegel found the greatest value in works of art that achieved self-consciousness without vanishing into silence, works that dealt in a mortal or sensuously embodied context with the ultimately nonphysical "Idea" they strove to represent. He respected works whose form most closely mirrored their content, and found a modified religious and philosophical expression in those works whose "Idea" was spirit:

> But inasmuch as the task of art is to represent the Idea to direct perception in sensuous shape, and not in the form of thought or pure spirituality as such, and seeing that this work of representation has its value and dignity in the correspondence and unity of the two sides, i.e. of the Idea and its plastic embodiment, it follows that the level and excellency of art in attaining a realization adequate to its Idea must depend upon the grade of inwardness and unity with which Idea and shape display themselves as fused into one.
>
> Thus the higher truth is spiritual being that has attained a shape adequate to the conception of spirit. This is what furnishes the principle of division for the science of art. For before the mind can attain the true notion of its absolute essence, it has to traverse a course of stages whose ground is in this Idea itself; and to this evolution of the content with which it supplies itself, there corresponds an evolution, immediately connected therewith, of the plastic forms of art, under the shape of which the mind as artist presents to itself the consciousness of itself.[13]

In the light of these remarks, it is possible to construct a dialectical history of literary form characterized by an increasing self-consciousness. The most advanced works would be those in which "the mind as artist presents to itself the consciousness of itself." That would, at least, be the most advanced concept available in the Romantic period. The literature of consciousness can, however, be seen to have progressed beyond that point, to a stage in which the mind of the text presents to itself the consciousness of itself, displaying on an "as if" basis its independence from the mortal artist. Of course it is still "the mind as artist" that is of central interest, but in this case both artist and audience may confront and celebrate an artifact that displays a greater degree of self-consciousness than is found in a work whose ontology appeals back to that of the artist. Whether or not Hegel envisioned a work like *The Book of Questions* or *The Unnamable* when making the following statement, he did provide a rationale for interpreting in spiritual terms the quality of systemic self-consciousness found there:

> The highest characteristic of spirit is self-consciousness. . . . The subject recognizes the absolute substance, in which it has to annul or lose itself, as being at the same time *its* essence, *its* substance, in which, therefore, self-consciousness is inherently contained. It is this unity, reconciliation, restoration of the subject and of its self-consciousness, the positive feeling of possessing a share in, of partaking in this absolute, and making unity with it actually one's own—this abolition of the dualism, which constitutes the sphere of worship. Worship comprises this entire inward and outward action, which has this restoration to unity as its object.[14]

The "dualism" to which Hegel refers is that between self and "other," a split consciousness that arises as long as there is any distinction between "the knowing spirit" and the infinitude of God. As long as the knowing spirit thinks of God, "God, as Idea" becomes an object, and absolute self-consciousness cannot be said to exist. Absolute self-consciousness, then, because it cannot include the separations inherent in thought, is ineffable.[15]

This beings us to a qualified refutation of Lacan, who has maintained that there is no self outside the network of language and therefore no possible "abolition of the dualism" or "restoration to unity." The following is a relatively accurate and readable paraphrase of Lacan's basic concepts:

Lacan distinguishes three levels within human reality. The first level is nature, the third is culture. The intermediate level is that in which nature is transformed into culture. This particular level gives its structure to human reality—it is the level of the symbolic. The symbolic level, or order, includes both language and other systems which produce signification, but it is fundamentally structured by language.

Lacanian psychoanalysis is a theory of intersubjectivity, in the sense that it addresses the relationship(s) between "self" and "other" independently of the subjects who finally occupy these places. The symbolic order is a net of relationships. Any "self" is definable by its position within this net. . . . The symbolic order is in turn structured by language. . . .

Thus for Lacan, unlike Descartes, the subject is *not* the fundamental basis of cognitive processes. First, it is only one of many psychological functions. Second, it is not an innate function. It appears at a certain time in the development of the child and has to be constituted in a certain way. It can also be altered, stop functioning, and disappear. Being at the very center of what we perceive as our self, this function is invisible and unquestioned. To avoid the encrusted connotations of the term "subjectivity," Lacan calls this function "the imaginary." It must be understood in a literal way—it is the domain of images. . . .

The imaginary is constituted through a process which Lacan calls the mirror-phase. It occurs when the infant is six to eighteen months old and occupies a contradictory situation. On the one hand, it does not possess mastery of its body; the various segments of the nervous system are not coordinated yet. The child cannot move or control the whole of its body, but only isolated discrete parts. On the other hand, the child enjoys from its first days a precocious visual maturity. During this stage, the child identifies itself with the visual image of the mother or the person playing the part of the mother. Through this identification, the child perceives its own body as a unified whole by analogy with the mother's body. The notion of a unified body is thus a fantasy before being a reality. It is an image that the child receives from outside.

Through the imaginary function, the respective parts of the body are united so as to constitute one body, and therefore to constitute somebody: one self. Identity is thus a formal structure which fundamentally depends upon an identification. Identity is one effect, among others, of the structure through which images are formed: the imaginary. Lacan thus operates a radical desacralization of the subject: the "I," the "ego," the "subject" are nothing but images, reflections. . . . The "subject" is no more than a unifying reflection.

The disappearance of the imaginary results in schizophrenia.[16]

The essential limitation of Lacan's "radical desacralization" is that although it may well be an accurate analysis of the formation and inaccessibility of the imaginary, it does not present any evidence or rationale for dismissing the existence of absolute subjectivity. It is primarily useful as a means of understanding how the "tabula rasa" of the conscious self arrives at a self-concept. In that light, it is effective as a rationale for the linguistically determined mind's inability to find words to express the nature of subjectivity. From the perspective of the imaginary, the self must remain ineffable. Lacan can serve as a bridge, then, between Hegel and both Heidegger and Derrida, but only if one is willing to admit into discussion the possible existence of innate subjectivity and its independence from the limits and proper functioning of the imaginary.

This quarrel with Lacan does, of course, have implications for literary criticism. Derrida, for instance, integrates aspects of Heidegger, Nietzsche, and Lacan into his conviction that there is no absolute center (of the self or anything else) and therefore that language is always held back from absolute saying; one circles around the absent center and, appropriately, never expresses that center. This leads him to what I take to be a serious misreading of Jabès. *The Book of Questions,* as we shall see later on, is self-consciously organized around the problem of the absence of an absolute knowledge of God—and by extension, the absence of an absolute knowledge of the existence of "the Book." ("The Book" in this context is *The Book of Questions,* history, the world, and the vehicle of subjective expression—the mind of the text.) Because it is so rigorous in what it excludes from the possibility of conscious affirmation, *The Book of Questions* would look the same whether or not Jabès believed in the existence of God. Derrida's conviction of the absence of any absolute center leads him to praise Jabès' expression of the nature of the centerless world/discourse. But it is entirely possible that what Jabès has done is to express the nature of the centered world whose center is ineffable. By the same logic, it is possible to analyze Darl's madness in *As I Lay Dying* as a schizophrenic reaction to the loss of the imaginary *without* ruling out the further and related possibility that Darl's madness represents the inability of his imaginary to deal adequately with his having glimpsed the transcendent aspects of the narrative system whose absent center is his dead mother or some unnamable narratorial consciousness.

All that is to anticipate considerably the arguments that will appear later in this chapter. At this point, I would like to suggest quite simply that a reexamination of Hegel may prove useful in grounding our discussion of the goals and processes of self-consciousness. Ihab Hassan has argued that "The (post)structuralist metaphysic of absence and its ideology of fracture refuse holism almost fanatically. But I want to recover my metaphoric sense of wholes."[17] I think Hassan is correct there, and trust that we can now return to Heidegger with a perspective that may help us discover an ideology of holism without doing too much violence to his and Derrida's more valuable insights into the nature of language.

One of Heidegger's crucial terms, "Saying" or "essential Saying," is closely related to Wittgenstein's notion that logical form is shown or mirrored in propositions and that "What finds its reflection in language, language cannot represent. . . . What *can* be shown, *cannot* be said."[18] In his essay, "The Way to Language," Heidegger writes:

> *The essential being of language is Saying as Showing.* Its showing character is not based on signs of any kind; rather, all signs arise from a showing within whose realm and for whose purposes they can be signs. . . . Self-showing appearance is the mark of the presence and absence of everything that is present, of every kind and rank. Even when Showing is accomplished by our human saying, even then this showing, this pointer, is preceded by an indication that it will let itself be shown.[19]

In this sense, the fact of language constitutes a Saying; language as a system—reflecting an underlying construct of what can present itself to be said—presents itself in much the same way Being does, and both are equally manifest and equally unable to account for themselves by subsystemic means or terms. Although particular signs convey particular meanings, Saying is an indexical sign for itself: it shows the realm of language. So irreducible is Saying that without it, Being cannot find "presence," cannot manifest itself to our awareness; in this sense, language does not simply name something but metaphysically precipitates it.

Without alluding to the Gospel of John, Heidegger finds in "Logos" an etymological link between Saying and Being that may prove useful in sorting out the question of just what it is that a self-conscious work might be conscious of. In his essay, "Words," he argues:

As mystery, the word remains remote. As a mystery that is experienced, the remoteness is near. . . . The treasure that never graced the poet's land is the word for the being of language. . . .

The word's rule springs to light as that which makes the thing be a thing. The word begins to shine as the gathering which first brings what presences to its presence.

The oldest word for the rule of the word thus thought, for Saying, is *logos:* Saying which, in showing, lets beings appear in their "it is."

The same word, however, the word for Saying, is also the word for *Being,* that is, for the presencing of beings. Saying and Being, word and thing, belong to each other in a veiled way, a way which has hardly been thought and is not to be thought out to the end.

All essential Saying hearkens back to this veiled mutual belonging of Saying and Being, word and thing. Both poetry and thinking are distinctive Saying in that they remain delivered over to the mystery of the word as that which is most worthy of their thinking, and thus ever structured in their kinship.[20]

According to Vine's *Expository Dictionary of New Testament Words,* there are two basic terms that can be translated as "word": Logos and Rhema. Rhema "denotes that which is spoken, what is uttered in speech or writing"—in the singular, "a word"; in the plural, "speech" or "discourse"; and in relation to the Bible, a particular fragment of Scripture. Logos "denotes the expression of thought, not the mere name of an object" as well as "the Personal Word, a title of the Son of God"; in relation to the Bible, it refers to Scripture as a whole, the word and "revealed will" of God (and in this final sense it refers to the universe).

Although any novel or speech act is in the first place an instance of Rhema, to the extent that it probes the question of its own ability to speak—probes "the mystery of the word," whose "remoteness is near"—it attempts to become an instance of "essential Saying." It tries to uncover the Logos that is precomprehended in Rhema, the sense of Being that it cannot declare completely but that it may manifest or show. The "veiled mutual belonging of Saying and Being" is the quest object of self-conscious discourse; Logos is the etymological intersection of Being and essential Saying. The being to which Heidegger refers Logos is "the presencing of beings"; it is the Being that is manifest and (up to a point) knowable, rather than the ultimate ground of Being.

For Saint John, however, the latter is one legitimate sense of the term "Logos," which is seen as the indispensable basis of the universe:

> In the beginning was the Word [Logos], and the Word was with God, and the Word was God. This is the One who was in the beginning with God. Through Him everything came into being and without Him nothing that exists came into being. In Him was Life, and the Life was the Light of men. The Light shines in the darkness and the darkness has not overcome it.[21]

John goes on to make the connection between Logos (as Christ) and "the true Light that illumines every person"[22]— the link between the energy of the higher self (or what is sometimes called Christ-consciousness) and the essential Being of the universe. In this respect, his gospel is not only a site of continuity among Christianity, Gnosticism, and the mystery religions but also a means of integrating Hinduism, wave mechanics, and systemically self-conscious fiction. Rhema shows Logos (the expression of thought), and Logos attempts to trace itself back to its more primary signified (that through which everything comes into being): the Light that is outside Plato's cave as well as the originator and dispeller of shadows, because it is also "the Light of men," indistinguishably without and within.

We can dance back and forth among all these systems because they all tend to deal, finally, with similar insights and a similar goal: to trace the language of beings back to Being. The difference between Rhema and the ultimate Logos (or transcendental signified) will always remain a basic property of language and of knowable being. As Saint Augustine observed:

> Have we spoken or announced anything worthy of God? Rather I feel that I have done nothing but wish to speak: if I have spoken, I have not said what I wished to say. Whence do I know this, except because God is ineffable? If what I said were ineffable, it would not be said. And for this reason God should not be said to be ineffable, for when this is said something is said. And a contradiction in terms is created, since if that is ineffable which cannot be spoken, then that is not ineffable which can be called ineffable. This contradiction is to be passed over in silence rather than resolved verbally. For God, although nothing worthy may be spoken of Him, has accepted the tribute of the human voice and wished us to take joy in praising Him with our words. In this way he is called *Deus*. Although He is not recognized in the noise of these two syllables, all those who know the Latin language, when this sound reaches their ears, are moved to think of a certain most excellent immortal nature.[23]

Between this meditation and the last sentence of the *Tractatus* not a great deal has changed: there is still much to be "passed over in silence." Augustine's contradiction can be dealt with only by considering "ineffable" a nonsensical term, a sign without a meaningful signified. What Augustine allows in prayer (and Beckett in fiction) is what Wittgenstein will not legitimate in philosophy: the use of failed language, used with a continual awareness of its inability to signify the transcendental and validated as a source of enjoyment and prompter of a state of mind. (It must be remembered, of course, that Wittgenstein's construction of the *Tractatus* as a self-consuming artifact enabled him to say things that were eventually pointed out as nonsensical and that the rigorously nonmetaphysical philosophy he recommended was not achieved in that book.) Within the context of an awareness of ineffability, the failure of language can be taken to validate "the tribute of the human voice," as the tribute is validated by the intuited authenticity of what its words cannot realize. As Saint Paul says in I Corinthians, the fragmentary is useful only until "the perfect is come." More than useful, it is in most cases all we have.

Systemic self-consciousness shows that for a word-system and for a mind, probing how and whence and when the Saying happens means probing the sayer, the being that speaks and acts. The link that this posits between the self-regarding text and the inward-turning mind opens the possibility of a shared self-consciousness, an existential compatibility, an analogous route to vision. It becomes possible to speak of "the mind of the text," a notion that goes beyond what is normally meant by "stream of consciousness" even though both of these textual systems imitate minds rather than have autonomy. The mind of the text is seen to be engaged in an act, however imitative, of self-declaration; it appears to be aware that it is a text as well as the process of some narrator's or character's mentation.

This acknowledging that it is a text is essential simply because it *is* a text. What many people dislike or find trivial about self-conscious fiction is that this acknowledgment of textuality can seem like a dead end, as if Federman or Beckett were solving only the problems of texts, raising tempests in teapots. Such readers miss the point of analogy, that we all work with what we actually are, and that for a text to pretend to be something else entirely—though this can generate many wonderful stories—is on some level to evade both the facts and an essential task.

Systemic self-consciousness refers, then, to the text's awareness, usually expressed through the narrator (who may at first appear to be simply a character but who comes to be seen as a vehicle for the text's imitation of self-expression), that it is a limited system. The text can say that it is limited only as long as it can say anything. In the books to be discussed in this chapter, the ineffable is not so much urgently prodding from behind the forehead of a white whale as it is present and silent at the center of personal/textual being. *This* silence is confronted not just when language fails to describe some outside and distant other but when language fails to describe itself and its own showing—when consciousness focuses on its own presence and activity and is unable to do more than assert them. When a text pays attention to the limits of its means of expression and the limits of its being—when its self-consciousness attempts self-expression—then the ineffable is most urgently at issue.

The text's awareness that there is a silence outside its expression and central to its being can simply be presented, or it can be pushed through. On "the other side" is the silent wholeness of Being. The point of the mind at which contradictions cease to conflict and differences merge is the point at which language vanishes, where it ceases to maintain its own inner divisions, where saying yields to showing. At that point (or stage of inner awareness), language's mechanism of fragmentation into terms and integration into statements might be perceived as inappropriate to an expression of the nature of absolute and irreducible unity were it not for the fact that the mind given over entirely to that unity is incapable of recognizing or analyzing, let alone of employing, *any* fragmentative process.

The self can "express" itself at that point only by being. And since the nature of its Being is the content of its insight, to *be* is an appropriate way to show—not to explain—what has been found. Being becomes recognized as *the* transcendental presentation, the showing of what *is* and of what can never be sorted out. From that perspective (looking around us at all this being), it is as if all of this has always been understood. As we begin to ask the right question, we notice the obvious answer; the "problem" vanishes.

Having clarified to the best of my ability what it means to say that the ineffable is self-evident, I would now like to set forward what I take to be the reason that the ineffable is ineffable. This insight, once achieved, is so obvious and simple that I cannot help but think that it is true. To explain it, however, requires a deconstruction of Derrida. (Because of its more ready comprehensibility, I will be citing not "Linguistics and Grammatology"[24] but Gayatri Spivak's paraphrase of its essential points.)

Although a sign is conventionally thought of as the point where signifier and signified are joined, Derrida argues that "the structure of reference works and can go on working not because of the identity between these so-called component parts of the sign, but because of their relationship of difference."[25] *Tree* declares, to the extent that it is perceived as a sign, that there is a difference between that leafy wooden thing outside and the signifier "tree."

> Armed with this simple yet powerful insight—powerful enough to "deconstruct the transcendental signified"—that the sign, phonic as well as graphic, is a structure of difference, Derrida suggests that what opens the possibility of thought is not merely the question of being, but also the never-annulled difference from "the completely other." Such is the strange "being" of the sign: half of it always "not there" and the other half always "not that." The structure of the sign is determined by the trace or track of that other which is forever absent. This other is of course never to be found in its full being. . . . Heidegger's ~~Being~~ might point at an inarticulable presence. Derrida's ~~trace~~ is the mark of the absence of a presence, an always already absent present, of the lack at the origin that is the condition of thought and experience.[26]

What Spivak means by "not there" and "not that" is that *tree* reminds us that the tree is "not there" (absent from the signifier) and that the signified, which is a concept-on-call rather than the thing itself, is "not that" (the physical tree is absent from the signified). Her related point is that signified and signifier are not each other and can never completely stand in for each other; their relation depends on their being different not only from the tree but also from each other. But because it makes my point easier to express and amounts to the same problem, I will reverse the terms, modify them slightly, and say: "tree" (signifier) is "not this" and the wooden leafy thing is "not here."[27] (It might help to imagine that one is in the presence of a physical tree and saying "tree." The signifier is "not this," one says, pointing at the tree; the signified is "not here," one says, contemplating the sign.) To show the sign as the site of an absence rather than the achievement of a presence, it might be appropriate to print "~~tree~~," to give the sign and take it back, except that this introduces problems of legibility. "~~Tree~~" is an instance of writing "under erasure," and Derrida asks us to consider all signs as being given and taken away in just this sense; this is not a special case of problematical signification but is, in fact, what Derrida means by the term "writing."

Without getting into a superfluous analysis of Derrida's complex system of thought, I would like to endorse his notions of the sign as the site of a paradoxical absence and his concept of *"différance"* (which carries the double sense of "differing" and "deferring"—an endless putting off of absolute presence and unity).[28] My only quarrel here is with his Nietzschean concept of "the lack at the origin that is the condition of thought and experience." His description of the nature of language is, I think, accurate, and the nature of language certainly dictates the conditions of thought. The origin, other, or absolute center will not "be found in its full being" *within this system.* Whether or not there *is* a transcendental signified or an ultimate ground of Being cannot—because of the action of *différance*—ever be established by either language or logical consciousness, as Derrida realizes. The problem is the concept of "experience." Derrida follows Freud in putting the psyche under erasure,[29] making con-

231

sciousness a process of *différance;* and as a semiotician, he perhaps unwittingly concentrates most of his analysis of conscious function on the left hemisphere of the brain. But although the left hemisphere, and perhaps even the unconscious, may always be determined by the limits and processes that Derrida posits, it remains possible for the right hemisphere (whether considered as a literal body part or as a metaphor for certain potentials of human consciousness) to achieve holistic intuitions, and there is no telling of what insights the transpersonal consciousness or "Beingness" is capable. Experience is a master category.

Language and thought operate, to return to Saint Paul, "indistinctly in a mirror" (sometimes translated as "through a glass, darkly") and are thereby capable of great mortal precision; direct spiritual insight is a matter of seeing "face to face." The visionary experience can be described in such nonsensical formulations as "being in a nowhere that is everywhere," but in the instant of its happening it would be more appropriate to use a pure expletive: ! The essence of the visionary experience—as, for instance, that of being in the presence of a simple achieved Oneness—is that the signifier is THIS and the signified HERE. "This is It!" would be verbose. And such insights are not thoughts. We have to "fall" from this point for thought and difference and deferrence (which sustain each other) to be possible.

The notion of the signifier's being "this" and the signified "here" is an ideal of language, and is in some ways the naïveté that Saussure reproved. Real human language depends on the relationship of *différance* between a signifier that is "not this"/ and a signified that is /"not here," and thus it is not equipped to express the visionary situation. The irony in this is wonderful, because a language in which the sign is fully achieved and is the site not of difference, perdurance, and division but of unity is a language of absolute expressivity—and one in which expression is unnecessary.[30] This is why so many mystical or metaphysical statements are simple, obvious, and tautological.[31] This is why they "say nothing." In the presence of the ineffable Oneness, there would be no "other" to mandate terminology, and no question of *différance*. If this experience is possible, it is not linguistic. Language limits its world. THIS/HERE, the completely and already expressed, is ineffable, and "not this"/"not here"— this failure, this referentiality—is language. The ineffable is characterized by absolute presence, the effable by *différance*. It is not that the ineffable is an illegitimate concern, but that language deals properly and only with what is not ultimately present. It is not that language fails to express the ineffable, but that the effable is the province of that failure which is language.

2. THE STREAM OF SELF-CONSCIOUSNESS

You are the one who writes and the one who is written.
                                        —Edmond Jabès, *The Book of Questions*

The term "stream of consciousness" was first coined by William James[32] and first critically applied to literature by the philospher/novelist May Sinclair in her 1915 review of the first volume of Dorothy Richardson's *Pilgrimage*.[33] It has come to refer to a method of presenting, as if directly and without mediation, the flowing or jagged sequence of the thoughts, perceptions, preconscious associations, memories, half-realized impressions, and so on, of one or more characters—the attempt, in fiction, to imitate the complete mental life as it manifests itself in the ongoing present. Its most accomplished practitioners are Gertrude Stein, James Joyce, and Virginia Woolf, though there are works in which William Faulkner, Samuel Beckett, Manuel Puig, and Tillie Olsen exploit the technique almost to the point of transfiguration. Its origins, however, lie in eighteenth-century fiction, and Dorothy Richardson herself cited Goethe's acknowledgment of the precursors of *Wilhelm Meister:*

233

In the novel, reflections and incidents should be featured; in drama, character and action. The novel must proceed slowly, and the thought-processes of the principal figure must, by one device or another, hold up the development of the whole. . . . Grandison, Clarissa, Pamela, the Vicar of Wakefield, and Tom Jones himself, even where they are not acted upon, are still retarding personalities and all the incidents are, in a certain measure, modelled according to their thoughts.[34]

The earliest formal justification of the technique appears in Samuel Richardson's preface to *Clarissa* (1747–1748), a novel pretending to collate the correspondence of four characters over a twelve-month/seven-volume period:

> All the letters are written while the hearts of the writers must be supposed to be wholly engaged in their subjects (the events at the time generally dubious): so that they abound not only with critical situations, but with what may be called instantaneous descriptions and reflections. . . .
>
> "Much more lively and affecting," says one of the principal characters, "must be the style of those who write in the height of a present distress, the mind tortured by the pangs of uncertainty (the events then hidden in the womb of fate), than the dry, narrative, unanimated style of a person relating difficulties and dangers surmounted, can be; the relater perfectly at ease; and if himself unmoved by his own story, not likely greatly to affect the reader."[35]

Because these letters are written as the situation develops, each of them declares and keeps pace with the developing state of mind and more or less instantaneous reflections of each character. *Clarissa* does not offer a continuous present (of the sort often found in the interior monologues and perceptual montages of *Ulysses* or *The Waves*) but an example of what Gertrude Stein called "beginning again and again,"[36] a continual starting over that is to the flow of consciousness in the unfolding present as a series of motion picture frames is to the movement of which they generate an impression. Looking back on *Clarissa* from a perspective enriched by Borges, Beckett, Federman, Márquez, and Jabès, one can note that from its outset this mode tended toward the reflexive, for Richardson cites one of his own characters as an authority for (and commentator on) the technique and gives both preface and letter the same parentheses at the same point in the development of each argument ["(the events at the time generally dubious)" and "(the events then hidden in the womb of fate)"].

Stream of consciousness also involves, though not so consistently, a confrontation with the ineffable, since it presents the operations of consciousness to itself. Though verbal consciousness is of the knowable, we have learned from Derrida that any presence is (to the extent of our ability to analyze it) the trace of an absence; we can talk only about what is "not there." And while Derrida is willing to follow Nietzsche in not looking for the ultimate "Other," he also follows Freud in recognizing that consciousness is "not there" to be observed by the mind.[37] The literature of consciousness always presents this absence and often calls attention to the nature of what is, from a transcendental perspective, its own failure. It becomes most exciting in the moments when it realizes what it is unable to do.

There are two arresting modes of absence in *Clarissa,* one of them omnipresent and one climactic. Any letter posits that the correspondents are not in each others' presence. The writer writes to a person who is not there at the time—but when the letter is received, it is the writer who is not present. This makes any letter the hinge of a double absence, and in that sense, a model for the sign in general, charged with the burden of attempting to join signifier and signified. To write a letter is to be immersed in what one is saying and to generate an image of the addressee, but it is also to confront one's own absence in the letter's future. This is the omnipresent process in *Clarissa,* the battle between psychologically accurate reporting and the drama of separation; it is appropriate (and implicitly reflexive) that letters and letter writing are themselves as important in the plot as any of its other events. The climax of the novel is a letter that Clarissa cannot write.

After Clarissa is drugged and raped, Lovelace sends to Belford a transcription of a letter and ten "Papers."[38] They are offered as evidence of Clarissa's distress and might simply be taken as Richardson's way of recording a mind too upset to compose a formal letter (a Joycean advance on the unmediated presentation of the montage of consciousness[39]), something they certainly accomplish. But it is crucial that what they record is a moment of breakdown, Clarissa's awareness (signified by her having torn up the papers, which Lovelace has had retrieved) that she is unable to find words adequate to her violation or to her present self-concept.

Clarissa's attempts have been preceded by a long silence. Lovelace writes:

Last night, for the first time since Monday last, she got to her pen and ink: but she pursues her writing with such eagerness and hurry, as show too evidently her discomposure. . . .

Just now Dorcas tells me that what she writes she tears, and throws the paper in fragments under the table, either as not knowing what she does, or disliking it: then gets up, wrings her hands, weeps, and shifts her seat all round the room: then returns to her table, sits down, and writes again.

From *"Paper I. (Torn in two pieces.)":*

MY DEAREST MISS HOWE,—O what dreadful, dreadful things have I to tell you! But yet I cannot tell you neither. . . .

I sat down to say a great deal—my heart was full—I did not know what to say first—and thought, and grief, and confusion, and (O my poor head!) I cannot tell what—and thought, and grief, and confusion, came crowding so thick upon me; *one* would be first, *another* would be first, *all would* be first; so I can write nothing at all. Only that, whatever they have done to me, I cannot tell; but I am no longer what I was in any one thing. In any one thing did I say? Yes, but I am; for I am still, and I ever will be,

> Your true—

It is at the point when she is about to affirm her still being herself that Clarissa tears up the letter. "I am no longer what I was in any one thing" is the closest she comes to describing her violation, and the vagueness of that line indicates her horrific repulsion against what she is trying to express as well as a failure of terms.

In *"Paper II. (Scratched through, and thrown under the table.),"* Clarissa attempts to address her father, first asking his forgiveness, then bursting into: "My name is—I don't know what my name is! I never dare to wish to come into your family again!" In *Paper III* she tells a story about a lady and a wild animal, implying that the victim is more to blame than her attacker—for although the lady is torn to pieces, "the brute" at least acted according to "its own nature." *Paper IV* is addressed to herself, as if it took vicious pride in the humbling of "thou proud Clarissa Harlowe"; this is both an imitation of her sister Bella's anticipated tone (as *Paper V,* addressed to Bella, suggests—though it is clear that Clarissa is addressing herself in *Paper IV*) and a great insight into the psychology of victimization. Clarissa's world-view and self-concept are both fracturing at once; at this point, she tries to save the former at the expense of the latter: "I must have been so! [that is, headstrong, vain, and foolish] My fall had not else been permitted." In *Paper VI* she laments the "happy life" and proper wedding she will never have; in *Paper VII* she reviles Lovelace. *Papers VIII* and *IX* continue her attack on Lovelace in a more controlled tone. *Paper X*[40]

PAPER X.

LEAD me, where my own Thoughts themselves may lose me,
Where I may doze out what I've left of Life,
Forget myself; and that day's guilt! ——
Cruel remembrance!···how shall I appease thee?

——Oh! you have done an act
That blots the face and blush of modesty;
Takes off the rose
From the fair forehead of an innocent love,
And makes a blister there! ——

Then down I laid my head,
Down on cold earth, and for a while was dead;
And my freed Soul to a strange somewhere fled!
Ah! sottish soul! said I,
When back to its cage again I saw it fly,
Fool! to resume her broken chain,
And row the galley here again!
Fool! to that body to return,
Where it condemn'd and destin'd is to *mourn*.

O my Miss Howe! if thou hast friendship, help me,
And speak the words of peace to my divided soul,
That wars within me,
And raises ev'ry sense to my confusion.
I'm tott'ring on the brink
Of peace; and thou art all the hold I've left!
Assist me in the pangs of my affliction!

When honour's lost, 'tis a relief to die:
Death's but a sure retreat from infamy.

Then farewel, youth,
And all the joys that dwell
With youth and life!
And life itself, farewel!

For life can never be sincerely blest.
Heaven punishes the *Bad*, and proves the *Best*.

Death only can be dreadful to the bad:
To innocence 'tis like a bugbear dress'd
To frighten children. Pull but off the mask
And he'll appear a friend.

I could a tale unfold
Would harrow up thy soul!——

By swift misfortunes
How am I pursu'd!
Which on each other are,
Like waves, renew'd!

Paper X, from the first edition of *Clarissa*, 5: 239.

is as extraordinary as any of Sterne's black or blank pages, a collage of poetic fragments written every which way across the page (and printed by Richardson himself at those angles), some of which come from her reading while some are original (see figure). The first line is: "Lead me, where my own Thoughts themselves may lose me"; perpendicular to this is, "Death only can be dreadful to the bad"; there are ten stanzas in all. The one that is nearly upside down and veers obliquely toward the right margin is: "I could a tale unfold—/Would harrow up thy soul!——"(the point being, of course, that she cannot unfold it).

At this point, Lovelace—who is a conspicuously reflexive observer and in that perhaps incarnates Richardson's sublimated sense of complicity (Lovelace later defends his "plots" and his "recourse to *art*" [drugs][41])—breaks in with the letter Clarissa finally wròte him. This letter and the earlier "Papers" are charged with the energy of the unspeakable; in fact, Lovelace cannot bear to transcribe them himself, so he has Dorcas do it. In his mocking way, he had earlier called Clarissa's letter too "extravagant" to copy for Belford and said further that "the original is too much an original to let it go out of my hands." (It is the energy of absolute origin that *is* at stake here, despite Lovelace's attempt to let "original" mean "unusual" or "cute.") After going through the "Papers," he now says they are "too affecting" to copy and goes on to enclose Dorcas' transcript.

Through this final involuted and fragmented letter, Clarissa's anger shines. Although she keeps forgetting what she has to say (and the disorder of this letter is extremely moving), she nearly comes to terms with the change in herself, which is not so much a matter of virginity or even of honor as it is her change in self-concept, the feeling that she somehow deserved this punishment and therefore could never again be who she thought she was (good and clear). "Alas!" she writes, "you have killed my head among you—." The most affecting indication that she is no longer present to herself is her request in this letter that she may be shut away in "a private madhouse" where she may write letters that need not be sent.

Richardson, in his use of fragmented and chaotic texts to imitate Clarissa's disoriented consciousness, may or at least ought to have been indebted to Jonathan Swift's *A Tale of a Tub* (1710). Although Swift's book presents itself as a parody of "modern" pamphleteering, its unnamed authorial persona is so clearly a fiction and the bizarre course of his argument so ironic a critique of his mental state that *A Tale of a Tub* must be recognized as the first English novel, and a self-conscious one at that. It is no more an essay than *Pale Fire* is a critical edition.

Swift's purpose in *A Tale of a Tub* (a title that looks forward to Sterne's closing auto-critique of *Tristram Shandy* as the story of "a COCK and a BULL") is "to expose the Abuses and Corruptions in Learning and Religion."[42] His announced strategy is to address the former in the "Allegory of the Coats, and the three Brothers" and the latter "by way of Digressions."[43] The digressive chapters and prefatory apparatus, however, do not discuss these abuses so much as act them out, and it becomes evident that the "Author" (unlike Swift but very like Nabokov's Kinbote) is mad. His disorientation is a property of the system and is indistinguishably an aspect of the Author's consciousness and the result of his attempt to critique the structures within which he functions. His "Bookseller's" dedicatory chapter is an analysis of how dedications proceed and a recounting of how this one came to be written as well as a self-consuming example of a vacuous dedication; its abuses are magnified in the Author's subsequent dedication to "Prince Posterity," which is itself succeeded by "The Preface" and "The Introduction." The many footnotes (some not written by Swift) incorporated into the 1710 edition are, in this context, further self-declarations of egotistical scholarly vacuity, not only in the Author but also in the establishments this book critiques, and thus serve as manifestations by the text of its essential point. The sane consciousness—that of the ideal reader—is extrasystemic; the madness of the Author is less discussed than shown. After all the introductory chapters, "Once upon a Time"[44] has lost its innocence and become an as-if-unconscious—in our terms, hilariously self-conscious—indication or showing of the fall from simple clarity. The "Digression in Praise of Digressions" *says* that digressions are necessary because "the Society of Writers would quickly be reduced to a very inconsiderable Number, if Men were put upon making Books, with the fatal Confinement of delivering nothing beyond what is to the Purpose,"[45] but what it *shows* is that the Author has nothing "to the Purpose" to say. It is followed by a dramatically ironic (that is, as-if-unconscious) critique of the animating Spirit or Breath of the world as "Wind,"[46] which connotes a host of vanities from flatulence to empty discourse and which the reader recognizes as the animator and essential quality of the Author's argument as well as Swift's critique both of the Author and of mystical religions. This leads directly into the "Digression on . . . Madness."

In this Digression, the Author presents the "Modern" interpretation of madness as "a Disturbance or Transposition of the Brain, by Force of certain *Vapours* issuing up from the lower Faculties" and presents the loud whispering of the Modernists (concerning the apparent madness of one of Swift's critics, a friend of the Author) as reaching "up to the very Garret I am now writing in."[47] This suggests that the Author's writing site is analogous to the brain disordered by the rising gas of an uncreative and involuted culture, and hence that his text is a site of madness. When he attempts to analyze madness, there is a five-line gap in the text,[48] indicating not only that the Author is not clever enough to "unravel this knotty Point" but also that he has reached the limits of the system. His "Faculties" are strained "to their highest Stretch" here because his madness is unable to analyze itself. By the end of the chapter, he is able to indicate that his friends consider him mad and his writing therapeutic, only within the context of a disclaimer (which immedi-

ately follows another breakdown of the text, a two-line silence complete with an uncomprehending footnote and the
superscription *"Heark in your Ear"):*

> That even, I my self, the Author of these momentous
> Truths, am a Person, whose Imaginations are hard-
> mouth'd, and exceedingly disposed to run away with
> his *Reason,* which I have observed from long Experi-
> ence, to be a very light Rider, and easily shook off;
> upon which Account, my Friends will never trust me
> alone, without a solemn Promise, to vent my Specula-
> tions in this, or the like manner, for the universal Ben-
> efit of Human kind; which, perhaps, the gentle, cour-
> teous, and candid Reader, brimful of that *Modern*
> Charity and Tenderness, usually annexed to his *Office,*
> will be very hardly persuaded to believe.[49]

The Author's final chapter, "The Conclusion," does not
summarize his argument but observes its own process of
ending the book (which is, of course, a self-conscious showing of what the argument—the fact of pointless textuality—
has been, and *is* therefore a summary conclusion.) When he
says, "I am now trying an Experiment very frequent among
Modern Authors; which is, to *write upon Nothing,"*[50] he is
referring not to the ineffable (nor to the gaps in the text,
which show silence rather than address it), but to the fact
that he has nothing more to say and is still writing. It is
clear, however, that this critique of his own process, revealing his madness without being able to analyze it, is an intrasystemic attempt to describe the narrating system and that
the Author has been led to this exhaustion by the intracta-
bility of that system's limits. The subject he has exhausted is
himself.

The connection between psychological investigation and
systemic reflexivity begun by Swift and Richardson was
pursued by Laurence Sterne in *Tristram Shandy* (1759–1767)
after Henry Fielding had established the basic link between
the novel (*Tom Jones,* 1749) and the self-conscious epic (*Don*

Quixote, 1605–1615).[51] Arthur Schopenhauer, who made much of the implicit correspondences between Kantian idealism and Hinduism, considered *Don Quixote, Tristram Shandy, La Nouvelle Héloise,* and *Wilhelm Meister* "the best of all existing novels," not just because they stress "inner" over "outer" life but because they contain "as good as no action at all."[52]

What Sterne presents is a text that behaves like a mind, and in this respect, *Tristram Shandy* is not far removed from *A Tale of A Tub.* The structure of Sterne's novel is, following John Locke, that of the association of ideas: one scene or concept suggests another in a labyrinth of parentheses and interjections. The center of the novel, Tristram Shandy, is almost absent from the plot except as a catalyst (through his being born, for instance) for the other characters' potentially infinite conversations.

Whether or not Tristram is absent from the book is another question, however, since he is very much present as the narrator: first, because he continually reminds the "Lady" reader that she (among others) is reading his book and that he is writing it; and second, because the events and meditations are presented in the order he deems fit. (Even if Tristram did not continually point this out and take responsibility for his shifts of attention, the reader's impatience or delight would continually raise the issue.) In the second sense especially, one is reading the contents of Tristram's mind, which *are* his "Life and Opinions." Extended and codified, this is the method of Robbe-Grillet's *Jealousy,* in which the narrator is so radically present—his perceptions and associations being the novel's only manifest content—that he appears at first to be absent from the plot. What Robbe-Grillet leaves out, of course, is Sterne's elegant and deliberate play between the narrator and his real or imagined audience.

What Sterne also presents is a mind that behaves like a text, and this is where the question of Tristram's "presence" becomes most interesting. *Tristram Shandy* teaches its reader

243

to think in systemic terms: to back off and regard the whole text as a mind or being in process and to advance into the labyrinth of cross-references to find that there is no discernible Minotaur (the sequence is infinitely self-deferring in a way Heidegger, Nietzsche, and Derrida would enjoy; the absolute ground of Being is not *in* the text). Tristram's center is nowhere and his circumference everywhere; he is a property of the text as a w/hole. By foregrounding the writing and reading that are always going on, Tristram does not allow us to consider his text as simply *like* a mind in process (much of Richardson's aim); one always remembers that it is a book, too, and that Tristram runs parallel with it:

> I will not finish that sentence till I have made an observation upon the strange state of affairs between the reader and myself, just as things stand at present—an observation never applicable before to any one biographical writer since the creation of the world, but to myself—and I believe will never hold good to any other, until its final destruction—and therefore, for the very novelty of it alone, it must be worth your worships attending to.
>
> I am this month one whole year older than I was this time twelve-month; and having got, as you perceive, almost into the middle of my fourth volume—and no farther than to my first day's life—'tis demonstrative that I have three hundred and sixty-four days more life to write just now, than when I first set out; so that instead of advancing, as a common writer, in my work with what I have been doing at it—on the contrary, I am just thrown so many volumes back— . . . as at this rate I should just live 364 times faster than I should write—It must follow, an' please your worships, that the more I write, the more I shall have to write—and consequently, the more your worships read, the more your worships will have to read.
>
> Will this be good for your worships eyes?

It will do well for mine; and, was it not that my OPINIONS will be the death of me, I perceive I shall lead a fine life of it out of this self-same life of mine; or in other words, shall lead a couple of fine lives together. -

As for the proposal of twelve volumes a year, or a volume a month, it no way alters my prospect—write as I will, and rush as I may into the middle of things, as *Horace* advices,—I shall never overtake myself—[53]

This passage is followed by Tristram's at last receiving a name, since one good self-definition deserves (or calls forth) another.

Though Tristram repeatedly attempts to join the time of events, the time of composing, and the time of reading into an autonomous time of the text (for instance, "She listened to it with composed intelligence, and would have done so to the end of the chapter, had not my father plunged . . ."[54]), he is never able to "overtake" himself because his human and textual beings are finally different, having begun in different years and proceeded at different rates. Still, his human and textual beings behave, or are constructed, according to the same Lockean model—and even this is not the limit of the analogy between the "couple of fine lives together." For the author is Sterne, not Tristram; Tristram *is* a textual entity. Although in reality Tristram is generated by the text, the text appears to be generated by him, and their orders of being are not only interdependent but perfectly analogous. "Let us leave, if possible, *myself*:—But 'tis impossible,—I must go along with you to the end of the work."[55] The actual moment of Tristram's birth is not described; at that point in the work there is instead "The Author's PREFACE."[56] Tristram does not say, or even think, that he is a book, because that would necessitate a vantage point outside textuality; in this context, that would be the ineffable insight. The exact nature of his being makes itself manifest (to return to Wittgenstein) as a property of the system; just as the eye is not within the visual field but can contemplate its image in a mirror, Tristram's "I" is available only through the mirror of textuality. He is beyond both the macro- and the micro-limits of the book, both outside the labyrinth and at the unfindable center of its parentheses; yet he, or something like him, is omnipresent.

Sterne pushes even this system to its limits by a strategy of private references to himself, not just as the author of certain sermons and as the unnamed object of similar roman-à-clef games, but by having Tristram make his (Sterne's) trip through Europe and by having Tristram name what may have been the actual date of a given chapter's being written.[57] Because Sterne does not point out these correspondences, they do not explode the text or undermine the distinction between textual and human being.

One author whose work attempts to do away with this distinction is Steve Katz. In *The Exagggerations of Peter Prince,* a contemporary American novel, Katz uses many of Sterne's devices of textual foregrounding—crossed-out pages, paralleled subtexts, announcements that certain vital transitions were not interesting enough to write down, and so on—but adds the devices of having some of the characters read or discuss *Peter Prince* and its sequel and of including "Steve Katz":

> Enough! Katz, you're making this all up. It doesn't make a bit of sense. It's not a promising beginning. Why can't you follow the instructions? You can't write whatever you want: Peter Prince Peter Prince Peter Prince. . . .
>
> This is serious, even if Katz is making it up. Who'd say he's making it up?
>
> I'd say he was.[58]

Sometimes Katz is "a serpentine river" flowing "down the valley into [the town of] Peter Prince,"[59] which is a relatively conventional authorial role; sometimes, when pressed for an explanation of "what's really happening," he describes the "air-conditioned library study" in which he is writing the novel and speculating on the difference it will make that he is composing by fluorescent light, whereas "the best books so far have been written by natural light, or long ago maybe by candle, oil or kerosene, and recently, incandescent."[60] This is like Sterne's many references to his goose-quill pens, except that those are presented as Tristram's pens; Sterne's reader could draw the analogy between narrator and author, but here Katz (like Ron Sukenick in his first novel, *Up*) joins the two directly.

This leaping back and forth across the border that conventionally separates fiction from the real activity of composition tends to make nonsense of that border. The fluorescent light affects Katz just as the buzzing of a fan in a room (and on the pages, in a superimposed column of *zzz*s and meditations) affects Peter Prince while he reads part of the manuscript.[61] The following passage is a clever example of the problems involved. A character named Philip Farrel is being questioned by some executives about his relationship with Peter Prince:

"I don't talk to him. It isn't that kind of novel."

"What do you mean, 'not that kind of novel'? What kind of a novel is there? It's a novel, isn't it?"

Philip Farrel sighed. "Yes. Right. But it's not what you think. I mean I don't understand it even that well myself all the time. I'm just there, that's all."

"You're trying to tell me that you spend a whole novel with Peter Prince and you don't get a line of dialogue, not one little joke to tell him, in the margin?"

"I don't talk to him at all. . . . I mean I drop a few words into the text while he's sleeping sometimes, but he never hears them."

"Philip Farrel," said the President . . . "We know better than that."

"Better than what?"

"We know that by the end of the book you speak to him at least once, perhaps more than once, and a conversation that has no little influence on him."

"Nonsense. The book is almost over. I understand my function in it and it's not to talk to Peter Prince. I know what I do by now. I wasn't hired as a talker to Peter Prince." Philip Farrel smoothed his sideburns. He could tell that things weren't going as he'd expected them to. He wasn't sure, flipping quickly back through the pages, that they ever did. Maybe he was wrong.

"You'll see," said the President.

"How can you say you know this?" It wasn't only Philip Farrel who was surprised and made uneasy by this presumptuous prediction. It stirred me up a little bit. I have nothing like a conversation in mind at all for these two, nothing like that. It sent a chill up my backbone to think that someone could be looking on like that at what I'm doing, a constant surveillance. Nothing makes me shake as much as spying. Even I wasn't sure. Maybe he did know something I didn't know, something my characters were going to do. Don't think it doesn't scare me.[62]

The changes of tense in that last paragraph are intricate. Katz, in the present of composing, with the end of the novel not yet written ("I *have* . . . in mind"), describes how he *was* stirred and *is* scared by the (past) scene he has just recounted. He speaks, however, of something his characters might have been going to do. So he is in the present of composition (with the novel's end still in the future) and within a past continuum. He is both the author of the system and inside it. This is more than just a matter of Katz's pretending to be out of control: it is the way he and Philip Farrel are in much the same position, each of them understanding, up to a certain point, that this (this situation, this novel, this life in general) is a book and that he plays a certain role in it, and furthermore that he can flip "back through the pages" (but

248

apparently not forward into the not-yet-written) to check things out. As it develops, the disputed "conversation" never occurs.

What Katz dares here is a systemic self-consciousness that includes its real author. The barrier between textual and human being is thus violated, but only to be established at a higher level. The text as a limited system includes Katz-at-the-time-he-was-writing, Katz the author as a construct by Katz the author. (Katz the man continued to exist as a person after the novel was printed, of course, and did other things than write during the years of composition; Katz is not a textual entity all the time, but in the moment of self-conscious composition he is largely that.) The self-consciousness of this occasionally silly novel goes as far as it can, and we must still observe that the complete or human Katz, the ground of being of the authorial construct Katz, is not *in* the text. There is no way he could be, because he is a limit of the system. Katz the author remains the image of the eye in the mirror, even if no temporal distancing and no lying are going on, and Katz the human being remains before the mirror, outside the textual field.

Katz does not confront the metaphysics of this encounter, but in the novel *Mist,* Miguel de Unamuno does. The main character, Augusto, at one point imagines that he is "a dream, an entity of fiction."[63] Augusto is willing to consider himself a dream by the author Unamuno only until it becomes clear that Unamuno is going to write him a death scene. Here is Robert Alter's fine summary of the implications of their encounter:

> The characters, who delude themselves into imagining they possess free will, are merely a dream of the author, who in turn, with his own illusions of autonomous existence, is merely a dream of God. Is what we think of as reality finally an infinite regress of dreams, or, alternatively, might the novelist's invention be more real than he himself is—the author, having imbued his fic-

tional world with independent life, reduced to a re-flected dream of that world?[64]

Unamuno tells Augusto, "you are only a product of my imagination" and that of the readers, but Augusto argues that *Unamuno* may be "the fictitious entity" and "nothing more than a pretext for bringing my story into the world." The point about these questions regarding the ontological nature of the author is that they cannot with any finality be answered. The author is one limit of the narrative system, and by paying attention to him, *Mist* and *Peter Prince* (and most of the fictions of Ron Sukenick, *Up* in particular) render themselves *realistic* self-conscious novels. They do not finally include their authors, but they are at least paying attention to a limit of their respective systems that actually exists; they do not cease to be self-conscious fictions because everything they include is or becomes textual. Augusto can attempt to check out his reality by conversing with a textual version of Unamuno, but Unamuno cannot resolve the question of whether he himself is a primary reality or a dream in the mind of God without transcending the system of *that* dream, the text of the world.

The stream of self-consciousness becomes a maximally re-alized analogy for human awareness when the "author" is not so cleverly brought into play. In many ways, it is easier for Unamuno to have Augusto confront Unamuno than for Being to have a human confront Being. It seems more dra-matically interesting to present a consciousness in the act of confronting the limits of its system and the nature of its own being as unknowns, to exclude the answers from the text, and thereby to preserve the integrity of the parallel, the ineffability of the extrasystemic.

I am not going to rehearse the whole history of stream of consciousness literature here, nor even the history of self-conscious literature, because much of that can be found in other books[65] and you will in any case be able to apply these observations to Stein, Proust, Dorothy Richardson, Joyce, and Woolf (the proper historical sequence) on your own. I will suggest only that within the twentieth century, the stream of consciousness mode has tended to evolve, or re-evolve, into the self-conscious mode. This is especially obvious in *Ulysses,* particularly in the "Aeolus" chapter, with its text/mind doubleness, and in Stephen's meditations on *Hamlet* and history, both of which are structures or scripts from which he is (as he says only of history) "trying to awake" and which control him until—or except to the extent that—he grows into his surrogate, Joyce, who dreams/creates the novel and so is safely outside it. This, of course, does not actually liberate or waken the character Stephen, and that points to the ways in which *Ulysses* is not as systemically self-conscious as *Peter Prince* or *Finnegans Wake,* although it is a definitive instance of authorial self-consciousness. I will, however, analyze the overlap of "stream of consciousness" and "mind of the text" in *The Sound and the Fury* and the metaphysics of *As I Lay Dying,* because these have not yet been adequately noticed and are keys to the works there is not room here to discuss. At that point it will be possible to consider Beckett and Jabès, who bring the device of systemic self-consciousness and the investigation of writing and Being to an extraordinary juncture.

3. FAULKNER, BECKETT, AND JABÈS

When we dream that we are dreaming, the moment of awaking is at hand.
—Novalis

The essence of the literature of consciousness is that it presents thought in written form. But the problem is that conscious activity is not always linguistic; it can include visual impressions, holistic intuitions, dreams, emotions to which words feel inadequate, and so on. It is also generally private, so that even when verbal or verbalizable thought is going

251

on, it is addressed to the originating subject. The way this was typically taken into account in the eighteenth-century novel was to place the character in a textual, narrating situation. Clarissa writes letters that keep pace with what has been happening to her and her thoughts on her situation; the Author of *A Tale of a Tub* writes a pamphlet whose disorganization reflects that of his mind; Tristram Shandy writes his *Life and Opinions,* which becomes his second life. The late nineteenth-century *Dracula* adheres to this pattern with its device of continuously updated journal entries.

Gertrude Stein made a radical leap forward with her concept of "listening and talking at the same time," whereby the narrating identity vanished into a narrative entity and the text took on a special ontological clarity; Proust's free-floating narrative consciousness may represent a comparable achievement. But the more characteristic attempt of twentieth-century stream-of-consciousness fiction (as typified in *Pilgrimage, Ulysses, Mrs. Dalloway,* and *Tell Me a Riddle*) is to present a flow of thoughts and impressions as if author and reader had gained privileged access to the insides of the characters' heads and hearts. This calls for more suspending of disbelief than the eighteenth-century approach since it is easier to accept a letter as a record of thought than to equate a page of *Ulysses* with thought itself, even if the latter is (once accepted on its own terms) often more psychologically "accurate" in its disjointed flux. In many ways, the most psychologically inaccurate and antiliteral texts are those of Faulkner. The question his most famous interior monologues raise is, "When is this being thought?" and the answers point to a textual construct of consciousness.

In the opening section of Faulkner's *The Sound and the Fury,* the world is presented in the way Benjy experiences it. A congenital idiot with no sense of linear time, Benjy is led from one scene and period to another by associations ("caddie" sounds like the name of his lost sister, Caddy; crawling under the fence now is like crawling under the

252

fence then), and the sequence of scenes *shows* his way of thinking. Benjy is not aware that X reminds him of Y and that he has an attitude toward the difference between X and Y (he does not say to himself that he misses Caddy, for instance). But the reader deduces the meaning of the juxtaposition of X and Y, which is his "thought," and his occasional bellowing can be taken as further evidence (that he misses the Caddy he "thought of" when he heard "caddie," though he cannot say this). Present and past scenes are equally accessible to Benjy and are experienced as if present; what is going on and what is remembered affect him in the same way, and so he does not have what is ordinarily called a "memory." Or perhaps he has only a memory. Here is a typical passage:

> I looked through the fence while Luster was hunting in the grass.
> "Here, caddie." He hit. They went away across the pasture. I held to the fence and watched them going away.
> "Listen at you, now." Luster said. "Aint you something, thirty-three years old, going on that way. After I done went all the way to town to buy you that cake. Hush that moaning. Aint you going to help me find that quarter so I can go to the show tonight."
> They were hitting little, across the pasture. I went back along the fence to where the flag was. It flapped on the bright grass and the trees.[66]

Faulkner is careful to give words only to what Benjy might understand and to include only what Benjy might notice. Because Benjy does not comprehend the game of golf or its terms, he says "hitting little" instead of "putting"; he recognizes a flag but not its function. Because he always attempts to deny loss (and because he would not have the proper term anyway), the golf course is still "the pasture" it used to be. He hears what Luster says, sees the flag flapping,

253

but does not notice his own bellowing or deduce its cause. Since Faulkner is so careful about all this, why is Benjy speaking in the past tense? And is he "speaking"?

To employ the past tense here is to imply that it has some analogous signified in Benjy's consciousness, just as "flag" does and "golf" does not. If the reader were meant to consider Benjy indiscriminately nonverbal, Faulkner would have included the golf terms along with the others. Everything Benjy notices is equally past, including what goes on in what for convenience we have to call the narrative present. It would seem altogether more appropriate and obvious for everything Benjy notices to be in the present tense (a device often used in *As I Lay Dying*). One could dismiss this use of the past tense as a novelistic convenience: everything had to be in the same tense (in the context of Benjy's consciousness), and the past is more manageable than the "I see this and he does that" of the continuous present. Yet Faulkner appears to want the reader to ask this question rather than gloss over it (along with the convention of Benjy's using words in the first place), for in the Quentin section he offers the past-tense stream of consciousness of a character who has committed suicide shortly after his final recorded thought and could not possibly be telling or remembering what he thought even if he *were* more able than Benjy to discriminate among past and present and fantasy. It is too glaring a problem to overlook.

Although much of Quentin's effort is focused on becoming free of linear time (which is why he starts his final day by breaking a watch), he never loses his ability to employ tenses. In the picnic fight scene, for instance (where Quentin's memory of fighting Dalton Ames is presented instead of his fight at the picnic, since the earlier fight is what Quentin is thinking about), what Faulkner gives is a verbal analogue to what the character is conscious of in the instant of its happening. One possible interpretation of Quentin's section has been offered by Sartre:

Faulkner's vision of the world can be compared to that of a man sitting in a convertible looking back. . . . All Faulkner's art aims to suggest to us that Quentin's soliloquy and his last walk *are already* his suicide. I believe we can explain in this fashion a curious paradox: Quentin thinks of his last day as being in the past, like someone who remembers. But who is it that remembers, since the last thoughts of the hero almost coincide with the sudden eruption and destruction of his memory? The answer lies in the novelist's skill in choosing the particular moment of the present from which he describes the past. . . . Faulkner has chosen for his present the infinitesimal instant of death. Thus, when Quentin's memory begins to enumerate his impressions . . . *he is already dead.*[67]

This seems a drastic example of reading-in, even if it does explain Quentin's use of the "continuous past" tense. One could argue that Quentin perceives reality as if it were past (sitting in the convertible looking back), but that does not really address the problem of Benjy, the essence of whose consciousness is that all his experience is equally available, that past and present are not different categories. Quentin's obsession with history and doom might account for his seeing everything as over with, but that, too, clearly cannot apply to Benjy (and I am relating these two characters to each other because they both operate in a continuous past that would make more sense as a continuous present). In fact, what makes the day of Quentin's suicide unusual for him is its *freedom* in time, a temporary Benjy-ness before the surrender to the pressures of his past (that is, of his own rigidity). Finally, the argument of Faulkner's having chosen for Quentin a present (the instant of death) in relation to which the pastness of the day can make sense can in no way apply to the living Benjy. A valid interpretation ought to explain both sections.

The first step must be to accept the unreality of the monologues rather than to invent a realistic context for them. Benjy has no sense of time and cannot possibly conceptualize pastness. Quentin dies shortly after the final page of his section and is not available to tell how he felt on his last day. Nor would either of them describe (that is, narrate as past from whatever vantage point) the ins and outs of their perception in such detail. These sections translate thought into discourse; they present each character's thinking as it proceeds. Quentin is not telling anybody anything, and Benjy is not addressing himself in words, let alone in the past tense. What, then, is the reader reading?

What one reads is the record of a mind that has become recordable. The past tense is a convenience of the transcriber, who is not a character but whose activity is manifest. Benjy cannot use words, but here are the words that he would use if he could. Quentin can use words but is too busy living his last day to be considered as telling anyone about it (even himself) as it proceeds. The thinker is extrasystemic (that aspect of Benjy that translates "caddie" into "Caddy" and decides to bellow is not in the record of his consciousness), as is the transcriber (who is probably Faulkner), yet the activities of both are manifest in the fact and processes of the text. The past tense, a convenience of the transcriber, is a way of rendering the equality of subjective time. It is also an indication that these sections are part of a completed story now to be told, rather than an imitation of some past-tense awareness on the part of the characters. Either way, the past tense belongs to the transcriber and not to the characters.

This transcriber could be an autonomous entity not mentioned in but manifested by the text (perhaps speaking in its own voice in the novel's fourth section) or it could be Faulkner; but if it is Faulkner, it is a Faulkner whose presence is manifest in the same way that this anonymous textual entity is, because the unrealistic and contradictory aspects of his transcriptive method are too obvious to be overlooked. Or

one could say, "yes, it's Faulkner, and he got it wrong."
Hugh Kenner has said that when Faulkner confronted the
students at the University of Virginia he felt "perhaps like a
shaman who has wandered into a conference of brain sur-
geons";[68] there is much danger in playing the brain surgeon
with his work, of taking him literally and inventing systems
he would never have had in mind. Faulkner may well simply
have gotten it wrong. His books, however, do manifest certain paradoxes that are worth taking up regardless of Faulkner's unknown intentions, and this question of the transcriber is one of them.

This transcriber may be described as the textuality of
Quentin's or Benjy's consciousness, or the agency of their
having been made textual. (He can as easily be seen in Jason's section, though Jason can be imagined as telling his
story aloud.) The reader must approach these sections as
texts *and* as imitations of ongoing mental processes. They
are not innocent examples of stream of consciousness whose
likeness to texts is to be ignored. They are interior monologue and narration, but there is no fictional situation in
which they are being offered by one mind to another.
Rather, they are self-consciously being presented as written
language; their textuality is an essential element of their presence. Their narrative present is a present of narrating, and
the events they record are simultaneous with their being
told. Quentin's day happens to him and to the reader at the
same time, while he is posited as being alive, and the same
is true of Benjy. The filter of the transcriber is manifest
throughout. What one reads is a mind and a text, a *self-consciously textual* analogue to a mind.

This represents a return, via Joyce, to the method of *Clarissa*, with the difference that transcription is not an event in
the plot. This self-consciousness is not passed back to the
characters; they do not conceptualize themselves as being in
a novel, or even in a limited system. The self-consciousness
is a property of the text. This is an irreducible junction of
the mind of the text and stream of consciousness: Benjy's

narrated mind and the narrating Benjy section. It is as true to say that Faulkner presents Benjy's mind as a text as it is to say that the Benjy section presents itself as a mind while reminding the reader that it is a text.

The notion of the mind of the text becomes more challenging and more useful when that mind attempts to define the limits of the narrative system and to speak of itself rather than simply manifest its presence—when it attempts to imitate self-awareness and self-description. In the title of *Absalom, Absalom!,* the mind of the text can be thought of as uttering the tragic awareness that escapes its characters. In *The Unnamable,* the character's self-descriptions vanish as the mind of the text asserts itself as a more radically pure narrative consciousness. There is one stage of awareness through which the mind of the text has to pass before it can engage in such forthright self-declaration, however, and this may be exemplified in *As I Lay Dying,* where it sets itself up at the periphery of the narrative system as well as at its center and says "I" for the first time in the history of fiction without passing that consciousness back to a character or invented narrator.

What I am suggesting here is that *As I Lay Dying* represents a simultaneous self—that it has not fifteen narrators but one larger, transcribing or fantasizing "I," who is named in the title and is the mind of the text. To clarify this, a brief review of the story and its organization may be helpful.

Addie, a schoolteacher, marries Anse Bundren, a poor farmer, and gives him four children: Cash, Darl, Dewey Dell, and Vardaman. Between the first two sons and the daughter, she has a third son, Jewel, by Preacher Whitfield. Of the five children, Addie feels that only Cash and Jewel are truly hers, and what unites them is their preference for silent action over empty words. She feels that Darl, an unwanted pregnancy, is a trick played by Anse and the word he hid in ("love"). She rejects Darl and resumes her search for a way out of language, first through her affair with Whitfield and second through what she calls her "revenge" on Anse—holding him to his promise to bury her in Jefferson with her relatives. (Ironically, she forces the language-insensitive Anse to "do" according to his "word.") All of Addie's children are like her in some ways, like Gestalt projections from her wholeness: Cash and Jewel are silent and grounded; Darl and Vardaman are vulnerable and given to trying to sort out their conflicts in words; Dewey Dell is the victim of her own exploited sexual fertility. Realizing that it is impossible to "straddle" the two lines of "words" and "doing," Addie chooses to do, to be. Eventually she feels ready to die, and while she lies in bed, Cash builds her coffin (and the novel starts).

The journey to Jefferson takes a long time, and along the way, the corpse begins to stink. Earlier, talking to her rather stupid friend Cora, Addie had called Jewel her salvation and had predicted that he would save her from the water and the fire; she turns out to have been right. Fording a river, the wagon is overturned and the coffin nearly lost. Jewel saves the coffin, but Cash's leg is broken. Anse cools and sets it with concrete, and gangrene develops. At this point, there is a hiatus.

Each chapter of *As I Lay Dying* is narrated by one of the characters, usually in the present tense, and most of them pick up the story where the earlier chapter has left off. Some are narrated in the past tense but occur in chronological sequence; presumably, they are being told in the story's future (which raises the question of the transcribing consciousness as collator). The chapter that occurs in this hiatus, however, belongs to no chronology and is spoken from no discernible vantage point. (One at least knows the date of Quentin's suicide.) It is preceded by Cora's "fire and water" chapter and followed by Whitfield's account of his hypocritical attempt at repentance (in other words, it is sandwiched between instances of the existential failure and gullibility of those who mistake language for primary being, which also demonstrate that Addie has failed to communicate with her peers). It is Addie's sole chapter, the keystone of the novel, the chapter in which she tells her own story; and it seems to disrupt not only the book's chronology but time itself. It is followed (after Whitfield's) by one of the only chapters that Darl narrates in an inappropriate past tense. After this hiatus, the main story continues.

With the suffering but good-natured Cash on top of the retrieved coffin, Anse sells Jewel's horse to buy a team to pull the wagon to Jefferson. Along the way, Darl believes he hears Addie talking in the coffin, begging to be hidden from the sight of men. When Anse leaves the team and wagon in a hospitable barn for the night, Darl sets fire to the barn—but Jewel proves Addie's prophecy right on both counts and saves her from the fire as he had from the water. The accuracy of this prediction has a way of reinforcing another: that Addie would take her revenge without Anse's ever knowing that she was taking it.

When the wagon arrives in Jefferson, Addie is buried, Cash is taken to a doctor, and Dewey Dell is taken advantage of by a druggist to whom she has gone for abortion pills. To save himself from being sued by the owner of the barn, Anse has Darl committed to an asylum. Then, in the novel's masterfully sick punch line, Anse buys the false teeth that were his main reason for undertaking the journey and remarries.

Darl is left in a state of complete hysteria, his identity split into "I" and "Darl." He speaks of himself in the third person and the first:

> Darl has gone to Jackson. They put him on the train, laughing, down the long car laughing, the heads turning like the heads of owls when he passed. "What are you laughing at?" I said.
> "Yes yes yes yes yes."[69]

This could simply be Faulkner's attempt to write about schizophrenia from the inside, but it has several provocative connections with Addie's chapter. Darl's "I" remains rational, while "Darl" is the one who goes crazy and is taken away. Psychologically, this may be a case of extreme withdrawal. Metaphysically, it may suggest that the ultimate inner self (the witness to experience) is not subject to the disruptions that consciousness may undergo. To a Lacanian this would be a classic example of the connection between schizophrenia and the disappearance or dysfunction of the imaginary. And all of these readings make sense. But in terms of narrative system, this could almost be—rather than withdrawal—an extreme *extroversion*, a movement toward third-person omniscience.

Until now, each of the narrators (even Addie, at first glance) has spoken from a rigidly limited point of view. No larger mind appears to connect these fifteen selves; there is no overview. Darl, who speaks one third of the novel's fifty-nine chapters, appears to be the principal narrator only in the statistical sense; there is no evidence that he has anything to do with the other two thirds. His abrupt split does, however, remind the reader that no such outside view—no view from outside the narrating persona—has appeared before. I suspect that the split between "I" and "Darl" is similar to that between "I" and "Addie": that it is "Addie" who dies and is buried and "I" who transcends those events and chapters to become, in effect, the narrator of the book. Darl is the reader's window on this transformation, destroyed by the attempt to "straddle" language and being; Addie has long preceded him on this route, first by her rejection of language and second by dying (becoming "was"), so that she may almost be said to inhabit the silence that words try to fill.

To Addie, the only significant communications are wordless: extreme sensuality, the ties of blood-consciousness, physical violence, and her more or less posthumous (thus unspoken) chapter. As a teacher, she is closest to her students when she whips them, for she imagines she feels the switch on her own back and becomes a permanent part of their "secret and selfish life." This fantasy of marking their blood with hers is a key to the silent bonds between Addie

and her children, who are both independent beings and fragments of her personality; she contacts others by establishing
her silence inside them. Whitfield misses the point of her
silence, Cora the point of her words; Darl is driven crazy by
his *différance* from her and from the silence of being that lets
her mother life. To Darl but not to Addie, origin is Other.
The integrity of Addie's aloneness is never "violated" by
words, let alone by Anse's sexual intrusions. (Anse's sexuality is reduced to an empty word, whereas Addie's putting
on and stripping away sinfulness with Whitfield lets her contact the "voiceless speech" of nature and action, which is
much more highly charged than "thin and harmless" potentially vacuous words.)

Addie explores two routes to aloneness. She is not returning to virginity, because the birth of Cash has awakened the
blood-consciousness that is the essence of one of those
routes; this "violation" has made her whole, drawing a "circle" outside which are "time, Anse, love, what you will"
and inside which is Addie and those with whom she communicates nonverbally. A word is just "a shape to fill a
lack." She suggests that the lack is best filled by a direct
experience of the signified; with that knowledge, the word
is unnecessary anyway. Her achieved silence is not a vacuum
but the wholeness of being that requires or allows no referential expression. But to a character like Darl, ontologically
insecure since the day Addie rejected him as the fruit of a
trick of language, to strip away words is to confront only
the lack and not the wholeness; his only hope is to transcend
the system. Darl, then, is language (Addie has made him
so), and its problems are his. If Addie's most successful
route to the silence is to give birth, to deconstruct sin, and
to die, her other route is to deconstruct language; these exercises are mutually supportive.

Sometimes I would lie by him in the dark, hearing the
land that was not of my blood and flesh, and I would
think: Anse. Why Anse. Why are you Anse. I would

think about his name until after a while I could see the
word as a shape, a vessel, and I would watch him liq-
uefy and flow into it like cold molasses flowing out of
the darkness into the vessel, until the jar stood full and
motionless: a significant shape profoundly without life
like an empty door frame; and then I would find that I
had forgotten the name of the jar. I would think: The
shape of my body where I used to be a virgin is in the
shape of a   and I couldn't think *Anse,* couldn't
remember *Anse.* It was not that I could think of myself
as no longer unvirgin, because I was three now. And
when I would think *Cash* and *Darl* that way until their
names would die and solidify into a shape and then fade
away, I would say, All right. It doesn't matter. It
doesn't matter what they call them.[70]

For the word that escapes her Addie offers a blank space in
the text—not a sign under erasure but a moment of stymied
language, a not-word. As the full jar is recognized as an
empty door frame, she forgets the name of the jar and gives
up language. Her experience finds expression in the energy
of notated silence, much like Ishmael's "dumb blankness,
full of meaning."

If this is the way Addie feels, why is she speaking? And
even if one justifies this apparent contradiction by accepting
the notion of the unseen transcriber who might be approxi-
mating Addie's insights into language, one would like to locate her chapter somehow in time and space. (Ishmael's shift
of narrative vantage after the "Mast-Head" chapter poses
just the same problems.) Perhaps a clue is its location in the
sequence of the text. Her chapter appears over one hundred
pages after her death, following (as if it were evoked by) the
fulfillment of her "water" prophecy. One might even suspect that the river disaster is a manifestation of her power,
an aspect of her "revenge." (Compare Ahab's "monomaniac
revenge" and its focus on action.) Does that mean that her
spirit is hovering around the coffin, provoking catastrophes,

and cannot rest until she is buried? Somehow, *As I Lay Dying* does not strike me as a ghost story. Darl does hear Addie talking in her coffin, but that may be because he has, or would like to have, some privileged access to the source of her speech. It may be that Addie would expect him to hear her and imagines his doing so in that "Darl" chapter; or it may be that Addie and Darl are in touch with an unseen periphery of consciousness that surrounds their actions as the heart of darkness envelops Marlow's tale, and which in parts of *Moby-Dick* proved a narrative vantage point. If Addie is not "alive" in her coffin, there seem to be only two possibilities: either she is still dying in her bed or she is within the circle to which time and ordinary language are exterior. Perhaps both apply.

The simplest way to interpret the novel's title is to accept it at face value: all the action takes place as Addie lies dying. (The immediate source of the title is a translation of the *Agamemnon* in which Agamemnon describes what he heard as he lay dying; his point in a similar passage from the *Odyssey* is not to trust women, but the emphasis in the *Agamemnon* is on Clytemnestra's refusal to close his dead eyes.[71]) While Addie lies in her bed, listening to Cash build her coffin, she imagines her revenge on Anse. Or she does this just after she has died, with "eyes" unclosed. The whole novel may be her fantasy. At the point where her imagined destruction of the family begins to come clear—the river disaster, from which, she dreams, Jewel saves her—she takes stock of herself and the sources of her power. Because of the intense nonverbal connections she has cultivated with life and with the "secret" centers of the personal being of others, she imagines her revenge from the most private viewpoints of her children and those they might encounter.

This interpretation offers one of the only explanations for the eloquence of the various narrators, unless Faulkner is randomly and even carelessly shifting between what the characters say and his own analogues for the essence of their thinking (which is certainly possible). Darl goes on about spatializations of time and even compares the coffin on its sawhorses to "a cubistic bug," while Cash breaks out of his simple diction to say things like: "But I aint so sho that ere a man has the right to say what is crazy and what aint. It's like there was a fellow in every man that's done a-past the sanity or the insanity, that watches the sane and the insane doings of that man with the same horror and the same astonishment."[72] While this is a nice analysis of Darl's ability to retain an "I" even while mad, and a good definition of what many mystics call the "inner witness," the last words of Cash's sentence are simply out of tone. And the only character likely to have any acquaintance with Cubism on an impoverished Southern farm in 1930 is Addie, who had been a schoolteacher and whose chapter begins with an echo of "The Waste Land" (though it is perhaps equally arguable that Darl encountered Cubism while a soldier in France). The logical conclusion is that these are not simply the characters' thoughts but may well be Addie's. In fact, the whole novel has a Cubist aspect, since it portrays one extended event from many different simultaneous viewpoints. The title may imply that Faulkner is presenting the "cubistic" fantasy of Addie's revenge that flashes through her mind as she lies dying. In some ways, the fulfillments of her predictions are too accurate and the characters' behavior too much in line with Addie's judgments of them for any other explanation to make sense.

The fact that the key word in the title is not "lie" but "lay" could simply be considered an instance of Faulkner's continuous past, if the reader were not forced to deal with Darl's lengthy meditation on the metaphysics of Addie's pastness. Though the interpretation I am about to offer may still leave Addie the narrator behind all these interior monologues, it locates her not (or perhaps not only) in bed but in the silence. Like Agamemnon, his eyes uncovered, something has kept Addie from completely dying; at question is the nature of her eternity.

Twenty pages after Addie's death, Darl predicates his existence on hers. The existence they have is a flowing kind, comparable to that of Proust's narrator in his dark bedroom: an "I" whose name is ambiguous or hidden and who can—at least in the opening pages of *A la recherche* and arguably in *As I Lay Dying*—be many people in many times. (In Heidegger's terms, Addie as Being is precomprehended in Darl's being and in his Saying.) This "I" comes into being as the named character—in this case, Darl—"empties himself for sleep":

> In a strange room you must empty yourself for sleep. And before you are emptied for sleep, what are you. And when you are emptied for sleep, you are not. And when you are filled with sleep, you never were. I dont know what I am. I dont know if I am or not. Jewel knows he is, because he does not know that he does not know whether he is not. He cannot empty himself for sleep because he is not what he is and he is what he is not. Beyond the unlamped wall I can hear the rain shaping the wagon that is ours, the load that is no longer theirs that felled and sawed it nor yet theirs that bought it and which is not ours either, lie on our wagon though it does, since only the wind and rain shape it only to Jewel and me, that are not asleep. And since sleep is is-not and rain and wind are *was,* it is not. Yet the wagon *is,* because when the wagon is *was,* Addie Bundren will not be. And Jewel *is,* so Addie Bundren must be. And then I must be, or I could not empty myself for sleep in a strange room. And so if I am not emptied yet, I am *is.*[73]

Darl here attempts to reason his way to the fact of his existence, which is also a search for the precomprehended foundation of language in time. His first step is to prove that Addie (as his mother, the literal source of his being, and as a felt absence, the transcendental signified) somehow exists; and since she has died, he has to reason out a limbo between *is* and *is-not* that somehow includes Being. Once he has done this, he can feel assured enough to notice that his being can be predicated on the fact that *he* is "not emptied yet," rather than on Jewel's ontological ties with Addie. (So this is, among other things, an all-time example of sibling rivalry.)

Darl sets up a spectrum of emptying for sleep that is analogous to the process of dying. To be awake is not to know very much—to be limited, like Montaigne, to questions ("Que sais—je?" as "what are you"). To be emptied for sleep is not to be. To be asleep or dead is more radically not to be ("you never were"). So he locates Addie in the middle of this spectrum and himself on the *is* side of her ("not emptied yet"). If he admitted Addie's being "filled with sleep," she would never have been and he could not be sure of his own existence.

Jewel, for his part, does not worry about whether he is or not, and so he can be described as grounded in Being but also as unenlightened; Jewel is not all he could be. Darl wants to know that he is, a self-awareness that has to begin with his admitting the limits of his knowledge of Being (a more or less Platonist perspective). The quest for Being makes emptying for sleep possible; there has to be something half-known-about to empty.

The load on the wagon is in a limbo between owners. To know about the load without knowing whose it is, is like sensing personal being without knowing its authentic name. Darl senses that he *is* but can prove it only by arriving at his own version of Addie's concept of language, whose implication is that he is the shape that fills his lack. He is not yet far enough along to consider this silence as the self-sufficiency of Being, but he is working in that direction.

Darl says that the rain is shaping the wagon, Addie that a word is a shape to fill a lack. Darl means two things: first, that he can hear the rain hitting the different altitudes and substances of the wagon and so can make out its shape the way a bat deduces from sonar the shape of objects in its path; second, that as far as he is concerned (that is, within the limits of his knowledge), the wagon takes its shape from a hole in the rain. There had to be a wagon to create that hole, just as there has to be some signified behind every signifier, some concept for the sign to address. But once a language exists, the holes become primary tools of reference and knowledge, and being is barred from the confrontation with absolute Being as long as it works within language. Darl takes comfort in deducing from the presence of the sign (even if it is a hole or an empty door frame) that the wagon exists. The wagon both abolishes and occupies the hole so that the hole both is and is not. For Addie the hole is lifeless, but for Darl it is a vital indication that an unseen thing is present. The wagon is known to be, because Darl and Jewel perceive the hole in the rain. In this sense, the hole in the rain creates the wagon, just as for Derrida the "central signified, the original or transcendental signified, is never absolutely present outside a system of differences."[74]

As they empty themselves for "sleep," Addie and Darl slip between "what are you" and "you are not." For Proust this was the stage where the anonymous consciousness could take on different identities, and Darl's "strange room" problem appears to be a deliberate reference to Proust.[75] It is as if the wagon could, in the process of vanishing, leave a protean hole in the rain. When Addie empties herself for death, it is possible that her "I" flows into the first-person viewpoints of all the novel's characters and partially becomes them. This is not the same thing as saying that she imagines her revenge from their individual points of view while having an Agamemnon-like vision of the fall of her House. It is not that she literally narrates their chapters but that she participates in or symbolizes the underlying ground of Being that makes itself manifest in each chapter's Saying and that must be "located" extratextually. If Darl is language, Addie is what mothers language. In such a case, all of these minds would be linked by the overarching consciousness of a supernarrator. A chapter like "Whitfield" or "Addie" would be a lower manifestation of the mind of the text than would the "I" of the title; in some of the "Darl" chapters, the self-consciously linguistic element of that "I" might be trying to sort itself out.

This mind of the text would be everywhere evident yet, in its fullest self-consciousness, necessarily outside the work; its only possible location would be the title, and even that is a form of cheating. ~~Addie~~ is the ground of Being, inside a circle whose center is everywhere and circumference nowhere, and from which time and language are excluded although it precomprehends and sustains them. It is not "Addie" the wagon but "I" the hole in the rain that originates these chapters, as Addie has mothered her children; it is the transcendent and anonymous consciousness that Darl's "I" touches when he is "crazy" or disoriented enough to know that he *is* and yet to discuss "Darl" as an other (a Laingian condition in which "Darl" cannot think but "I" is clear). If one locates Addie in this kind of ubiquitous narrative space, her chapter can appear at any point in the novel whether or not "Addie" is dead, just as Godot's messenger boy can show up in act after act for what will always be the first time (an essential privilege of coming from outside time). This makes the novel a simultaneous self with an unnamable first-person narrator.

It is not clear why Darl considers rain and wind to be *was* unless one takes his meditation as a key not only to the "I" but also to the "lay" of the title. Darl must not let Addie be *is-not,* so that which shapes the wagon (the wagon being here an analogue for her knowable presence and for whatever can be posited as existing) must also be. The completely past cannot help to signify something present; the creation of presence must happen in the present (or, put another way, the signifier and signified must share the same order of time, as language and what language creates must be of the same order). This leads Darl to argue that the wagon *is* and therefore that its shapers cannot be the forces of an utter pastness.

Darl's anxiety prompts him to introduce a stage between two kinds of past, like that between "you are not" and "you never were," one of which allows for a paradoxical presence that could just as easily be described as the "felt absence" of the transcendental signified. The nearest linguistic equivalent to this temporal ambiguity would probably be the imperfect tense, or a participial structure that would indicate a perhaps-not-finished continuity; hence "as I lay dying." At this point, the deep relevance of Proust becomes most striking. What Darl appears to be saying is that between *is* and *is-not* is *was*. Darl *is,* because he is not yet filled with sleep; Addie is dead, but in a state of *was* rather than of *is-not.* She must *be,* for such manifestations of her life and consciousness as Jewel and Darl—and their chapters—to be. (If she were indirectly narrating Darl's meditation here, the point would be that she cannot imagine herself as absolutely not being.) She must be dead and yet not filled with sleep, not all the way into "you never were." The only way she can be is to be *was.* One good solution to the Benjy/Quentin quandary, then, may be that Faulkner found the quality of eternity to be best suggested by an unanchored past tense as well as by a paradoxically unanchored locus of narrativity. If Addie is omnipresent in this book, or even if she is simply to be real to Darl, the time of her presence must be *was,* or *lay.* The temporal is posited on the extratemporal, which Darl cannot define further; the italics indicate the failure of his terms. Addie can be physically dead and metaphysically present, but only in the self-consuming time sense of Darl's wildly complicated paragraph and Faulkner's simple title.

The best evidence I can offer that "I" is at the ubiquitous narrative center of this novel is Darl's madness. When he is forced to *be* without Addie, he loses his verbal skills, and his "I" appears nearly to join the superconsciousness that could speak of all these characters in the third person or in the first in the present tense or in the past, at will. The price of contacting the ultimate ground of Being, in this context, is for language to fail and the limited sense of identity to be discarded. (It would be entirely proper to call this "limited sense of identity" the imaginary, as long as one continued to admit the possibility of an underlying ground of Being.)

And it will be noted that in his final chapter Darl speaks of himself not only in the third person but also in the past tense.

The title can be seen as summarizing all this. "As" is process, a continuity of being and doing. "I" is the mind of the novel. "Lay" suggests that the novel's consciousness-complex and its process are being viewed from some exterior perspective; it locates the "I" in bed or in the silence and declares that she does not exist as a living being in the simple present. "Dying" unites "as" and "lay" in perfect ambiguity, since it could refer to a finished or an unfinished process (like the opening of *A la recherche*), and links "I" to Addie, since she is the only character in the novel who dies.

If Addie were still alive and imagining her revenge, and if some of the characters began to probe the limits of her dream from within (that is, if they became systemically self-conscious), that dreaming mind would be unnamable and extrasystemic in exactly the same way it would be if Addie were dead and the novel self-narrating and self-naming. Addie has earned her privileged access to the origin of her world's being because she has gone past words. Jewel and Cash cannot follow her, even though they are materialists, because they have not dealt with the problem of language and self-consciousness (and, of course, Addie is not a materialist but an essentialist). The projections of Addie's language-probing side, however, make progress. Vardaman's final chapter is full of gaps; and Darl has gone past him, destroying and being destroyed by language in search of the absent Other that his existence both depends upon and attests to, finding "I" at the expense of "Darl," and perhaps realizing his connection with the overarching narrative consciousness rather than continuing to imagine, for instance, that he has heard a corpse in her coffin—as the reader may have imagined hearing Addie's chapter in some conventional time of the story. It is possible that in his final chapter Darl is Marlow to Addie's Kurtz, penetrating the realm of her experience at the expense of his sanity. What sets Faulkner's work apart from Conrad's, however, is that the enveloping haze has been given consciousness. *As I Lay Dying* has a peripheral narratorial energy, a transcendent consciousness that is the mind of the novel and is the true occupant of the hole in language designated "I." (Its pastness is only a diegetic function of Addie's death and Darl's anxiety; the point is its being liberated by the liminal "emptying for sleep.") It is like the eye outside the mirror: a limit of this novel, unable to speak adequately about itself. It can speak about "Addie" and is subject to reflection in the indirect apprehensions and eventual example of Darl, but the novel as a whole remains the "visual" field from which the "eye" is excluded.

What kind of book would result if this kind of "I" felt the tension of its own self-consciousness and tried to declare it within the text instead of in the title? *As I Lay Dying* points to what is at its own periphery but can hardly address it directly. It is not clear whether "Addie" is aware of the "I" in the title—whether the dream-self has an inkling of its dreamer-self. It is not clear whether Darl could remain both aware of the whole system and sane. In his trilogy, Beckett deals with analogues to most of these questions.

Whether by intention or coincidence (I did not plan this), the sequence of narrative structures in Beckett's works, from *Watt* through *Molloy* and *Malone Dies* to *The Unnamable,* exactly duplicates the sequence in which formal narrative structures have been discussed in this book and culminates, like them, in the potential for maximal self-consciousness. This suggests that this sequence has some inherent legitimacy. As a secondary first-person novel, *Watt* allows the mysteries of language and of inexplicable phenomena to be pondered by an overreacher who is himself pondered by the narrator (himself a parody of authorial consciousness). The next step is for the elements of this hierarchy to be condensed into variants of one self who examine each other and the mystery in similar terms, which is what happens in *Malone Dies.*

Molloy is a brilliant and efficient link between *Watt* and

Malone Dies because it can be analyzed both as secondary first-person narration and as an instance of the simultaneous self. Molloy is the original quest-hero, attempting to understand how he came to be in his mother's room and telling the story of his journey—a journey that left him immobile at the bottom of a ditch (if he did get to his mother's room—the locus of his narrating, rather like the locus of the "I" in *As I Lay Dying*—he must have arrived there by a quantum leap or transcendence that the novel could not include). Moran is the more "methodical" investigator who tells the story of his quest for Molloy; he also begins by writing in a room after the journey is over, and his journey has left him, too, in a crippled condition. Moran's task becomes to write the report of his search, and he deliberately does so in fiction:

> I have spoken of a voice telling me things. I was getting to know it better now, to understand what it wanted. It did not use the words that Moran had been taught when he was little and that he in his turn had taught to his little one. So that at first I did not know what it wanted. But in the end I understood this language. I understood it, I understood it, all wrong perhaps. That is not what matters. It told me to write the report. Does this mean I am freer now than I was? I do not know. I shall learn. Then I went back into the house and wrote, It is midnight. The rain is beating on the windows. It was not midnight. It was not raining.[76]

Though Moran begins as more Nick than Gatsby, more acculturated and practical then Molloy, he undergoes an analogue to Molloy's journey and disintegration, a disintegration that can suggest transcendence or pointless scattering (it is the essence of Beckett not to argue which, since there is in any case no way to know and since his comedy depends on the interchangeability of hope and despair), and offers the story of his own quest as his report on Molloy. That is classic secondary first-person narration. But several things make

273

Molloy different. First, it includes Molloy's first-person account—which takes the reader only a little farther along than Moran's version since it does at least begin in the mother's room though it cannot say how it got there. Second, Moran's account deliberately presents itself as fiction (systemic self-consciousness). Further, the "voice" Moran hears does not speak his native language and must be intuited. Moran describes himself, as listener, in the third person. And finally, Molloy and Moran are easily viewed as aspects of the same character.

The extrasystemic voice prompts self-conscious fiction as a quest for truth. Moran wonders whether he has "invented" Molloy: "I mean found him ready made in my head. There is no doubt one sometimes meets with strangers who are not entire strangers, through their having played a part in certain cerebral reels."[77] Hugh Kenner has observed that "Molloy and Moran are more or less the author's Irish and French selves respectively."[78] And Moran says that the stories he has failed to tell include those of "Murphy, Watt, Yerk, Mercier and all the others."[79] So if there is a simultaneous self at work, it is probably that of "Beckett," the authorial construct, masked down into Molloy and Moran as he had earlier parodied himself in the Sam of *Watt*. But it may also involve that "voice" that demands that the narrator actualize it in fiction ("It told me to write the report"). This helps lay the foundations of the all-encompassing self-consciousness of the trilogy as a whole, in which what declares itself is indistinguishably the mind of the text, the sublimated self-awareness of the author, and the stream of consciousness of the characters, subsuming authorial into systemic self-consciousness. The liminal experience of violating the margin of the text has proved itself a viable rite of passage.

Just as in Gestalt psychology the recognition and re-owning of projections leads to the self's discovery of its wholeness, the hierarchy of displacement in secondary first-person narration yields to the more inter-equivalent structure of the simultaneous self, in which the projections confront each other more or less as comparable aspects of a whole. These partial selves are like the elements of a system that is greater than the sum of its parts, so they must search for the intangible that makes them a system rather than a heap (or a sum of component parts). In *As I Lay Dying,* that intangible is "I" and the character/chapters are the parts. In *A la recherche* (and it should be remembered that Beckett's Master's thesis was on Proust), the intangible is the timeless self to which the metaphorizing anonymous narrative consciousness is analogous, and the more knowable components are the active narrator, the experiencing self, and the reexperiencing self. The simultaneity of these last three (diegetically, in involuntary memory; systemically, in the hero's becoming able to narrate the book of his life) liberates the transcendental awareness that is outside the system's expression and that motivates the expression of the system. The "voices" that Moran and other of the trilogy's narrators hear, motivating the discourse to continue, are an important element of the system, almost its basic-self life force, keeping the body (the written novel) in a state of continual regeneration even if the conscious self is exhausted and the higher self indefinable and apart. These voices do not speak in ordinary words but are felt to be present. For Beckett, textuality is mortality, just as pointlessly tiring and just as indisputably the fact of our process on this level; it accomplishes little or nothing, yet without it nothing can even begin to be dealt with. The texts start themselves and their characters into life, the voices demand that the narrators "go on," and the task is always to describe the real and speak the silence in one and the same impossible gesture, which may or may not create freedom.

Malone Dies offers an extreme compression of the elements of this system in a drive to fulfill that gesture. Moran *may* have invented Molloy, but Malone clearly *does* invent Macmann. As Hugh Kenner Shandeanly summarizes it:

Let the serpent commence swallowing his tail, and let this process continue to some ideal limit: then ultimately the tip of his tail (who doubts it?) must end up stuffed as far back inside the serpent as it is possible to reach: i.e., inside the tip of his tail. In the same way, Molloy's narrative, composed in bed, of the events which brought him to this bed, must one day be brought down in time to the moment when it was itself commenced; and then discuss the writing of its own first paragraph; and so at last traverse itself to that limit where the writing of the word now written becomes its own subject. This is what in fact happens in *Malone Dies,* the man in bed writing about himself in bed writing, and proposing to track himself to his own death, so that his last word may be about his last word—better, may *be* his last word; as a spring with no thickness, wound sufficiently tight, will become a point. Malone even introduces a new train of terms to converge on this limit, the sequence of fantasies about Macmann, who if all goes well (and it seems to) will die when he does.[80]

The irreducible problem is that the spring does have a thickness, as language is not silence and the novel not "a point" but a one-hundred-page involuted aspiration. Macmann is Malone's attempt to create a fiction that parallels himself, whose quest will end at an identical (not at a displaced) vanishing point. Whereas *Molloy* has a two-"chapter" structure, *Malone Dies* is a single monologue that dances between the converging/parallel lines of Malone and his invented surrogate (compare Tristram Shandy's "couple of fine lives together"). The "exercise-book" in which Malone writes, urged "on"ward by murmuring voices, is his life, the locus of self-description.[81] His notes and his life are equally self-consuming ("But my notes have a curious tendency, as I realize at last, to annihilate all they purport to record"[82]), and what they aspire to is a state of transcendental synchrony in which the absolute convergence of recording and recorded will free him from his task, a perfect expression that will be instantaneously transfigured into the silence (Malone's death, the end of the novel, the fully achieved hole in the rain). But this is either not achieved or not enough, for there comes quite suddenly another novel.

The Unnamable attempts to become a single line, toying with parallels only to reject them, a self whose simultaneity is so radical that all sense of componency vanishes and "I" is left facing the silence that is itself, as what is said steps utterly aside for what is shown and what is shown remains ineffable.

The Unnamable is a consciousness. It is hard to say whether he can express himself only in words, or whether he *is* only words, for we encounter him in a book made up entirely of his monologue and he continually discredits any process but that of his own speaking. The problem is the same, of course, whether he is a thinking book or a mind that can only speak; that is the essence of systemic self-consciousness here. He has to be content with the word "I" when he wants to refer to himself, but he senses that his identity can be found only beyond the reach of words and that even the referentiality of "I" is a self-declaring failure. (To express the ineffable mandates no referentiality, even within the component parts of the sign.) He expects to find timelessness and silence and himself all at once, and his fate is to speak until words evoke that silence. He does not share Malone's relatively easy solution of being able to die, since his *only* mortality is textuality and since he may even be a postincarnate Malone, the inhabitant of fiction's Purgatory. He must speak until there is no need to speak; he must say "I" until he has defined himself. Restricted to language, he has no way of going beyond "I" to what it represents; restricted to his own consciousness in a Cartesian nightmare, he has no way of establishing anything about himself except that he *is* conscious. So in this novel, the tension of an unnamable speaker exactly overlaps the tension of ineffable

277

subject matter. *The Unnamable* is a limit of the novel, an extraordinary resource for the future of fiction. It is the Logos that reanimates the genre.

The Unnamable has no discernible plot, no namable character, no describable setting, no clockable time. All it has is a voice, or mind, speaking in the continuous present. Three-fourths of its length is occupied by a single paragraph. Its stream of sentences and fragments, separated more often by commas than by periods, exactly expresses the movements of the narrator's mind and records his every thought. He does not think his sentences out in advance; he is unable to silence himself long enough to compose. Something compels him to speak and prevents him from doing anything else, so that it is as true to call him a verbal consciousness as to call him language made self-conscious. The progress of his self-awareness is worth describing.

In his own "Call me Ishmael," the narrator labels himself "I," immediately putting that sign under erasure: "Where now? Who now? When now? Unquestioning. I, say I. Unbelieving. Questions, hypotheses, call them that. Keep going, going on, call that going, call that on."[83] He is awakened from sleep or death or blank paper, but in any case from silence. He is Beckett's archetypal character, a life force that had underlain such heroes of the earlier fictions as Belacqua, Watt, Murphy, Molloy, Moran, and Malone (who all resemble him) and that is now being forced to awaken into a new but more accurate manifestation. The karma of his failures at self-description is inseparably that of Beckett, who has in all those novels failed to describe him; reincarnation, so to speak, is mandated. The narrator seems to be asking the forces that have animated him, "What situation am I in now? Who am I supposed to be this time? What time is it?" When he gets no answers, he gives in, takes a deep breath, and makes the old inevitable definition: I will call myself I, without believing it. He feels commanded to "keep going on" but makes it clear that he is only settling for the terms "going" and "on." He makes the reader aware that every word in this book is in quotation marks or under erasure, that each is a little wrong. Not even his speaking is free of *différance:* "I seem to speak, it is not I, about me, it is not about me."

The narrator has a collective name for his fictional alternates or pseudoselves: Mahood. At first he feels he has two alternatives to the articulate darkness in which he appears to be. He can be a name, Mahood, and be the subject of more stories, or he can be Worm, an unspeakable negative. (He is never called "the Unnamable" except in the book's title, but many critics have found it convenient to call him that.) These alternates represent poles of language. If he were Worm, he would not speak at all, even to try to name himself; he would just be Worm, the existential equivalent of a Black Hole. When words try to deal with Worm, they address not the silence, in which there may be some kind of Being, but absolute negation. When they handle Mahood, they are on holiday, spinning stories, their nouns and verbs apparently applying to real things and actions in a welcome escape from self-consciousness. The Unnamable occupies a middle ground. It is difficult for words to find something to say about him because he has no story, but relatively easier and more valuable than to surrender to Worm, the antithesis of being. When the Unnamable rejects both Worm and Mahood and decides to seek the silence on his own, to talk not about them but about "I," the history of fiction enters a climatic phase—or perhaps a better term for this stage would be "peripeteia." It is as if *The Unnamable* were the novel (as a genre) awakened into self-consciousness, just as its narrator is roused from a dream of Molloy and Malone. Groping through its new awareness, the novel nearly succumbs (like *As I Lay Dying*) to the temptations of Mahood—nearly constructs a Moby-Dick and an Ahab and an Ishmael so that it can discuss itself in more familiar terms. (And most of the criticism of this novel has fallen for the game, insisting that Malone is orbiting or that there is a jar outside a restaurant, whereas all of these are irrefutably dispensed with in the course of the book.) But it sees that such a solution is evasive, that the quietus at which it arrives is only the blank space between novels, between new and compulsory dreams (the echoes of "To be or not to be" are mine, not Beckett's). If language is ever to know itself, if the novel is ever to learn to speak on its own, *The Unnamable* must pursue its self-consciousness to the root and speak from that base. The heart of darkness must not manifest itself down into Kurtz and Marlow; the heart in the darkness must reveal itself to itself.

Until he can arrive at the door that he imagines opening on himself and the silence, the Unnamable is doomed to keep talking, like a man whose one necessary task is to drill a well but whose only tool is a paintbrush. Language always has these problems but tends to ignore them; Beckett is neither obscuring the function of literature nor spinning death dirges, as many critics have suggested (Wylie Sypher, for instance, considers *The Unnamable* an extreme case of "loss of the self," an anonymous complaint against life[84]). On the contrary, he is awakening language from a drugged sleep, infusing it with new potential—and in these early stages, the oversleeper may be forgiven some grogginess. Literature is addicted to Mahood, and the doctor who attempts to introduce it cold turkey into the real world is liable to encounter the most resistance from the patient. This new art must begin by talking about itself in order to be itself—to come to terms with the self-consciousness that allows it to be both abstract and factual, even if those terms are under erasure.

All the terms of the Unnamable's compulsion are arrived at instantly, just as the life-functions of a child are breathed into motion at birth. Within fifteen pages of beginning, he abandons his "puppets":

> All these Murphys, Molloys and Malones do not fool me. They have made me waste my time, suffer for nothing, speak of them when, in order to stop speaking, I should have spoken of me and of me alone. . . .

> They never suffered my pains, their pains are nothing, compared to mine, a mere tittle of mine, the tittle I thought I could put from me, in order to witness it.[85]

So he begins the attempt again: "I, of whom I know nothing."[86] He knows that his use of words makes him appear to be like them and subject to their limits, but he is contemptuous of that assumption: "It's a poor trick that consists in ramming a set of words down your gullet on the principle that you can't bring them up without being branded as belonging to their breed."[87] His salvation is that he fails to understand or remember most of the words he uses, so that his processes are able to function in an ever-renewed present tense, not bound by previous identities or assertions, or by the lies and evasions that come from speaking an inadequate language. He is constantly free to experiment, to seek that impossible point where the closed system comes to terms with the animating metaconsciousness.

Somehow, between the words, the Unnamable finds that point. The novel ends with a four-page sentence in which he starts his attempt all over again, defining the place of his confinement as the inside of his head and allowing the words to tell him what to do. What he encounters is a manifestation that releases him from his task and appears to proceed from outside him. His attempt brings him to the edge of silence, where he is up against the same limits but where he feels something outside the closed system taking place— something that has slipped between the lines and brought him to an intuition.

The novel reaches its climax not in an impossible statement but in the narrator's sense that he is at the door that leads to his true self, that he is waiting for himself in the silence, that his true self will speak itself by speaking silence. In great excitement, the narrator feels himself waiting for an ineffable language to manifest itself so that he can be done with his saying and join what his saying has continuously shown:

281

he is made of silence, there's a pretty analysis, he's in the silence, he's the one to be sought, the one to be, the one to be spoken of, the one to speak, but he can't speak, then I could stop, I'd be he, I'd be the silence, I'd be back in the silence, we'd be reunited, his story the story to be told, but he has no story, he hasn't been in story, it's not certain, he's in his own story, unimaginable, unspeakable, that doesn't matter, the attempt must be made, in the old stories incomprehensibly mine, to find his, it must be there somewhere, it must have been mine, before being his, I'll recognize it, in the end I'll recognize it, the story of the silence that he never left, that I should never have left, that I may never find again, that I may find again, then it will be he, it will be I, it will be the place, the silence. . . .[88]

He was booted out of the silence by an author who made him speak, by an author who woke him from the blank pages that followed *Malone Dies*—or perhaps by an incomprehensible birth that filled him with words and made him subject to the compulsions of the murmuring voices. There is no way he can speak the "I" of the metaphysical self (both "he" and "I," and of course, beyond either term), but he can bring himself to a point where he will be ready for that self to accept him into its totality. Of course, that self, incomprehensibly his, has manifested itself throughout the work, but the words have not been able to declare it (the self is a limit of the world).

Arriving at an intuition that cannot be included in the text, the Unnamable finds himself suddenly at "the door." He feels the words giving out and the silence coming over him, but the words—necessarily unable to attain silence—declare up to the very last their compulsion to "go on." Up to the final printed moment, he remains verbally conscious; thus he never has an overview, never knows whether the silence that may be coming will be "the one that lasts" or only the space between literary incarnations. In the extraordinary moment that ends the novel, he accepts this compulsion as his own:

> you must go on, I can't go on, you must go on, I'll go on, you must say words, as long as there are any, until they find me, until they say me, strange pain, strange sin, you must go on, perhaps it's done already, perhaps they have said me already, perhaps they have carried me to the threshold of my story, before the door that opens on my story, that would surprise me, if it opens, it will be I, it will be the silence, where I am, I don't know, I'll never know, in the silence you don't know, you must go on, I can't go on, I'll go on.[89]

He accepts his vocation, and the pseudoexternal command, "you must go on," ceases. He has apparently discovered that the voices that force his expression are his own, that he is the entire narrating system and not just its mouthpiece. This instant of absolute systemic self-consciousness is not described in the text but is shown by the disappearance of "you must go on"; it is prompted by his intuition of being at the door, to which he has been brought by sheer persistence; and it immediately yields to the silence that may show his perfect integration (there is no way, of course, to know exactly what that silence "means").

The Unnamable is a record of turmoil, the birth-pang of the mind of the text, which occurs as the conscious self beats at the limits of apprehension that divide it from the metaphysical self. Beckett does not invent a silent language here, but he brilliantly dramatizes the limits of self-consciousness. In so doing, he creates a new character—the "I" that attempts to speak itself—and summons the "I" in common usage to an awareness of its possibilities. This self-conscious pronoun can prove the basis of a revolution in literature. "I" is not only the manifestation of human consciousness in language; it can now be seen or employed as *language's* attempt at self-consciousness. Written by Beckett, *The Unnamable* is a work that speaks itself, and in a much more recognizable

283

manner than *As I Lay Dying*. The sequence of internal filters and presenters has been dispensed with; the only "telescope" or displacement structure that remains is the fact of language, interposed between the will to expression and the metaphysical self, and now allowing "I" to be recognized as a direct manifestation of the presence of being, relentlessly unnamable and ubiquitous. What this revolution implicitly accomplishes, then, is to put the mind of the text on much the same level as human consciousness. The work remains able to speak in fictions; it does not have to be simply the factual record of its author's speech or the gropings of its narrator to apply words to his situation. But in an important sense, it can never again be innocently regarded as fiction, for it has become *autobiography*.

It is autobiography because it speaks in its own voice and records its own life. The fact that it may also be the first-person account of an invented narrator becomes a coincidence. Its "I" cannot wholly be assigned to Addie or Darl or Ishmael, any more than the Unnamable can give himself over to Mahood and find fulfillment. "Ishmael" and "Addie" are pasteboard masks for the minds of their novels. The reader can acknowledge these minds' struggles for coherent self-expression as much as their authors', particularly in the context of a battle with silence, for it is in such battles that the human mind (to invoke Stein) brings its principal tool up to its own existential level and enlists it in a struggle that takes place at their common boundary: the limits of apprehension. Within those limits, art has as much right as its author to self-awareness.

One possible implication of this line of thinking is that other forms and genres have undergone similar metamorphoses that, in the absence of an adequate critical understanding of self-consciousness, have not previously been recognized. There may come a point where any system—whether self, genre, or polis—becomes aware of its limits and intuits what must lie beyond them. At that point, it may break down—even appear to "go mad," as in the case of both *The Golden Notebook* and its hero, as we shall see later on—and grow; it may achieve an integration best described as a different structuring principle, another form.

To put this another way: systemically self-conscious fiction is a different category of expression from first-person narration. Goaded by many challenges—in particular, the problem of dealing with the ineffable and the related problem of dramatizing personal identity—the self-conscious novel has developed a means of dramatizing its own limits. Just as *Hamlet*, overburdened with Humanist self-consciousness, could not function as a conventional tragedy and therefore found itself dealing more with the nature of theatre than with the problem of revenge (Lionel Abel has called *Hamlet* the first work of "Metatheatre"), *The Unnamable* appears consumed in self-analysis and preoccupied by failure—an analysis and a failure that are inseparable from its awareness of the limits of language and from its awareness that the only alternatives it has to its current paradoxical state of being are to achieve silence or to lapse into conventional fiction.

New genres seem to arise not just when certain highly innovative authors become dissatisfied with the limitations imposed on them by existing narrative methods but when these authors arrive at their new methods by dramatizing the limits of the old from *within* those existing structures, so that the new genre appears to create itself out of the old. Thus the Greek drama may date from a hypothetical moment when certain voices split off from the Chorus and imitated the autonomy, will, and introspection of character, grappling with the problems of self-determination and helping to transform one kind of public religious ceremony into another. (Something similar apparently happened in the transition from chant to oratorio to opera.) Thus, too, metatheatre evolved out of the perceived limits of tragedy. *Don Quixote* can be seen in this context as a self-conscious romance: aware of the limits of its parent form; caricaturing its conventions while groping toward the social perspective, narrative range, and introspective psychology of the novel; and playing all the while with its own self-conscious project. Montaigne, transforming the epistle into the essay, appears centrally concerned with the feat of *trying* ("essayer") and with his own role as narrator and subject. And in *A Tale of a Tub*, Swift takes the essay form well past those limits, using irony and digression and the device of a maddened pamphleteer to create the first English novel. In other words, it is possible to suggest that most genres evolve out of a self-consciousness achieved within the context of their parent forms. This would give the lie, once and for all, to any notion that modern fiction is structured by "exhaustion" or even by a "postmodern" conviction of the negative artificiality of literary efforts. We are at a crucial and vitally exciting juncture in the history of the novel and perhaps in our cultural and linguistic paradigms.

In *The Book of Questions* Edmond Jabès lets the metaphysics of self-consciousness assume its maximum scope to date. In order to help explicate his masterful demonstration that at the end of the Unnamable's tunnel there is a Light that unifies language, life, theology, and silence—the non-place of the word in the Book—I would like to turn for a moment to a discussion of the Kabbalah.

Leo Schaya's *The Universal Meaning of the Kabbalah* argues that the monotheism of the Jewish mystics shares the basic insight of most major spiritual traditions: that God is the One and that the illusion of multiplicity in phenomena and language is a veiled manifestation of that One. Schaya offers a fascinating exposition of the Zohar and related texts that can be taken as an analogue to Shankara's Hinduism, to Buddhism, to Neo-Platonism, to Blake's cosmology, to Hegel's dialectic of self-consciousness, to Sufism, to Gnosticism, to John-Roger's MSIA, to the "tao of physics," as well as to such less esoteric expressions as the Koran and the Old and New Testaments. Since his book appeared in France in 1958,[90] it may well have been one of Jabès' sources

(and I will be using it as if it were—Jabès does in any case
operate in the space between Kabbalah and Derrida).

One of the most interesting aspects of Kabbalist thought
is the notion of the *Sefiroth,* the ten archetypal aspects of
God, which form a hierarchy that is mirrored throughout
the universe but particularly in humanity (recall Pynchon's
linking of the *Sefiroth,* the Tree of Life, the Tarot, and the
Countdown). The task of the "lower man" is to transcend
thought to a direct spiritual intuition of the One and so to
become more fully the "higher man," in whom *"kether* is
the 'hidden and superintelligible brain'; *hokhmah,* the 'right
brain,' which sees only the One; *binah,* the 'left brain,' the
principle of all distinction,"[91] and so on. Noting the comparable descriptions of the specialized functions of the
"right" and "left" brains here and in contemporary psychological research, let us examine the interplay of these
three highest *Sefiroth* in the self-knowledge of God, a systemic self-consciousness in which the "higher man" aspires
to participate:

> *Kether,* the "crown" . . . is the uncreated and infinite
> all-reality of God . . . pure selfness, superintelligible
> essence, unity without trace of duality. It is reality with-
> out condition, without definition, in which God is what
> he is, beyond being; for Being is not the absolute reality
> as such, but its first affirmation. . . . *Hokhmah,* "wis-
> dom," or the first divine emanation, issues from the
> more than luminous "nothingness" of *kether* as an infi-
> nitely radiant sun . . . the radiation of the divine being,
> in which he contemplates himself. . . . In *hokhmah,*
> God knows himself as being all that is, and all that is
> knows itself as God. There, no difference in being or in
> knowledge exists between him and one or another es-
> sence; for *hokhmah* is the eternal resolution of opposi-
> tions. . . . It issues from the divine being, yet without
> issuing from it; in its infinity, it is hidden in *kether—*

287

which is itself contained in *ain,* the absolute and super-conscious self—while at the same time, in becoming conscious of all its knowable possibilities, it is as it were outside of *kether.* . . . Before manifesting itself to the worlds, the divine being reveals itself, in its wisdom, its act of pure knowledge, to itself, that is, to its own receptivity, its "intelligence": *binah.* . . . Thus *hokhmah* pours out all the intelligible possibilities of *kether* into the midst of *binah* in a single undifferentiated emanation. . . . *Kether, hokhmah* and *binah* are the one and only God revealing himself to himself. . . . "The Creator's knowing (his consciousness or knowledge) is not like that of his creatures; for in creatures the knowing is distinct from the subject and is brought to bear on objects which are likewise distinct from the subject. This is expressed by the three terms: thought, that which thinks, and that which is thought. On the contrary, the Creator is himself knowledge, that which knows, and that which is known all at the same time. His way of knowing does not consist of applying his thought to things outside himself; by knowing himself and perceiving himself, he knows and perceives all that is."[92]

God's systemic self-consciousness (compare the ending of the *Paradiso*) is utterly nonverbal, and the triad of *kether, hokhmah,* and *binah* in which Being is manifest to itself is a subsystem or activity transcended by *kether,* the ultimate ground of which Being is an affirmation. The human intuition of Oneness is a stage in the return to the heart of God, which can also be facilitated by the chanting of God's name (a current issuing from and returning to God; this is, doubtless, the most important reason God's name is not to be taken in vain). The transcendental man—in which the higher self is linked to the soul, which has never entirely left God and which sends its wavelike emanations down into the higher self, the conscious self, the basic self, and the physical body—contemplates his *kether* through the intuitions of spirit rather than through an analysis of the multiplicity of the world. The *kether* of transcendental man is to Atman as the *kether* of God is to Brahman, and the ultimate metaphysical fulfillment is the instantaneous vanishing of the personal One into the "One without a second," the "I AM THAT I AM" of God, which involves a transcending of the illusions of all temporal and phenomenal and linguistic difference into the simultaneous or eternal unity of the absolute.

When a narrator/character becomes systemically self-conscious, realizing that he is within the system of his own expression, he does not begin to reenter the heart of God (unless God takes equal account of all creations, even those that are not alive). To argue that he did would be to mistake the finite for the infinite, which to the Kabbalists (as to Plato, who considered art the shadow of a shadow), would be a fundamental error. A systemically self-conscious work can, however, be used as a tool to prompt the reader to his or her own self-discovery, particularly since the novel and the thinking consciousness can be presented as equally responsive to holistic extrasystemic intuitions that each is, for analogous reasons, unable to sort out within the system. It is in this sense that the mind of such a text is on the same level as the mind (especially the *binah*) of man. *Malone Dies* parodies the dream of having the account of an object "distinct from the subject" facilitate the Godlike unity of thought and thinker. *The Unnamable* goes further by showing the failure of expression (since the medium is language rather than divine self-awareness), even where the thought and the thinker are *one* in a way the thinker cannot formulate. Beckett, after all, studied Dante as closely as he did Proust.

The Book of Questions says that the book in question is not a poem-novel by "Jabès" but a complex analogue to the Book of God, the universe. In this context, systemic self-awareness is not a stage within literature but a stage in the human condition. The Book of the universe is written not in words but in divine emanations, the word as Logos or as an aspect of God's self-contemplation. The characters are made of the same substance that the Book is and are capable of analogous acts of generation ("You are the one who writes and the one who is written"). To be aware of one's role in *The Book of Questions* is to be a systemically self-conscious element of Jabès' text (like the Unnamable), but it is also to show the limits of self-awareness of the linguistic being who is written in the Book of God.

The Book of Questions is an auto-ontological world in which reader, text, characters, and God are able to meet. It consists of three volumes: *The Book of Questions, The Book of Yukel,* and *Return to the Book.* As a whole, the system is self-narrating. On the next level down, the narrator is Jabès, an Egyptian Jew living in "exile" in Paris, who takes the name "Yukel" in homage to the pain of one of his characters (Yukel) and who examines his own role in the creation of the book (a role that often involves stepping aside so that the work may discover its own form as the words advance on the void they seek to express). The manifested form is a dialectic, a collage of poetic fragments and commentaries in search of the synthesis that is the book—an aspiration toward systemic self-consciousness that closes the circle:

> The story of Sarah and Yukel is the account, through various dialogues and meditations attributed to imaginary rabbis, of a love destroyed by men and by words. It has the dimensions of the book and the bitter stubbornness of a wandering question.[93]

The book is full of questions to which the book is the answer.

The Kabbalist axiom that God exists in the silence of his own complete self-knowledge finds its challenge in the limits of human knowledge and in the atrocities of history, whose site is the Jew, the zone of the question of Being. In an attempt to utter the silence that is analogous to God's word, language can only question. The alternative to the mystical Kabbalah is the questioning Talmud, a dialogue of commentary and symbolic interpretation whose center is the sacred text. *The Book of Questions* is by turns Kabbalist and Talmudic in point and method. Commentary yields to further commentary as one question leads to another. One learns not from the answers but from "the order of the questions"[94] and from a look at the whole:

> "I have turned all the pages of the book without finding hope."
> "Perhaps hope is the book."[95]

The Kabbalist ideal, in which the higher man's assured awareness of being is comparable to that of God, is revised here so that what man, God, and language share is the same degree of paradoxical absence. Although God is absent from man, who "moves within the eye of God fixed on His own image," it is also argued that "God loses His life on the shores of His sovereign voice" and that the site of that loss is where man calls to himself.[96] The world allows God to be in exile from himself in a place where his name is unpronounceable; thus he is unknowable in the Void and unnamable in the world, which is his Book. The author is in the same situation:

> So ever since the book my life has been a wake of writing in the space between limits, under the resplendent sign of the unpronounceable Name. . . . Repetition is man's power to perpetuate himself in God's supreme speculations. To repeat the divine act in its First Cause. Thus man is God's equal in his power to choose an unpredictable Word which he alone can launch.[97]

It is not just that the writer attempts to imitate God but that to write is to create a world and that from that instant forward the world creates the writer. (Borges would doubtless agree with this, though his perspective is more limited.) The writer's quest begins as an attempt to offer an adequate sign for what he or she means, but it is reversed in the moment of the text so that it is not the meaning but the sign

291

that exists—and further, the sign exists only insofar as it is able to create meaning. This involuted system is like the world, "written" by God as an expression of his presence but from which he is perceived as an absence; from within the world, one concludes that the world creates life as the text creates meaning—not some preexisting meaning in the intentions of the author, but something newly created by the interaction of text and reader (who is continually acknowledged as an element of Jabès' system). "The book is the work of the book."[98] In his final sentences, Jabès observes: "Man does not exist. God does not exist. The world alone exists through God and man in the open book."[99] This might be interpreted to mean that the book is the primary reality, since it contains the world and is the site of the confrontation between its otherwise absent elements, God and man; but whichever is primary, it is the interaction between these elements "in the open book" that lets the world exist.

The book is aware of its limits; and this awareness of its being coextensive with the world, this systemic self-consciousness, is continually referred back to the question of silence. Silence is the limit of speech but is also one of its elements, as the absence of God is an element of his presence in the world. This is a book that fits into Derrida's system (and it is Derrida who has written the first strong essay on Jabès[100]) since each of its signs is charged with the unsaid and every answer is another question. Words aspire to perfect significance, but meaning is often in what they do not say:

> And Reb Hati: "The pages of the book are doors. Words go through them, driven by their impatience to regroup, to reach the end of the work, to be again transparent.
> "Ink fixes the memory of words to the paper.
> "Light is in their absence, which you read."[101]

In the Zohar it is said that the "black fire" of the words of Scripture is written on the "white fire" of the parchment, the latter of which is not just blankness but the transcendental luminosity of the ideal Scripture, the ineffable Word; the black fire is an interpretation, an attempt to translate into the terms of the world. The Torah is its own failed commentary, an aspiration toward its own higher self, the first Talmud. Jabès' words—available to the reader only in the ink that shows the traces of their passage (they are already gone)—communicate through the context of their absence. The reader reads the black fire but, in search of the white, reads with an awareness that one must see past the ink, which is only the corpse of signification. This is how a self-aware limited system prompts the reader to look past it into the silence, and it is the way one reads the whole book and participates in the creation of meaning.

It is clear how all this applies to the quest for self, for in the Book, the self is a name—especially if one starts from the Jewish assumption that one is written in the Book of God, so that to be in the world and to be written in the Book of God are identical. For a character in *The Book of Questions,* to write one's name is an existential affirmation and to read one's name is to question the limits of being and the intentions of God. To understand one's role in this book is exactly analogous to understanding one's place in the universe—even if both the book and the universe are conceivable only as structures of self-questioning. The "problem vanishes" when one sees that the book is the answer to its quest. (This is not to imply that the atrocities of history vanish, for they do not; the task is rather to put them in context, to see them as questions in the Book, in their own way as unfathomable as the question of Being.) This is where the self-narrating quality of the system becomes most intriguing, for Yukel's probings of silence and atrocity and Jabès/Yukel's analyses of the system he is helping to voice are both subsumed within the mind of the text.

The Book of Questions begins with a dedication to its characters, to its project, and to the reader, all of which participate in the site of signification that is the book. In the chapter "At the Threshold of the Book," the mind of this phase of the text is questioned by a voice that is about to enter the book (a surrogate of the reader):

> "What is your lot?"
> "To open the book."
> "Are you in the book?"
> "My place is at the threshold."
> . . . "What is your story?"
> "Ours, insofar as it is absent."
> . . . "Where are you?"
> "In what I say."[102]

This is the clearest possible example of a systemically self-conscious utterance by the mind of the text and of how in this book to speak is to be. The reader objects that the self-sufficiency of the text's voice is a dead end and that it ought to tell one something beyond that it is there:

> "What can you do for me?"
> "Your share of luck is in yourself."
> "Writing for the sake of writing does nothing but show contempt."
> "Man is a written bond and place."[103]

So the text's being is no more a dead end than is existence, and the voice of the text knows much in accepting its role. By now the reader wishes to come into the lighted house of the book, looks forward to *living in* the book, but the voice responds accurately that a different role awaits: "You will follow the book, whose every page is an abyss where the wing shines with the name."

A few pages later, other sentences declare their roles and simultaneously carry them out:

> To be in the book. To figure in the book of questions, to be part of it. To be responsible for a word or a sentence, a stanza or a chapter.
> To be able to say: "I am in the book. The book is my

world, my country, my roof, and my riddle. The book is my breath and my rest."

I get up with the page that is turned. I lie down with the page put down. . . . I will evoke the book and provoke the questions.

If God is, it is because He is in the book. If sages, saints, and prophets exist, if scholars and poets, men and insects exist, it is because their names are found in the book. The world exists because the book does. For existing means growing with your name.

The book is the work of the book.[104]

It will be noted that each of these sentences speaks the absolute truth, from the perspective of a sentence *in* this book.

Soon this voice declares its proper name. It declares its awareness that it can pretend to be the vehicle of other voices, including those of the "wound" it would express and of the reader, but that what it is, is textuality. The parallels with *The Unnamable* are striking:

I say "I," and I am not "I." "I" means you, and you are going to die. You are drained.

From now on, I will be alone.

. . . You are walking toward death. . . . And it is I who force you to walk. I sow your steps.

And I think, I speak for you. I choose and cadence.

For I am writing

and you are the wound.

. . . Forgive me, Yukel. I have substituted my inspired sentences for yours. You are the toneless utterance among anecdotal lies.[105]

The reader, the narrator (Yukel), the character (Yukel), the painful act of signification (the wound), history (the wound)—all of these are the "you" that the "I" of the text expresses, and here the "I" assumes the burden of self-consciousness as a real voice and as the medium of fiction (an-

295

ecdotal lies), the responsibility for all communication and failure. Its name is "I," and it is writing. Yukel, the rabbis, and the reader look for their names in the book and discover that they are "written"—that textuality (existence) is manifesting itself as themselves, that they are organized expressions of the consciousness of the system, that Being masks itself in them (as in time) to allow the system's self-questioning to continue. The book is in this sense acting like God, the underlying ground of Being that masks itself in Saying and phenomena to further its own self-realization. Every pronoun in this book is superimposed on the unspoken, "absent," "I" of the text.

The task of the characters is to see that the existence of the whole system is the answer to all the questions that are not answered within it. The book ends when the three most "essential" questions have been formulated: those of the self, the world, and the void.[106] To ask questions, to write, is to mirror "the divine gesture" and to discover that the void that this act opens is both being and the answer to being:

The invisible form of the book is the legible body of God. . . .

We are at the heart of creation, absent from the All, in the marrow and moire of Absence, with the Void for recourse, for a means to be and to survive. So that, in the creative act, we are and even surpass the Void facing the restoring All.

Book rejected and reclaimed by the book. The word, for which I was pain and meditation, discovers that its true place is the non-place where God lives resplendent with not being, with never having been. . . .

The work imposes its choices on us. Only much later the writer becomes aware of this. . . .

"In the book reality learns and reveals what it is: a visible irreality which we confront with itself, with its base in the summoned word."[107]

296

Reality is "irreal" in the same sense that a word is an absence, and language's facing language reveals that language and reality share the same "non-place" in which only paradoxical terms can describe what it means to be. The "visible irreality which we confront with itself" returns us, of course, to the "dumb blankness, full of meaning" that was the goad to *Moby-Dick*'s self-conscious project, but with a more practical understanding of the problem of "atheism." To create in what can be *known* only as an existential vacuum informed by a rupture is to create God—not as a lie but as an unfiction who is as real as man and language (if God is more than that, one cannot say—and Derrida interprets Jabès as saying "No"— but the wholeness of the self-conscious system suggests an answer). The book confronts that it is a structure of words and declares in the same instant that it is a world as real as any other.

The "I" that has suffered and meditated so that the word might arrive is indistinguishably Jabès and the mind of the text. If one could see the "form of the book," one could "read" God, who is not in the text but whose absence may be his clearest manifestation. Even if there is no God, one is left with the same set of self-answering questions. The probing of the relations between language and silence, and the attempt to see the system as a limited whole, have issued in the reclamation of the book, not as an act of "contempt" but as a profound exploration of the nature and condition of man. In the rigor of these correspondences, it is an augury of the future of self-conscious fiction.

Literature's self-questioning is the path of its self-renewal, its regeneration. Like *The Unnamable, Identity A Poem, The Divine Comedy, Moby-Dick, As I Lay Dying,* and numerous other works haunted by the inexpressible and by themselves, *The Book of Questions* shows how systemic self-consciousness and intuitions of the metaphysical inadequacy of language—both of which reflect an awareness of limits—reinforce each other in the creation of a world whose radical autonomy and beauty find their only adequate parallel and antecedent in life, which is Light, which is love.

4. FEMINISM AND THE DIS-COVERY OF SELF

Spinsters spin and weave, mending and creating unity of consciousness. In doing so we spin through and beyond the realm of multiply split consciousness.

—Mary Daly, *Gyn/Ecology*

Every woman who writes is a survivor.

—Tillie Olsen, *Silences*

If the metaphysical insight is so radically self-sustaining and holistic, one might reasonably ask where a literature organized around that insight is capable of going. Once Saying has pointed past itself to Being, what is there to say? But this is much like arguing that once one knows who one really is, one has nothing to do. One *can* do more than bask in Being, however; one can act, grounding action in the centered recognition and energy resource of systemic completeness. The same is true of the self-conscious novel, which can address from its holistic and ~~fictional~~ perspective the problems of the real world. The literature of radical feminism has evolved in much the same way that the literature of the ineffable has and offers a clear example of the politics of self-consciousness.

For a better understanding of the appropriateness of reflexive literary structures to woman's quest for authentic self-recognition and self-expression, it is necessary to examine the limits not just of the personal but also of the patriarchal system. Some limits are inevitable, but others are blinders, taboos, artificial limits that serve the convenience of those in power. That which is genuinely "off limits" will take care of itself; there will be no means to describe it, no social order on hand to reinforce it. Feminist literature chal-

298

lenges the second order of limitation, confronting both political and metaphysical boundaries together—for what is at issue in both confrontations is the nature of the self.

There has been built into most languages and patriarchal cultures a wall, on one side of which woman is defined as Other, as she who differs, as she whose creativity is founded on self-absence and whose uterus is not an organ but a void. As outlined by Mary Daly, among others, the feminist "journey" involves violating the boundaries of patriarchal space and finding on the other side of the wall the Self that is not Other. From this freedom come new and subversive acts of naming, his/hers designations that can appear inconvenient or trivial, breakthroughs that can look like madness, terrible powers of rage and love, self-definition founded not on negation but on plenitude. What may begin in a revolt against "the language" opens a space in which a woman can enter her wholeness and go on to consider that in her which transcends language (thus dealing with the Derridean Other rather than the "feminine" Other). No one can be free or self-knowing, can truly be said to have addressed the limits of language and consciousness, who has also accepted as a limit the half world of patriarchy, the domain of the halves and half-nots. It is not that language is patriarchal but that patriarchy has long presented itself as the world's language.[108]

In his *Philosophical Investigations,* Wittgenstein substituted for the notion of a limited language the notion of an extensive cluster of language games, each with its own rules. I have already suggested that whatever the validity of this later work, the *Tractatus* remains essentially accurate, if only as a model of the most fundamental and all-embracing of language games (whose irreducible, tautological, and final rule is that the ineffable is ineffable). What Mary Daly, Susan Griffin, Adrienne Rich, and Monique Wittig are showing is that the language of patriarchy is a language game and that the game must be seen through and its limits addressed if there is to be a literature that accurately corresponds to, celebrates, and critiques the real existence of women. Adrienne Rich's "silence" is not that of the ineffable but that of women declining, unable, or forbidden to speak.[109] Susan Griffin's *Woman and Nature*[110] offers a deconstruction of patriarchal assumptions and vocabulary that emerges with a new energy of naming and of world-definition. In *Gyn/Ecology*,[111] Mary Daly critiques the pronominal code, the uses of the passive voice, the deliberate abuses of scholarship, the atrocities of erasure and the erasure of atrocities, in an unrelenting and often hilarious "dis-covery" that is also a model of the "Journey into the Background."

One of the ways Daly breaks ground for a radical lesbian/ feminist language game is to pun, hyphenate, capitalize, invent, recontextualize, and scrutinize words so that they reveal new meanings, latent meanings, or etymologically and historically suppressed meanings, which become keys that can stimulate new perspectives. This conjunction of radical insight and transfigurative language makes Daly's work comparable to that of Emily Dickinson. The title *Gyn/Ecology*, for example—"a way of wrenching back some word-power"[112]—critiques and unmasks the "gynocidal" and "phallocratic" practice of gynecology while affirming an ecology ("the complex web of interrelationships between organisms and their environment") of woman. The slash mark becomes a site of linguistic reflexivity and deconstruction. The new word is useful in naming a new program of thought: "Gyn/Ecology is by and about women a-mazing all the male-authored 'sciences of womankind,' and weaving world tapestries *of our own kind*. That is, it is about dis-covering, de-veloping the complex web of living/loving relationships *of our own kind*. It is about women living, loving, creating our Selves, our cosmos."[113] Undoing the patriarchal labyrinth ("a-mazing") is one element of the journey into what Daly and Denise Connors call "the Background": "the realm of the wild reality of women's Selves."[114] The "Background" is a place of power and authenticity (Margaret Atwood's *Surfacing* is one fictional treatment of how it might feel to touch this energy), and "Selves" is capitalized as a way of signifying the unmediated truth of the personal center, a selfhood that predates socialization, myth, or personality—an enspiriting holistic energy. Although this energy is closely related to the higher self as well as to the freed and unconflicted basic self, and although it focuses via the conscious self in writing and in comparable social expressions, the woman who deeply contacts it is often called "mad" or "a witch," so that even if she is not socially persecuted she may internalize this rejecting attitude and become so double-binded and depressed that she will retreat from this threatening energy and suffer a kind of death.

It is common both in literature and in psychiatric clinics to find women who experience themselves as split between a madwoman and a social being. The madwoman, or the woman going through a mad phase, often has great freedom to see and speak clearly (examples range from Cassandra in *The Trojan Women* to Linda in *The Four-Gated City*) and is sometimes presented as a spiritual figure, especially in the works of Doris Lessing and others influenced by R. D. Laing. In some cases, the madwoman is understood as a split-off projection from the immanent or foregone wholeness of the protagonist's Gestalt (as in Charlotte Perkins Gilman's "The Yellow Wallpaper"), and in others, as an independent personality who is also an avowed/disavowed element of the protagonist, like Bertha Mason Rochester in *Jane Eyre,* the paradigmatic "madwoman in the attic."[115] Emily Dickinson noted, as Laing would later, that one needs "a discerning Eye" to recognize that "Much Madness is divinest Sense," that to be mad may be to be deeply in touch with a transcendent understanding.[116] It is this form of madness one finds in Ahab and Darl. As Dickinson argues in a later poem, the only way to escape the insights and demands of the Self may be to self-destruct:

> . . . since Myself—assault Me—
> How have I peace

Except by subjugating
Consciousness?

And since We're mutual Monarch
How this be
Except by Abdication—
Me—of Me?[117]

The relegation of woman to "Other" has, of course, encouraged this self-abdication, both psychologically and po-
litically as well as metaphysically. Simone de Beauvoir puts
this clearly:

> Every individual concerned to justify his existence feels
> that his existence involves an undefined need to tran-
> scend himself, to engage in freely chosen projects.
>
> Now, what peculiarly signalizes the situation of
> woman is that she—a free and autonomous being like
> all human creatures—nevertheless finds herself living in
> a world where men compel her to assume the status of
> the Other. They propose to stabilize her as object and
> to doom her to immanence since her transcendence is to
> be overshadowed and forever transcended by another
> ego *(conscience)* which is essential and sovereign. The
> drama of woman lies in this conflict between the fun-
> damental aspirations of every subject (ego)—who al-
> ways regards the self as the essential—and the compul-
> sions of a situation in which she is the inessential.[118]

It is one thing to say that woman is "other than male" (a
difference that, freely explored, may lead to a clear self-affir-
mation) and something entirely different to say that woman
is "the Other," since the true Self is properly defined as the
irreducible THIS/HERE of Being. For Monique Wittig, it is
impossible even to say "I" in a language predicated on her
not being a self-authenticating "subject," so she writes "J/e"
as a "symbol of the lived, rending experience which is m/y
writing."[119] It is not necessary, however, to stop at the perception of fragmentation.

Because the writer confronts herself and the world both as
creator and as subject, writing is a special and charged means
of defining and healing the self. This is one reason "Every
woman who writes is a survivor" and the most obvious reason that women's writing—recognized however unconsciously as subversive—has been suppressed, whether the re-
pressive agent be the writer's mate, her internalized self-
rejection, or the critical establishment that decides what is
published and generates canons. A typical example of modern canonization is the elevation of D. H. Lawrence—whom
I consider not only a demonic incompetent but also the only
human ever genuinely to have suffered from penis envy[120]—
and the near obliteration of Kate Chopin and Dorothy Richardson; a more damning story is that of Margery Kempe,
author of the first extant autobiography in English, whose
work was broken off when her male scribe died.[121] Virginia
Woolf's evocation of Shakespeare's sister brings into the
group of women writers those who "never wrote a
word,"[122] and the number of works written but never published is inestimable. A typical defense of such suppression
can be found in the *Journal* of John Winthrop, Puritan Gov-
ernor of the Massachusetts Bay Colony at Boston (instru-
mental, seven years earlier, in the banishment of Anne Hut-
chinson):

> [April 13, 1645] Mr. Hopkins, the governor of Hartford
> upon Connecticut, came to Boston, and brought his wife
> with him, (a godly young woman, and of special parts)
> who was fallen into a sad infirmity, the loss of her un-
> derstanding and reason, which had been growing upon
> her divers years, by occasion of her giving herself
> wholly to reading and writing, and had written many
> books. Her husband, being very loving and tender of
> her, was loath to grieve her; but he saw his error when
> it was too late. For if she had attended her household
> affairs and such things as belong to women, and not
> gone out of her way and calling to meddle in such

things as are proper for men, whose minds are stronger,
etc., she had kept her wits and might have improved
them usefully and honorably in the place God had set
her.[123]

Some 240 years later, in Philadelphia, the internationally
famous nerve specialist Dr. S. Weir Mitchell applied much
the same level of insight to the economist and novelist Charlotte Perkins Gilman. The treatment he administered nearly
drove her mad, for, of course, it is not writing that leads to
madness—though it is often involved in such rites of passage
as those undergone by the liminal protagonists of *Surfacing*
and *The Golden Notebook*—but writing that clarifies and
heals, and internalized self-rejection/denial that often pro-
motes madness and fragments consciousness.[124] (The threat
of a "rest cure" modeled on Mitchell's apparently contributed to Virginia Woolf's decision to kill herself.) Although
it is most likely that what had brought on Gilman's initial
fits of helpless depression and fatigue was her discomfort
with the institution of marriage, Mitchell assumed that what
she needed was to do no writing. After a month of bed rest
in his sanitarium, as Gilman recounts in her autobiography:

> . . . he sent me home, with this prescription:
> "Live as domestic a life as possible. Have your child
> with you all the time." (Be it remarked that if I did but
> dress the baby it left me shaking and crying—certainly
> far from a healthy companionship for her, to say noth-
> ing of the effect on me.) "Lie down an hour after each
> meal. Have but two hours' intellectual life a day. And
> never touch pen, brush or pencil as long as you live."
> I went home, followed those directions rigidly for
> months, and came perilously near to losing my mind.[125]

In her story "The Yellow Wallpaper," Gilman presents
the hidden journal of a woman whose husband, a doctor,
imposes a similar treatment on her. This nameless woman
reveals in many ironic remarks that her feelings of guilt and

exhaustion stem from repressed anger at her husband's denying the validity of her perceptions and restricting her healthy impulses. Her remark that "He is very careful and loving, and hardly lets me stir without special direction,"[126] for instance, recalls Winthrop and indicts a virulent "crazymaking" that insists on calling an evil (domination) by its opposite (love). Laing has shown that the schizophrenic in a schizophrenogenic family is often its most sensitive and perceptive member, whose fragmented consciousness is a scapegoat manifestation of the unacknowledged contradictions by which the family insists on living.[127] Since her husband "hates to have me write a word," the woman conceals her journal, which becomes the place where she most directly confronts her situation (this is in itself an authorially self-conscious presentation of the embattled role of women's writing within a patriarchy). She is confined to a barred room with "atrocious" yellow wallpaper, behind which she comes to imagine there is a woman, her own maddened split-off self whom in the course of the story she virtually becomes. Between these women is an ugly decorative barrier that must be peeled away if the mad self is to be acknowledged and the social self to be healed—a healing that would depend on the integration of the woman's Gestalt. (At one point the narrator begins to feel healthy "*because* of the wallpaper.") Because of the intense suppression of the woman's autonomy and process, however, the rebellious, imprisoned projection (sometimes seen as many women trying to climb through a strangling pattern[128]) is not holistically re-owned—or rather, the socialized linguistic self surrenders to her silent sister. She does, however, continue to write in her journal, so that it remains ambiguous whether her madness will eventually develop, as a rite of passage, into a new perspective. In both its positive and negative aspects, then, "The Yellow Wallpaper" becomes a horror story, a self-conscious example of that stage of feminist literature in which writing and the risk of madness are inseparable, yet in which writing is still a "relief."

305

The self is fragmented when it is replaced by a cluster of roles, and to recognize this fragmentation can strike one as the first stage of madness. To have an insight of the extra-systemic existence of wholeness and then to be unable to exercise that wholeness in action—to be thrust back into the firelit Cave—is to feel trapped in fragmentation and not necessarily to discover the personal resources or sustaining vision necessary to transcend that fragmentation. These remarks apply as well to Ahab and Darl as they do to those who have been socialized to consider the face as an accretion of masks, who are on the verge of discovering that the Self is not Other but who have internalized the rules of self-*différance*. The threat of madness often intervenes between the vision of wholeness and the world of unexamined limits, and madness figures regularly in the literature of the ineffable as well as that of feminism because it can characterize, in both contexts, the aspirations and contradictions of being at once inside and outside the Cave.

It is clear that not all madness is psychosis and that there are many dark and frightening aspects of authentic self-discovery. On an initial level, one might have to acknowledge that one has behaved unacceptably in certain situations, has lied to oneself, has acted against one's own or others' best interests; one might have to confront the fear of aloneness and take the risk of abandonment and rejection; one might have to overcome the fear of change itself. On a more metaphysical level, many people engaged in such meditative disciplines as Self-Realization Exercises[129] report a phase of blackness, a void of nonbeing, a frightening or else neutral pseudodeath that must be entered before the higher self steps forward. As in "The Yellow Wallpaper," the madness that is often addressed in fiction by women tends to be doubly determined: by social pressures against role breakdown (pressures whose rigidity makes role breakdown one of the few healthy options), and by the dynamic energy of the self that seeks to transcend fragmentation. These are closely related traumatic/fulfilling situations, and they each have linguistic effects, which may be schematized, respectively, as the verbal exuberance of naming with new rules and the breakdown of language in the face of the ineffable. The woman who transcends her socially reinforced fragmentation and its metaphysical complement is in a position to be healthy and creative; she is also in a position to explore the wholeness of Being.

In Lessing's *The Golden Notebook*, for instance, Anna Wulf goes through a stage of madness when she attempts to integrate all the aspects of herself, each of which writes in a different notebook as a different kind of writer. In the central, "golden" notebook in which she achieves this integration, she has moments of transcending language entirely. This process leaves her cured of a writer's block, and she goes on to compose a short novel called *Free Women*. This is a clear example of the ways the themes of madness, fragmentation of consciousness, the limits of language, and the discovery of an integrated self go together. Because it also shows the relation of systemic self-consciousness to these concerns, *The Golden Notebook* is worth turning to at some length.

Throughout much of her writing career, Anna keeps four notebooks. To each she commits the notations of one of her self-aspects. In one notebook, she writes as a novelist, in one as a diarist, and so on. She comes to terms with her experience as an African Communist, for example, first by writing a novel about it, then by rejecting the novel's falsehoods and attempting to set down what "really" happened; she also describes a long love affair both from the perspective of a fictional alter ego and as it happened to her everyday self. When she becomes involved in an intense love relationship that, in connection with her writer's block, makes her aware of the failure of these selves to cohere, she begins a fifth, golden notebook—an attempt to put "all of me in one book." This golden notebook is something of a red herring because it is in part a collaboration with the lover (also a writer); it becomes clear on reflection that *The Golden Note-*

book as a complete system is the book that somehow manifests Anna's wholeness.

In the golden notebook, the critical stage of her self-discovery, Anna writes:

> During the last weeks of craziness and timelessness I've had these moments of "knowing" one after the other, yet there is no way of putting this sort of knowledge into words. Yet these moments have been so powerful, like the rapid illuminations of a dream that remain with one waking, that what I have learned will be part of how I experience life until I die. Words. Words. I play with words, hoping that some combination, even a chance combination, will say what I want. Perhaps better with music? . . . Anything at all, but not words. The people who have been there, in the place in themselves where words, patterns, order, dissolve, will know what I mean and the others won't.[130]

If one goes completely through this "craziness and timelessness" whose insights are ineffable, Lessing argues, one may discover a new autonomy based on integration, a personal completeness in which freedom is natural and creativity is possible. Rather than stop, as Beckett often does, at the silence of the silence, Lessing goes on to examine the fullness of the personal and literary system that has been transfigured by this confrontation with the silence, demonstrating clearly that self-consciousness is not a dead end but the foundation of another literature.

Anna emerges from her limit-shattering experience as a whole person, as an identity freed from her roles yet in no way "reduced." The novel she writes uses her own name and those of her friends; it is a success in that it integrates the many kinds of writing explored in the notebooks, but a disappointment in that it is a rather ordinary piece of fiction without much of a sense of what it might mean to be a free woman.[131] In the context of *The Golden Notebook,* however,

Free Women has a more interesting function; its importance lies in its *being* a fiction.

Lessing has repeatedly said that the form of *The Golden Notebook* is its major achievement and that *Free Women*'s inadequacy is itself a comment on "the conventional novel"; she has described her aim as "to shape a book which would make its own comment, a wordless statement: to talk through the way it was shaped."[132] That form is an assemblage of the writings of a fictional character. One reads a chapter from *Free Women,* then a long excerpt from each of the four notebooks in turn, then another chapter of *Free Women,* and so on, with the golden notebook occurring as its own section near the end. One assumes at first that *Free Women* is by Lessing only and not by Anna—that it is "the truth"—partly because it is in the thrid person, uses "real" names, and begins on page one with no overt framing. But when one discovers at the end that *Free Women* is the fiction written after the golden notebook experience, its "Anna" becomes a character in the reader's mind and the "real Anna," the writing Anna, jumps to the limits of the whole system one has been reading. She is the eye, and all these writings are her visual or expressive field.

The Golden Notebook is the record of *Free Women*'s genesis; it is also a self-conscious critique of the limits of fiction and a celebration of its own struggle toward completeness. The mind of this text is inseparably that of a self-conscious novel and that of the writing Anna. The organization of the book manifests, in Wittgenstein's sense, how Anna as a complex or a system is a whole; this is what its "shape" *shows*. It is as accurate to say that *The Golden Notebook* narrates itself as to say that it is narrated by an Anna who appears nowhere in the book, a narrating intelligence at the periphery of the system, everywhere evident yet nowhere defined. The complete Anna and the mind of the text are emblems for each other, and the simultaneous selves of the notebooks and *Free Women* fuse past themselves into that double emblem.

Although Lessing's work is by her own admission not feminist,[133] it shares much with feminist literature in that it does clarify the relation between self-realization and writing, the necessity to speak from wholeness. Lessing shows how confrontations with the ineffable and the self are coterminous and how the form of a self-conscious novel is analogous to the system of consciousness (with the ultimate self outside the boundaries of each and everything namable within; because the golden notebook occurs inside the limits of the system, it does not analyze its "moments of 'knowing'"). What this shows is that the self-conscious novel has resources that may prove useful to the feminist imagination, where self-definition is a matter of creative, linguistic, and political urgency. Just as feminist literature may gain from the juncture of self-consciousness and the unnamable that informs this fiction, the literature of self-consciousness may find in much feminist writing an example of its relevance to the lived-in world, despite the determination of most critics and many novelists to limit it to a solipsistic narcissism.

The Golden Notebook is a systemically self-conscious novel that involves a confrontation with the ineffable but is not programmatically feminist. Joanna Russ's *The Female Man,* by contrast, is a systemically self-conscious novel that is programmatically feminist but does not involve a confrontation with the ineffable, though it does address clearly the importance and the problem of writing and most emphatically organizes itself around the quest for the true self. These novels, whose structures are remarkably similar,[134] may be considered the poles of the argument I am advancing in this part of the chapter: that systemic reflexivity naturally accompanies many attempts to discover the limits of the self; that whether or not one chooses to adopt a metaphysical perspective on that problem, the self will be most effectively presented as a limit of the narrative system and of its conscious analogues; and that feminist literature often works with these structures and implicitly demonstrates their relevance and utility. Before discussing *The Female Man* in depth,

310

however, I would like to set Russ's work in the context of feminist science fiction.

In an important essay, "What Can a Heroine Do? or Why Women Can't Write," Russ argues the value of what she calls the "lyric mode" for feminist writing:

> If *the narrative mode* (what Aristotle called "epic") concerns itself with *events* connected by the *chronological order* in which they occur, and *the dramatic mode* with *voluntary human actions* which are connected both by *chronology and causation,* then the principle of construction I wish to call *lyric* consists of *the organization of discrete elements* (images, events, scenes, passages, words, what-have-you) *around an unspoken thematic or emotional center.* The lyric mode exists without chronology or causation; its principle of connection is *associative.*[135]

Offering Virginia Woolf as an example of a lyric novelist, and implicitly engaging such structures as those of *As I Lay Dying* and *The Golden Notebook,* Russ finds that "the unspeakable and unembodyable," the "action-one-cannot-name," can be manifested or approached not in "discrete elements" of the text but as a property of the system, as something those elements *"add up to."*[136] But Russ is interested not only in woman's struggle to discover and name the unspeakable center of the Self who is not Other but also in the politics of that discovery. One advantage of science fiction is that its stories are not "about men *qua* Man and women *qua* Woman; they are myths of human intelligence and human adaptability. They not only ignore gender roles but—at least theoretically—are not culture-bound."[137] In another essay, "The Image of Women in Science Fiction," she adds that science fiction rises to the challenge of "genuine speculation: how to get away from traditional assumptions which are nothing more than traditional strait-jackets."[138] It is common, of course, to find in most science fiction an unexamined extension of its writer's traditional assumptions into some other time or place, and it could easily be argued that

311

much contemporary feminist science fiction simply extends the present feminist struggle in a similar manner.

While some science fiction (notably Ursula K. LeGuin's *The Left Hand of Darkness*) is worthy of Russ's idealistic project—and most is not—there is a particularly interesting body of work that employs a dialectic between some story elements that are culture-bound and some that are not, thereby "adding up to" a program that cannot yet be satisfactorily imagined. Two stories contributed by Dr. Alice B. Sheldon[139] to the science fiction anthology *Aurora: Beyond Equality*[140] fall into this category; each depends on an inner dialectic between what is and what might be, and taken together, they project a synthesis of feminist consciousness that is also the unnamed totality of the author. The author offers one story under the female pseudonym "Raccoona Sheldon" and the other under the male pseudonym "James Tiptree Jr." (It used to be said that all the best science fiction writers in America were female, except for Samuel R. Delany and James Tiptree.)

In the "Sheldon" story, "Your Faces, O My Sisters! Your Faces Filled Of Light," a mental patient imagines that she lives in a world where all humans are sisters so that there are "No dangers left at all, in the whole free wide world!" She goes running through a major American city at night, a sandaled courier; some people think her crazy, most agree that she is vulnerable; finally a group of males assaults her. The story alternates between third-person scenes anchored in the "real" world and point-of-view passages that dramatize the woman's free experience. This brilliant story raises many of the issues addressed by Susan Griffin in *Rape: The Power of Consciousness*:

What does the inside of my mouth feel like when even the memory of rape has vanished. And how is it then, walking into the night, the first steps into the sweet, safe, covering darkness? And where do these steps take us? Are there mysteries outside our windows which will

312

be revealed to us when we know the air is safe there? Who are we when we are finally safe with our own kind? Our kind. And what of the silence when there is no more such cruelty even imaginable as rape, what is the softness like inside such a silence, such a solitude. I have a taste of it now; it brings me near tears. I know this world we see the edges of is real. And because we see this world, we can make it be.[141]

The "power of consciousness" rises in that last sentence, and one of its implications might be that feminist science fiction can help prompt us into first imagining, then seeing, then precipitating into full being a new world. The largest sense of the words "to create" is active in this argument, for one of Griffin's strongest affirmations is that politics and spirit are inseparable in the unnamable reaches of the self, that their modes of discourse support each other, and that together they have a power of wholeness that is transfigurative.[142]

In this light, we can see the irony in Sheldon's double perspective. The courier's imagination creates her world and may point the reader toward precipitating that vision into reality—but the reader also understands that the courier, first institutionalized and then raped, cannot completely enjoy her freedom until the world she imagines comes to pass. So this is also a story about the plight of the feminist science fiction author, free to imagine a better world but not yet free to live in it. The hero is like a visitor from a future society. The story develops its resonant seriousness from the fact that the heroine is not from that future and that the reader wishes she were.

In the "Tiptree" story, "Houston, Houston, Do You Read?" (whose last word I take as a pun: does NASA pay attention to the messages of feminist fiction?), three spacemen find themselves jogged into the future by a solar flare; they are rescued by a crew of women. (This is similar to Charlotte Perkins Gilman's recently republished *Herland,* but it is more likely a response to such misogynist science fiction as John Wyndham's "Consider Her Ways.") Hundreds of years before this, a plague had wiped out all the males; now reproduction is accomplished through cloning and artificial impregnation.[143] The central male figure, Dr. Lorimer, is made to understand the danger (the shared theme of these stories) that he and the other two males represent to this female society. The captain wants to reestablish patriarchal Christianity; the pilot wants to reestablish rape; Lorimer himself responds to male authority and feels comfortable protecting (that is, dominating) women, so even if he considers himself a "humanist"—or perhaps because he does— he is equally a threat. When one of the women collects a sperm sample from the rapist, the means for regenerating a heterosexual society are at hand, and "Tiptree" makes sure that the reader will consider this regeneration as much of a danger as the others.

"Houston" and "Your Faces," then, form a diptych: in the former, the visitor (Lorimer) *is* from another world, and that world is "ours"; it is the free women, this time, who live in the genuine world. From each perspective, the message is the same. It is significant that the first constellation Lorimer sees out the window of his damaged spacecraft is the Pleiades, a sisterhood in space; as a feminist science fiction metaphor, that seems basic, and it brings us back to Russ.

The Female Man uses the "parallel worlds" device to explore an identity construct similar to that of Anna in *The Golden Notebook* and makes much the same point: that the self must confront its own divisions and the causes of those divisions if it is to achieve wholeness, if it is to learn how to *be*. In both novels, the hero is split four ways; in both, a fifth, self-conscious presence projects their integration; and in both, that wholeness of self and vision is made manifest by the form of the novel as a self-conscious system. In *The Female Man,* the reader is introduced gradually to four instances of the same woman, each living in a different but

314

parallel universe. The first, Joanna, lives in something very like our own world; the second, Jeannine, lives in what our world might be like if there had never been a Second World War; the third, Janet, lives on the planet Whileaway, an all-female utopia (first explored in Russ's story, "When It Changed"); and the fourth, Jael, an ethnologist who brings these, her alternate selves, together for comparison, is based in the fortieth year of a total war between the sexes.

This novel is written (like *As I Lay Dying*) in a circulating first person, but the "I" is not, at least at first, extrasystemically identified. This allows Russ to perform some dazzling shifts among her personae; the "I" can leap from Joanna to Janet to Jeannine within a few pages, emphasizing that these are variants of one self—or from Joanna to a disembodied Joanna, more like a ghost-narrator than a fantasy projection. And of course, at key moments, the "I" is that of the self-conscious author, Joanna Russ—who is the fifth presence, the one who helps pay "our quintuple bill" for the luncheon at Schrafft's that concludes the novel: "We got up and paid our quintuple bill; then we went out into the street. I said goodbye and went off with Laur, I Janet; I also watched them go, I, Joanna; moreover I went off to show Jael the city, I Jeannine, I Jael, I myself."[144] One has the feeling throughout, but especially in this passage, that the author is dealing seriously with her own alternate selves—in fact *is* one of her own alternates—rather than intruding as the "solution" to the complex. The novel is narrated by an "I" that includes all five women and that slips from one to the other as appropriately as Anna closes the black notebook and opens the red.

Each of the worlds these women inhabit has its own sexual politics and produces its own woman: Jeannine is repressed, oppressed, depressed; Jael is a bad angel, ironic and ruthless, "luminous with hate"; Joanna struggles with a sense of enlarged possibilities; Janet is strong and free. These connections between character and world are explored in much the same manner as are those in *Gulliver's Travels,* but with more "collision" (Eisenstein's term) among the elements of the montage. The synthesis of this dialectic, the integrative concept,[145] is the feminist self and its world.

Toward the end of the novel, Joanna recreates a conversation she once had with her mirror. After having been told (in college) that "Woman is purity; Woman is carnality; Woman has intuition; Woman is the life-force; Woman is selfless love, and so on," she says:

> "I am the gateway to another world," (said I, looking in the mirror) "I am the earth-mother; I am the eternal siren; I am purity," (Jeez, new pimples) "I am carnality; I have intuition; I am the life-force; I am selfless love." (Somehow it sound different in the first person, doesn't it?)
>
> Honey (said the mirror, scandalized) Are you out of your fuckin' *mind?*
>
> I AM HONEY
> I AM RASPBERRY JAM
> I AM A VERY GOOD LAY
> I AM A GOOD DATE
> I AM A GOOD WIFE
> I AM GOING CRAZY
> Everything was preaches and cream.[146]

It certainly does sound different in the first person, and it is clear why she is going crazy. It is one thing to integrate the true aspects of one's Gestalt and another to try to integrate a contradictory cluster of false images. Each of the things Joanna is told to be contradicts most of the others, so each self or self-aspect modeled on each of these instructions from the patriarchy (and the women who support it) has to remain a fragment, and to that extent—compared with the whole, true self—a fiction, especially since these fragments are *in themselves* unreal. The woman who follows all these instructions—Daly calls her "the totaled woman"—cannot, inside herself, be more than a colony of fictions (and the imperialist metaphor is intentional). To perceive the extent

316

of this fragmentation is to feel, desperately, that one is not all there; so as Laing has noted and as much of this fiction demonstrates, the term "madness" is often applied to the healthy experience of becoming aware of fragmentation, and genuine insanity is often the result of attempts to adapt to impossibly contradictory demands. The good news is that such an awareness is possible only when one begins to see beyond one fragment to others. One gropes for a context that could embrace all the fragments that feel valid and for a language that could describe that integration. Until the larger self is discovered and the new data fall into place, one's identity remains a montage, but at least there is the sense of systemic interconnection, even if aspects of that wholeness are projected into the future.

In the meantime, one can confront the fragments and be sustained in that attempt by the energies of anger, wit, aspiration, desperation, and genius—all of which apply here. Looking into the mirror of her novel, Russ finds Jeannine: a passive, low-energy figure who is afraid of both feminism and herself. Jeannine turns into Jael's convert, discovering anger and power. Joanna is more won over by Janet, whose anger is in balance with the rest of her energies (Janet has killed but is not murderous, for instance; she is assertive and aggressive, but not "luminous with hate"). But Russ suggests, toward the end of the novel, that without the Jael stage the Janet stage is not possible: it was apparently Jael who started the plague on Whileaway that wiped out the males. Whether or not one is supposed to believe that last story about Jael (an intentional ambiguity in the novel), it is clear that Russ considers anger a healing force not just for her character-selves but for herself as an artist. In her greatest moments of wit and fury, she seems to expect that some reviewer or colleague is going to call her a hysterical bitch or dismiss the daring form of her novel as one of the "tired tricks of the anti-novelists."[147] So she writes their reviews and puts them in the text, thus refusing to let them have power over her, especially the power of definition. In this free space, she goes on confronting her selves and exploring their complex interdependence.

One of the major therapeutic strategies in Gestalt psychology is to urge the client to re-own projections by speaking in the first person from each of their points of view; this is the project that motivates Russ's circulating first person. "To resolve contrarieties," she says as Joanna, "unite them in your own person." She continues:

> Well, I turned into a man.
>
> We love, says Plato, that in which we are defective; when we see our magical Self in the mirror of another, we pursue it with desperate cries—*Stop! I must possess you!*—but if it obligingly stops and turns, how on earth can one then possess it? . . . There is one and only one way to possess that in which we are defective, therefore that which we need, therefore that which we want.
>
> Become it.[148]

Because sex-role stereotyping is a major splitting-off force in patriarchal culture and because Joanna has been denied the autonomy, power, and centrality associated with maleness, as part of her project she turns into a man: not "The Man," but "the female man," as totalized a being as the author can imagine. It is not simply Janet who is the female man (as the opening pages of the novel might suggest) and not simply Joanna Russ; it is the complete narrative system of which they are elements, and which speaking in Joanna says:

> For years I have been saying *Let me in, Love me, Approve me, Define me, Regulate me, Validate me, Support me.* Now I say *Move over.* If we are all Mankind, it follows to my interested and righteous and rightnow very bright and beady little eyes, that I too am a Man. . . . Give me your Linus blanket, child. Listen to the female man.
>
> If you don't, by God and all the saints, *I'll break your neck.*[149]

In the end, Russ concedes that "we don't believe in" Janet, although the fantasy of her is inspiring, and urges her "daughter-book" to "take your place bravely on the book racks of bus terminals and drugstores," to "live merrily . . . even if I can't and we can't; recite yourself to all who will listen."[150] The book ends, as Russ has said, in the reader's lap, which is just where it should. It does not end on While-away, where the self-actualized Joanna is not to be found in any case; the only present world that can generate such a healthy and powerful figure turns out to be that of the self-conscious novel, reciting herself to all who will listen.

Both as an independent object and as an authorial rite of passage, *The Female Man* demonstrates many of the literary applications of Daly's vision of the Spinster's "whirling movement of creation":

> The play is part of our work of unweaving and of our weaving work. It whirls us into another frame of reference. We use the visitation of demons to come more deeply into touch with our own powers/virtues. Unweaving their deceptions, we name our Truth. Defying their professions we dis-cover our Female Pride, our Sinister Wisdom. Escaping their possession we find our Enspiriting Selves. . . . Avoiding their elimination we find our Original Be-ing. Mending their imposed fragmentation we Spin our Original Integrity.[151]

"Spinning" is one of the essential terms Daly rouses from "the spell of brokenness" of patriarchal language:

> Thus, the Latin term *texere,* meaning to weave, is the origin and root both for *textile* and for *text.* It is important for women to note the irony in this split of meanings. For our process of cosmic weaving has been stunted and minimized to the level of the manufacture and maintenance of textiles. . . . "Texts" are the kingdom of males.[152]

319

Daly is not arguing that women should shift from one aspect of the "split" to another, writing rather than weaving, but that women should "mend [the demons'] imposed fragmentation" and spin in the largest sense: to create threads, to make connections, to generate fabrics of meaning and relation. It is not just writing, but writing in the service of the dis-covery of the Original Integrity of the Enspiriting Self, that "whirls us into another frame of reference." Griffin's *Woman and Nature* employs intertextuality as weaving in this sense, interrelating threads of male and female discourse until woman "sees through her own eyes" a world "no longer his," a world of "The Separate Rejoined" in which the inevitable distinctions of language refer back to and are posited on the ineffable unity of Being:

> *and all that we say we are saying around that which cannot be said, cannot be spoken. But in a moment that which is behind naming makes itself known. Hand and breast know each one to the other. Wood in the table knows clay in the bowl. Air knows grass knows water knows mud knows beetle knows frost knows sunlight knows the shape of the earth knows death knows not dying. And all this knowledge is in the souls of everything, behind naming, before speaking, beneath words.*[153]

Because patriarchal constructs are often mispresented as natural and its taboos as facts of language, the literature that attempts to violate political boundaries often employs the same strategies and structures as that which batters the limits of language in the largest (that is, not culture-bound) sense. The other side of the false split is often experienced as nameless, not because it is ineffable, however, but because it has never been named. It is experienced as madness because the culture is informed by a narrow sense of the rational; it is experienced as a dis-covery of self, with that self presented as outside the system of the text or as an unnamable property of the system, because the political self has been artificially excluded from the available structures of naming as rigorously as the metaphysical self is inherently outside that structure. Writing is one aspect of spinning into a holistic frame of reference (the left brain in the service of the right, perhaps) in which naming can be based on a vision of unnamable wholeness.

In Wittig's *Les Guérillères*, the "O" is the central symbol of this frame of reference—not the zero of nothingness, but the circle that is also an invocation, a symbol of the notnamed and of enspiriting completeness. For Daly, the "O" represents "the power of our moving, encircling presence, which can make nonbeing sink back into itself."[154] For Wittig, the "O" is also "the vulval ring," "that infinite sphere whose centre is everywhere, circumference nowhere," and a key to such gynocentric symbols of the ineffable as the Grail ("They say it is impossible to mistake the symbolism of the Round Table that dominated their meetings. They say that, at the period when the texts were compiled, the quests for the Grail were singular unique attempts to describe the zero the circle the ring the spherical cup containing the blood").[155] The "O" is the realm of the non-gap:

> They say, the language you speak is made up of signs that rightly speaking designate what men have appropriated. Whatever they have not laid hands on, whatever they have not pounced on like many-eyed birds of prey, does not appear in the language you speak. This is apparent precisely in the intervals that your masters have not been able to fill with their words of proprietors and possessors, this can be found in the gaps, in all that which is not a continuation of their discourse, in the zero, the O, the perfect circle that you invent to imprison them and to overwhelm them.[156]

Within this circle is a new energy of naming. Wittig does not imply that everything can be named once the spell of patriarchy is broken but offers a full-page "O" at many

321

points in the novel as a symbol of wholeness that transcends the language in which the book is necessarily written. On the final page she invokes:

LACUNAE LACUNAE
AGAINST TEXTS
AGAINST MEANING
WHICH IS TO WRITE VIOLENCE
OUTSIDE THE TEXT
IN ANOTHER WRITING
THREATENING MENACING
MARGINS SPACES INTERVALS
WITHOUT PAUSE
ACTION OVERTHROW[157]

In the current state of textuality, it is in the lacunae of patriarchy that women find much of their power and "outside the text" that this power projects its fulfillment.

This fulfillment is inseparably political and personal. As Griffin writes:

And have we not then, in the stripping away of the voices of patriarchal authority from our minds in order to make ourselves essential once again, established for ourselves a direct relation with our own hearts, our spirit which is the same as the universe, the spirit?[158]

To establish a direct relation with the metaphysical self is to become one with an all-inclusive silence, a silence that may appear from the perspective of rational numbers to be a zero but that is recognized from within as "that infinite sphere." The original integrity that charges consciousness and transfuses being, that is outside language and beneath all acts of naming, is the central energy of the self. The integrity of the literature of self-consciousness and the ineffable is not in the rigor of its exclusions from discourse but in the wholeness it manifests in response to that sense of limits, which is based in the indescribable experience of the fullness of the silence. As art is about what is important to us, so the art of self-realization—whose limits expand its range to all that is knowable and allow it to point beyond, to manifest that of which it cannot speak—is vital as goad and guide, testimonial and proving ground, stimulating and thereby helping to create both a greater awareness in its readers and a culture that respects and nurtures on all levels the autonomous, spirited, unpredictable, creative, and loving Self.

NOTES

CHAPTER ONE: NOTES ON A HAUNTED FORM

1. Please note that throughout this book "man," "he," "him," and "his" are often —and I hope self-evidently—intended to refer to persons of both sexes. As a male reader I have sometimes found "the reader/he" a comfortable formula, and as a stylist I have tried not to weigh down some of my more intricate sentences under a series of alternate pronouns, but I have no intention of excluding the female reader or author.

2. John Barth, "The Literature of Exhaustion," reprinted in *Surfiction: Fiction Now and Tomorrow . . .,* ed. Raymond Federman (Chicago: Swallow Press, 1975).

3. Herman Melville, *Moby-Dick,* ed. Harrison Hayford and Hershel Parker (New York: W. W. Norton, Norton Critical Edition, 1967), p. 163.

4. Norman Mailer, *Why Are We In Vietnam?* (New York: G. P. Putnam's Sons, Berkley Medallion, 1968), p. 22. The other narrator is a crippled Black living in Harlem; the reader does not know which of these narrators might be inventing the other.

5. Ludwig Wittgenstein, *Tractatus Logico-Philosophicus,* trans. D. F. Pears and B. F. McGuinness (London: Routledge and Kegan Paul, 1961), 5.633–5.6331.

6. Dante, *Paradiso,* ed. and trans. John D. Sinclair (New York: Oxford Univ. Press, Galaxy Books, 1961), p. 483.

7. *Ibid.,* p. 485.

8. Wittgenstein, *Tractatus,* 6.45. For a good introduction to systems theory, see Ervin Laszlo, *The Systems View of the World* (New York: George Braziller, 1972).

9. Shunryu Suzuki, *Zen Mind, Beginner's Mind* (New York: Weatherhill, 1970), p. 35.

10. Edmund Husserl, "Phenomenology," *Encyclopedia Britannica* XVII (1953), 701. "Eidetic" here refers to the "essence" evident within a structure.

11. Pirandello, by contrast, is never this realistic. There is no reason the protagonists of *Six Characters in Search of an Author* or

Tonight We Improvise should repeat their investigations of how and where they exist once each play's puzzle has been solved.

12. Robert Alter, *Partial Magic: The Novel as a Self-Conscious Genre* (Berkeley: Univ. of California Press, 1975), pp. x–xi.

13. Alter, *Partial Magic,* p. 245.

14. Jorge Luis Borges, "Partial Magic in the Quixote," *Labyrinths,* ed. Donald A. Yates and James E. Irby (New York: New Directions, 1964), p. 197.

15. Actually, "Borges and I" can make sense as nonfiction in two ways: as a manifestation of an authentic textual predicament, and as a direct statement of how Borges feels about being both a mortal and an abstract entity who exists as the author of "Borges' " works. Once the living man has signed his name to a story, that story is "by 'Borges'," and the existence of "Borges" is predicated upon the story. "Borges," then, is created by the interaction between the reader and "what 'Borges' has written," which means that "Borges" is a fiction created by his own fictions. In this sense, "Borges and I" is both authorially self-conscious and a statement of fact; when I spoke with him about it, he maintained emphatically that "Borges and I" was no more than a simple description of how he felt about what it means to be an author. It should also be noted that, because Borges has worked as a librarian, there is an authorially self-conscious aspect to "The Library of Babel." In a less paradoxical tone, Orson Welles used to complain that he resented people who wanted to talk not to *him* but to "Orson Welles." "The Library of Babel" and "Borges and I" can be found in *Labyrinths,* ed. Yates and Irby.

16. Alter, *Partial Magic,* p. 134. The context is a discussion of Melville's *The Confidence-Man.*

17. Ferdinand de Saussure, *Course in General Linguistics,* excerpted in Michael Lane, *Introduction to Structuralism* (New York: Harper and Row, 1970), pp. 43–45. This relationship is conventionally notated as an equation:

$$\text{Sign} = \frac{\text{signifier}}{\text{signified}} \text{ or } S = \text{sr/sd.}$$

For further reading in this area, see John Lyons, *Introduction to Theoretical Linguistics* (Cambridge: Cambridge Univ. Press, 1968).

18. William Faulkner, *As I Lay Dying* (New York: Random House, Modern Library, 1967), p. 163.

19. James Agee and Walker Evans, *Let Us Now Praise Famous Men* (Boston: Houghton Mifflin, 1941), p. 13. Compare the happy failure of language in the marvelous conclusion, pp. 463–71.

20. See Rubin Rabinovitz, "*Watt* from Descartes to Schopenhauer," in *Aspects of Irish Literature: Essays in Honor of William York Tindale,* ed. James Brophy and Raymond Porter (New Rochelle, NY: Iona College Press, 1972), esp. pp. 286–87. For the influence of Fritz Mauthner on Beckett, see Linda Ben-Zvi, "Samuel Beckett, Fritz Mauthner, and the Limits of Language," *PMLA* 95(1980): 2, 183–200.

21. *Chuang Tzu: Basic Writings,* trans. Burton Watson (New York: Columbia Univ. Press, 1964), pp. 39–40.

22. Wittgenstein, *Tractatus,* 5.631–5.632.

23. *Labyrinths,* ed. Yates and Irby, p. 247.

24. *The Republic of Plato,* ed. and trans. F. M. Cornford (New York: Oxford Univ. Press, 1945), pp. 230–31.

Chapter Two: Metaphysical Heroism

1. *The Shorter Oxford English Dictionary.*

2. See the discussion of Bulkington and "right reason" in Charles Olson's *Call Me Ishmael* (San Francisco: City Lights, 1947), p. 57.

3. Carlos Castaneda: *The Teachings of Don Juan: A Yaqui Way of Knowledge* (New York: Simon and Schuster, Pocket Books, 1974), p. 193. Because Castaneda does not allow direct citations from his works, I have had to resort to footnotes and paraphrase more than the reader might have wished. An "escogido" is one chosen by a higher power as a proper apprentice—one who, possessing some of that special power already, is different from other people and (from the start) more than a mere apprentice.

4. Herman Melville, *Moby-Dick,* ed. Harrison Hayford and Hershel Parker (New York: W. W. Norton, Norton Critical Edition, 1967), p. 144.

5. Ibid., p. 467. As in *King Lear,* the metaphor of physical blindness is here coupled with a growth in insight. (*Lear* seems a more likely source than *Oedipus Rex.*) Another complementary figure

is the metaphysical hero in Plato's allegory of the cave, who is blinded by his first exposure to the light outside that cave.

6. Melville, *Moby-Dick,* p. 417.

7. In *Call Me Ishmael,* pp. 53–54, Olson implicitly compares the Parsee to the Weird Sisters in *Macbeth.* For Shakespeare's general influence on Melville, see Olson, passim. The reader will note that I make no attempt in this chapter to refer to or incorporate the entire canon of Melville criticism, but simply point to those sources that are most closely related to my own arguments about narrative structure.

8. Melville, *Moby-Dick,* p. 147. Melville's original notes for the novel include the words "madness is undefinable" (see Olson, *Call Me Ishmael,* p. 52).

9. Melville, *Moby-Dick,* p. 139.

10. Ibid., p. 140.

11. Ibid., p. 155.

12. Ibid., p. 160.

13. Ibid., p. 162.

14. Ibid., p. 163.

15. Ibid., p. 169.

16. Ibid., p. 354. Ishmael navigates the novel in precisely the same manner, with the same effects.

17. Joseph Conrad, *Heart of Darkness,* in *Three Novels by Joseph Conrad,* ed. Edward Said (New York: Washington Square Press, 1970), pp. 176–77.

18. Ibid., p. 150. Conrad's first draft read " . . . kernel but outside in the unseen, . . ."

19. Ibid., p. 226.

20. Ibid., p. 230.

21. Ibid., p. 230.

22. Ibid., p. 229.

23. Ibid., p. 231.

24. Ibid., p. 232. The quality of his distance from others here echoes Ishmael's view of himself as a "wanderer," or liminal figure.

25. Ibid., pp. 176, 239. Compare the way Philip Marlowe becomes "part of the nastiness now" in Chandler's *The Big Sleep*—a connection that suggests, among other things, how Chandler may have selected his detective's name.

26. Conrad, *Heart of Darkness,* p. 240.

27. Ibid., p. 148.

28. Ibid., pp. 148, 240.

29. Seymour Gross has made a similar observation in his excellent article, "A Further Note on the Function of the Frame in 'Heart of Darkness'," *Modern Fiction Studies* 3: 167–70.

30. Conrad, *Heart of Darkness,* p. 202.

31. Ibid., p. 150.

32. James Guetti, *The Limits of Metaphor: A Study of Melville, Conrad, and Faulkner* (Ithaca: Cornell Univ. Press, 1967), p. 35.

33. Guetti, *The Limits of Metaphor,* p. 28.

34. The narrator of *Madame Bovary,* of course, is entirely reticent about his own involvement and never commits himself to a personal observation, but much can be deduced from the ways he opens and closes the novel. He is evidently irritated at Homais' receiving the Legion of Honor, for instance (an event that might have provoked his telling the story of his old schoolmate and the latter's wife, to set the record straight—but in its own terms, not in his). I am not suggesting that *Bovary* is an example of secondary first-person narration.

35. Samuel Beckett, *Watt* (New York: Grove Press, Evergreen, 1959), p. 30.

36. Ibid., p. 62.

37. Ibid., p. 76.

38. Ibid., p. 77.

39. Ibid., p. 248.

40. Ibid., p. 81.

41. Ibid., p. 82. The essential point is not that Watt *is* in ineffable territory but that *he feels* that the things around him consent to be named "with reluctance." Whether or not Watt is deluded, Sam is interested in his friend's perplexity, just as Ishmael is attentive to Ahab's; it would destroy the evocative balance of the novel for Beckett (or Melville) to pronounce on the validity of his hero's insight. (This does not rule out parody; Watt can be both comical and correct. In Beckett, the reduction to absurdity is often simply a closing in on the essence of the problem.)

42. Compare the situation of the narrator in Borges' "The Library of Babel," *Labyrinths,* ed. Donald A. Yates and James E. Irby (New York: New Directions, 1964), pp. 51–58.

43. Beckett, *Watt,* p. 200. For the uses of repetition in *Watt* and their relationship to time and silence, see Bruce F. Kawin, *Tell-*

ing It Again and Again: Repetition in Literature and Film (Ithaca: Cornell Univ. Press, 1972), pp. 128–44.

44. Beckett, *Watt,* p. 51. He even *says* "turn and turn about" but proceeds to note each one.

45. Ibid., p. 75. Compare the opening of Joseph Conrad's *Under Western Eyes* (Garden City: Doubleday, Anchor, 1963).

46. Beckett, *Watt,* p. 201.

47. Thomas Mann, *Doctor Faustus: The Life of the German Composer Adrian Leverkühn as Told by a Friend,* trans. H. T. Lowe-Porter (New York: Alfred A. Knopf, 1948), p. 504.

48. Ibid., p. 504.

49. Ibid., p. 452.

50. Boris Pasternak, *Selected Writings* (New York: New Directions, 1958), pp. 13–14.

51. Conrad, *Under Western Eyes,* p. 1.

52. For a more complex reading, see Julia Bader, *Crystal Land: Artifice in Nabokov's English Novels* (Berkeley: Univ. of California Press, 1972), pp. 31–56.

53. Vladimir Nabokov, *Pale Fire* (New York: G. P. Putnam's Sons, 1962), pp. 28–29.

54. Ibid., p. 13.

55. Carlos Castaneda, *Journey to Ixtlan: The Lessons of Don Juan* (New York: Simon and Schuster, 1972), p. 108.

56. In *Telling It Again and Again,* I made a similar point about repetition: that it is an effective device for imitating a sense of timelessness; that it has been shown through the use of mantras as well as psychological experiment to be capable of actually inducing a change in one's subjective orientation to time; and that it is arguable, both through philosophy and through modern physics, that there is a direct and literal connection between repetition and the underlying structure of the universe. It may be argued that this connection is the ultimate justification, or even the prompter, of the literary technique.

57. Carlos Castaneda, *A Separate Reality: Further Conversations with Don Juan* (New York: Simon and Schuster, Pocket Books, 1972), p. 15.

58. Castaneda, *Journey to Ixtlan,* pp. 11–13. Also see Carlos Castaneda, *Tales of Power* (New York: Simon and Schuster, Pocket Books, 1976), pp. 229–60.

59. Castaneda, *Journey to Ixtlan,* p. 167 and passim.

60. Castaneda, *The Teachings of Don Juan,* p. 193. Also see note 3, above.
61. Castaneda, *Journey to Ixtlan,* p. 252.

CHAPTER THREE: THE SIMULTANEOUS SELF

1. "Transpersonal Psychology is the title given to an emerging force in the psychology field by a group of psychologists and professional men and women who are interested in those *ultimate* human capacities and potentialities that have no systematic place in positivistic or behavioristic theory . . . classical psychoanalytic theory . . . or humanistic psychology. . . . The emerging Transpersonal Psychology . . . is concerned specifically with the *empirical,* scientific study of . . . ultimate values, unitive consciousness, peak experiences, B-values, ecstasy, mystical experience, awe, being, self-actualization . . . maximal interpersonal encounter, sacralization of everyday life, transcendental phenomena, cosmic self-humor and playfulness . . . and related concepts, experiences, and activities." (Condensed from Anthony Sutich's effusive definition in the *Journal of Transpersonal Psychology* [Spring 1969]; cited in full on p. 3 of Charles T. Tart, *Transpersonal Psychologies* [New York: Harper and Row, Colophon, 1975].)
2. Carlos Castaneda, *Tales of Power* (New York: Simon and Schuster, Pocket Books, 1976), pp. 174–76, 199.
3. Ludwig Wittgenstein, *Tractatus Logico-Philosophicus,* trans. D. F. Pears and B. F. McGuinness (London: Routledge and Kegan Paul, 1961), 4.1212.
4. Castaneda, *Tales of Power,* pp. 95, 123–28, 175–76, 178, 191, 208, 243, 250–56, 272–78.
5. Carlos Castaneda, *The Second Ring of Power* (New York: Simon and Schuster, 1977), p. 282.
6. Castaneda, *Tales of Power,* pp. 272–78.
7. Ibid., pp. 140–41.
8. Ibid., p. 269.
9. Ibid., pp. 268–74.
10. Andrew Marvell, "A Dialogue Between the Soul and Body."
11. Wittgenstein, *Tractatus,* 6.121–6.13.

12. For a guide to the controversy, see Daniel C. Noel, ed., *Seeing Castaneda: Reactions to the "Don Juan" Writings of Carlos Castaneda* (New York: G. P. Putnam's Sons, Capricorn Books, 1976), which is in any case worth consulting for its intelligent complex of articles. It is perhaps inevitable that the reader who *needs* to know how much of Castaneda's work cannot be true be referred to Richard de Mille's overcute "exposé," *Castaneda's Journey: The Power and the Allegory,* 2nd ed. (Santa Barbara: Capra Press, 1978).

13. Castaneda, *Tales of Power,* p. 253.

14. *Brain/Mind Bulletin* IV, 5 (January 15, 1979), p. 3.

15. Castaneda, *Tales of Power,* p. 277.

16. See S. J. Dimond and J. G. Beaumont, eds., *Hemispheric Function in the Human Brain* (London: Eleck Science, Ltd.; and New York: Wiley, 1974) for a careful and wide-ranging examination of brain lateralization theory. For a general introduction, see M. C. Wittrock's special issue of the *UCLA Educator* (1975), "Education and the Hemispheric Process of the Brain," as well as *Brain/Mind Bulletin* (passim). The latter is especially valuable for recent developments. In the issue of May 11, 1981, for example, *Brain/Mind Bulletin* notes that the "assumption that reading was exclusively a left-brain activity" has been "discredited." The notion of left-hemisphere *dominance* in reading and related sequential processing, however, still appears valid at this time, even if such activities as recognizing the shapes of letters and responding to sentence rhythms involve the right hemisphere.

17. Castaneda, *Tales of Power,* pp. 275–76.

18. Ibid., pp. 192–94, 202.

19. Ibid., p. 202.

20. "Upward and Juanward: The Possible Dream," in Noel, ed., *Seeing Castaneda,* p. 114.

21. Castaneda, *Tales of Power,* pp. 268–69.

22. Ibid., p. 292.

23. William James, *The Varieties of Religious Experience: A Study in Human Nature* (London: Collins, Fontana Library, 1960), pp. 219–57 (Lecture X).

24. Ibid., pp. 235–37.

25. Ibid., p. 242. The "subconscious region" James describes is, in John-Roger's system, the "high self."

26. Alan W. Watts, *The Book: On the Taboo Against Knowing Who You Are* (New York: Macmillan, Collier Books, 1967), p. 130.

27. Wittgenstein, *Tractatus*, 3.032.

28. Ibid., 1.13.

29. Ibid., 5.6–5.61

30. Ibid., 4.115.

31. See Joseph Margolis' excellent essay, "Don Juan as Philosopher," in Noel, ed., *Seeing Castaneda*, pp. 228–42.

32. Wittgenstein, *Tractatus*, 4.121.

33. Ibid., 4.116–4.1212.

34. Watts, *The Book*, pp. 130–31. Also see p. 140 and compare I Corinthians 13:12.

35. Wittgenstein, *Tractatus*, 5.43.

36. Ibid., 6.54.

37. Ibid., 6.45.

38. Ibid., 4.461–4.464. It must be noted that "$x = 2$" does not, like "$x = x$," admit all possible situations, since it excludes "$x = 3$" and so forth. So although the form of any equation is tautological, one can ignore that in the interest of describing a particular situation.

39. Ibid., 6.51–6.522.

40. T. S. Eliot, *Collected Poems 1909–1962* (New York: Harcourt, Brace, and World, 1963), p. 180 ("Burnt Norton," V). This might also serve as a useful gloss on Wagner's *Parsifal;* Pierre Boulez' DGG recording is recommended.

41. Eliot, *Collected Poems 1909–1962*, p. 177 ("Burnt Norton," II).

42. See *Shankara's Crest-Jewel of Discrimination*, ed. Swami Prabhavananda and Christopher Isherwood (New York: New American Library, Mentor Books, 1970) for the title piece, a clear introduction to Shankara's philosophy, and "A Hymn." See also Alan Watts's paraphrase in *The Book*, pp. 11–14. The game might be compared to blind man's bluff.

43. Wittgenstein, *Tractatus*, 4.461.

44. John Ashbery, *Some Trees* (New Haven: Yale Univ. Press, 1956), pp. 32–33. This poem is also available in Donald M. Allen's *The New American Poetry 1945–1960* (New York: Grove Press, Evergreen, 1960), p. 271.

45. Henri Bergson, *An Introduction to Metaphysics*, 2nd ed., trans. T. E. Hulme (Indianapolis: Bobbs-Merrill, Library of Liberal Arts, 1955), p. 21.

46. Ibid., p. 24.

47. Ibid., pp. 23–24.

48. Ibid., p. 42.

49. Ibid., p. 57.

50. Ibid., p. 53.

51. Ibid., p. 53.

52. See W. Brugh Joy, *Joy's Way: A Map for the Transformational Journey* (New York: St. Martin's Press; and Los Angeles: J. P. Tarcher, Inc., 1978).

53. This may explain the function of meter in helping poets and reciters (working in an oral tradition) to remember a given poem (see M. C. Wittrock, "The Generative Processes of Memory," in the *UCLA Educator* (1975), "Education and the Hemispheric Process of the Brain"). For further work on the relations between the right hemisphere and the arts, see Bruce Kawin, "Right-Hemisphere Processing in Dreams and Films," *Dreamworks* II, 1 (1982).

54. Watts, *The Book*, p. 133.

55. Joy, *Joy's Way*, p. 5. Joy sees his rhetoric as a dialectic of left- and right-hemisphere terminology. He offers terms like "Beingness" that are "beyond the left brain" but that, as Whitman put it, "itch at your ears till you understand them."

56. *Shankara's Crest-Jewel of Discrimination*, ed. Prabhavananda and Isherwood, p. 72. Also see pp. 13–22.

57. Ibid., p. 73.

58. Bruce F. Kawin, *Telling It Again and Again: Repetition in Literature and Film* (Ithaca: Cornell Univ. Press, 1972), pp. 107, 170–76.

59. The question of frustration is dealt with at length in Chapter Four.

60. Thornton Wilder's Introduction to Gertrude Stein, *The Geographical History of America or The Relation of Human Nature to the Human Mind* (New York: Random House, Vintage Books, 1973), p. 44. See also William Gass's Introduction to that same volume, one of the better pieces ever written on Stein. For the record, the very best still seems to be Donald Sutherland, *Gertrude Stein: A Biography of her Work* (New Haven: Yale Univ. Press, 1951).

61. Gertrude Stein, *What Are Masterpieces?*, ed. Robert Bartlett Haas (New York: Pitman, 1970), p. 103.

62. Stein, *The Geographical History of America*, p. 105.

334

63. Stein, *What Are Masterpieces?*, p. 92. Most mystics, of course, have argued that this neutral unnamable entity is the opposite of the mind; Stein's term is idiosyncratic.

64. Thornton Wilder, "Introduction to Miss Stein's Puppet Play," in the Gertrude Stein issue of *Twentieth-Century Literature*, ed. Edward Burns, XXIV, 1 (Spring 1978), p. 94. This same issue contains a relevant article on *Ida* by Cynthia Secor (pp. 96–107).

65. Text from Stein, *What Are Masterpieces?*, pp. 71–79.

66. Stein, *What Are Masterpieces?*, pp. 90–91.

67. See Thornton Wilder's Introduction to Gertrude Stein, *Four in America* (New Haven: Yale Univ. Press, 1947), pp. v–vi; and Gertrude Stein, *Lectures in America* (Boston: Beacon Press, 1957), p. 119.

68. Stein, *What Are Masterpieces?*, p. 72.

69. Ibid., p. 74.

70. Ibid., p. 75.

71. Ibid., p. 75.

72. Ibid., p. 76. The text in that edition actually reads "no left of right"; the comparable passage in the *Geographical History* reads "no left or right" (p. 109). My guess is that the former is an interesting typo.

73. Stein, *The Geographical History of America,* p. 112. For the short version, see Stein, *What Are Masterpieces?*, p. 77.

74. Stein, *What Are Masterpieces?*, p. 78.

75. Ibid., p. 78.

76. Ibid., p. 86. Stein does, however, allow the possibility of knowing that there is no identity (pp. 90–91), a slightly different issue.

77. "Henry James" is a chapter in Stein's *Four in America.* It is more widely available in *Gertrude Stein: Writings and Lectures 1909–1945,* ed. Patricia Meyerowitz (Baltimore: Penguin, 1971); this passage can be found on p. 292 of the latter. Regarding Heisenberg, see Kawin, *Telling It Again and Again,* pp. 30–31.

78. Stein, *What Are Masterpieces?*, p. 89.

79. Ibid., p. 93.

80. Itzhak Bentov, *Stalking the Wild Pendulum: On the Mechanics of Consciousness* (New York: E. P. Dutton, 1977), pp. 63–64.

81. Rhondell (pseudonym of Dr. Bob Gibson), *Headlines: A workbook concerning the discovery of the inner man* (USA [n.p.], 1976), pp. 14 and 68. This obscure book is worth tracking down.

82. The following observations concerning the higher self are

partly an attempt to integrate what has been said on the subject by others and partly firsthand impressions. The term "higher self" is comparable to William James's subliminal doorway ("a subconscious region which alone should yield access to . . . higher spiritual agencies"). In most systematizings of the structure of metaphysical consciousness, there is a distinction between the higher self and the soul, and I have respected that distinction. Where some confusion may have entered my presentation is in the qualities of completeness and transcendent love I have ascribed to the higher self, qualities usually reserved for descriptions of the soul.

The soul is understood to be an entirely "positive" energy untouched by the problems of mortality, as if it were a cell in the divine organism. The rest of the self, in many of these systems, is understood to bear a "negative" charge (as in the analogy of battery terminals, not in the sense of good and bad) and to include—in order of increasing "negativity," or sympathy with the energies of the planet—1) the higher self; 2) the conscious self or the mind; 3) the reactive mind or the preconscious; 4) spinal reflex activity, shared by the lower vertebrates; 5) the unconscious or subconscious mind; and 6) the basic self, which is a body consciousness oriented toward survival and the site of many deep emotional reactions, as well as the vehicle through which the higher self often finds expression. According to John-Roger (who outlines this hierarchy in many of his works), the soul, the higher self, and the basic self "meet" before birth and agree on the karmic burdens and goals to be dealt with upon incarnation. The basic self is more or less conscious of this project until the conscious mind (born, as John Locke argued, "tabula rasa" or like a "blank slate") comes to the fore in late childhood; Wordsworth argued something similar in his "Ode: Intimations of Immortality from Recollections of Early Childhood," and in the "Myth of Er" near the end of the *Republic,* Plato endorsed the notion that we know the outlines of our destiny before we are born. The higher self, on the other hand, never forgets the karmic project and acts as a gateway for spiritual energies, precipitates those apparently fortuitous situations that in retrospect often seem "fated," and conducts what might be called a holding action by keeping the ultimate accessible (as the soul is in most cases not accessible) center of personal being in a state of clarity and unconditional love. At death, the energy pattern of the higher self is changed as the experience of the being is integrated (lifted up) into it, and that energy is further lifted into the soul, which has thus gained its earthly experience.

What all this implies is that the higher self is subliminally accessible to mortal consciousness. The problem is how to describe that aspect of inner being. It is not enough for the mind to synthesize a number of verbal descriptions in a scholarly context, let alone in a work of fiction; in that case one would be faced not only with the limitations of language but also with having avoided the essence of the experience, which is a matter of making *direct contact* with the energy or personal element in question. I realized, in writing this section of the book, that I was in danger of alienating a scholarly audience by indulging in the poetic and personal, but decided that it was more important to follow out my conviction that intuition and reason are linked in the investigation of the ineffable, so that I would be justified in probing my own intuitions here. And since there is no substitute for firsthand direct research in the tackling of any important subject, it seemed obvious to follow advice as old as that in *The Cloud of Unknowing* by investigating my own experience of my higher self. I have spared the reader the autobiographical saga and reported here only those descriptions that seemed of general interest and application.

The other problem I naturally encountered was that of nonsense, tautology, and contradiction in the terms of that description, and the solution I discovered seems of considerable relevance to the mechanics of writing about the ineffable. I found, as I wrote the 300 words or so that follow this footnote in the main text, that I experienced a rise in energy of the sort I was describing. I took that as an indication that what I was writing was calling forth, or bringing into synchronization, my subliminal gateway. Something inside me was pleased with these particular formulations. It seemed, in conclusion, that the higher self can watch and guide the part of the self that uses words, and can indicate by a shift in energy level which of the mind's nonsensical and unprovable statements is closer to the truth. This seems comparable to the experience Dante had when writing the end of the *Paradiso:* "in telling of it I feel my joy expand." There is no way for me to be sure that this passage will evoke the same experience for another reader, but you might find it valuable to attempt a similar description. I think this is the way one writes about the ineffable with a minimum of distortion and pomposity, though the logical problems are in no way dismissed.

83. Notably John-Roger, founder of MSIA (Movement of Spiritual Inner Awareness). Two of his most interesting books are *The Sound Current* and *Dreams* (New York: Baraka Press, both 1976). A cassette tape, *The Three Selves* (available through MSIA: P.O. Box 3935, Los Angeles, CA 90051), offers a discussion of the higher, conscious, and basic selves, though John-Roger touches on the question throughout his work; his fullest discussions are contained in a series of "Discourses" that are available through MSIA only by subscription and from which quotation is prohibited.

84. W. B. Yeats, *Selected Poems and Two Plays of William Butler Yeats,* ed. M. L. Rosenthal (New York: Macmillan, Collier Books, 1966), p. 125. The poem's first part is a dialogue between "My Self" and "My Soul"; the "Soul" urges the "Self" to cultivate detachment from love, war, honor, and so forth, and instead to concentrate on "that quarter where all thought is done," where "intellect" is unable to make terminological distinctions. The conflict between these rather tense and ponderous voices seems entirely conscious and overdetermined. In the second part of the poem "My Self" alone speaks, rehearsing the painful and humiliating experiences he has suffered until he arrives—with what strikes me as deep emotional conviction—at a willingness to suffer reincarnation. The "Soul" had earlier encouraged him to meditate in such a way that he would be freed from the pulls of earth and no longer have to incarnate, but the "Self" finds that a cold solution and chooses life instead. It is when the "Self" lets go of its "remorse" that the heart opens, and it is only at that point, I argue, that the energy of the higher self is brought into play in this poem. "So great a sweetness flows into the breast," he says, that "We must laugh and we must sing,/We are blest by everything,/Everything we look upon is blest." One of John-Roger's arguments is that the higher self often finds expression through the basic self (a more or less body- and survival-oriented consciousness dominant in children and fundamentally emotional, whereas the higher self is impersonal and neutral in its unconditional love); in this poem it appears that "My Self" is

primarily the basic self, touched at the end by the energy of the higher self, and that "My Soul" is the conscious self's image of what a properly neutral soul ought to *think*.

85. Walt Whitman, *Leaves of Grass: The First (1855) Edition,* ed. Malcolm Cowley (New York: Viking Press, 1959), p. 28 (lines 65–72). Cowley's excellent introduction places "Song of Myself" in the context of Eastern thought.

86. Ibid., p. 29 (lines 90–91).

87. Ibid., pp. 30 (line 112), 31 (lines 124–29), and 81 (line 1242).

88. The Lacanian aspects of this phase are worth pursuing, especially in terms of the relation between conscious self-awareness and mirror–identification. Of course the self that emerges is more than the Lacanian "imaginary."

89. Whitman, *Leaves of Grass,* pp. 84–85 (lines 1288–1308). The bracketed ellipses indicate my own deletions; the others are Whitman's.

90. Lewis Carroll, *Alice in Wonderland,* ed. Donald J. Gray (New York: W. W. Norton, Norton Critical Edition, 1971). pp. 145, 208 (*Through the Looking-Glass,* chapters IV and XII). See also Bruce F. Kawin, *Mindscreen: Bergman, Godard, and First-Person Film* (Princeton: Princeton Univ. Press, 1978), pp. 55, 103–42.

91. Marcel Proust, *Swann's Way,* trans. C. K. Scott Moncrieff (New York: Random House, Vintage Books, 1970), p. 3.

92. Proust, *Swann's Way,* p. 5.

93. Marcel Proust, *The Past Recaptured,* trans. Andreas Mayor (New York: Random House, Vintage Books, 1971), p. 147 (slightly rephrased).

94. Proust, *Swann's Way,* pp. 64, 73.

95. See Kawin, *Telling It Again and Again,* pp. 182–85, and Jorge Luis Borges, "A New Refutation of Time," in *Labyrinths,* ed. Donald A. Yates and James E. Irby (New York: New Directions, 1964), pp. 217–34.

96. Proust, *The Past Recaptured,* p. 133.

97. Ibid., p. 272.

98. Ibid., pp. 133–34. For a more complex reading of Proust, especially with regard to the systemic autonomy of *A la recherche* in a reinterpreted Platonist context (e.g., "There is no Logos, there are only hieroglyphs," p. 167), see Gilles Deleuze, *Proust and Signs,* trans. Richard Howard (New York: George Braziller, 1972).

CHAPTER FOUR: FRAMES UNDER PRESSURE

1. Alan Greenberg, *Heart of Glass* (Munich: Skellig Edition, 1976), p. 198. For the scene quoted at the beginning of this chapter, see p. 36.

2. Thomas Pynchon, *Gravity's Rainbow* (New York: Viking Press, 1973), p. 760. "Preterite" means passed over.

3. Herman Melville, *Moby-Dick,* ed. Harrison Hayford and Hershel Parker (New York: W. W. Norton, Norton Critical Edition, 1967), p. 147.

4. William Faulkner, *Absalom, Absalom!* (New York: Random House, Modern Library, 1951), pp. 263–65.

5. F. Scott Fitzgerald, *The Great Gatsby* (New York: Charles Scribner's Sons, Scribner Library, 1925), p. 1.

6. Fitzgerald, *The Great Gatsby,* p. 2.

7. After he leaves Gatsby's set and returns to the Midwest, Nick responds to strangers almost as Marlow did on his return from the Congo: "I felt that I wanted the world to be in uniform and at a sort of moral attention forever" (ibid., p. 2).

8. Ibid., p. 149.

9. Ibid., p. 99.

10. Ibid., p. 97.

11. Ibid., p. 99.

12. Ibid., p. 99.

13. Ibid., p. 182.

14. See Bruce F. Kawin, *Faulkner and Film* (New York: Ungar, 1977), pp. 145–46, and Kawin, *Mindscreen: Bergman, Godard, and First-Person Film* (Princeton: Princeton Univ. Press, 1978), pp. 23–44. For an interesting variation on reflexivity and hero-making, see the first Sherlock Holmes novel, *A Study in Scarlet,* where the reticent Holmes, filled out by Watson, appears to consider Poe's Auguste Dupin as real as himself.

15. This point about the relations between Logos and dialogue is drawn from a lecture by Frank McConnell. The Greek word *dialogos* is actually subject to two possible analyses: 1) *dia* (one with another) + *logos* (speech, word, reason, cosmic Word), or 2) *dia* + *legesthai* (from *legein,* to tell or talk). The second and more widely received derivation takes "dialogue" as meaning the act of talking with one another; the first suggests that underneath

a conventional understanding of the interchange, the cosmic *Logos* is finding expression through the dialectic of serious conversation.

16. *The Republic of Plato,* trans. F. M. Cornford (New York: Oxford Univ. Press, 1945), p. 262. For a comparable reading of the *Phaedrus,* see Stanley E. Fish, *Self-Consuming Artifacts: The Experience of Seventeenth-Century Literature* (Berkeley: Univ. of California Press, 1972), pp. 9–21.

17. *The Republic of Plato,* p. 141.

18. Ibid., p. 217.

19. Ibid., p. 217.

20. Rhondell (pseudonym of Bob Gibson), *Headlines: A workbook concerning the discovery of the inner man* (USA [n.p.], 1976), p. 62. In *Physics* II, 3, Aristotle arrived at a very similar breakdown of the four "causes" of any natural phenomenon: material, efficient, formal, and final.

21. Faulkner, *Absalom, Absalom!,* p. 7. On Faulkner's use of oxymorons and dialectics, see Bruce F. Kawin, "The Montage Element in Faulkner's Fiction," in *Faulkner, Modernism, and Film,* ed. Evans Harrington and Ann. J. Abadie (Jackson: Univ. Press of Mississippi, 1979), pp. 103–26.

22. Alain Robbe-Grillet, *For a New Novel: Essays on Fiction,* trans. Richard Howard (New York: Grove Press, Black Cat, 1965), pp. 138–39, 151–54.

23. See, in particular, Steven Marcus, *The Other Victorians: A Study of Sexuality and Pornography in Mid-Nineteenth-Century England* (New York: Basic Books, 1966).

24. The novel begins with Catherine Earnshaw. Heathcliff's "demonic" energy, infused into the world-system of Wuthering Heights, must be purged. Catherine cannot survive her internal tension; a tamer part of her, born as Catherine Linton, can patch up the damage she and Heathcliff have done, while her wilder self can go on to become a ghost. By marrying Hareton, the second Catherine becomes Catherine Earnshaw once again; the Linton marriage has been unmade, Heathcliff has been exorcised, and the household itself has moved from the Heights to the Grange.

25. Dorothy Van Ghent, *The English Novel: Form and Function* (New York: Harper and Row, Torchbooks, 1961), pp. 153–70.

I am clearly indebted to Van Ghent's argument and will simply refer the reader to her essay as a whole, which is, I think, by far the best piece of criticism yet written on *Wuthering Heights*.

26. Emily Brontë, *Wuthering Heights,* ed. V. S. Pritchett (Boston: Houghton Mifflin Company, Riverside Editions, 1956), pp. 20–21.

27. Brontë, *Wuthering Heights,* pp. 140–41.

28. Compare the ending of Buster Keaton's film, *Sherlock Junior* (see Kawin, *Mindscreen,* pp. 61–63). There is a further parallel with the projector breakdown at the hinge point of *Persona* (see *Mindscreen,* p. 127).

29. It is not a question of directorial talent, either, since two of these were directed by Wyler (1939) and Buñuel (1952). (The others include a well-acted TV version starring Claire Bloom, made sometime in the 1960s, and a negligible 1970 film directed by Robert Fuest. Unfortunately, I haven't seen the British silent versions.) Wyler's deep-focus approach has been highly praised by Bazin and other critics on its own merits, but it poses special problems in relation to Brontë's achievement. Deep focus generally implies that all the elements of the visual field are accessible and interrelated—though Bazin argued that in Renoir, for instance, this opened possibilities of transcendental intuition—and is classically opposed to the montage aesthetic of fragmentation and extratextual synthesis. Fragmentation, displacement, synthesis, filtering, and narrative distancing are all crucial to this novel and ought to have mandated montage and involution rather than Wyler's direct appeal to nature and integration. *Citizen Kane,* by contrast (shot by Gregg Toland, who also shot Wyler's film), employs a montage of relativist narrations *and* a deep-focus cinematography that together generate an ironic dialectic on the problem of truth; I imagine both Bazin and I would have been pleased by such a treatment of *Wuthering Heights*.

30. The reader is left to imagine how powerful must any good, non-Gothic interpretation of the primary experience of Catherine and Heathcliff have been, and beyond that how the experience might have felt. The knowledge that such a description would be impossible is part of the evocative mechanism. The reader is not left imagining better ways of writing the novel.

31. See Walter Slatoff, *Quest for Failure: A Study of William Faulkner* (Ithaca: Cornell Univ. Press, 1960).

32. Shakespeare (cf. *Sutpen*) had twin children named Hamnet and Judith, made a name for himself in the big city in spite of his relatively unsophisticated rural background, and used much of his fortune to build New Place. Faulkner would be familiar with Shakespeare's biography from Chapter 9 of *Ulysses* if nowhere else. The Quentin/Henry/Hamlet connections are obvious both here and in *The Sound and the Fury* and probably take their cue from the Stephen/Hamlet connections in *Ulysses;* the introduction of Henry's sister Judith clinches the brother-sister connection with Hamnet that might complete the Quentin/Hamlet connection (Hamlet has no sister), and to relate Sutpen to Shakespeare has, from that point on, manifest advantages, one of which is to echo Joyce's reflexive use of Shakespeare-as-King-Hamlet (rather than Prince Hamlet, which in terms of *Absalom* has to be Quentin's role rather than Sutpen's) in *Ulysses*.

33. Compare Faulkner, *Absalom, Absalom!*, p. 249: "A very condensation of time which was the gauge of its own violence." Faulkner once said that writing a novel was like nailing a henhouse together in a hurricane.

34. Ibid., p. 263.

35. Ibid., p. 265.

36. Ibid., pp. 7–8.

37. See Kawin, "The Montage Element in Faulkner's Fiction," in *Faulkner, Modernism, and Film,* ed. Harrington and Abadie, pp. 112–14, and Sergei Eisenstein, "The Cinematographic Principle and the Ideogram," in *Film Form: Essays in Film Theory,* ed. Jay Leyda (New York: Harcourt, Brace, and World, Harvest, 1949), p. 30.

38. Faulkner, *Absalom, Absalom!,* pp. 8–9.

39. Ibid., p. 9.

40. Ibid., p. 258.

41. Ibid., p. 303.

42. Edgar Allan Poe, "The Man of the Crowd," in *Terror!,* ed. Larry T. Shaw (New York: Lancer Books, 1966), p. 40.

43. Wayne C. Booth, *The Rhetoric of Fiction* (Chicago: Univ. of Chicago Press, 1961), pp. 311–16. For a much more satisfying reading of the ambiguities of this novel, see Shoshana Felman,

343

"Turning the Screw of Interpretation," *Yale French Studies* 55/56: 94–207.

44. F. W. Dupee, *Henry James* (New York: Dell, Delta, 1965), pp. 159–60.

45. Henry James, *The Turn of the Screw and Daisy Miller* (New York: Dell, 1954), p. 8.

46. Ibid., p. 27.

47. Ibid., p. 28.

48. Ibid., p. 29.

49. Ibid., p. 43. Compare p. 95, where she describes Miles as living "in a setting of beauty and misery that no words can translate."

50. Ibid., p. 44.

51. Ibid., p. 61.

52. Ibid., p. 124.

53. H. P. Lovecraft, *The Lurking Fear and Other Stories* (New York: Ballantine Books, 1971), pp. 99–106.

54. H. P. Lovecraft, *At the Mountains of Madness and Other Tales of Terror* (New York: Ballantine Books, 1971), p. 5.

55. Jorge Luis Borges, "Tlön, Uqbar, Orbis Tertius," in *Labyrinths,* ed. Donald A. Yates and James E. Irby (New York: New Directions, 1964), pp. 3–18.

56. Edgar Allan Poe, *Narrative of A. Gordon Pym,* in *The Complete Tales and Poems of Edgar Allan Poe* (New York: Random House, Modern Library, 1938), p. 748.

57. Lovecraft, *At the Mountains of Madness,* p. 100.

58. Robert W. Chambers, *The King in Yellow and Other Horror Stories,* ed. E. F. Bleiler (New York: Dover, 1970), p. 23. The original volume appeared in 1895.

59. Ibid., p. 39.

60. Ibid., p. 17.

61. Ibid., pp. 91–92.

62. Mary Shelley, *Frankenstein, or, The Modern Prometheus,* with an afterword by Harold Bloom (New York: New American Library, Signet, 1965), pp. 16, 20–22, 25–26, 206.

63. Ibid., p. 204.

64. Ibid., pp. 20–21, 37, 106.

65. The closest that Frankenstein comes to understanding his kinship with the Monster is to insist on his own responsibility

for the murders—another irony on Shelley's part (see ibid., pp. 69–74).

66. Ibid., pp. 210–11.

67. Ibid., p. 114.

68. John-Roger, *Dynamics of the Lower Self* (New York: Baraka, 1976); *The Consciousness of Soul* (New York: Baraka, 1976); and *Sex, Spirit, and You* (New York: Baraka, 1977), pp. 15–16. Similar structures are discussed in any number of esoteric works, but this seems to me the most economically phrased and widely applicable (see Chapter Three, notes 82 and 83).

69. Pynchon, *Gravity's Rainbow*, p. 400.

70. Mark Richard Siegel, *Pynchon: Creative Paranoia in "Gravity's Rainbow"* (Port Washington, NY: Kennikat Press, 1978), pp. 68–69.

71. Siegel, *Pynchon*, pp. 11, 22. For the term "mindscreen," see Kawin, *Mindscreen*, p. xi.

72. Pynchon, *Gravity's Rainbow*, p. 404; Siegel, *Pynchon*, p. 70.

73. These remarks are necessarily addressed to the reader who is familiar with *Gravity's Rainbow;* the novel is too complex to summarize here. For the best short discussion of this novel see Frank D. McConnell's *Four Postwar American Novelists: Bellow, Mailer, Barth, and Pynchon* (Chicago: Univ. of Chicago Press, 1977), pp. 174–97. The only full-length study, so far, is Siegel's *Pynchon,* and it is excellent.

74. Pynchon, *Gravity's Rainbow*, pp. 163–67.

75. Ibid., p. 85.

76. Ibid., p. 49.

77. Ibid., pp. 754–59. Slothrop is attuned to the Rocket via his spontaneous erections.

78. Ibid., p. 638.

79. Ibid., p. 727.

80. Ibid., p. 637.

81. Ibid., p. 590.

82. Ibid., p. 663.

83. Ibid., pp. 737–38. For an important interpretation of Slothrop's Tarot that casts light on the Jungian side of the narrator, the relation of Slothrop's story to that of Parsifal, the Hermit aspects of Slothrop's isolation and perhaps of Pynchon's reclusiveness, and the possibilities for spiritual fulfillment and psychic

integration of Slothrop and his time, see Siegel's *Pynchon,* pp. 67–68. According to Bruce Bassoff, the kreplach story is an old Russian Formalist joke.

84. Pynchon, *Gravity's Rainbow,* pp. 159, 510, 754, 760. The upcoming discussion of Heidegger and Derrida reaches a similar conclusion.

85. Ibid., p. 760.

86. Ibid., p. 159.

87. Ibid., p. 407.

88. Hugo Münsterberg, *The Film: A Psychological Study* (New York: Dover, 1970), p. 30.

89. Pynchon, *Gravity's Rainbow,* p. 159.

90. Ibid., p. 753.

91. Ludwig Wittgenstein, *Tractatus Logico-Philosophicus,* trans. Pears and McGuinness (London: Routledge and Kegan Paul, 1961), 3.032.

92. Pynchon, *Gravity's Rainbow,* p. 758. See also pp. 747–48.

93. Ibid., p. 760. Compare the figure of Dr. Mabuse (played by Rudolf Klein-Rogge, who also played the mad scientist in *Metropolis* and is, one black glove and all, the antecedent of Dr. Strangelove, who is as much a Pynchon figure as possible); in Part II of Lang's *Dr. Mabuse der Spieler,* Dr. Mabuse causes his audience to hallucinate a film on a stage while he prepares to murder the policeman via hypnotic control.

CHAPTER FIVE: THE MIND OF THE TEXT

1. "Burnt Norton" II, in T. S. Eliot, *Collected Poems 1909–1962* (New York: Harcourt, Brace, and World, 1963), p. 177.

2. Georges Poulet, *The Metamorphoses of the Circle,* trans. Carley Dawson and Elliott Coleman (Baltimore: Johns Hopkins Univ. Press, 1966), pp. xvii, 37–38.

3. Stanley E. Fish, *Self-Consuming Artifacts: The Experience of Seventeenth-Century Literature* (Berkeley: Univ. of California Press, 1972), pp. vi, 13, 41–42.

4. Martin Heidegger, *Identity and Difference,* trans. and intro. by Joan Stambaugh (New York: Harper and Row, Torchbooks, 1974), p. 13.

5. Ibid., p. 71.

6. Ibid., pp. 17, 70–73. Heidegger's argument in this book is that "Being is neither present nor outside difference" (to quote Alan Bass). Also see Gayatri Chakravorty Spivak's Introduction to Jacques Derrida, *Of Grammatology,* trans. Spivak (Baltimore: Johns Hopkins Univ. Press, 1976), p. xiv.

7. Martin Heidegger, *Being and Time,* trans. John Macquarrie and Edward Robinson (New York: Harper and Row, 1962), p. 34.

8. Ibid., p. 488. Heidegger and Shankara would disagree, of course, on whether Being is fundamentally or secondarily actualized in time.

9. Heidegger, *Identity and Difference,* p. 73.

10. Heidegger, *Being and Time,* pp. 55–58. Also see "Word" in W. E. Vine, *An Expository Dictionary of New Testament Words* (Iowa Falls: Riverside Book and Bible House, 1952).

11. Heidegger, *Being and Time,* p. 486.

12. Derrida, *Of Grammatology,* p. xiv.

13. G.W. F. Hegel, *On Art, Religion, Philosophy: Introductory Lectures to the Realm of Absolute Spirit,* ed. J. Glenn Gray (New York: Harper and Row, Torchbooks, 1970), pp. 108–109.

14. Ibid., pp. 188–89.

15. Ibid., p. 189. This passage appears as the epigraph to Chapter Two, section three (pp. 62–63) of the present book.

16. Daniel Dayan, "The Tutor-Code of Classical Cinema," in *Movies and Methods,* ed. Bill Nichols (Berkeley: Univ. of California Press, 1976), pp. 441–42.

17. Ihab Hassan, *The Right Promethean Fire: Imagination, Science, and Cultural Change* (Urbana: Univ. of Illinois Press, 1980), p. 56. For a holistic reading of dialectics, see John Berger, *The Look of Things,* ed. Nikos Stangos (New York: Viking Press, A Richard Seaver Book, 1974).

18. Ludwig Wittgenstein, *Tractatus Logico-Philosophicus,* trans. Pears and McGuinness (London: Routledge and Kegan Paul, 1961), 4.121–4.1212.

19. Martin Heidegger, *On the Way to Language,* trans. Peter D. Hertz (New York: Harper and Row, 1971), p. 123. Note the similarity with Poe's "The Man of the Crowd" in that last sentence. See also p. 126, "Saying is showing"; and p. 146, "The word first bestows presence, that is, Being in which things appear as beings."

20. Ibid., pp. 154–56.

21. The Gospel According to Saint John I: 1–5.

22. The Gospel According to Saint John I: 9.

23. St. Augustine, *On Christian Doctrine,* trans. D. W. Robertson, Jr. (Indianapolis: Bobbs-Merrill, Library of Liberal Arts, 1958), I, 6, pp. 10–11. Compare Dante's acceptance of his failed tribute at the end of the *Paradiso,* and Hegel on the problem of noticing God's infinitude.

24. Derrida, *Of Grammatology,* pp. 27–73, esp. pp. 49–51.

25. Ibid., p. xvi.

26. Ibid., p. xvii.

27. My formulation preserves the notion that the tree is absent from the signifier (which is "not this") and from the signified (which is "not here").

28. Derrida, *Of Grammatology,* pp. xliii–xliv.

29. Ibid., pp. xli–xlii.

30. Expression in this case would be redundant. This is, in fact, the language of repetition and the point at which all discrete units merge into a unity best described *as* repetition. (See Bruce F. Kawin, *Telling It Again and Again: Repetition in Literature and Film* [Ithaca: Cornell Univ. Press, 1972], pp. 184–85.) When the Other is found in its full being, when the self entirely and with awareness inhabits its wholeness, who would express the insight, and to whom? And when signifier and signified are so radically present, what would be the need of reference, even within the components of the sign? The question is, happily, moot, since not even the sign could have components.

31. This is also, in a roundabout way, why so many of them are contradictory—koans in particular. These statements use the awareness of difference that is basic to language, deliberately overdoing it so that one can see language for what it is, so that one can have a vantage point exterior to language and in contact with Unity. In this sense, the only legitimate statements are those that annihilate language.

32. William James, *The Principles of Psychology* (New York: Henry Holt and Co., 1890), I, 239. For useful excerpts, see Robert E. Ornstein, *The Nature of Human Consciousness: A Book of Readings* (San Francisco: W. H. Freeman, 1973), pp. 153–66.

33. The review is excerpted by Walter Allen in his Introduction to Dorothy Richardson, *Pilgrimage* (New York: Popular Library, 1976), I, 4–5.

34. Richardson, *Pilgrimage* I, 11 (Richardson prints "retarding personalities," which may be a misprint for "regarding").

35. Samuel Richardson, *Clarissa: Or, the History of a Young Lady* (New York: Dutton, Everyman's Library, 1932), I, xv.

36. See "Composition as Explanation" in Gertrude Stein, *What Are Masterpieces?,* ed. Robert Bartlett Haas (New York: Pitman, 1970), esp. pp. 29–33; Donald Sutherland, *Gertrude Stein: A Biography of her Work* (New Haven: Yale Univ. Press, 1951), pp. 51–52; and Kawin, *Telling It Again and Again,* p. 119.

37. Derrida, *Of Grammatology,* pp. xxiv–xli. See also "Freud and the Scene of Writing" in Jacques Derrida, *Writing and Difference,* trans. Alan Bass (Chicago: Univ. of Chicago Press, 1978), pp. 196–231.

38. Lovelace's letter of "Friday, June 16," in Samuel Richardson's *Clarissa* III, 203–17. If for no other reason, this section should be consulted as the best analysis of the psychology of rape (both roles) before those made by contemporary feminism. Lovelace, for instance, is explicit about rape as an exercise of power and envy, "subduing one of that exalted class" (p. 203).

39. For the term "montage of consciousness," see Bruce F. Kawin, "The Montage Element in Faulkner's Fiction," in *Faulkner, Modernism, and Film,* ed. Evans Harrington and Ann J. Abadie (Jackson: Univ. Press of Mississippi, 1979).

40. Samuel Richardson, *Clarissa* III, 209. Clarissa's name, of course, suggests how important and characteristic it is for her to be "clear," how unusual it is for her articulation and perceptiveness to fail her.

41. Ibid., pp. 213–14.

42. Jonathan Swift, *A Tale of a Tub,* in *The Writings of Jonathan Swift,* ed. Robert A. Greenberg and William Bowman Piper (New York: W. W. Norton, Norton Critical Edition, 1973), p. 270.

43. Ibid., p. 265.

44. Ibid., p. 301.

45. Ibid., p. 337.

46. Ibid., pp. 340–45.

47. Ibid., pp. 349–50.

48. Ibid., p. 350.

49. Ibid., p. 355.

50. Ibid., p. 370.

51. On Fielding, Cervantes, and Sterne, see Robert Alter, *Partial*

Magic: The Novel as Self-Conscious Genre (Berkeley: Univ. of California Press, 1975), pp. ix–56.

52. *The Art of Literature,* in Arthur Schopenhauer, *The Pessimist's Handbook: A Collection of Popular Essays,* ed. Hazel E. Barnes and trans. T. Bailey Saunders (Lincoln: Univ. of Nebraska Press, 1964), pp. 491–92.

53. Laurence Sterne, *The Life and Opinions of Tristram Shandy, Gentleman,* ed. James Aiken Work (Indianapolis: Bobbs-Merrill, Odyssey Press, 1940), pp. 285–86. Also see pp. 515–16 and 533.

54. Ibid., p. 370.

55. Ibid., p. 442.

56. Ibid., pp. 192, 214.

57. Ibid., pp. 533 and xxxiv, 600 and xxxviii.

58. Steve Katz, *The Exagggerations of Peter Prince* [*The Novel by Steve Katz*] (New York: Holt, Rinehart and Winston, 1968), pp. 3, 9. The bracketed subtitle began as a compositor/designer's error, and Katz retained it.

59. Ibid., p. 22.

60. Ibid., p. 61.

61. Ibid., pp. 214–29.

62. Ibid., pp. 179–80.

63. This summary is condensed from Alter, *Partial Magic,* pp. 154–56.

64. Ibid., p. 155. Also see pp. 57–83 for a relevant analysis of Diderot's *Jacques le fataliste.* (Katz has said that his two models for *Peter Prince* were *Tristram Shandy* and *Jacques le fataliste.*)

65. Notably Alter, *Partial Magic;* Robert Humphrey, *Stream of Consciousness in the Modern Novel* (Berkeley: Univ. of California Press, 1954); and Dorritt Cohn, *Transparent Minds: Narrative Modes for Presenting Consciousness in Fiction* (Princeton: Princeton Univ. Press, 1978). There is a useful and relevant overview of Joyce and Woolf in Keith Cohen, *Film and Fiction: The Dynamics of Exchange* (New Haven: Yale Univ. Press, 1979), and of cinematic consciousness and self-consciousness in Bruce F. Kawin, *Mindscreen: Bergman, Godard, and First-Person Film* (Princeton: Princeton Univ. Press, 1978).

66. William Faulkner, *The Sound and the Fury* (New York: Random House, Modern Library College Editions, n.d. [facsimile of first 1929 printing]), pp. 1–2.

67. Jean-Paul Sartre, "Time in Faulkner: *The Sound and the Fury,*"

in *William Faulkner: Three Decades of Criticism,* ed. Frederick J. Hoffman and Olga W. Vickery (New York: Harcourt, Brace, and World, Harbinger, 1963), pp. 228–30.

68. Hugh Kenner, "Faulkner and the Avant-Garde," in *Faulkner, Modernism, and Film,* ed. Harrington and Abadie, p. 186. Also see Kenner's "Faulkner and Joyce" in the same volume, esp. pp. 28–29.

69. William Faulkner, *As I Lay Dying* (New York: Random House, Modern Library, 1967), p. 243. Laing would endorse the notion that this schizophrenia might be a response to a transcendental intuition.

70. Faulkner, *As I Lay Dying,* p. 165. For a very good analysis of this passage and for a Derridean interpretation of the whole novel, see Richard Godden, "William Faulkner, Addie Bundren, and Language," *Studies in English* 15 (University of Mississippi, 1978): 101–23, esp. pp. 111–13, 116–17.

71. Joseph Blotner, *Faulkner: A Biography* (New York: Random House, 1974), I, 74 (note to p. 502). Blotner got this information from Faulkner himself.

72. Faulkner, *As I Lay Dying,* p. 228. For Darl's cubist sawhorse, and so on, see pp. 139, 209.

73. Ibid., p. 76. Faulkner is said to have written this passage when drunk and to have been unable to explain it later; it is just as likely that he told such a story to ward off critics.

74. Jacques Derrida, *Speech and Phenomena and Other Essays on Husserl's Theory of Signs* (Evanston: Northwestern Univ. Press, 1973), cited by Richard Godden on p. 116 of his article.

75. Marcel Proust, *Swann's Way,* trans. C. K. Scott Moncrieff (New York: Random House, Vintage, 1970), pp. 3, 8, and elsewhere.

76. The final sentence of Samuel Beckett, *Molloy,* in *Three Novels by Samuel Beckett* (New York: Grove Press, Evergreen, Black Cat, 1965), p. 176.

77. Ibid., p. 112.

78. Hugh Kenner, *Samuel Beckett: A Critical Study* (Berkeley: Univ. of California Press, 1973), p. 57.

79. Beckett, *Three Novels,* p. 137.

80. Kenner, *Samuel Beckett,* p. 79. Compare Sterne, *Tristram Shandy,* pp. 285–86.

81. Beckett, *Three Novels,* pp. 269, 274, 277, 280, and elsewhere.

82. Ibid., p. 259.

83. Ibid., p. 291.

84. Wylie Sypher, *Loss of the Self in Modern Literature and Art* (New York: Random House, Vintage Books, 1962), pp. 147–58.

85. Beckett, *Three Novels,* pp. 303–304.

86. Ibid., p. 304.

87. Ibid., p. 324.

88. Ibid., p. 413.

89. Ibid., p. 414.

90. As *L'Homme et l'Absolu selon la Kabbale* (Paris: Editions Buchet/Chastel, Corrêa, 1958).

91. Leo Schaya, *The Universal Meaning of the Kabbalah,* trans. Nancy Pearson (Baltimore: Penguin, The Penguin Metaphysical Library, 1973), p. 35. The *Sefiroth* are, in descending order: *kether* (crown), *hokhmah* (wisdom), *binah* (intelligence), *hesed* (grace), *din* (judgment), *tifereth* (beauty), *netsah* (victory), *hod* (glory), *yesod* (foundation), *malkhuth* (kingdom—or *shekinah,* immanence).

92. Schaya, *The Universal Meaning of the Kabbalah,* pp. 35–42. In the last part of this passage, Schaya is quoting from Moses Cordovero's *Garden of Pomegranates.*

93. Edmond Jabès, *The Book of Questions,* trans. Rosmarie Waldrop (Middletown, MA: Wesleyan Univ. Press, 1976), p. 26.

94. Edmond Jabès, *The Book of Questions II & III: The Book of Yukel and Return to the Book,* trans. Rosmarie Waldrop (Middletown, MA: Wesleyan Univ. Press, 1977), p. 207. This volume is continuously paginated, but future references will be keyed either to *The Book of Yukel* or to *Return to the Book.*

95. Jabès, *Return to the Book,* p. 178.

96. Ibid., pp. 228–29. Compare with Jabès, *The Book of Yukel,* pp. 86–87, 104.

97. Jabès, *Return to the Book,* pp. 162–63.

98. Jabès, *The Book of Questions,* p. 31.

99. Jabès, *Return to the Book,* p. 236.

100. Jacques Derrida, "Edmond Jabès and the Question of the Book," in *Writing and Difference,* trans. Alan Bass (Chicago: Univ. of Chicago Press, 1978), pp. 64–78. Also see "Ellipsis," pp. 294–300, on Jabès' *Return to the Book.* Derrida stops short, of course, of endorsing the immanence of the transcendental signified—so it may be that he fits Jabès into a Procrustean bed.

101. Jabès, *The Book of Questions,* p, 25.

102. Ibid., pp. 16–18.

103. Ibid., pp. 18–19.

104. Ibid., p. 31. For comic relief, compare Tom Robbins, *Even Cowgirls Get the Blues* (Boston: Houghton Mifflin, 1976), p. 108—a sequence of playful self-declarations ("This sentence can do the funky chicken," etc.) ending with: "This sentence is proud to be a part of the team here at *Even Cowgirls Get the Blues.* This sentence is rather confounded by the whole damn thing."

105. Jabès, *The Book of Questions,* pp. 32–33.

106. Jabès, *Return to the Book,* pp. 206–11, 235.

107. Ibid., pp. 231–35. A Lacanian might call all this "the symbolic in search of the imaginary," or perhaps the reverse.

108. This sentence contradicts the dominant line of thought in poststructuralist French feminist theory.

109. Adrienne Rich, *On Lies, Secrets, and Silence: Selected Prose 1966–1978* (New York: W. W. Norton & Company, 1979), especially pp. 184–97, 204, 223–58. Also see Adrienne Rich, *The Dream of a Common Language: Poems 1974–1977* (New York: W. W. Norton & Co., 1978), which is in my opinion her best work to date. I hope it is clear that the purpose of this chapter is not to rehearse the entire history of feminist theory but to focus on—and demonstrate the relevance of—feminist analyses of the nature of the self, particularly in the context of the social, personal, and narrative politics of women's writing.

110. Susan Griffin, *Woman and Nature: The Roaring Inside Her* (New York: Harper and Row, Colophon, 1980).

111. Mary Daly, *Gyn/Ecology: The Metaethics of Radical Feminism* (Boston: Beacon Press, 1978).

112. Ibid., p. 9.

113. Ibid., pp. 10–11.

114. Ibid., p. 2.

115. See Sandra M. Gilbert and Susan Gubar, *The Madwoman in the Attic: The Woman Writer and the Nineteenth-Century Literary Imagination* (New Haven: Yale Univ. Press, 1979): and R. D. Laing, *The Politics of Experience* (New York: Ballantine, 1968).

116. Emily Dickinson, *Complete Poems,* ed. Thomas H. Johnson (Boston: Little, Brown & Co., 1960), # 435.

117. Dickinson, *Complete Poems,* # 642.

118. Simone de Beauvoir, *The Second Sex,* trans. H. M. Parshley (New York: Bantam, 1961), p. xxvii. This Other-ness is entirely different from the delta-t of Derridean "absence," which is posited as universal.

119. Monique Wittig, *The Lesbian Body,* trans. David Le Vay (New York: Avon, Bard, 1976), p. x.

120. In conversation, Sandra Gilbert suggested I add "womb envy" to this statement; I agree.

121. See Joan Goulianos, *by a Woman writt: Literature from Six Centuries by and about Women* (Baltimore: Penguin, 1974), pp. 3–20.

122. Virginia Woolf, *A Room of One's Own* (New York: Harcourt, Brace, and World, 1929), pp. 117–18. Also see Tillie Olsen, *Silences* (New York: Dell, Delta, 1978).

123. *Anthology of American Literature,* ed. George McMichael (New York: Macmillan, 1974) I, 68.

124. For a good introductory discussion of madness in *Jane Eyre, Mrs. Dalloway, The Four-Gated City,* and *Surfacing,* as well as of R. D. Laing, see Barbara Hill Rigney, *Madness and Sexual Politics in the Feminist Novel* (Madison: Univ. of Wisconsin Press, 1978). For the devastating effect of Mitchell's treatment on Virginia Woolf, see Elaine Showalter, *A Literature of Their Own: British Women Novelists from Brontë to Lessing* (Princeton: Princeton Univ. Press, 1977), pp. 274–78.

125. Charlotte Perkins Gilman, *The Living of Charlotte Perkins Gilman* (New York: Harper and Row, Colophon, 1975), p. 96.

126. Charlotte Perkins Gilman, *The Yellow Wallpaper* (Old Westbury, NY: Feminist Press, 1973), p. 12.

127. See R. D. Laing, *Self and Others* (Baltimore: Penguin, Pelican, 1971); R. D. Laing and A. Esterson, *Sanity, Madness and the Family: Families of Schizophrenics* (Baltimore: Penguin, Pelican, 1970); R. D. Laing, *The Divided Self: An Existential Study in Sanity and Madness* (Baltimore: Penguin, Pelican, 1965); and R. D. Laing, *The Politics of Experience.* A movie that dramatizes many of these insights, based on David Mercer's BBC teleplay, *In Two Minds,* and sometimes called *Wednesday's Child,* is Ken Loach's *Family Life* (Great Britain, 1971).

128. Gilman, *The Yellow Wallpaper,* p. 30.

129. Originally formulated by Yogeshwar Muni, director of the Sanatana Dharma Foundation. As described by Francesca Erbsenhaut, to whom I wish to acknowledge my gratitude and indebtedness: "Participants choose partners and take turns being

speakers and listeners. A listener delivers the instruction, 'Tell me who you are.' The speaker receives the instruction, then contemplates and remains open to direct experience of who s/he is. S/he communicates as fully as possible to the silent, attentive partner any thoughts, feelings, sensations, or other phenomena of which s/he may become aware. After five minutes the listener thanks the speaker and prepares to receive the instruction. This alternating sequence continues for approximately forty-five minutes with a given partner. A typical day might involve ten such sessions." The goal of the Self-Realization Intensive is direct experience of pure consciousness, "unrelated to the physical body and transcending the mind" (quoting Ramana Maharshi).

130. Doris Lessing, *The Golden Notebook* (New York: Bantam, 1973), pp. 633–34.

131. This "disappointment" is, of course, the proper response to an irony Lessing intended.

132. Doris Lessing, *A Small Personal Voice: Essays, Reviews, Interviews,* ed. Paul Schlueter (New York: Random House, Vintage, 1975), pp. 32–33 (from the "Preface to *The Golden Notebook*"); also see pp. 51, 65.

133. Lessing, *A Small Personal Voice,* pp. 25–29.

134. In conversation, Joanna Russ told me that she had not yet read *The Golden Notebook* but had been strongly influenced by Laing's *The Divided Self* (which, of course, has also been an important work to Lessing).

135. Both this and the next-mentioned essay can be found in *Images of Women in Fiction: Feminist Perspectives,* ed. Susan Koppelman Cornillon (Bowling Green, OH: Popular Press, 1972); this passage is on p. 12.

136. Ibid., p. 14.

137. Ibid., p. 18.

138. Ibid., p. 91.

139. See Robert Silverberg's unconsciously hilarious speculations on Tiptree's identity ("It has been suggested that Tiptree is female, a theory I find absurd, for there is to me something ineluctably masculine about Tiptree's writing") and his later recantation ("She fooled me beautifully [sic], along with everyone else, and called into question the entire notion of what is 'masculine' or 'feminine' in fiction") in his Introduction to James Tiptree Jr., *Warm Worlds and Otherwise* (New York: Ballantine, 1979 edition).

140. *Aurora: Beyond Equality,* ed. Vonda N. McIntyre and Susan

Janice Anderson (Greenwich: Fawcett, Gold Medal, 1976), pp. 16–98.

141. Susan Griffin, *Rape: The Power of Consciousness* (New York: Harper and Row, 1979), pp. 67–68.

142. Griffin, *Rape: The Power of Consciousness*, pp. 37–47.

143. Shulamith Firestone's *The Dialectic of Sex: The Case for Feminist Revolution* (New York: William Morrow & Co., 1970), by deconstructing fixed assumptions about "the means of reproduction," has had considerable influence on feminist science fiction, as elsewhere; though the all-female world has been a recurrent theme in science fiction for over 100 years (from Gilman's *Herland* to Wyndham's "Consider Her Ways") and parthenogenesis has been around for thousands, the contexts and specific technologies have clearly changed.

144. Joanna Russ, *The Female Man* (New York: Bantam, 1975), p. 212. "Laur," by the way, was not at the meal.

145. See "The Cinematographic Principle and the Ideogram" and "A Dialectic Approach to Film Form" in *Film Form*, pp. 28–63.

146. Russ, *The Female Man*, p. 205. For the other side of the socialization disaster, see Herb Goldberg, *The Hazards of Being Male: Surviving the Myth of Masculine Privilege* (New York: New American Library, Signet, 1976).

147. Russ, *The Female Man*, p. 141.

148. Ibid., p. 139.

149. Ibid., p. 140.

150. Ibid., pp. 212–13.

151. Daly, *Gyn/Ecology*, p. 423.

152. Ibid., pp. 4–5.

153. Susan Griffin, *Woman and Nature*, p. 191. Also see pp. xv–xvii, 116–19, 159–69, 187, 195, 202–203, and 227.

154. Daly, *Gyn/Ecology*, p. 11. She uses "O" to mean both "zero" and "the letter O."

155. Monique Wittig, *Les Guérillères*, trans. David Le Vay (New York: Avon, Bard, 1973), pp. 7, 14, 27, 30, 45, 69, and passim.

156. Ibid., p. 114.

157. Ibid., p. 143.

158. Griffin, *Rape: The Power of Consciousness*, p. 44.

SELECTED BIBLIOGRAPHY

Abel, Lionel. *Metatheatre: A New View of Dramatic Form.* New York: Hill and Wang, Dramabook, 1963.

Agee, James, and Walker Evans. *Let Us Now Praise Famous Men.* Boston: Houghton Mifflin, 1941.

Alter, Robert. *Partial Magic: The Novel as a Self-Conscious Genre.* Berkeley: University of California Press, 1975.

Arberry, A. J. *Sufism: An Account of the Mystics of Islam.* New York: Harper and Row, Torchbooks, 1970.

Atwood, Margaret. *Surfacing.* New York: Popular Library, 1976.

Augustine, Saint. *On Christian Doctrine,* translated by D. W. Robertson, Jr. Indianapolis: Bobbs-Merrill, Library of Liberal Arts, 1958.

Bader, Julia. *Crystal Land: Artifice in Nabokov's English Novels.* Berkeley: University of California Press, 1972.

Barth, John. "The Literature of Exhaustion." In *Surfiction: Fiction Now and Tomorrow* . . . , edited by Raymond Federman. Chicago: Swallow Press, 1975.

Barthes, Roland, *Writing Degree Zero and Elements of Semiology,* translated by Annette Lavers and Colin Smith. Boston: Beacon Press, 1970.

————. *The Pleasure of the Text,* translated by Richard Miller. New York: Hill and Wang, 1975.

Beauvoir, Simone de. *The Second Sex,* translated by H. M. Parshley. New York: Bantam Books, 1961.

Beckett, Samuel. *Proust.* New York: Grove Press, Evergreen, 1957.

————. *Watt.* New York: Grove Press, Evergreen, 1959.

————. *Waiting for Godot.* New York: Grove Press, Evergreen, 1954.

————. *Three Novels by Samuel Beckett.* New York: Grove Press, Black Cat, 1965.

————. *Rockaby.* New York: Grove Press, 1981.

Benjamin, Walter. *Illuminations,* edited by Hannah Arendt, translated by Harry Zohn. New York: Schocken, 1969.

Bentov, Itzhak. *Stalking the Wild Pendulum: On the Mechanics of Consciousness.* New York: E. P. Dutton, 1977.

357

Ben-Zvi, Linda. "Samuel Beckett, Fritz Mauthner, and the Limits of Language." *PMLA* 95 (1980): 2, 183–200.

Berger, John. *G.: A Novel*. New York: Pantheon, 1980.

————. *The Look of Things*, edited by Nikos Stangos. New York: Viking Press, A Richard Seaver Book, 1974.

Bergson, Henri. *An Introduction to Metaphysics*, 2nd ed., translated by T. E. Hulme. Indianapolis: Bobbs-Merrill, Library of Liberal Arts, 1955.

Borges, Jorge Luis. *Labyrinths*, edited by Donald A. Yates and James E. Irby. New York: New Directions, 1964.

Blotner, Joseph. *Faulkner: A Biography*. 2 vols. New York: Random House, 1974.

Brain/Mind Bulletin. [P. O. Box 42211, Los Angeles, CA 90042.]

Brée, Germaine. *The World of Marcel Proust*. Boston: Houghton Mifflin, Riverside Studies in Literature, 1966.

Brontë, Emily. *Wuthering Heights*, edited by V. S. Pritchett. Boston: Houghton Mifflin, Riverside Editions, 1956.

Brunton, Paul. *The Secret Path: A Technique of Spiritual Self-Discovery for the Modern World*. New York: E. P. Dutton, 1935.

Capra, Fritjof. *The Tao of Physics: An Exploration of the Parallels Between Modern Physics and Eastern Mysticism*. Boulder, CO: Shambhala, 1975.

Castaneda, Carlos. *The Teachings of Don Juan: A Yaqui Way of Knowledge*. New York: Simon and Schuster, Pocket Books, 1974.

————. *A Separate Reality: Further Conversations with Don Juan*. New York: Simon and Schuster, Pocket Books, 1972.

————. *Journey to Ixtlan: The Lessons of Don Juan*. New York: Simon and Schuster, 1972.

————. *Tales of Power*. New York: Simon and Schuster, Pocket Books, 1976.

Cavell, Stanley. *The World Viewed: Reflections on the Ontology of Film*, enlarged ed. Cambridge: Harvard University Press, 1979.

Cervantes, Miguel de. *The Adventures of Don Quixote*, translated by J. M. Cohen. Baltimore: Penguin, 1950.

Chambers, Robert W. *The King in Yellow and Other Horror Stories*, edited by E. F. Bleiler. New York: Dover, 1970.

Christie, Agatha. *The Murder of Roger Ackroyd*. New York: Simon and Schuster, Pocket Books, 1939.

Chuang Tzu. *Chuang Tzu: Basic Writings,* translated by Burton Watson. New York: Columbia University Press, 1964.

The Cloud of Unknowing and the Book of Privy Consciousness, edited by William Johnston. Garden City: Doubleday, Image, 1973.

Cohn, Dorritt. *Transparent Minds: Narrative Modes for Presenting Consciousness in Fiction.* Princeton: Princeton University Press, 1978.

Connell, Evan S., Jr. *Mrs. Bridge.* Greenwich, CT: Fawcett, Crest, 1970.

—————. *Mr. Bridge.* Greenwich, CT: Fawcett, Crest, 1970.

Conrad, Joseph. *Heart of Darkness.* In *Three Novels by Joseph Conrad,* edited by Edward Said. New York: Washington Square Press, 1970.

—————. *Lord Jim.* New York: Bantam Books, 1957.

—————. *Under Western Eyes.* Garden City: Doubleday, Anchor, 1963.

Cornillon, Susan Koppelman. *Images of Women in Fiction: Feminist Perspectives.* Bowling Green, OH: Popular Press, 1972.

Daly, Mary. *Gyn/Ecology: The Metaethics of Radical Feminism.* Boston: Beacon Press, 1978.

Dante. *The Divine Comedy,* edited and translated by John D. Sinclair. 3 vols. New York: Oxford University Press, Galaxy Books, 1961.

Deleuze, Gilles. *Proust and Signs,* translated by Richard Howard. New York: George Braziller, 1972.

Derrida, Jacques. *Writing and Difference,* translated by Alan Bass. Chicago: University of Chicago Press, 1978.

—————. *Of Grammatology,* translated by Gayatri Chakravorty Spivak. Baltimore: Johns Hopkins University Press, 1976.

Dickinson, Emily. *Complete Poems,* edited by Thomas H. Johnson. Boston: Little, Brown and Co., 1960.

Dimond, S. J., and J. G. Beaumont, eds. *Hemispheric Function in the Human Brain.* London: Eleck Science, Ltd.; and New York: Wiley, 1974.

Dinnerstein, Dorothy. *The Mermaid and the Minotaur: Sexual Arrangements and Human Malaise.* New York: Harper and Row, Colophon, 1977.

Doyle, Sir Arthur Conan. *A Study in Scarlet and The Sign of Four.* New York: G. P. Putnam's Sons, Berkley Medallion, 1975.

Dupee, F. W. *Henry James.* New York: Dell, Delta, American Men of Letters Series, 1965.

Einstein, Albert. *Relativity: The Special and the General Theory,* translated by Robert W. Lawson. New York: Crown, 1961.

Eisenstein, Sergei. *Film Form: Essays in Film Theory,* edited by Jay Leyda. New York: Harcourt, Brace, and World, Harvest, 1949.

Eliot, T. S. *Collected Poems 1909–1962.* New York: Harcourt, Brace, and World, 1963.

Ellmann, Mary. *Thinking About Women.* New York: Harcourt Brace Jovanovich, 1968.

Faulkner, William. *The Sound and the Fury.* New York: Random House, Modern Library, n.d. [facsimile of 1929 ed.]

———. *As I Lay Dying.* New York: Random House, Modern Library, 1967.

———. *Absalom, Absalom!* New York: Random House, Modern Library, 1951.

Federman, Raymond. *Surfiction: Fiction Now and Tomorrow . . .* Chicago: Swallow Press, 1975.

———. *Take It or Leave It: an exaggerated second-hand tale to be read aloud either standing or sitting.* New York: Fiction Collective, 1976.

———. *The Voice in the Closet.* Madison: Coda Press, 1979.

Felman, Shoshana. "Turning the Screw of Interpretation." In *Literature and Psychoanalysis. The Question of Reading: Otherwise,* edited by Shoshana Felman. *Yale French Studies* 55/56: 94–207.

Ferguson, Marilyn. *The Aquarian Conspiracy: Personal and Social Transformation in the 1980s.* Los Angeles: J. P. Tarcher, 1980.

Ferguson, Mary Anne. *Images of Women in Literature,* 2nd ed. Boston: Houghton Mifflin, 1977.

Fish, Stanley E. *Self-Consuming Artifacts: The Experience of Seventeenth-Century Literature.* Berkeley: University of California Press, 1972.

Fitzgerald, F. Scott. *The Great Gatsby.* New York: Charles Scribner's Sons, Scribner Library, 1925.

Ford, Ford Madox. *The Good Soldier: A Tale of Passion.* New York: Alfred A. Knopf, 1951.

Gardner, Helen. *The Metaphysical Poets.* Baltimore: Penguin, Penguin Poets, 1966.

Genet, Jean. *The Blacks: A Clown Show,* translated by Bernard Frechtman. New York: Grove Press, Evergreen, 1960.

Gilbert, Sandra M., and Susan Gubar. *The Madwoman in the Attic: The Woman Writer and the Nineteenth-Century Literary Imagination.* New Haven: Yale University Press, 1979.

Gilman, Charlotte Perkins. *The Yellow Wallpaper.* Old Westbury, NY: Feminist Press, 1973.

Godden, Richard. "William Faulkner, Addie Bundren, and Language." *Studies in English* 15 (1978): 101–23.

Goldberg, Herb. *The Hazards of Being Male: Surviving the Myth of Masculine Privilege.* New York: New American Library, Signet, 1976.

Gornick, Vivian, and Barbara K. Moran. *Woman in Sexist Society: Studies in Power and Powerlessness.* New York: New American Library, Signet, 1972.

Goulianos, Joan. *by a Woman writt: Literature from Six Centuries by and about Women.* Baltimore: Penguin, 1974.

Griffin, Susan. *Rape: The Power of Consciousness.* New York: Harper and Row, 1979.

———. *Woman and Nature: The Roaring Inside Her.* New York: Harper and Row, Colophon, 1980.

Gross, Seymour. "A Further Note on the Function of the Frame in 'Heart of Darkness.'" *Modern Fiction Studies* 3: 167–70.

Guetti, James. *The Limits of Metaphor: A Study of Melville, Conrad, and Faulkner.* Ithaca: Cornell University Press, 1967.

Harrington, Evans, and Ann J. Abadie. *Faulkner, Modernism, and Film: Faulkner and Yoknapatawpha, 1978.* Jackson: University Press of Mississippi, 1979.

Hassan, Ihab. *The Right Promethean Fire: Imagination, Science, and Cultural Change.* Urbana: Univ. of Illinois Press, 1980.

Hegel, G.W.F. *Phenomenology of Spirit,* translated by A. V. Miller, introduced by J. N. Findlay. Oxford: Oxford Univ. Press, 1977.

———. *On Art, Religion, Philosophy: Introductory Lectures to the Realm of Absolute Spirit,* edited by J. Glenn Gray. New York: Harper and Row, Torchbooks, 1970.

Heidegger, Martin. *Being and Time,* translated by John Macquarrie and Edward Robinson. New York: Harper and Row, 1962.

———. *Identity and Difference,* translated by Joan Stambaugh. New York: Harper and Row, Torchbooks, 1974.

———. *On the Way to Language,* translated by Peter D. Hertz. New York: Harper and Row, 1971.

Hoffman, Frederick J., and Olga Vickery. *William Faulkner: Three*

Decades of Criticism. New York: Harcourt, Brace, and World, Harbinger, 1963.

Humphrey, Robert. *Stream of Consciousness in the Modern Novel.* Berkeley: University of California Press, 1954.

Jabès, Edmond. *The Book of Questions,* translated by Rosmarie Waldrop. Middletown, MA: Wesleyan University Press, 1976.

————. *The Book of Questions II and III: The Book of Yukel and Return to the Book,* translated by Rosmarie Waldrop. Middletown, MA: Wesleyan University Press, 1977.

James, Henry. *The Turn of the Screw and Daisy Miller.* New York: Dell, 1954.

James, William. *The Principles of Psychology.* 2 vols. New York: Henry Holt and Co., 1890.

————. *The Varieties of Religious Experience: A Study in Human Nature.* London: Collins, Fontana Library, 1960.

John-Roger. *Awakening into Light.* New York: Baraka Press, 1976.

————. *The Consciousness of Soul.* New York: Baraka Press, 1976.

————. *Dynamics of the Lower Self.* New York: Baraka Press, 1976.

————. *Inner Worlds of Meditation.* New York: Baraka Press, 1976.

————. *The Sound Current.* New York: Baraka Press, 1976.

————. *MSIA Soul Awareness Discourses.* [By subscription: Movement of Spiritual Inner Awareness, P.O. Box 3935, Los Angeles, CA 90051.]

Joy, W. Brugh. *Joy's Way: A Map for the Transformational Journey.* New York: St. Martin's Press; and Los Angeles: J. P. Tarcher, 1978.

Joyce, James. *Ulysses.* New York: Random House, Vintage, 1961.

————. *Finnegans Wake.* New York: Viking Press, Compass, 1958.

Katz, Steve. *The Exagggerations of Peter Prince* [*The Novel by Steve Katz*]. New York: Holt, Rinehart & Winston, 1968.

————. *Creamy and Delicious.* New York: Random House, 1970.

————. *Saw.* New York: Alfred A. Knopf, 1972.

————. *Moving Parts.* New York: Fiction Collective, 1977.

Kawin, Bruce F. *Telling It Again and Again: Repetition in Literature and Film.* Ithaca: Cornell University Press, 1972.

————. *Mindscreen: Bergman, Godard, and First-Person Film.* Princeton: Princeton University Press, 1978.

Kenner, Hugh. *Samuel Beckett: A Critical Study,* 2nd ed. Berkeley: University of California Press, 1973.

Koedt, Anne, Ellen Levine, and Anita Rapone. *Radical Feminism.* New York: New York Times Book Co., Quadrangle, 1973.

Lacan, Jacques. *The Language of the Self: The Function of Language in Psychoanalysis,* translated by Anthony Wilden. New York: Dell, Delta, 1975.

Laing, R. D. *The Divided Self: An Existential Study in Sanity and Madness.* Baltimore: Penguin, Pelican, 1965.

———. *The Politics of Experience.* New York: Ballantine, 1968.

Lakoff, Robin. *Language and Woman's Place.* New York: Harper and Row, Colophon, 1975.

Laszlo, Ervin. *The Systems View of the World.* New York: George Braziller, 1972.

Lerner, Eric. *Journey of Insight Meditation: A Personal Experience of the Buddha's Way.* New York: Schocken, 1977.

Lessing, Doris. *The Golden Notebook.* New York: Bantam Books, 1973.

———. *The Four-Gated City.* New York: Bantam Books, 1970.

———. *A Small Personal Voice: Essays, Reviews, Interviews,* edited by Paul Schlueter. New York: Random House, Vintage, 1975.

Lovecraft, H. P. *The Dunwich Horror and Others,* edited by August Derleth. Sauk City, WI: Arkham House, 1963.

———. *At the Mountains of Madness and Other Tales of Terror.* New York: Ballantine, 1971.

Lyons, John. *Introduction to Theoretical Linguistics.* Cambridge: Cambridge University Press, 1968.

McConnell, Frank D. *Four Postwar American Novelists: Bellow, Mailer, Barth, and Pynchon.* Chicago: University of Chicago Press, 1977.

McIntyre, Vonda, and Susan Janice Anderson. *Aurora: Beyond Equality.* Greenwich, CT: Fawcett, Gold Medal, 1976.

Machado de Assis, Joaquim Maria. *Dom Casmurro,* translated by Helen Caldwell. Berkeley: University of California Press, 1966.

Mailer, Norman. *Why Are We In Vietnam?* New York: G. P. Putnam's Sons, Berkley Medallion, 1968.

Mann, Thomas. *Doctor Faustus: The Life of the German Composer Adrian Leverkühn as Told by a Friend,* translated by H. T. Lowe-Porter. New York: Alfred A. Knopf, 1948.

Márquez, Gabriel García. *One Hundred Years of Solitude,* translated by Gregory Rabassa. New York: Avon, Bard, 1971.

363

Maslow, Abraham H. *Toward a Psychology of Being,* 2nd ed. New York: D. Van Nostrand, Insight, 1968.

Melville, Herman. *Moby-Dick; or, The Whale,* edited by Harrison Hayford and Hershel Parker. New York: W. W. Norton, Norton Critical Edition, 1967.

Mill, John Stuart, and Harriet Taylor Mill. *Essays on Sex Equality,* edited by Alice S. Rossi. Chicago: University of Chicago Press, 1970.

Miller, Jean Baker. *Toward a new psychology of women.* Boston: Beacon Press, 1977.

Millett, Kate. *Sexual Politics.* New York: Avon, 1971.

More, Sir Thomas. *Utopia,* translated by Robert M. Adams. New York: W. W. Norton, Norton Critical Edition, 1975.

Morgan, Robin. *Sisterhood is Powerful: An Anthology of Writings from the Women's Liberation Movement.* New York: Random House, Vintage, 1970.

————. *Going Too Far: The Personal Chronicle of a Feminist.* New York: Random House, Vintage, 1978.

Münsterberg, Hugo. *The Film: A Psychological Study.* New York: Dover, 1970.

Nabokov, Vladimir. *Pale Fire.* New York: G. P. Putnam's Sons, 1962.

————. *Ada or Ardor: A Family Chronicle.* New York: McGraw-Hill, 1969.

Nichols, Bill. *Movies and Methods: An Anthology.* Berkeley: Univ. of California Press, 1976.

Nicoll, Maurice. *Living Time and the Integration of Life.* London: Watkins, 1976.

Noel, Daniel C., ed. *Seeing Castaneda: Reactions to the "Don Juan" Writings of Carlos Castaneda.* New York: G. P. Putnam's Sons, Capricorn, 1976.

Olsen, Tillie. *Tell Me a Riddle.* New York: Dell, Delta, 1971.

————. *Silences.* New York: Dell, Delta, 1979.

Olson, Charles. *Call Me Ishmael.* San Francisco: City Lights, 1947.

Pagels, Elaine. *The Gnostic Gospels.* New York: Random House, 1979.

Pears, David. *Ludwig Wittgenstein.* New York: Viking Press, Modern Masters, 1970.

Perls, Frederick S. *Gestalt Therapy Verbatim,* edited by John O. Stevens. New York: Bantam Books, 1971.

Plato. *The Republic of Plato,* translated by Francis MacDonald Cornford. New York: Oxford University Press, 1945.

Poe, Edgar Allan. *The Complete Tales and Poems of Edgar Allan Poe.* New York: Random House, Modern Library, 1938.

Poulet, Georges. *The Metamorphoses of the Circle,* translated by Carley Dawson and Elliott Coleman. Baltimore: Johns Hopkins University Press, 1966.

Pritchard, James B. *Ancient Near Eastern Texts Relating to the Old Testament,* 3rd ed. with supplement. Princeton: Princeton University Press, 1969.

Proust, Marcel. *A la recherche du temps perdu,* edited by Pierre Clarac and André Ferré. 3 vols. Paris: NRF, Bibliothèque de la Pléiade, 1963.

—————. *Swann's Way,* translated by C. K. Scott Moncrieff. New York: Random House, Vintage, 1970.

—————. *The Past Recaptured,* translated by Andreas Mayor. New York: Random House, Vintage, 1971.

Puig, Manuel. *Betrayed by Rita Hayworth,* translated by Suzanne Jill Levine. New York: Avon, Bard, 1973.

—————. *Heartbreak Tango: A Serial,* translated by Suzanne Jill Levine. New York: Random House, Vintage, 1981.

—————. *The Buenos Aires Affair: A Detective Novel,* translated by Suzanne Jill Levine. New York: Random House, Vintage, 1980.

—————. *Kiss of the Spider Woman,* translated by Thomas Colchie. New York: Random House, Vintage, 1980.

Pynchon, Thomas. *Gravity's Rainbow.* New York: Viking Press, 1973.

Rajneesh, Bhagwan Shree. *The Psychology of the Esoteric: The New Evolution of Man,* edited by Ma Satya Bharti. New York: Harper and Row, Colophon, 1978.

Rhondell (pseudonym of Bob Gibson). *Headlines: A workbook concerning the discovery of the inner man.* USA (n.p.), 1976.

Rich, Adrienne. *Of Woman Born: Motherhood as Experience and Institution.* New York: W. W. Norton, 1976.

—————. *The Dream of a Common Language: Poems 1974–1977.* New York: W. W. Norton, 1978.

―――. *On Lies, Secrets, and Silence: Selected Prose 1966–1978*. New York: W. W. Norton, 1979.

Richardson, Dorothy. *Pilgrimage*. 4 vols. New York: Popular Library, 1976.

Richardson, Samuel. *Clarissa: Or, the History of a Young Lady*. 4 vols. New York: E. P. Dutton, Everyman's Library, 1932.

Rigney, Barbara Hill. *Madness and Sexual Politics in the Feminist Novel: Studies in Brontë, Woolf, Lessing, and Atwood*. Madison: University of Wisconsin Press, 1978.

Robbe-Grillet, Alain. *Jealousy*, translated by Richard Howard. New York: Grove Press, Black Cat, 1978.

―――. *For a New Novel: Essays on Fiction*, translated by Richard Howard. New York: Grove Press, Black Cat, 1965.

Roberts, Jane. *The Nature of Personal Reality: A Seth Book*. Englewood Cliffs, NJ: Prentice-Hall, 1974.

Russ, Joanna. *The Female Man*. New York: Bantam Books, 1975.

Satprem. *Sri Aurobindo or The Adventure of Consciousness*, translated by Tehmi. New York: Harper and Row, Lindisfarne, 1974.

Schaya, Leo. *The Universal Meaning of the Kabbalah*, translated by Nancy Pearson. Baltimore: Penguin, Penguin Metaphysical Library, 1973.

Schreiner, Olive. *Dreams*. Pacific Grove, CA: Select Books, 1971.

Shah, Idries. *The Way of the Sufi*. New York: E. P. Dutton, 1970.

Shankara. *Shankara's Crest-Jewel of Discrimination*, edited by Swami Prabhavananda and Christopher Isherwood. New York: New American Library, Mentor, 1970.

―――. *The Vedanta Sutras of Bādarāyana, with the Commentary by Śaṅkara*, translated by George Thibaut. 2 vols. New York: Dover, 1962.

Shattuck, Roger. *Proust's Binoculars: A Study of Memory, Time, and Recognition in "A la recherche du temps perdu."* New York: Random House, 1963.

Shelley, Mary. *Frankenstein, or, The Modern Prometheus*. New York: New American Library, Signet, 1965.

Showalter, Elaine. *A Literature of Their Own: British Women Novelists from Brontë to Lessing*. Princeton: Princeton University Press, 1977.

Siegel, Mark Richard. *Pynchon: Creative Paranoia in "Gravity's Rainbow."* Port Washington, NY: Kennikat Press, 1978.

Slatoff, Walter. *Quest for Failure: A Study of William Faulkner.* Ithaca: Cornell University Press, 1960.

Stein, Gertrude. *The Geographical History of America or The Relation of Human Nature to the Human Mind.* New York: Random House, Vintage, 1973.

———. *What Are Masterpieces?,* edited by Robert Bartlett Haas. New York: Pitman, 1970.

———. *Selected Writings of Gertrude Stein,* edited by Carl van Vechten. New York: Random House, Modern Library, 1962.

———. *Gertrude Stein: Writings and Lectures 1909–1945,* edited by Patricia Meyerowitz. Baltimore: Penguin, 1971.

———. *Selected Operas and Plays of Gertrude Stein,* edited by John Malcolm Brinnin. Pittsburgh: University of Pittsburgh Press, 1970.

Sterne, Laurence. *The Life and Opinions of Tristram Shandy, Gentleman,* edited by James Aiken Work. Indianapolis: Bobbs-Merrill, Odyssey Press, 1940.

Stevens, Wallace. *The Palm at the End of the Mind: Selected Poems and a Play,* edited by Holly Stevens. New York: Random House, Vintage, 1972.

Stoker, Bram. *Dracula.* New York: Random House, Modern Library, n.d.

Stone, Jon. *the MONSTER at the end of this Book.* New York: Western Publishing Company, Sesame Street Books, 1977.

Sukenick, Ronald. *Up.* New York: Dial Press, 1968.

———. *The Death of the Novel and Other Stories.* New York: Dial Press, 1969.

———. *Out.* Chicago: Swallow Press, 1973.

———. *98.6.* New York: Fiction Collective, 1975.

Sutherland, Donald. *Gertrude Stein: A Biography of her Work.* New Haven: Yale University Press, 1951.

Suzuki, Shunryu. *Zen Mind, Beginner's Mind.* New York: Weatherhill, 1970.

Svevo, Italo. *Confessions of Zeno,* translated by Beryl De Zoete. New York: Random House, Vintage, n.d.

Swift, Jonathan. *The Writings of Jonathan Swift,* edited by Robert A. Greenberg and William Bowman Piper. New York: W. W. Norton, Norton Critical Edition, 1973.

Tart, Charles T. *Transpersonal Psychologies.* New York: Harper and Row, Colophon, 1975.

Thomas, D. M. *The White Hotel*. New York: Viking, 1981.

Turner, Victor. *The Ritual Process*. Chicago: Aldine, 1969.

Van Ghent, Dorothy. *The English Novel: Form and Function*. New York: Harper and Row, Torchbooks, 1961.

Waley, Arthur. *The Way and Its Power: A Study of the Tao Tê Ching and Its Place in Chinese Thought*. New York: Grove Press, Evergreen, 1958.

Watts, Alan W. *The Book: On the Taboo Against Knowing Who You Are*. New York: Macmillan, Collier, 1967.

Whitman, Walt. *Leaves of Grass: The First (1855) Edition,* edited by Malcolm Cowley. New York: Viking Press, Compass, 1959.

Wittgenstein, Ludwig. *Tractatus Logico-Philosophicus,* translated by D. F. Pears and B. F. McGuinness. London: Routledge and Kegan Paul, 1961.

———. *Philosophical Investigations,* translated by G.E.M. Anscombe, 3rd ed. New York: Macmillan, 1975.

———. *Lectures & Conversations on Aesthetics, Psychology and Religious Belief,* edited by Cyril Barrett. Berkeley: University of California Press, 1972.

Wittig, Monique. *Les Guérillères,* translated by David Le Vay. New York: Avon, Bard, 1973.

———. *The Lesbian Body,* translated by David Le Vay. New York: Avon, Bard, 1976.

Wittig, Monique, and Sande Zeig. *Lesbian Peoples: Material for a Dictionary*. New York: Avon, 1979.

Wittrock, M. C. "Education and the Hemispheric Process of the Brain." Special issue of *UCLA Educator*. Los Angeles, 1975.

Wood, Ann Douglas. "'The Fashionable Diseases': Women's Complaints and Their Treatment in Nineteenth-Century America." In *Clio's Consciousness Raised: New Perspectives on the History of Women,* edited by Mary S. Hartman and Lois Banner. New York: Harper and Row, 1974.

Woolf, Virginia. *Mrs. Dalloway*. New York: Harcourt, Brace, and World, Harvest, n.d.

———. *To the Lighthouse*. New York: Harcourt, Brace, and World, Harvest, n.d.

———. *Orlando: A Biography*. New York: New American Library, Signet, 1960.

———. *A Room of One's Own*. New York: Harcourt, Brace, and World, 1929.

————. *Jacob's Room and The Waves*. New York: Harcourt, Brace, and World, Harvest, n.d.

————. *Three Guineas*. New York: Harcourt, Brace, and World, Harbinger, n.d.

Yeats, W. B. *A Vision*, 2nd ed. New York: Collier Books, 1966.

————. *Selected Poems and Two Plays of William Butler Yeats*, edited by M. L. Rosenthal. New York: Macmillan, Collier Books, 1966.

INDEX

Abel, Lionel, 285
Aeschylus, 264–65, 351
Agamemnon, King, 172, 179, 264.
    See also Aeschylus.
Agee, James, 24, 26, 327
Alter, Robert, xiv, 16–21, 249–50,
    349–50
Aristotle, 311, 341
Arnold, Matthew, 158
Ashbery, John, xiv, 108
Atwood, Margaret, 300–301, 304,
    354
Augustine, St., xi, 9, 66, 227–28
Aurora: Beyond Equality, see Sheldon

Bader, Julia, 330
Barth, John, 5
Bass, Alan, 347, 349
Bassoff, Bruce, xiv, 346
Bazin, André, 342
Beckett, Samuel, ix, xiii, 5, 20,
    24–26, 98, 99, 101, 132, 143, 217,
    227–28, 233, 235, 251, 272–85,
    289, 308, 327, 350–51
    Malone Dies, 118, 272–73,
        275–78, 282, 289
    Molloy, 70, 118, 272–75, 278, 351
    Proust, 275
    The Unnamable, x, 7, 12, 18–19,
        21, 33, 37, 70, 90, 98, 100–101,
        118, 136, 167, 220, 258, 272,
        277–86, 289–90, 295, 297
    Waiting for Godot, 128, 140, 269
    Watt, 22, 33, 64–70, 104, 115,
        146–47, 167, 272, 274, 278,
        329–30

Bentov, Itzhak, 126
Ben-Zvi, Linda, 327
Berger, John, 347
Bergman, Ingmar, x, 142
    Persona, 22, 342
Bergson, Henri, 110–12, 115–16,
    136, 138, 171
Berne, Eric, 197
Blake, William, 25, 113, 286
Bloom, Harold, 344
Blotner, Joseph, 351
Bonaventure, St., 214
Booth, Wayne, 182
Borges, Jorge Luis, xiv, 17, 19,
    74–76, 143, 187–89, 235, 291,
    326, 329, 339
    "Borges and I," 19, 32–33, 326
Boswell, James, 151
brain lateralization, 83, 91–93, 95,
    113, 232, 287, 321, 332, 334
Brontë, Charlotte, 301, 354
Brontë, Emily, xiv, 26, 70, 142,
    147–49, 151, 156–71, 183, 198,
    341–42
Browning, Robert, 158
Buñuel, Luis, 342

Cage, John, 211–12
Capra, Fritjof, 286
Carlyle, Thomas, 158
Carroll, Lewis, 134, 143, 158
Castaneda, Carlos, xi, 34, 36–37,
    42, 53, 56, 74–80, 83–97, 99, 102,
    122, 128, 140, 211, 327, 332–33
Cervantes, Miguel de, 16, 20,
    242–43, 285, 349–50

371

Library of Congress Cataloging in Publication Data

Kawin, Bruce F., 1945–
   The mind of the novel.

   Bibliography: p.
   Includes index.
   1. Fiction—History and criticism. 2. Self
in literature. I. Title.
PN3352.S44K3   809.3'9353   81-47927
ISBN 0-691-06509-8   AACR2